THE NEXT GREAT
BUBBLE BOOM

HOW TO PROFIT FROM THE
GREATEST BOOM IN HISTORY:
2006–2010

HARRY S. DENT, JR.

FREE PRESS

NEW YORK   LONDON   TORONTO   SYDNEY

FREE PRESS
A Division of Simon & Schuster, Inc.
1230 Avenue of the Americas
New York, NY 10020

First Free Press trade paperback edition 2006

FREE PRESS and colophon are trademarks
of Simon & Schuster, Inc.

Designed by Lisa Chovnick

For information regarding special discounts for bulk purchases,
please contact Simon & Schuster Special Sales at 1-800-456-6798
or business@simonandschuster.com

The following are registered trademarks of
The H. S. Dent Foundation and Bill Good Marketing, Inc.:
H. S. Dent Adviser's Network®
Roaring 2000s®
Investment Strategies for the Roaring 2000s®
The Spending Wave®
H. S. Dent®
R2Ks®
Helping People Understand Change®

Manufactured in the United States of America

5   7   9   10   8   6   4

ISBN 13: 978-0-7432-2299-0
ISBN 10:   0-7432-2299-7
ISBN 13: 978-0-7432-8848-4 (Pbk)
ISBN 10:   0-7432-8848-3 (Pbk)

To my father, Harry S. Dent, Sr.
To my wife, Jean-ne Carmichael Dent

Acknowledgments

Thanks to my literary agent, Susan Golomb; my marketing agent, Harry Cornelius. For research, thanks to Rodney Johnson, Stephanie Morgan, Eva Sturm-Kehoe, and Vladimir Bulatovic. For PR and promotion thanks to Sandi Mendelson, Mariah Leeson, and Terry Reid. And special thanks to Bill Good and the members of the H. S. Dent Advisers Network.

Contents

THE NEXT GREAT
BUBBLE BOOM

BUBBLE AFTER BUBBLE IN THE ONGOING BUBBLE BOOM

Oil Bursts, the Housing Bubble Fades, and Stocks Emerge Into a Greater Bubble That Finally Ends in 2010

BEGINNING IN APRIL 2005 we gave a series of updates in our newsletter that showed how the oil and housing bubbles were holding back the acceleration we had been predicting in stocks by early 2005, but that stated we were still very closely following the trends in the 1920s recovery and bubble boom, now on an eighty-one-year lag. This is a summary of those updates as of early August 2005 for this paperback edition. We have left the text of the original book published in September 2004 the same, with the exception that we have revised the dates for our new forecasts included in this update to avoid confusion. Make sure to read this important update carefully and don't give up on the "Next Great Bubble Boom" unless our warning signs at the end of this update are violated. The last great buy opportunities since October 2002 occurred in April 2005 and October 2005 as we strongly warned. Early 2006 and late 2006 should also give attractive buying opportunities ahead of what is likely to be the greatest bubble boom since 1925 to 1929.

The theme of *The Next Great Bubble Boom* is that it is a terrible misperception that we've seen a bubble in stocks and that now it's over. The truth is that we are in a bubble boom that is very different from the last generation's boom from 1942 to 1968. First, the generation driving this boom is much larger than those that came before it and its purchasing and investment power drive every trend to extremes, one after the other. Second, and more important, bubbles are more likely when radical new technologies, infrastructures, and business models are first moving into the mainstream economy. This also occurred eighty years ago with automobiles, phones, and electricity—especially from 1914 to 1929, which saw the last two technology bubbles in stocks.

It is critical to see this boom since the mid-1970s or early 1980s as a series of bubbles: in inflation, stocks, real estate, technology, and other sectors like oil. It's not that we have seen a bubble burst . . . but that we are in an ongoing bubble boom!

In fact, the first bubble was the huge inflation trend that ushered the baby boomers and their new technologies and consumer trends into the workforce and economy. The inflation rates that peaked in 1980 dwarfed past inflation cycles. And with that inflationary trend came the first oil bubble and the gold bubble that peaked in 1980. Do you remember when oil was at $40 and forecast for $100 plus, and when gold was at $800 and expected to go to $5,000? There was also a minor bubble in housing prices driven by inflation trends into 1981 (and we will show later that housing prices correlate most with inflation trends long term). Then the boom started in early 1983 and we saw the first bubble in the stock market emerge quickly into 1987 out of the twin stock market corrections and economic declines in 1980 and 1982. Then we saw a stronger technology-led stock bubble into early 2000, out of the ashes of the twin stock corrections in 1987 and 1990, and the mild recession into early 1991.

Now we are projecting a third, even steeper tech-led bubble into 2010 and another great boom ahead.

Baby boomer demand and falling mortgage rates have created two real estate bubbles since the first peak in 1981 with peak inflation trends. The next occurred with the baby boom starter-home cycle that peaked in 1990. That was followed by the next and greater bubble, with trade-up home and vacation buying that is likely to peak by late 2005 or early 2006 at the latest. Now we have another oil bubble that will likely have peaked in late August of 2005, at least for now, echoing the first oil bubble with inflation back in 1980.

Note that most of these bubbles come in pairs: two bubbles in oil over a sixty-year inflation and Kondratieff cycle, two bubbles in real estate, and two tech-stock bubbles over an eighty-year generation-driven New Economy cycle. Also note that the second bubble tends to be more dramatic than the first. This confirms our model of a growth boom and maturity boom with a shakeout in between. Most economists assume that you only see one major bubble, only very infrequently, and then it's all over. But that is not typically the case, especially for technology bubbles as we show in Chapters 1 and 2.

Most analysts think we are crazy for predicting another bubble in stocks to follow the recent one, because obviously we have learned our lesson and wouldn't let such a thing happen again so soon. But that argument already looks weak after seeing the run-up in Google and other new growth stocks recently, and the dramatic housing bubble since 2000 directly after stocks peaked. What do you mean when you say we learn our lessons? As long as growth and returns are there, investors will chase increasing bubbles. One bubble followed by the next stronger one, is actually what more often occurs in history until the longer trends driving them peak, as we have shown with the twin tech-stock bubbles that peaked in late 1919 and late 1929 before the most devastating long-term downturn in U.S. history followed from 1930 to 1942.

We as investors need to first accept that we are in a bubble boom, and hence, should continue to expect stronger booms and busts in rotating sectors until this growth boom or bubble stage in the eighty-year New Economy cycle is over around 2010, when baby-boom spending and new technology penetration rates are projected to peak.

It will be over, at least in North America and most of the Western world, when these new technologies have penetrated around 90% of households by around late 2009, and when the massive baby-boom generation finishes its spending cycle around 2010. And it is the first half of the eighty-year New Economy cycle when new technologies are first emerging into the mainstream that we get these growing series of bubble booms and busts with increasing upside and downside volatility in the markets. This occurred in the last technology revolution from 1900 to 1942, including two bubbles in tech stocks from 1914–1919 and 1925–1929, and a bubble bear market rally in stocks from mid-1932 to early 1937. After the next crash into early 1942, we entered a more orderly boom without major bubbles or busts into 1968. That is why the boom from 1942 to 1968 and even the downturn from 1969 to 1982 to follow were so different from what we are seeing in recent decades—and what we will see in the next stage of this continued boom and the extended bust to follow.

In this update to *The Next Great Bubble Boom*, we are going to look at the peaking of the oil and housing bubbles and how investors will naturally switch back into stocks again when the current oil and housing bubbles burst or slow—and the next growth sectors, led by technology, take off again with a very strong economy from mid-2006 into 2010.

It wasn't a coincidence that home prices started accelerating when stock prices failed and interest rates dropped with the slowing economy that followed. In this bubble boom, the massive rising incomes and assets of baby boomers, leveraged by falling interest rates and liberal lending policies, keep chasing the next hot sector after the last one bursts. And the game is not over yet!

The demographic trends have been slowing for housing, but speculation has continued to thrive with lower interest rates and rising prices, especially in large urban coastal areas, condos, and vacation sectors. Interest rates cannot continue to fall much longer, while demographic trends in overall home buying that peaked in late 2003 will weaken further. A booming stock market again may be the greatest impetus for cooling the speculation in housing in 2006, as the next bubble game starts building and looks more attractive.

MAJOR REVERSAL IN MANY TRENDS IN LATE 2005/EARLY 2006

The point now is that we see many trends reversing in the second half of 2005. Oil appears to have peaked in late August 2005. This peak should hold at a minimum for a few years, and it could possibly represent a very long-term top. Bond yields have been falling until just recently, giving housing prices a final burst of strength into the summer of 2005. Housing prices could continue to rise into the stronger fall season of 2005, or into the strongest spring season of 2006 at the very latest. Then they should decelerate rapidly and fall in the most overvalued areas. Bond yields should edge up gradually for nearly five years as the economy, stocks, and the dollar boom again. Gold and commodity prices should slow for a year or more to come, similar to oil. And finally, stocks will surge again between late 2005 and early 2006 to new extremes into 2010.

That will cause a number of leading stock sectors in the past few years, such as oil, commodities, and housing, to lag and possibly crash. Large- and small-cap growth stocks, especially technology, are going to take the stage again and lead the next bubble driven by the second stage, or maturity boom, of the S-curve technology cycle in Internet, wireless, broadband, and digital devices. Again, the sharp bubble in oil prices into August 2005 has put a damper on the stock rally that attempted to accelerate from early 2005 on. Stocks should rally more strongly in the latter part of 2005 and early 2006 from extreme oversold levels in late April 2005 and 40% undervaluation levels compared to bonds (the highest since late 2002). But there may continue to be some minor bumps along the way until oil prices finally begin to retreat convincingly and investors see a clear end to the Fed tightening cycle by January 2006.

At this stage in our generation and technology cycles, things continue to evolve very much as they did about eighty years ago in the last New Economy cycle. This recent tech and stock bubble peaked 80.5 years after the comparable bubble in late 1919. But the bottom in the recent crash came more like 81.0 years after the bottom in late 1921 (actually, the Dow bottomed in mid-1921 and the Automotive Index in early 1922—or around late 1921 on average). It took almost three years for stocks to start to accelerate after an initial strong recovery rally in 1922. The 81.0-year lag now looks to be the trend and it should be early to mid-2006 before the Dow finally makes a new high with the next convincing acceleration in stock prices that should begin by November 2005.

In *The Next Great Bubble Boom,* we forecast that the markets would accelerate again by early 2005. Our recent analysis, given the oil and housing bubbles, now suggests that should occur by mid- to late 2005 instead. The Dow making a new high will be an important event since it will dispel most of the "this is just a bear market rally" forecasts and convince more investors that we are in the next major bull market. This is now most likely to occur between January and March 2006, or May 2006 at the latest. Most investors have not noticed that the small- and mid-cap stock indices have already made new highs from the peaks in 2000, confirming the next bull market.

Since late April 2005, we have seen the downside risks for investors as very limited and the upside potential over the next one to five years as enormous! We have been warning our newsletter subscribers to buy on minor corrections and that October 2005 would likely be the last chance to buy stocks at levels near 10,000 on the Dow. Similarly, we would now advise new readers to be buying on any moderate short-term corrections in early 2006, and especially on more substantial corrections that are likely to occur between August and October 2006 on the four-year Presidential Cycle covered in Chapter 3.

THE OIL BUBBLE: THE BIGGEST MARKET HURDLE IN 2005

In the April 2005 issue of the *H. S. Dent Forecast* we showed how oil seemed to be moving into a near-term bubble and peak with one more wave up. We were forecasting in early August 2005 that oil prices were likely in their last rally to peak by mid-August or soon after. The peak finally occurred with Hurricane Katrina, near $71.00. We are in a period wherein supply is clearly somewhat fixed short term with demand growing due to the world recovery, especially in the U.S., and with China's continued very high growth. But rising prices stimulate new investment in supply over time. Oil, like housing currently and stocks back in 1999, was being driven more by short-term speculation than fundamentals.

According to analysis from Don Hayes at Hayes Advisory, there was something else going on that has been steadily tipping the balance ever so slightly toward rising demand and prices. That stimulus has been just enough to cause rising speculation beyond the fundamentals of supply and demand in oil, especially with stagnant stock prices and falling interest rates since 2000. Since 9/11, the U.S. and other major oil-importing countries were building their strategic reserves to prepare for terrorist attacks that could temporarily shut down oil supplies. Figure F.1 looks at a very clear correlation between the rise in the U.S. Strategic Petroleum Reserve and the price of oil.

The U.S. has added 155 million barrels since 9/11 or about 3.3 million barrels per month. And remember that other countries are doing this as well, so the stockpiling is much higher on a global level. Also note that the oil markets now carry a rising premium on their own for growing terrorist

FIGURE F.1 Crude Oil Versus Strategic Petroleum Reserve

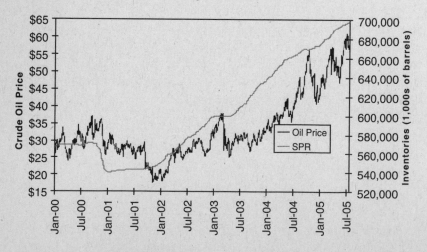

Source: Energy Information Administration

risks, and those risks are likely to fall in the future as terrorist attacks continue to be more minor and more accepted as a fact of life. Hence, 9/11 has nearly as much to do with this bubble as does rising demand in a world of constrained supply. However, the U.S. was due to hit its new targets for capacity and stop stockpiling by mid-August 2005. That should put mild downward pressure on oil prices to follow.

To get the broadest view, Figure F.2 looks at oil prices on a logarithmic chart over a longer period of time. This chart would suggest that since World War II we have seen a clear five-wave Elliott Wave pattern forming with the third-wave peak in 1980 and a long eighteen-year fourth-wave correction into late 1998 that tested the $10–$11 level twice. That would put us in a final broader fifth wave up and a long-term peak in this decade. Either we could see 1) a significant correction ahead for a year or so, and a final minor and major fifth-wave peak around 2010 (into the peak of economic activity in the next great boom); or 2) the broader fifth-wave could have been a peak in late August 2005.

In the first scenario (Figure F.2) we show a minor fourth-wave correction back to around $40 for one to two years and then we could see a final surge to $80 to $100 into around 2010. That would be followed by a long-term collapse back toward $40, and possibly as low as $10, in the downturn to follow from 2010 to 2022. The argument for this scenario would be that

FIGURE F.2 Historical Price of Oil, 1946–Present

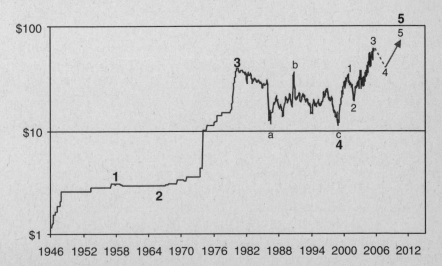

Source: Dow Jones Energy Service

oil is overvalued now due to speculation and needs a correction, but stronger U.S.–led growth in the next bubble boom, and continued extreme growth in China and Asia, would lead to strong pressures on supply again—and a final bubble would form. Although there are credible new supply alternatives emerging and strong price incentives, they will likely take years to make a significant difference.

The argument against this scenario would be that without another major terrorist threat that would disrupt oil supplies and stimulate further buildups in strategic reserves, it would be hard to see oil getting that high when fair value now is estimated to be between $25 and $40 by many experts, with present options for drilling deeper in many areas and the Canadian tar sands at higher price incentives. Also in the final larger fifth wave of many Elliott Wave patterns, the top is more anticipated and the final minor fifth wave often does not manifest, so that this apparent third wave of the larger fifth wave could represent the longer-term peak. We tend to lean more strongly toward the first scenario with a significant retreat in oil prices into 2006 or so and then one more bubble into 2010 before a worldwide slowdown in economic growth and more credible long-term solutions to the oil shortage emerge, such as the gasification of coal.

Long-term 28–30-year (minor) and 55–60-year (major) Kondratieff Wave peaks in commodity prices and inflation rates would also suggest a peak in oil and commodity prices (on the minor cycle) closer to 2010. We published a new special report in late 2005 on our Web site at www.hsdent .com that looks at how the Kondratieff Wave cycle of the past has been increasingly supplanted by the new forty- and eighty-year Generation Wave cycles, yet the two cycles are still interacting.

The second scenario (Figure F.3) is that we are presently seeing a peak in oil prices and we will see further weakening when the U.S. stops buying extra oil for its strategic reserve after mid-August. In this case oil could drop to $25 to $30 a barrel over the next few years, have a bear market rally into the strongest years of the boom into early 2010 or so, and then collapse back to its $10–$11 lows of the 1990s in the great downturn from 2010 to 2022. This scenario is less likely but would be confirmed if oil prices drop below $38 (the last first-wave high in late 2000) in the next year or two.

Figure F.4 shows a more realistic long-term picture using inflation-adjusted oil prices. Despite the recent bubble, we are still more than $25 below peak prices, just over $90 in today's 2005 dollars back in 1980 (the major top of the Kondratieff Wave cycle) when OPEC had a greater stranglehold on oil supplies and broad commodity and inflation rates were at a major peak (in line with both our eighty-year generation-driven New

FIGURE F.3 Historical Price of Oil, 1946–Present

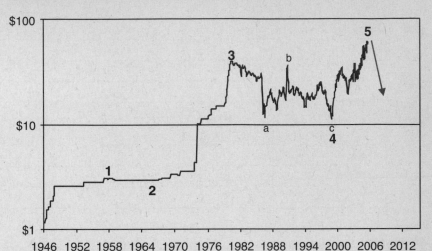

Source: Dow Jones Energy Service

Economy Cycle and the sixty-year Kondratieff Cycle). In this chart it would be more likely that this present top would represent a bear market rally that would peak in a "B" wave in late 2005 and then we would see a long "C" wave back toward $10–$11 from 2005 into as late as 2022 to 2023 or so. But it is also possible that we could see higher prices, or even a slight new high, around the end of this decade. A new high would suggest that oil prices would have to get to over $100 per barrel with future inflation adjustments, in order to get above the highs adjusted for inflation in 1980 (scenario 1). That would be in line with the first scenario we outlined earlier.

But either scenario—a long-term peak now, or a final peak toward the end of this decade after a major correction in the next year or two—could occur for oil prices. The next year should tell us which scenario is more likely, depending on whether we break below or hold above the critical support for oil prices between $38 and $40.

If we look at the Amex Oil Index for stocks since the broader boom started in 1983 (Figure F.5), we also get a stronger suggestion for the case that oil prices were close to peaking in August 2005. Oil stocks were moving into an exponential bubble that appeared to be near a fifth-wave peak. Oil stocks have actually underperformed the S&P 500 since the early 1980s and we continue not to recommend commodity-based sectors long term, despite short-term bubbles in these sectors that are harder to predict. Demographic and new technology trends favor new growing sectors of our

FIGURE F.4   Oil: Adjusted for Inflation, 1970–Present

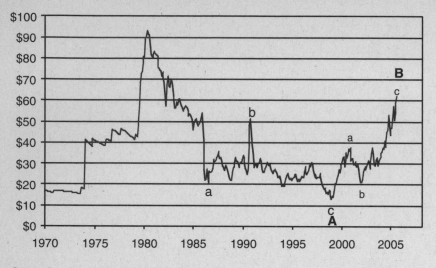

Source: Bureau of Labor Statistics; Dow Jones Energy Service

economy that have increased steadily in stock market capitalization trends, sectors such as technology, health care and financial services—and they are easier to project.

This would suggest a substantial correction ahead for oil stocks and a shakeout in that industry over the next few years—much like what the airlines went through after 9/11.

So it clearly appears that the next bubble in this "Great Bubble Boom" has already peaked and that a leading sector of the last few years may become a laggard or even a big loser quickly. This index looks like it could peak at or just above 1,000, and then could fall as low as 400 to 600 in the next year or so—during a continued economic boom! That could represent as much as a 40% to 60% correction, although likely less, much like what the home-building stocks experienced after their 1990 bubble and peak, as we show in Chapter 1.

Another bubble is very likely to burst for now, and perhaps long term, in oil and commodity prices, while the bubble boom goes on!

Our message to investors, especially since 2001 (in our special report "The Buy Opportunity of a Lifetime") is that you have to understand and accept that we are in a long-term bubble boom and that we will continue to see high volatility for this decade (during the boom) and the next (during the bust). Now we are seeing continued bubbles and potential busts in sectors like oil and commodities near-term, despite strong demographic and

FIGURE F.5 Amex Oil Index, Aug 1983–Present

Source: Yahoo Finance

technology trends for the next five years or so. Housing should be the next sector to see a shakeout and setbacks in stock prices, while the broader economy and stock market advances. Then we will see another major bubble in stocks peak by 2010 and then burst between 2010 and 2014, along with most sectors of our economy.

Welcome to the most exciting and volatile bubble boom since 1914 to 1929! We can't change the nature of this boom, but we can react more intelligently than the great majority of investors, who keep chasing hot sectors and then fall off the cliff with them. In the last few years, investors have run into energy stocks, real estate, home-building stocks, REITs, and bonds. We see all of those trends reversing between mid-2005 and early 2006. Most investors will get burned again.

In past issues of our newsletter we talked about supply and demand for oil being able to create the needed investment to sustain long-term trends at more like $30–$35 per barrel, according to most intelligent long-term analysts. Lee Raymond, CEO of Exxon Mobil, recently stated strongly that oil at these prices is clearly due to speculation, not fundamentals. But many long-term fundamentals point toward higher oil prices. The real question is what should the price of oil be? The markets are likely to tell us this in the next year or shortly thereafter.

A substantial break below $38 in the next year or so would strongly suggest that oil has peaked long term. Similarly, if the Amex oil stock index were to fall substantially below 600 that would similarly suggest

the oil bubble is over. Otherwise, we are likely to see another oil bubble into around 2010.

More fundamentals suggest that oil will fall into late 2005 and 2006. Don Hayes at Hayes Advisory presents another interesting analysis. In Figure F.6 he shows a strong correlation with oil prices and a reverse scale of U.S. inventories of crude oil, not including the strategic reserve that we hold and build for crisis times. The reverse scale is used because rising inventories would show higher supply and lead to lower prices and vice versa. Clearly, oil prices have been diverging from this trend very dramatically with the recent speculative bubble. This chart would suggest that oil prices could fall to as low as $25 to $30 unless inventories fall substantially. But inventories are actually more likely to rise and oil prices could fall even further. Again, since the U.S. will not have to buy additional oil for its reserve after August, that will take some pressure off oil demand and prices, and only serve to raise inventories.

In summary, oil prices look very likely to fall substantially in the next year and a shakeout is imminent in the oil and energy sectors. It is more of a question of whether oil prices will fall back to around $40 and then advance again (more likely), or peak here long term and perhaps fall as low as $25 to $30. If we do see $80 plus oil prices and a final bubble in oil, we don't think that will have a major impact on the stock market, since we will be in a stronger phase of earnings and growth by then and oil will continue to be

FIGURE F.6 Oil Prices Versus Oil Inventories

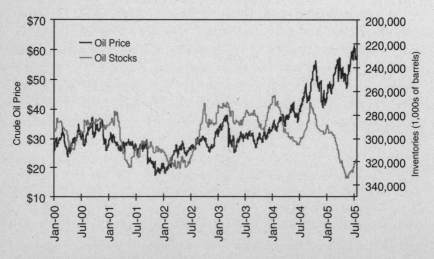

Source: Energy Information Administration

a smaller part of our economy, as it has been for decades. But it would be at least a mild negative if and when it occurred, just as the recent oil bubble has probably set stock prices back about 5% to 8% from where they would have been in 2005 without it (which would have had the Dow testing its 2000 highs earlier, which is what we were first expecting).

The scenario for a long-term peak in oil prices near-term would be better for the broad stock market and bonds, but it would suggest an even more severe shakeout and downside for oil and energy stocks over the next two years. We see the potential for as much as a 40% to 60% decline in oil stocks in the next year or so but likely less, and that is likely to affect such stock indices as the Dow and S&P 500 a bit more than the technology, health care, financial services, Asia, and small-cap sectors that we focus on for investment strategies in this continued bubble boom ahead.

BONDS AND INTEREST RATES

Before we look at the other great bubble in housing, let's look at the trends in bonds, which have seen a long-term bull market due to falling interest rates since 1981. Interest rates will be affected a bit by the peaking oil bubble, and falling interest rates are another factor driving home prices at this late stage in that bubble. We have seen somewhat volatile movements into 2005 in long-term interest rates like the 30-year and 10-year Treasury bonds. They first spiked up, as usual, with the strengthening recovery in 2003 and early 2004, anticipating rising inflation rates and Fed tightening. Most economists were surprised to then see long bond yields decline despite the Fed raising short-term rates from mid-2004 into 2005.

Why? Modest inflation from high productivity and excess capacity, and a moderate economic recovery for years at first, as our models suggested. But the bond markets have been telling the Fed that it is going too far in raising short-term interest rates out of misplaced inflation fears, as it has tended to do in the past. We are also seeing strong flows into bonds internationally from lower interest rates in Europe and growing trade imbalances with Asia (to compensate), as well as the fact that corporations are not fully investing their growing profits and are saving more than investing until they see more convincing signs of long-term growth and work off their excess capacity from the last bubble. That will change in 2006 as companies start investing in capacity aggressively to catch up with consumer demand.

In early 2004, with the sharp rise in oil prices and increasing speculation in long bonds, rates first jumped 0.65% in the 10-year Treasury and near 0.5% in the 30-year. But they came down again to as low as 3.80% on the 10-year Treasury bond with the slowing recovery into the second quarter of 2005 that we had been predicting since late 2004. With economic growth picking up a bit since June 2005, we will likely see the Fed raise short-term rates to between 4.25% and 4.50% by January 2006. But then the Fed should stop with another slowing in the economy into very early 2006. But moderating oil and commodity prices ahead should both lessen inflation fears and increase the perception that the economy will strengthen long term. Hence, inflation pressures have likely peaked for now, and rising productivity from the next technology-led boom should keep inflation moderate, although it is likely to rise a bit down the road due to mildly rising workforce entry from the echo-boom generation (as we outline in our books) and the next potential oil/commodity boom into 2010.

There are opposing forces—rising productivity of the aging baby boomers, and potentially falling oil and commodity prices on the disinflationary side versus stronger economic growth from early 2006 on, and the rising entry of the echo boom into the workforce growth on the inflationary side—in the years ahead for inflation, interest rates, and bond yields. The inflationary trends are likely to win out ultimately, but with interest rates rising only modestly in the years ahead. That will still work against strongly rising home prices.

In the 1920s bond yields continued to decline into 1928 due to rising productivity and declining immigration and workforce growth, despite accelerating economic growth. But workforce growth shows the highest correlation with inflation rates in our research. Our models show slightly greater workforce entry from the echo boom than baby boom retirement over the rest of this decade. And it is still likely that we will see a third bubble later in this decade in oil and commodity prices, unlike the 1920s. Hence, we think that inflation will be a bit higher than in the 1920s, rising very modestly, but still restrained to very low levels. Inflation rates are likely to remain contained to the 1% to 3% range, especially given lower outsourcing costs from emerging countries like China and India and a rising dollar that lowers our import costs and attracts greater foreign investment flows into our stock and bond markets.

Figure F.7 represents a very interesting long-term trend in bond yields that is similar to other channels we have used in the past, such as the Dow Channel. Since the late 1980s, the 30-year Treasury yield has been declining in an increasingly narrow channel or wedge pattern. We've hit peaks in yields in late 1987, late 1994, and early 2004 during periods when the econ-

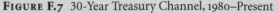

FIGURE F.7 30-Year Treasury Channel, 1980–Present

Source: Yahoo Finance

omy was accelerating and/or when the Fed was shifting toward a strong tightening policy in short-term rates. We hit the bottom of this channel in early 1986, late 1993, late 1998, and early 2003 when the economy was decelerating and the Fed was easing more.

The good thing about channels that are this consistent over long periods of time is 1) you can predict major reversals from high or low areas of the channel, and 2) the trends are likely to continue in the direction and parameters of the channel until the channel is clearly broken. With the first slowing of growth into mid-2005, 30-year Treasury bond yields fell near the bottom of this channel to near 4.10% and could retest these levels by early 2006, when the economy is likely to slow briefly again. That would represent the last great opportunity to refinance home and business mortgages. But it is more likely that we hit the bottom end of this channel for the last time in early 2003 and refinancing even at slightly higher levels by early 2006 should be advantageous.

Only a very strong surge in productivity that reduces inflation substantially and outweighs mildly higher workforce growth could cause long-term interest rates to trend lower in the next few years, and that would also dictate a possible easing in short-term rates by the Fed from early 2006 onward. That is possible with the strong productivity we are predicting in the next technology boom, but we wouldn't want to bet on that scenario, given the potential of rising workforce growth and rising oil prices later (although lower long-term interest rates did occur into the late 1920s bubble). In early

2006, investors should increasingly switch from longer-term maturities to shorter term in their portfolios, as we recommended in mid-2005, due to the likelihood that modestly rising rates ahead will penalize long-term bonds. Why take the longer-term risk when short-term rates are similar?

A break up through the top of this channel in the next year or two (above 5.2% by early 2006) would signal a somewhat stronger trend of rising interest rates into 2010 or so, and the greater likelihood that oil and commodity prices rise to new highs in the latter years of this boom. That would also lead to a greater slowdown in home prices.

Figure F.8 shows the Weekly Leading Index (from www.businesscycle .com) as of late July 2005. We have found it to be the best indicator for forecasting the economy around eight months ahead to get a better idea of how trends in the economy and interest rates are likely to go near term. This leading index forecast that economic growth was likely to weaken a bit into mid-2005, before beginning to strengthen again. But this indicator also suggests that growth should pick up into late 2005 and then slow one more time into January or February 2006 before we see stronger and more sustainable growth from mid-2006 to 2010, as occurred from 1996 to 2000 in the last bubble cycle. That is the reason that we have been warning of this slowing in the recovery since late 2004 in our newsletter. It is also natural for economic growth to slow after surging strongly in the early stages of a recovery. The Fed tightens in reaction to the strong initial growth and al-

FIGURE F.8 Weekly Leading Index (Growth Rate)

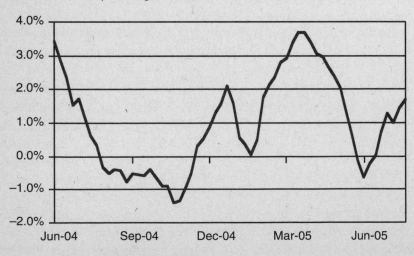

Source: Economic Cycle Research Institute

ways goes a bit too far. If inflation rates fall in the years ahead due to very high productivity, the Fed would likely ease a bit—and that would be even more bullish for stocks.

Homeowners and businesses should be looking to refinance mortgages, as we already recommended, between 3.7% and 4.0% on the 10-year Treasury into early 2006, optimally on a 5/1 ARM rate, especially if 30-year Treasury rates fall into the 4.1% to 4.4% range, or 10-year rates fall to 3.9% to 4.2%. That mortgage strategy will lock in fixed rates in a likely mildly rising inflation trend during the boom, and then convert you to short-term rates that should be declining sharply from late 2010 or early 2011 onward in the downturn to follow—the best of both worlds!

In *The Next Great Bubble Boom,* we forecast that the lows in long-term rates were likely to occur between late 2005 and early 2006, given the trends in past recoveries. That likely already occurred in June 2005, but we should get ready for another opportunity for refinancing by early 2006. Most investors can't understand how long-term bond rates could be falling amid rising short-term rates and a growing economy. This is because long-term rates follow more the trends in inflation and short-term rates are affected more by Fed policies and short-term demand/supply economics.

Figure F.9 shows the spread between 10-year and 3-month Treasury yields since 1980. This spread averages 2.0% over time, but in a steady boom with low inflation trends and expectations it can average 1.0% (between 0.5% and 1.5%), as occurred during the last bubble from 1995 to 1999. That is the "sweet spot" for stocks and the economy. But this "yield curve" will almost always invert—with lower long-term yields than short term—when the Fed is tightening to slow the economy down from overexpansive growth, or when long-bond traders expect a slowdown after an expansion period.

Note that the strong recession into late 1982 was preceded by the strongest inversion in rates. Then a flat yield curve in late 1989 would have forecast the slowdown into early 1991. A slight inversion in rates forecast the slowdown into 2001 and 2002. But also note that in the early stages of recoveries such as 1983, 1992, and early 2004, the yield curve or spread tends to hit its peak, between 3.75% and 5.0% at the extreme in 1983. We already hit near 4% in this spread in early 2004! The spreads are only likely to narrow into a range of 2.0% maximum and 0.0% minimum or around 1.0% to 1.5% for the years to come in the next boom, and again, that is the best range for stocks. In a slowing just after a recovery we can experience a near inversion that does not signal a recession, but is rather just the final slowing

FIGURE F.9 Spread Between 10-Year and 3-Month Yields

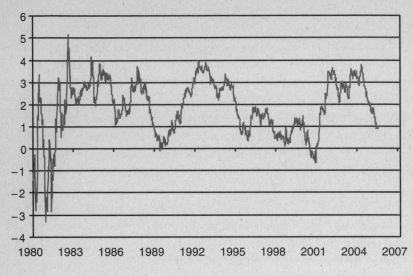

Source: Yahoo Finance

before the economy takes off again. We would be concerned if we did see an actual inversion in rates by early 2006.

   Long-term bond yields are likely to stay within a narrow range for years with a slight rising bias, unless the 30-year Treasury Channel is broken on the upside with yields above 5.2% by early 2006. Still, inflation should be tame and yields should only advance modestly. A 30-year yield above 6.0% and 30-year mortgages above 7.5% would be unlikely in the late stages of the boom ahead even if we break out of this channel on the upside. There is no chance that we would break below this channel and we have already likely seen the last test of the bottom of this channel in early 2003. A retest at 3.9% to 4.20% from early 2006 on would be very bullish for stocks, especially if short-term rates declined in reaction.

HOME PRICES: THE NEXT BUBBLE TO DEFLATE— BUT NOT A CRASH UNTIL 2011/2012

The financial news has continued to abound with stories of the housing bubble. We have said in the past that that was reason enough to think it was not going to bust quite yet. But our analysis continues to suggest it is now coming closer to late 2005 and by mid 2006 at the latest, and you would expect much more awareness and coverage of this bubble after the dramatic recent crash of the stock bubble. From 1996 to 1998 more analysts warned about the stock and tech bubble, but most started giving up by 1999— except for Robert Shiller, who came out at the right time with his book *Irrational Exuberance*. There have been increasingly worrisome signs in housing markets that Shiller and many others have been very vocal about. In Chapter 4 (and in our special report, *Demographic Trends in Real Estate*, in July 2003) we show very conclusively that the momentum in baby-boom home buying and trade-up homes climaxed back in mid- to late 2003. Mortgage interest and buying drops off significantly after age forty-two, and the peak numbers of baby boomers have since passed this age.

So why were house prices and demand still rising as we moved into mid- to late 2005? The truth is that speculation has increasingly replaced slowing fundamental demand since 2000 when the stock market failed. And interest rates continued to decline into June 2005 and increasingly liberal lending policies kept home prices and sales rising at least into the summer. They could continue to rise into the fall of 2005 at lower rates of growth, or at the very latest the spring of 2006 before speculation drops off more dramatically with rising interest rates and a booming stock market again. Often homebuyers and owners looking to refinance will make one last rush into the market when they sense that interest rates have bottomed and will be rising. Housing trends are also slower to react than stock and commodity trends. Low interest rates keep housing affordable despite skyrocketing valuations based on rents and incomes. But the real secret to the continued strength in housing despite waning demographic trends is the same factor as in the recent oil or stock bubbles. And that is, of course, speculation in the late stages!

The National Association of Realtors reported in mid-2005 that an estimated 25% of home sales are now bought as an investment, with 10% or higher as vacation homes. Typically vacation homes represent 6% of the market, with vacation homes appreciating recently at twice the rate of primary homes due to stronger demographic trends, as we forecast. And why not speculate with a poor stock market in the last five years and falling interest rates? Single-family homes are also slowing while condos continue to grow faster in price at three times the rate of primary homes. Condos are easier to buy preconstruction, with low down payments, and then sell when completed at a profit, and they are more likely to be in vacation/second home markets (including in large downtown areas of cities) that have had the strongest demographic trends. Hence condos and vacation areas are where the greatest speculation and risks are, despite the fact that demographic trends continue to favor vacation, resort, and retirement areas for years to come.

Again, remember that we are in a bubble boom. As incomes and assets rise and interest rates fall, investors keep chasing the strongest areas of appreciation and profits until they become overvalued. That has been happening in housing and oil stocks since 2000 when stocks crashed and forced investors to reallocate their investments. Now vacation homes and condos represent the greatest part of the recent housing bubble and have growing risks, despite stronger demographic trends than primary homes.

The best illustration of how extreme the speculative trends have gotten in a normally stable and moderate growth market comes from Robert Shiller in Figure F.10. This chart shows long term, and especially since the 1950s, that home prices simply correlate with inflation and construction/replacement costs, except for minor bubbles in demand like the early 1950s, late 1970s, and late 1980s—and the more extreme bubble now that is coming both from speculation and from increasingly limited land for development in more urban areas. But this increase is coming from rising land prices, not from rising construction costs! And land prices can deflate rapidly in a slowing market or economy, just like stock valuations! In fact, Shiller shows brilliantly in his recent revised edition of *Irrational Exuberance* that construction costs (after correlating strongly with housing prices and inflation since 1890) have been rising less than inflation since 1980, while home prices have been rising faster and accelerating dramatically since 2000. This is a sign of an extreme bubble, like stocks growing much faster than earnings.

The real pizzazz in housing, outside of bubbles like this one, is simply that they are bought on leverage through mortgages—and hence, are a leveraged hedge against inflation. In strongly rising inflation trends like the 1970s, housing performed better than stocks and most investments. In a boom like this one, with falling mortgage rates and growing demand versus supply, home prices tend to grow faster than inflation due to falling financing costs and scarcity of land for development and environmental restrictions. But that would conversely mean that home prices would also fall with reverse leverage during a deflation in prices, as they only last did significantly in the early 1930s, and a slowing in the economy and demographic demand. And that is what we are forecasting from 2011 on.

There are two camps in the housing bubble debate: The "it's a bubble camp" is led most credibly by Shiller, and the "it's not a bubble camp" includes Greenspan and argues that there are only bubbles in a narrow range of local markets. We ultimately agree with the bubble camp, but more so with Shiller, who argues this is the greatest bubble ever in housing. We have shown precedents like 1914–1919 and 1925–29 for the recent tech-driven bubble in stocks. We see no precedent in modern history for the recent bubble in housing prices across the Western world. And it was a minority of large-cap growth and technology stocks that caused the recent bubble in stocks, as Jeremy Siegel has pointed out. But we agree a bit with the not-a-bubble camp in that we don't see a crash near term, just a flattening in most home prices due to a strong economy and continued low interest rates ahead. After a minor crash in the most overvalued areas just ahead, we see a broad crash between 2011 and 2022, especially between 2011 and 2014.

Most forecasters in both camps will be wrong about the scenario in housing ahead. We will not see the broad crash in the coming years that the bubble camp predicts. But there will be a dramatic flattening near term and a broad crash from around 2011 into 2014, on a lag from the stock crash and economic slowdown from 2010 on, which the not-a-bubble camp does not see. Yet the most overvalued areas in the Northeast, California, and South Florida will likely see minor declines in the coming years, along with more substantial declines in the hottest high-end vacation and condo markets.

FIGURE F.10 House Prices and Costs
Adjusted for Size and Quality, 1890–2004

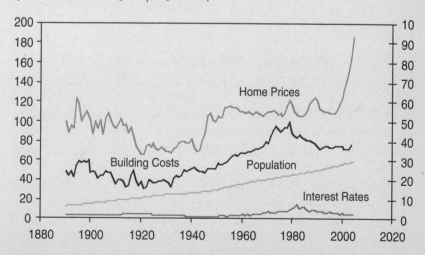

Source: Robert J. Shiller, *Irrational Exuberance,* 2nd edition, Princeton University Press, 2005.

Shiller brings excellent analysis in Figure F.10 by adjusting the change in home values for both inflation and changes in construction quality and size. This chart represents the deviation from inflation and quality trends, or simply, replacement costs. Note that when the trends were more disinflationary at first from 1920 to 1929, and then deflationary from 1930 to 1933, home prices underperformed even the broad price trends. The worst performance with the largest decline in modern history was between 1930 and 1933. And we have a deflationary period ahead of us again from 2011 to 2023 by our demographic forecasts. Hence, our much stronger warnings for real estate losses in that time period. But the most important insight here is that home prices have gotten way ahead of inflation and quality trends, far more than at any time in the last century.

This is not just another bubble—it is the greatest bubble we have ever seen in housing prices. And it is occurring around the developed world from Australia to South Africa to Western Europe. Appreciation rates are already slowing dramatically in London and Sydney, with Australia seeing 20% annual increases diminish to near 0% in just the last year and England seeing 25% growth rates drop to 5% in the last few years as we show in Figure F.11. That is similar to what we see happening in the U.S. over the next year or so.

With demographic demand trends waning and interest rates likely to rise mildly in the years ahead, the real question is not whether this bubble in strong home price rises is sustainable, but simply whether home prices

FIGURE F.11 Home Price Appreciation
Britain, Australia, and U.S., 1998–2005

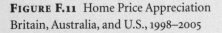

Home prices, % increase on a year earlier

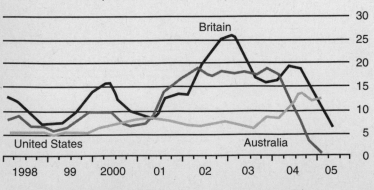

Source: Economist

are overvalued enough yet—given that most bubbles last longer than we
would think. Most analysts say yes. But one means of analysis still says . . .
not quite yet. Figure F.12 and Figure F.13 show two different measures of
home valuation and affordability. The first (Figure F.12) is the more typical,
with home prices divided by incomes (home prices divided by rents is the
other common measure). This valuation model says housing prices are
more overvalued than at any other time in U.S. history: 30% higher than
the norm on average, and that is extreme for housing. The ratios are very
similar when home prices to rents are measured.

But the second chart (Figure F.13) shows that housing prices are still
relatively affordable to new homebuyers and owners. It measures home
payments to incomes, and mortgage payments have continued to decline
due to falling long-term interest rates and innovative short-term ARM,
interest-only, and no–down payment loans. These products have lowered
the costs near term while incomes have continued to rise more modestly.
This chart says that the average family can still afford a home at today's
prices, but that would be less so if interest rates were to rise substantially, or
home prices were to continue to rise at high rates without a dramatic corresponding fall in interest rates, which is simply not possible. This chart
suggests that home prices could at best rise with rising income levels in the

FIGURE F.12 Home Price to Income

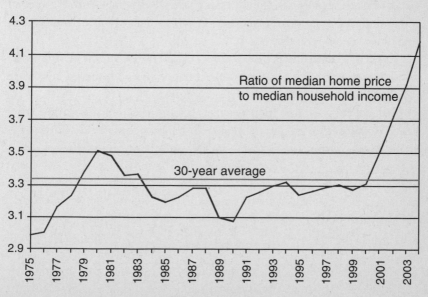

Source: U.S. Census Bureau; National Association of Realtors

FIGURE F.13 Home Payment to Income

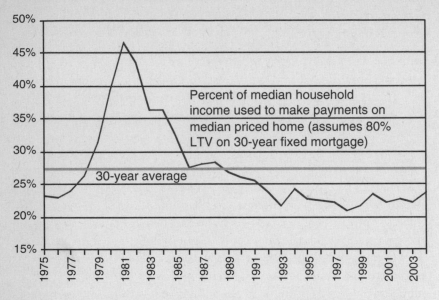

Percent of median household income used to make payments on median priced home (assumes 80% LTV on 30-year fixed mortgage)

30-year average

Source: U.S. Census Bureau; National Association of Realtors; Mortgage Rates for Federal Reserve

future if mortgage rates were flat, and that is a possibility for the next year or so. If interest rates rise, then housing levels will struggle to rise at even the underlying inflation or construction cost trends, which are more moderate than income trends.

Even with continued supply limitations in development, appreciation rates are clearly not sustainable short term and housing prices are not sustainable long term.

Hence, they are due to at least slow more dramatically in the years ahead toward more moderate inflation rates or income gains. But the extreme overvaluation today argues that they should slow more than that and flatten generally, with moderate declines in the most overvalued markets, as occurred in the early to mid-1990s. In the last slowdown the most overvalued markets in the Northeast and California declined between 10% and 20% as most housing markets simply grew very slowly from 1990 to 1997. High-end homes in those areas declined 20% to 40% in that time period. Hence, there are real risks ahead in these overvalued areas.

The mortgage payments are more the reality for homebuyers and their ability to afford a house, at least in their short-term thinking, especially for speculators. But the truth is somewhere in between as property taxes and insurance can run 35% to 45% above the mortgage and are not cushioned by falling interest rates. And most buyers don't fully consider that, as Suze Orman is always warning. So, the truth is that housing is extremely over-valued versus incomes and rents, and even more so versus inflation and construction costs. Hence, the especially strong rising trend since 2000 is not sustainable unless interest rates continue to fall—and that is not likely to occur past this year or very early 2006.

We expect incomes to keep rising and more strongly in the great boom ahead. But short-term interest rates are only going to rise modestly, hurting the 40% of new home buyers that use 1-year ARM rates currently, along with increasing trends in interest-only mortgages and low to zero down payments that are fueling the bubble. These unprecedented liberal policies in lending are also a sign of an extreme bubble that is not sustainable. And long-term interest rates are likely to follow upward, but also very modestly after a near-term modest fall again. So the truth is that home prices will be at more of a stalemate in the years ahead at best, and weaken more so if in-terest rates rise more than modestly. Given that home prices are so overval-ued, they should grow very modestly at best on average, and could decline modestly at worst over the next 1–5 years.

Figure F.14 shows that new-home sales have started to become more volatile, and slowed a bit into June 2005. Figure F.15 shows that new-home prices have been similarly volatile and weakened sharply from March 2005

FIGURE F.14 New-Home Sales, 1990–Present

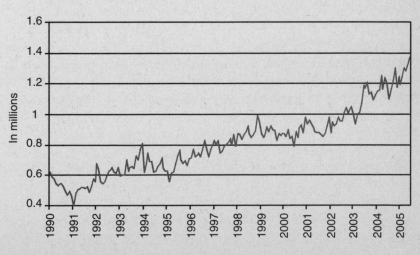

Source: U.S. Census Bureau

FIGURE F.15 Median New-Home Prices, 1990–Present

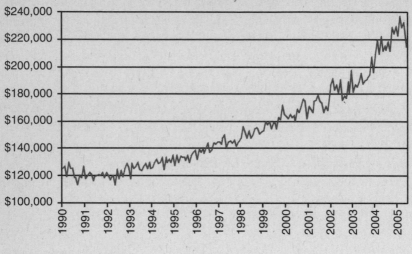

Source: U.S. Census Bureau

into June 2005 while existing-home prices and sales kept rising to new highs. This is a divergence that suggests a top approaching in appreciation rates by late 2005 or so. If appreciation rates do fall dramatically over the coming year, as we forecast, then speculation in housing will quickly lose its appeal and that will take the last air out of the housing bubble.

The housing bubble has gotten more extreme in the last year and has shifted more from California to Florida. Figure F.16 shows the top twenty markets for appreciation from March 2004 into March 2005. Bradenton, Florida, led with 45.6% growth and has been catching up with the adjacent hot market in Sarasota, which grew at 36.0%. California, the Northeast, and Las Vegas continue to show very strong gains, but California prices are so high that they simply can't grow as much as the up-and-coming markets in Florida. This last strong surge in Florida is a sign to us of the last stages of this bubble. Florida is simply catching up with the overvaluation levels in the hottest coastal areas of the Northeast and California.

We have presented many overvaluation indicators for different markets over the last year that all point to the same overvalued areas. Most of them are based on prices versus incomes or rents. Figure F.17 shows an analysis of the markets with the highest risk of declines based on job growth, past volatility, and overvaluation from Private Mortgage Insurance. Mortgage insurance companies bear the bottom-line risk from housing price volatil-

FIGURE F.16 Top 20 Markets for Home Appreciation
Annual Percentage Change, 1st Quarter 2005

Metro Area	State	Percent Change	Median Price
Bradenton	FL	45.60%	$275,100
Sarasota	FL	36.00%	$326,300
W. Palm Beach/Boca Raton/Delray Beach	FL	35.90%	$362,800
Riverside/San Bernardino	CA	32.60%	$343,400
Ft. Lauderdale/Hollywood/Pompano Beach	FL	31.80%	$320,700
Las Vegas	NV	29.40%	$291,000
Melbourne/Titusville/Palm Bay	FL	29.30%	$184,000
Orlando	FL	28.70%	$194,400
Miami/Hialeah	FL	28.40%	$315,700
Ocala	FL	27.00%	$122,200
Sacramento	CA	26.90%	$352,900
Honolulu	HI	26.00%	$529,100
Ft. Myers/Cape Coral	FL	25.60%	$215,700
Phoenix	AZ	24.40%	$193,800
Atlantic City	NJ	23.20%	$217,400
Washington	DC/MD/VA	22.70%	$369,000
Norfolk/Virginia Bch/Newport News	VA	22.20%	$174,000
Los Angeles Area	CA	21.10%	$474,700
San Diego	CA	20.90%	$584,100
New York/Monmouth/Ocean	NY/NJ	20.30%	$358,500

Source: U.S. Census Bureau

ity and hence should be the best gauge of overvaluation risks. This chart gives a slightly different ranking in risk with the Northeast the highest, then California, with South Florida substantially lower due to higher job growth and migration rates.

The highest-risk market at 55.3% is Boston, due to the highest prices in the Northeast and slower job growth and higher past volatility. That is followed by Nassau/Suffolk in New York at 54.0%, and then a host of California markets led by San Diego between 41.9% and 52.8% risk. The biggest surprise is that markets like Minneapolis and Detroit come in at high risks due to slowing job growth, despite not being as overvalued by most other measures. And Florida, despite high valuations versus incomes, comes in as more moderate, ranging from 21.9% in Fort Lauderdale to 16.6% in Miami and Tampa due to higher migration and job growth.

But as with oil stocks, Figure F.18 shows what looks to be a bubble nearing a peak in home-building stocks as of late July 2005. Since home-building stocks started to lead in 2000, we see that we were in the final stages of a clear five-wave rally. This chart would suggest that this could be a top with rising interest rates again since June 2005. But when interest rates ultimately start to rise again after early 2006 and home prices slow further, housing stocks should continue to lag. We could see as much as a 40% to

FIGURE F.17 Top 25 Markets for Risk of Home Price Declines

Rank	City	Risk Index
1	Boston-Quincy, Mass.	55.30%
2	Nassau-Suffolk, N.Y.	54.00%
3	San Diego-Carlsbad-San Marcos, Calif.	52.80%
4	San Jose-Sunnyvale-Santa Clara, Calif.	51.30%
5	Santa Ana-Anaheim-Irvine, Calif.	51.20%
6	Oakland-Fremont-Hayward, Calif.	50.90%
7	Cambridge-Newton-Framingham, Mass.	46.90%
8	San Francisco-San Mateo-Redwood City, Calif.	45.90%
9	Providence-New Bedford-Fall River, R.I.-Mass.	43.20%
10	Riverside-San Bernardino-Ontario, Calif.	42.20%
11	Los Angeles-Long Beach-Glendale, Calif.	42.10%
12	Sacramento-Arden-Arcade-Roseville, Calif.	41.90%
13	Edison, N.J.	36.40%
14	New York-Wayne-White Plains, N.Y.-N.J.	32.60%
15	Detroit-Livonia-Dearborn, Mich.	29.50%
16	Newark-Union, N.J.-Penn.	25.10%
17	Minneapolis-St. Paul-Bloomington, Minn.-Wis.	24.90%
18	Fort Lauderdale-Pompano Beach-Deerfield Beach, Fla.	21.90%
19	Washington-Arlington-Alexandria, DC-Va.-Md.	20.90%
20	Denver-Aurora, Col.	16.90%
21	Warren-Farmington Hills-Troy, Mich.	16.80%
22	Miami-Miami Beach-Kendall, Fla.	16.60%
23	Tampa-St. Petersburg-Clearwater, Fla.	16.60%
24	Las Vegas-Paradise, Nev.	13.00%
25	Baltimore-Towson, Md.	12.40%

Source: USA Today, PMI Mortgage

45% drop from near 1,000 back to the strongest support around 550 in the next year or so, but likely a bit less with the growing overall boom ahead in stocks.

Another bubble is about to end in real estate, while the bubble boom moves on.

But we will likely only see declines in the most overvalued areas, while most homes simply slow, flatten, or decline modestly in price trends in the years ahead. The economy and interest rates will still generally be favorable for housing so we won't likely see a broad decline. But slowing demographic demand, modestly rising interest rates, and strong stock appreciation will increasingly work against continued strong price increases for homes. The real crash in housing—and the final burst of the greatest bubble in housing in history—will come in the downturn we project for 2011 to 2022 when we see an extended deflationary downturn, like the one Japan saw from 1990 to 2003. Home prices have fallen in Japan 40% on average since 1992 and as much as 80% in the most overvalued areas. So much for the argument that real estate can't go down because it is only getting more scarce. There are few countries with scarcer land versus population than Japan.

FIGURE F.18 Dow Jones U.S. Home Construction Index, Feb. 2000–Present

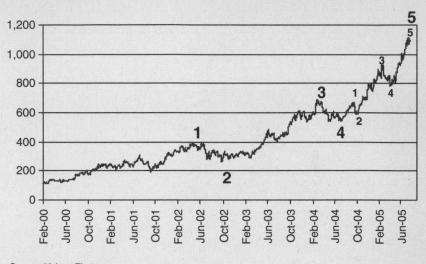

Source: Yahoo Finance

Figure F.19 also shows that home-building stocks were approaching their highest price/earnings (P/E) levels near 10 times earnings in mid-2005. Some analysts were already saying that home-building stocks are in a new era of ever-tightening supply and ever-expanding demand, but the smart money knows better, given the strong cyclicality of this industry—and would very likely take this as a sell signal confirming that a peak was at hand in late July 2005.

But to keep a larger perspective on home prices and why we see more limited downside for years to come, we present Figure F.20. It shows median prices of existing homes back to 1968. Using median prices takes out the bias that more expensive and volatile homes have on the market and thus more clearly shows what happens to the typical house, which is more stable in price. This chart demonstrates how stable median housing prices are even after bubbles, compared to stock and commodity prices. In this strong boom with falling interest rates, home prices have tended to slow or flatten rather than drop off significantly, since they have rising inflation rates and replacement costs, as well as supply limitations during boom times, underlying them. The demand cycle will slow increasingly even in this continued boom, and those inflation rates and replacement costs will decline more significantly in the downturn and deflationary cycle as we are forecasting from 2011 on. But again, remember that high valuation

FIGURE F.19 Price/Earnings Ratio, Home-Building Stocks

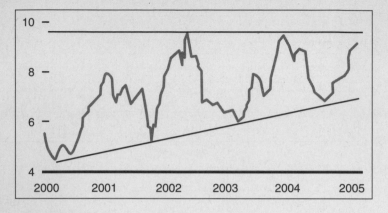

Source: Barron's

areas like the Northeast and California did see even median home prices drop 10% to 20% from 1990 to 1997, with high-end sectors dropping 20% to 40%.

After the peaking of trade-up home buying in late 2003 and then the slowdown in speculative buying from 2006 onwards, the greatest long-term trend in real estate and demographic trends will come from the continued "convection current" of younger graduates and new households migrating from higher cost and less favorable climate areas in the Northeast, upper Midwest, and California into the Southeast and Southwest—much more than the overhyped retirement trends of the baby boomers.

Eleven times more 20–29-year-olds moved out of state than retirees ages 60–69 between 1995 and 2000. The emerging echo boom will be accentuating this demographic cycle into around 2029, providing growth during the boom and even in the slowdown after 2010—but only in the southerly and favorable states and cities (like Nevada, Arizona, Florida, Georgia and North Carolina) that attract these younger people through lower-cost housing and infrastructure, growing jobs, and better schools. But the massive baby boom will also be moving into its retirement phase from 2000 into 2028 and they will move in smaller numbers into very concentrated areas like Arizona, Nevada, the Carolina coasts, and Florida. Thus they will continue to have a high impact on those areas. After 2028 to 2029 our nation will increasingly slow down in growth and move less. We summarized these trends in the October 2005 issue of *The H. S. Dent Forecast.*

FIGURE F.20 Median Existing-Home Prices, 1968–Present

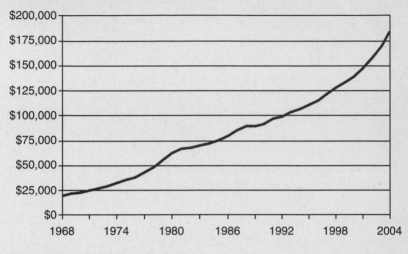

Source: National Association of Realtors

You can download a free sample of *The H.S. Dent Forecast* at www.hsdent .com. Our subscribers also have access to back issues, including our many reports on real estate trends over the last three years.

THE NEXT GREATER BUBBLE EMERGING IN STOCKS

Since the market slowed in January 2005 we have continued to evaluate the patterns to better predict when we would see a stronger liftoff and to monitor if we were still on track for the next great bubble boom. Once bubbles get started, as in early 1995, they tend to build momentum, and corrections, even strong ones like 1998, are sharp but brief. This clearly had not occurred as of August 2005 in this new bull market cycle, but it appears to have been building since late April 2005.

Since the bottom in October 2002, the market has been playing the "catch me if you can" game, moving up rapidly in short surges like 2003 and then moving sideways for many months to wear investors out before surging up again and leaving investors behind in the next surge. Most investors are seeing the long sideways correction after the strong recovery rally in 2003 as a sign that stocks have little potential. But such a scenario is precisely what preceded the last two great bubbles from 1995 to 1999 and 1925 to 1929!

The market has been holding its gains well given the oil bubble, but hasn't clearly moved into the next bubble phase of more consistent momentum as of early August 2005. We think that has possibly begun since late April, but it could be until October 2005 before we see the next very strong acceleration truly begin. Our analysis was correct in predicting the strong rebound in 2003 and the flat trading range in 2004. We were also correct in giving a strong buy signal in August 2004, right at the bottom of that trading range at 9,700 on the Dow. But the Decennial Cycle (in Chapter 3) would strongly suggest that a stronger liftoff would occur in 2005, and more on the earlier side, but the oil bubble thwarted that. The panic selloff in mid-April 2005 back to 10,000 on the Dow finally gave us much higher confidence that we could move forward more strongly and consistently from there on, and so we gave very strong buy signals there again. Hence investors should be buying stocks on short-term pullbacks ahead of the next acceleration between October 2005 and February 2006.

In the panic selloff in April 2005, everyday investors (Figure F.21) at the American Association of Individual Investors (AAII) got nearly as bearish as they did in late 2002 and early 2003, which marked the beginning of this bull market and a very strong rally from early 2003 into early 2004 that most investors missed. Note that high readings in this chart are bullish because investors are very bearish. These everyday investors are the last to

FIGURE F.21 AAII Sentiment Surveys, % Bears to Bulls

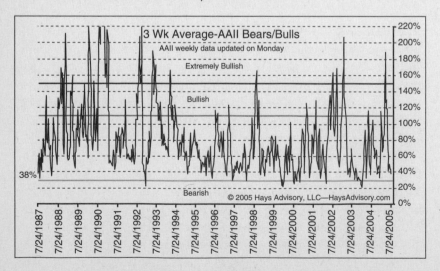

Source: Hays Advisory Inc., www.haysmarketfocus.com

panic and extreme bearish readings of this nature have always come at major bottoms.

This extreme bearishness by everyday investors in April 2005 is the greatest indication we are ready to more convincingly begin the next bubble market in stocks around October 2005, with a strong advance that will last into mid-2006.

Figure F.22 shows how closely this recovery rally on the Dow has been following the one from the tech crash in the early 1920s, on an approximate eighty-one-year lag (on our eighty-year New Economy Cycle in our books). We show in *The Next Great Bubble Boom* how tech stocks recently followed very closely the tech bubble that emerged and peaked in late 1919, and the crash that followed into mid-1921–early 1922. The first bubble peak in early 2000 followed the first bubble peak in late 1919 by about 80.5 years. But the bottom of the crash around late 1921, followed close to 81.0 years later. Now the markets are following the recovery from the early 1920s crash on a near 81.0-year lag. This chart would suggest that we put in a significant bottom in late April 2005 and that will see an acceleration by October of 2005.

Our Dow Channel from Figure 2.16 on page 99 shows we were very near the bottom trend line at around 9,700 in the selloff in April 2005. This would also strongly suggest another stellar buy opportunity for stocks and that we have put in a bottom in April with very little downside ahead for in-

FIGURE F.22 Dow Jones Industrials, 1920s Recovery Versus 2000s Recovery

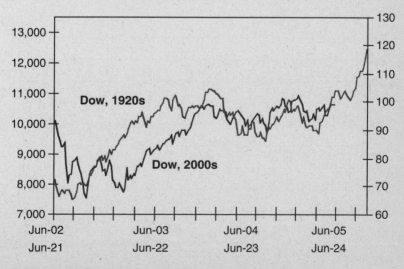

Source: www.globalfindata.com; Yahoo Finance

vestors. This trend line rises at about 12% per year as we move forward and would suggest that any corrections ahead should see higher lows. However, breaking below this bottom trend line would be a worrisome sign. That trend line will rise to 10,000 in October 2005 and 10,400 by February 2006. This should give the market strong support and very minor downside with a rising bias for correction lows.

If the Dow today continues to follow the patterns of the 1920s in the next year, then we should see strong rallies in late 2005 and the Dow should break to new highs, at 12,000 plus, by early 2006, or mid-2006 at the latest.

Figure F.23 shows an 81.0-year lag on the Dow from the 1920s moving out further to a projected potential peak, and would suggest the top should come around mid- to late 2010. If the Dow continues to follow the bubble scenario of the 1920s, as we roughly expect, then we could see 14,000 to 15,000 by as late as August 2006 when the four-year Presidential Cycle is likely to set in for a brief period, but then a sharp correction back to as low as 12,000 into October or so. We would finally hit 20,000 by late 2008 and then see the sharpest bubble from early 2009 into early to mid-2010. And yes, that scenario would suggest a peak around 40,000 similar to our Dow Channel. Our alternative scenario closer to 1995 to 1999 growth rates would project a Dow of 32,000-plus by 2010.

The greatest sign of a stronger bull market ahead is the fact that the

FIGURE F.23 Dow Jones Industrial Average
Lagged 81 years, 2005–2011

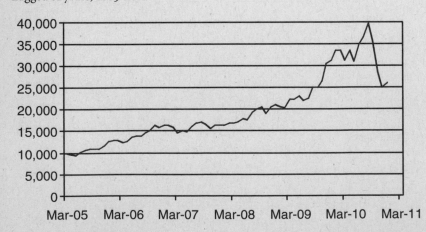

Source: Yahoo Finance

FIGURE F.24 Dow Versus Nasdaq Versus Russell 2000, April 2005–July 2005

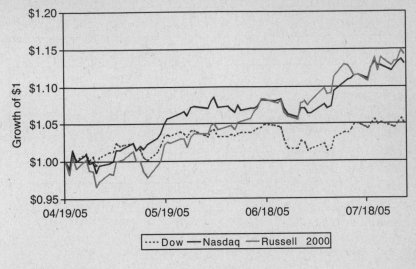

Source: Yahoo Finance

Nasdaq has been leading again since the late April 2005 correction, and small-cap stocks (Russell 2000) continue to lead as we show in Figure F.24. The next resistance points in the Dow will come at 11,300, where many bear market highs were made in 2000, and then the all-time highs at 11,770. Once we break above there, likely in early to mid-2006, the markets will clearly be in a broad new bull market and will be free to accelerate further into mid- to late 2006 before the four-year Presidential Cycle hits between August and October 2006. Then we should see increasing bubble surges from very late 2006 into 2010 before it peaks as high as 40,000.

A BULL MARKET IN THE DOLLAR AHEAD

Many analysts, including Warren Buffett, had been predicting in early 2005 that the U.S. dollar would continue to fall well into the future due to rising trade and budget deficits, while we were predicting a bottom and a major new bull market. The dollar already looks like it has made a bottom, completing a near perfect Elliott Wave pattern of decline in Figure F.25. A rising dollar will attract more foreign capital into the U.S. stock and bond markets and give us an extra boost. We expect a strong five-year bull market in

Figure F.25　Euro/Dollar, 1995–Present

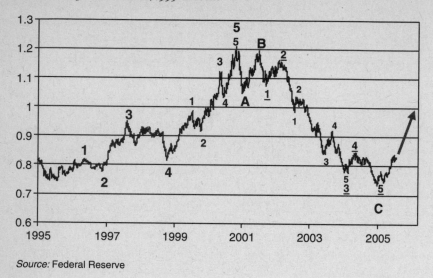

Source: Federal Reserve

the dollar similar to what occurred from 1995 to 2000. That means that travel overseas should be more affordable in the next five years as well.

Summary Recommendations

Don't give up on the next great bubble boom with the second "investment opportunity of a lifetime" that very likely occurred in late April 2005 and October 2005 and has very little downside risk going forward. This bull market is likely to be even greater than 1995 to early 2000, and should rival the mid-1924 to late 1929 bubble. Our projected peak for the Dow and broader markets is now between March and September 2010, likely closer to September. Our targets for the Dow are still 32,000 to 40,000—and around 13,000 for the Nasdaq. But note from Figure 3.14 in Chapter 3 that tech and small-cap growth stocks are likely to peak about a year earlier, or around mid to late 2009 in our updated projections in this special report.

The danger signs that would cause us to reconsider our forecasts near term would be 1) we see a significant break below 9,500 on the Dow in late 2005, or 2) we see the markets fail to have a strong rally by March 2006.

We would start to become more concerned if we broke much below the lower Dow Channel trend line (at 10,000 in October 2005 or 10,400 in February 2006). Otherwise, the trends are playing out very much in line with the recoveries in the 1920s and 1990s that led to very strong bubble-boom markets in line with our demographic and technology cycles.

Don't wait for greater proof of this bull market into next year and miss a potential 40% to 50% rally (greater on the Nasdaq and small-cap markets) from late 2005 into mid-2006, as investors did in 2003 after our extreme buy signals in early October 2002 and March 2003—as long as our downside risk targets above are not violated. The Nasdaq has already doubled from its late 2002 low and the Dow has seen 50% gains thus far, but which most investors have already missed. Our targets for mid to late 2006 are 14,000 to 15,000 on the Dow and 3,500 on the Nasdaq.

The sectors to focus on include large- and small-cap growth, technology, financial services (investment banking, management, and brokerage—but not mortgage lending), health care and biotech, leisure and gaming, upscale consumer products and services, consumer cyclicals (outside of housing construction), and Asia. Technology, small-cap growth, and biotech should be the best sectors to add near term. For fixed income, investors should focus on shorter-term maturities to protect against the likelihood of gradually rising long-term rates into 2006. And it is high time to sell investment or unnecessary vacation real estate by the fall or the spring of 2006 at the latest—or to even consider selling, moving from, or renting in the most overpriced coastal urban markets in the Northeast, California, and South Florida.

THE NEW SCIENCE

How Simple, Predictable Principles Drive Complex Change

WE ARE ALL REACTING to the "great bubble" in the stock market and business and its collapse in the early 2000s, wondering why we could have been so stupid to have believed in it and if we will see growth like this again for many decades. The common wisdom is that once you've seen a "bubble" it's all over for many years or decades. But the economic and stock market recovery from late 2002 into late 2005 has caused more people to wonder if this bull market is not going to continue.

We have a clear answer: There will be another great bull market into the end of this decade that is likely to be even stronger than the 1990s bull market.

In this book we will explain why the current perception that "we've seen a bubble burst and it's over" is not true when it comes to technology bubbles, why technology bubbles are different from other bubbles in history—and why such bubbles as well as strong consolidations and "tech wrecks" like those we have recently seen are necessary to major advances in human progress throughout history.

The truth is that there are at least two bubbles before a final peak in a major new technology expansion cycle is reached. We are forecasting the least suspected but greatest bull market in history—similar to the greatest bull market in U.S. history that occurred from 1922 to 1929 (the Roaring Twenties) after a very similar "technology" bubble and crash from late 1919 into early 1922. We have always compared this decade to the Roaring Twenties, and the truth is that decade started off almost exactly like this one.

Scientists and economists are experts in looking at a very complex world and coming up with complex explanations for it. But we often know different from our common-sense experience. Human beings have their own individual strengths and weaknesses and use them to survive as best they can. The people we know more often than not do predictable things most of the time, just like the planets predictably revolve around the sun, and the sun comes up every morning and the tides come and go, and so on. When many human beings do such predictable things in large numbers we can predict events such as when they will die on average—as life insurance actuaries have been doing for many decades.

But now for the first time since the early 1980s, when the first annual Consumer Expenditure Surveys were conducted by the U.S. Bureau of Labor Statistics, we can increasingly predict when people will do all types of things from growing up (at great expense to parents, the government, and businesses) to workforce entry (where they finally become productive) to earning to spending to borrowing to saving to retirement, as well as when they spend money on all types of things from cradle to grave. It simply wasn't possible to know these statistics before the recent information age began.

But in broader terms, in recent decades information technologies have allowed us to analyze all types of phenomena from the "big bang" and the evolution of our universe to the evolution of our planet and all of the flora and fauna that have developed over millions of years to the DNA code and how humans have developed and migrated around the earth over the last 80,000 years. Although we have always wanted to believe what we wanted to about the past to fit our personal, ethnic, and religious ideologies, we can increasingly see the greater reality of evolution and economic progress over long periods of time today. We have, predictably, fought most new scientific insights throughout history, such as the earth being round and revolving around the sun, but that hasn't changed reality. The people that have most understood reality throughout history have progressed the most, and even more so in recent decades! For the first time in history, from many angles, we can see where we have come from, how we have evolved, and where we are likely going—from the longest- to the shortest-term cycles. For a more in-depth analysis of human evolutionary cycles, you can download a free special report on our website at www.hsdent.com at "The Long View" under "Key Concepts."

THE ATTITUDE THAT "NO ONE CAN FORECAST THE FUTURE"

Today in economics and in many fields of politics, sociology, and science, there is an attitude that "nobody can predict the future past a certain point"—there are too many complex variables that could impact it—hence we can only learn from the past. But this is obviously nonsense as more and more fields of science have become capable of predicting more phenomena for centuries as our knowledge of the universe has grown exponentially. We have been saying something very different in economics for more than two decades with greater degrees of long-term predictability than other economists. Increasing advances in many fields of science are only validating this concept. There are more and more simple cause-and-effect factors that we can identify from evolutionary stages to planetary cycles to genes to early-life character developments in psychology to predictable life cycles in humans, natural systems, and technologies. And the most fundamental factors we have found to be critical in economics are so large that they overwhelm smaller factors and more random events.

No matter what we learn, there will always be factors that we don't understand yet, seemingly random factors—such as the September 11, 2001, terrorist attacks. But the truth is that even such factors may not be as random as we think. Our research has shown that incidents such as 9/11 are much more likely to occur when other factors, such as the economy, are weak or in down cycles—much like Hitler and World War II, which followed the Great Depression. Even the weather has become more predictable, both short term and long term, in recent decades. We can now track the climate and the movement of the continents over millions of years through drilling into glacial ice formations and many other means. And climate has been the greatest single factor driving the rise and fall of species over time.

But scientists, political scientists, and sociologists would ask, "How can you account for the great variability of events that have occurred in modern times?" The truth is that we can't be 100 percent certain, but we can better approximate the most fundamental trends that have driven past changes and will very likely drive our future. The two trends beyond climate that are most applicable to human and economic progress in the last 10,000 years are demographic trends in population and aging, and technological innovation. We have been predicting the most basic trends in economics since the late 1980s with greater and greater accuracy, just like weather trends. And we keep learning more and predicting more long term and short term, and again we will never get it totally right. But the people who have listened to us have made much better decisions than others over the last fifteen to twenty years.

Some of the greatest insights into predictability recently have come from DNA research. Despite our different environments growing up, we can more closely predict our personalities and characteristics from our DNA—and we will be able to change them in the future if we choose. We can now track the migrations of past ethnic groups around the world with much greater accuracy than through anthropological finds—through DNA tracing. But perhaps the greatest insight comes from Stephen Wolfram, author of *A New Kind of Science*. He has shown that the most complex patterns and cycles in nature actually evolve from very simple formulas or patterns that repeat and evolve over long periods of time.

Complexity evolves from simple factors through growth and replication over increasing periods of time, not complex causes or factors. **The truth is that life is complex but evolution and human nature over time are simple. Progress is also very clearly exponential, not linear. And we don't think that way.**

More progress has been made in our relative standard of living in the past 200 years than in the 10,000 years previously, and more progress was made in the past 10,000 years than millions of years before. Hence, the history of progress is clearly exponential beyond our present conceptions. In this book, as in many past books, we look at more and more trends that we can predict (despite seemingly random short-term events) well into the future that will affect our economy, our investments, our lives, our businesses, our children's educations and careers, our real estate and living circumstances—as well as many other aspects of our lives. And we use very commonsense indicators like when the average family spends the most money in their lifetime, which any of us can readily understand as we do similar things in our lives.

Imagine living in the Stone Age and not understanding how and why our seasons of weather change every year and being shocked by the advent of winter. We are charting the seasons of our economy in a way that has never been done before but is proving to be increasingly accurate. Many of the same types of things that occurred eighty years ago are recurring today—including the recent tech crash and terrorist strikes. All of our books have emphasized an approximate two-generation or eighty-year cycle in the emergence of radical new technologies and new economies and ways of living and doing business. The tech wreck and terrorist crisis of the early 1920s was followed by the greatest bull market in history and advances in our standard of living to follow from the late 1930s into the 1970s that literally no one would have forecasted back then. For the first time in history, we don't have to be "surprised" when spring or summer turns to fall or winter in our economy!

These seasons in our economy, as well as longer-term advances in technologies and our standard of living, are largely predictable. In this book we will look at how our economy and stock market will very likely evolve over the coming decade—when we will see the greatest bull market in history— and over the decades to follow, when we will see one of the greatest downturns in history in the United States and the Western world. These trends have already been set into motion by the massive baby-boom generation's spending and productivity cycle and the information revolution since the advent of microchips in 1971. All we have to do is understand how our consumer and technology life cycles coincide. And if we understand such trends and life cycles we should be preparing for the last *great* bull market in U.S. history (not the last bull market) and a downturn to follow that will compare to the Great Depression—in some ways worse, in some ways perhaps better.

Why We Will See the Dow at 40,000 Near the End of This Decade

Since the early 1980s, we have been conducting increasing research into demographic, generational, and technology cycles that are the fundamental generators of economic growth and stock market advances, despite and beyond political and random events such as 9/11, or short-term over- and undervaluation cycles in the stock market as we have recently seen and as we saw in 1987. People who are born into a highly productive economy, such as that of the United States and most developed countries around the world, do fairly predictable things as they age. Once radical new technologies emerge in clusters they grow in a four-stage life cycle, creating new growth industries and the reengineering of older industries much like the seasons of our own lives (youth, adulthood, midlife crisis, and late adulthood).

The most important premise of this book is that despite the crash of 2000–2002, the greatest economic boom and bull market is not over! The demographic wave of earning and spending of the largest generation in history, the baby boomers, never stopped during the downturn of 2000–2002 and will continue until 2009 or 2010. The greatest technology revolution since electricity, the automobile, and the telephone—and perhaps since the printing press in the late 1400s—will not see its first major peak until late in this decade as well and will resurge surprisingly in the second half of this decade into another strong growth boom in productivity and another bubble in the stock markets. It just had to go through a consolidation phase after the first rapid growth stage of the late 1990s.

It's not that we've seen a bubble burst, but that we are in an extended "bubble boom." We will show in Chapter 1 how this bubble boom has been evolving since the early 1980s, and in Chapter 2 how a greater bubble boom has been evolving since the steam engine and Industrial Revolution of the late 1700s. The first bubble in this boom occurred into 1987, the second into early 2000. The third and last is just ahead. This decade will resemble the Roaring Twenties as we have always been forecasting. That decade started out with a "tech wreck" that followed an initial tech bubble, as we will document in detail in Chapters 1 and 2 of this book. But after the stock crash in the early 1920s a greater bubble and expansion period followed into late 1929, the greatest eight-year bull market in U.S. history–"the buy opportunity of a lifetime" back then and the best of the entire last century. The Roaring Twenties bull market was the least anticipated in history due to the devastating technology bubble and crash that preceded it.

But that great bull market was finally followed by the Great Depression, the worst economic period in U.S. history. We continue to see a similar downturn from 2010 to 2022 or so. These predictable and tumultuous cycles will affect your investments, your business, and your life more than any other events in our lifetimes. We will present a much more comprehensive analysis of demographic, technology, and cyclical trends to allow you to prosper and adapt over the next two decades, which will continue to defy economic forecasts and normality as we have known it. But, more importantly, we will outline the most comprehensive forecasts and long-term systems for investment, business, and life planning ever offered. It's up to you to spend the time to examine our new logic and determine if it's worth applying to your life, career, and investments.

In *The Roaring 2000s,* published in early 1998, we followed our demographic analysis in *The Great Boom Ahead* (published in late 1992) and forecasted that the Dow Jones Industrial Average could reach as high as 35,000 or 40,000 by late 2008 or 2009. There is not an economist or analyst anywhere that we are aware of who thinks that is remotely possible today. This continues to be our forecast, and it bodes well for a very strong economy and returns for investors similar to or better than in the second half of the 1990s. Most investors and businesspeople were very skeptical of our forecasts in the late 1980s that the Dow would reach 10,000 or higher, especially after the early 1990s recession, S&L crisis, stock crash, and Iraqi war. But we have found through studying very long-term trends that the fundamental ones we identify win out over time and are clearly the best way to invest and make plans for the future.

The recent great stock crash bottomed in early October 2002, when we gave the strongest buy signal in the history of our newsletter, *The H. S. Dent Forecast.* The recovery in the stock market and economy since then has been persistent, although it stalled a bit, as we forecasted from early to late 2004. That was just the first wave in the last great bull market we will see for the rest of this decade. The greatest part of this bull market is still ahead, between late 2005 and mid- to late 2010. This is the last chance you have as an investor or businessperson to take advantage of the greatest boom in history. From late 2010 on, we will see a long-term economic downturn, as Japan saw from 1990 to 2003 and more similar to what the United States saw from 1930 to 1942. Why? Trends in spending and technology cycles will turn down. And if you thought political problems and terrorist threats were scary in the early 2000s—they will only intensify in such a prolonged downturn.

A NEW SCIENCE: DEMOGRAPHICS

Most people are not clearly aware of the full range of breakthroughs that have occurred in all types of sciences in the last two or three decades with the advent of the recent information and computer revolution that still has many more decades to deliver advances and results beyond most of our imaginations. This Information Revolution, which began with the first computer in 1946 and extended into microchips in 1971, personal computers by 1976, advanced software operating systems by 1981, then the Internet by 1993 and broadband in recent years—represents the capacity for communications, collaboration, and access to research that is spawning major advances in all of science, business, sociology, and personal lifestyles. Demographics represents just one new science that first emerged in the 1970s with demographic and lifestyle models such as PRIZM (from Claritas) and TAPESTRY (from ESRI) that could project consumer spending propensities down to counties and then zip codes and now neighborhood blocks.

We followed with macroeconomic models starting in the late 1980s, showing that incomes, spending, borrowing, investing, innovation, productivity (and inflation), and power shifts (business model and political changes) were predictably generated by demographic and generational cycles. William Strauss and Neal Howe documented these generation cycles since the late 1400s in great detail in *Generations* (1991) and other books. Strauss and Howe showed that there is a four-stage generation cycle that corresponds to the evolution of political, social, and economic cycles in our economy over approximately two generations, or eighty years or so.

The point is that there is a new information-based science built on predictable cause-and-effect impacts of how we change as we age that is just as predictable on average as life insurance actuarial tables for when we will die. That represents a major breakthrough, especially as computer and information technologies now allow us to analyze and project such predictable impacts decades in advance and down to zip codes and neighborhood blocks! Economists, business forecasters, and stock market analysts are still unaware of this new, simple science. Hence, they have been wrong about most fundamental trends for decades and will continue to be wrong about the prognosis for the rest of this very bullish decade and the very difficult decade to follow.

You as an investor, businessperson, or individual cannot afford to wait for the economic elite to recognize this new science or wait to see the results and scenario we have been and are continuing to successfully forecast. Your life may very well depend on understanding why we are in the most volatile period of expansion in history and how it will unfold on both the upside and downside in the next two decades and beyond. You are in a position to understand the simple, commonsense, and profound implications of some fundamental principles that most experts have not grasped and will not grasp as they continue to defend the economic principles of the past.

Demographics as a new science is the greatest breakthrough we have seen in economics. It is inherently very simple and understandable in principle as we all do these predictable things to some degree or another as we age. But these simple principles, when analyzed and projected in greater depth, allow us to see not just the simple trends, but the more complex unfolding of our economy and lives over time. Hence, our economy is far more predictable than we have been led to believe by economists.

A NEW KIND OF SCIENCE ALTOGETHER

In *A New Kind of Science,* Stephen Wolfram proposes the same principle we are proposing—that simple factors drive predictable long-term and complex trends, but on a much broader and more sophisticated level. Wolfram has used high-powered computers to demonstrate a new principle of science and evolution. He shows that very complex patterns of nature from snowflakes to seashells to zebra coats to coastlines to mountain ranges can be generated from very simple mathematical formulas that are repeated over long periods of time. They start out very simple but end up very complex in appearance. They seem unpredictable and random at first glance, but they end up highly predictable from such simple formulas if understood and applied rigorously over time.

Our evolution started out at the simplest level with the big bang and has expanded into an ever-growing and complex universe ever since. Life has emanated from very basic quarks, atoms, and molecules that evolved into very simple single-cell organisms (which are all still the building blocks of life today). These simple forms have evolved over time into very complex natural systems, reptiles, mammals, and human beings as the seemingly highest form of evolution to date. And our evolution as humans has evolved from very small populations at simple survival levels of existence, from migrating hunting tribes to small agricultural towns and into very complex societies, economies, and cultures. So, from a long-term point of view this should be obvious. Simple forms or formulas evolve into complex forms and manifestations through predictable cycles of growth and evolution over time. The key to understanding change and forecasting future trends is not to understand their apparent complexity but the inherently simple principles and formulas driving such change. The truth is that you can't understand the "whole" by merely analyzing all of the parts. "The whole is greater than the sum of the parts."

This may sound preposterous, but both Wolfram's new research and ours strongly suggest that nothing is random if you fully understand the simple factors driving growth and evolution and how they combine and evolve over time. We can get better at doing that but will likely never get it 100 percent right! But there have been major breakthroughs in the last few decades in many sciences, including research in economics.

It's just that we haven't begun to understand that this is the case until now, and of course, we still haven't fully understood how to determine them, combine them, and project them into the future. And again, we probably never will altogether. But we are beginning to, and in our long-term forecasts we have already made many major successful projections against the grain of opinion in the last two decades! Even Stephen Hawking, author of *A Brief History of Time*, stated that the future is inherently a mirrorlike projection from the past. Our research continues to confirm that point of view.

After forecasting the incredible bull market of the 1990s in the late 1980s and early 1990s, we also forecasted a correction in 2000, but at first we missed the severity of the 2000–2002 crash in the stock markets. But ours was the first research, using the same simple fundamental demographic and technological cycles, to explain by mid-2001 why the tech wreck of 2000–2002 was predictable and why it would lead to the last great bull market and bubble in our lifetimes in the United States. That will be covered in detail in Chapter 1. We had to learn from changes in events in order to refine the simple models we already had, in this case not the demographic model of consumer spending, but the four-stage technological life cycle model we have featured in our past books.

THERE IS NO END TO FORECASTING CAPACITIES, AND THAT IS THE KEY TO OUR EVOLUTION AND STANDARD OF LIVING

The truth is that what we are saying here is not new at all. From the measurable levels of human history we have advanced by learning more about our environment, developing new technologies, and forecasting more of what will come and how to better adapt to change. How long did it take us to discover fire, the wheel, or metal tools and weapons? How long did it take us to realize that there were predictable tides down to the minute every day and seasons every year? Now spring, summer, fall, and winter are totally obvious and predictable, although each season brings some new nuances. But even short-term weather patterns and hurricane probabilities and patterns are now becoming highly discernable.

How long did it take us to realize that the earth revolves around the sun and then the planetary motions of our solar system? Now we can launch spaceships to the moon or Mars with high precision! We have shown that the economy and the stock markets follow predictable economic seasons every eighty years and that long-term economic booms and busts follow projectable generational spending waves about every forty years. And we are now becoming increasingly capable of measuring when our stock markets are overvalued or undervalued in shorter-term cycles and when during each year and each Presidential Cycle and in each decade the stock markets will perform better or worse (Chapter 3).

What Stephen Wolfram is doing on a much broader basis is what we are now doing with economic trends and basic human evolution. We start this book with the very simple basics of natural and human evolution, starting in Chapter 1 by explaining why the tech wreck of 2000–2002 was a natural and inevitable part of the evolution of the baby-boom generation's economic and technological cycle and why we have a great bull market and bubble still ahead before we collapse into the most severe downturn since the Great Depression, and in some ways it could be more severe and longer in scope.

Our research increasingly shows that we may not see new highs after 2009 or 2010 in the broad stock markets for the rest of our lifetimes, although we will see another substantial boom from 2023 or so into the early 2040s after the great crash from 2010 to 2022. Similarly, after the peak in late 1989 Japan is not likely to see new highs for several decades—and we were one of the few forecasters to predict that Japan would decline in the 1990s and early 2000s, when it appeared to be on top of the world in the late 1980s.

In this book we will show not only where the best business and investment sectors will be in the great boom and bust ahead, but how to determine by using demographics in your local areas where the best areas for home appreciation or business opportunities will be. It is the most comprehensive guide to financial and life planning ever presented. Demographics (and technology life cycles) are destiny, and we take demographic models and logic and go beyond the most fundamental trends in spending, productivity, and inflation that we have been forecasting for decades now and apply them right down to the dynamics of your local economy and home market. We will give you more tools than you have dreamed of for seeing future trends and successfully adapting in good times and bad if you will take the time to read this book and apply it to your life—or find a financial adviser who understands our tools and logic.

We will show that we as humans have a profound and persistent tendency to view the world and progress in a linear fashion, whereas it actually occurs in clear cyclical and exponential growth trends until new limits are hit—and then, of course, progressive contractions follow. We are in denial about life and death, growth and progress—and that represents our greatest liability in planning for the future and making effective decisions.

We have been in a "bubble boom" since the big bang. The human bubble in population accelerated with the Agricultural Revolution 10,000 years ago, and has been accelerating even more since the Industrial Revolution in the late 1700s and the Information Revolution in the last century. We are at a very auspicious and potentially ominous time in human history now that birth and demographic trends are slowing for the first time in modern history.

Understanding the most fundamental cycles driving our growth will be key to surviving in a more volatile up-and-down future—for the next two decades in particular. The future is not going to be what you expect it to be. We can help you anticipate and adapt with simple indicators of future growth you can readily understand!

In Chapters 1 to 3 we will look at why the tech wreck occurred in the early 2000s, why the fundamental trends we projected in the past are still in force, and why the "investment opportunity of a lifetime" that we first called in late 2002 will still be very advantageous into late 2005. In Chapters 4 and 5, we will look at the trends in real estate and how to plan your entire life cycle and decisions around the predictable trends we can project in many areas for decades to come. In Chapters 6 and 7, we will take the most in-depth look at risks and returns in different investment sectors and show how to build portfolio strategies for the very different seasons of our economy. There will be the most significant season change since the late 1920s and early 1930s around the end of this decade and your investment strategies will have to change big time now and then. In Chapter 8 we will look at the business opportunities in the "new millionaire economy." We may see the highs for the Dow for many decades to come by 2010, just as we saw for the Nikkei in Japan by late 1989.

If you can find a book more important to your long-term success and survival, we would like to see it! Give yourself the time to read this entire book, not just the first chapter or the headings. You will see that the future is much more projectable than economists have led us to believe, now that we have clear demographic information comparable to learning that the earth revolves around the sun.

Our promise: If you study this book and apply its principles, you will make different decisions in the future than you have in the past. You will be able to create a more predictable and a better future for yourself in good times and bad—and we will certainly see both in the next two decades!

But it is also time for traditional economists and forecasters to start taking this new science of demographics and technology life cycles more seriously. If we are right about the next two decades, as we have been about the past two decades, then they will no longer be able to discount these new theories as overly simplistic. We continue to believe and prove that the complex changes in our economy and lifestyles are a result of simple and forecastable cause-and-effect factors. We urge you to consider this reality before the experts finally catch on.

We urge you to begin to accept the reality of exponential growth and cyclical change versus your preference for a linear world where we get better and better over time and then go to Heaven and stay there! Living in reality may be difficult at times, given what actually occurs in this world, but it makes you more responsible and more effective in all aspects of life. That is what this book is all about.

Chapter 1

THE INVESTMENT OPPORTUNITY OF A LIFETIME

Uncanny Parallels with the "Tech Wreck" of 1919–1922 and the Roaring Twenties "Bubble Boom" That Followed

THE INITIAL REBOUND in the stock market in 2003 after the crash in October 2002 is a harbinger of the next great bull market in stocks and the last stage of the greatest boom in history. This should not be a surprising forecast to our past readers, given our long-standing forecasts that the massive baby-boom generation would drive an unprecedented boom into 2008 or 2009 with their predictable spending and productivity trends. But it is crucial to understand that this is your last chance to profit from this extraordinary bull market that has raised more people than ever into the status of millionaire and affluent households. And the extreme crash of 2000–2002 makes the next stage of investment opportunities even more compelling! We are predicting that from the lows in late 2002 into around 2010, you as an investor are likely to achieve as high or higher average annual compound returns than you did in the unprecedented bull market of the 1990s. How many experts, economists, and investment strategists are predicting that?

This may sound astounding in light of the incredible crash in technology stocks and the terrorist attacks on September 11, 2001. You might ask, "After this incredible bubble and crash, how could we even think of seeing such returns in the coming decade?" Even Warren Buffett and Sir John Templeton, two of the most successful long-term investment gurus, are predicting much slower growth in the economy and in stock returns for many years to come! Buffett claims that you will, at best, see low-single-digit returns for this decade, and Templeton claims you would be lucky to break even in stocks during this time period.

But first remember that we stood almost alone in predicting the incredible boom of the 1990s in *The Great Boom Ahead,* published in late 1992—when most people were nearly as pessimistic as now. After all, *Bankruptcy 1995* was at the top of the best-seller lists at the time. We had just seen the extreme 1987 crash, collapsing housing prices, the S&L crisis, the Persian Gulf War, the collapse of Japan's economic, stock, and real estate bubble, the greatest government deficit ever, and a similar recession from late 1990 into mid-1991. Who would have thought that the 1990s could have seen greater stock returns and economic growth than in the 1980s? The truth is that every decade of this unprecedented boom has started out weak. Remember the early 1980s? The early 1990s? Most decades start by consolidating the strong gains from the previous decade before moving on again, due to a recurring corporate planning cycle that we will cover in Chapter 3.

We forecasted then that the decline in Japan, of which we were warning in the late 1980s, would continue and that America would see the greatest boom in history. We forecasted that inflation would fall to near zero and that we would balance the government deficit by 1998 to 2000. We said to "get ready"! But most people didn't realize the significance of the 1990s boom until the latter 1990s, just as that incredible expansion was increasingly due for a necessary consolidation to prepare for the next and greatest decade to come, just as occurred in the early 1990s, after the great 1980s expansion. The good news is that the fundamental trends we track and forecast have not changed despite the crash of 2000–2002.

We didn't title our early 1998 book *The Roaring 2000s* for nothing. We have been and are continuing to predict that this coming decade will be the greatest in history and will closely parallel the Roaring Twenties—the last time a major technology revolution moved fully mainstream while a new generation hit the peak of its spending and productivity cycle. That decade determined the leaders in most industries and technologies for many decades, into the 1970s and beyond! This time the generation is much larger and the technologies are even more powerful. So we are saying "get ready" again, as we did in late 1992 in *The Great Boom Ahead,* and we have much more evidence for why the economy and the technology revolution will continue to boom, including why we saw such a dramatic technology crash in 2000–2002. That was just the end of the first phase of the acceleration of new technologies into the mainstream of our economy. And the 1990s boom created the second bubble in stocks, concentrating largely in Internet and technology stocks, to follow the first bubble, which peaked in 1987.

The second stage of the technology revolution is coming. The same "tech wreck" scenario occurred eighty years ago, between late 1919 and early 1922, when automobiles and many other new technologies were growing rapidly and hit the same 50% penetration point of adoption by consumers. The incredible boom that followed that extreme and extended crash were indeed the infamous Roaring Twenties! In fact, we have identified a four-year cycle and a decade pattern of stock movements that have recurred regularly for more than fifty years. After another key four-year cycle hit in late 2002, there is only one more cycle due in mid- to late 2006. Otherwise, the coast appears to be clear for another strong decade of expansion.

Did you realize that almost every decade sees recessions, consolidations, and stock declines in its first few years and that most of the gains are made in the second half of the decade? In the next chapter we will look at why we are still predicting a Dow as high as 38,000 to 40,000. We will give you a more detailed road map for how the bull market will unfold over the rest of this decade, in large-cap stocks, small-cap stocks, bonds, real estate, and international markets. We will look at the sectors of the stock market that are being driven by the demographic trends and technology revolution. But expect the technology sectors to accelerate strongly again and lead the stock markets from mid-2005 into late 2009 or early 2010, just as they did from 1995 through 1999 and early 2000. Hence, even if you missed the great buying opportunity in late 2002, the best of the bull market is still ahead!

If you had bought stocks, and in particular auto and new technology stocks, at the bottom of the "tech wreck" in late 1921–early 1922, you would have seen gains of six times in the Dow, twelve times in the auto index, and twenty-two times in General Motors in just eight years. That was after a 45% crash in the Dow, a 70% crash in the auto index, and a 75% crash in General Motors that closely paralleled the crash of early 2000–late 2002. In fact, we will show that Intel's stock chart from 1992 to 2000 looked almost identical to General Motors' from 1912 to 1919. In late 1921–early 1922 it looked just like the beginning of the Great Depression. Unemployment hit 12% in the United States and 18% in Great Britain. There was deflation in prices for the first time in decades. Germany was about to collapse even further from hyperinflation in 1922 and 1923.

There was even the first modern terrorist strike: a bomb exploded on Wall Street in late 1920. There was an incredible reaction to new immigrant and ethnic groups, including the explosion of the Ku Klux Klan's membership to 5 million, or almost 23% of households, by 1924. The 1920s became the anti-immigration decade. But despite such extreme economic, political, international, and social conflicts, the Roaring Twenties saw the greatest bull market and decade of economic productivity and progress in U.S. history—that is, prior to the 1990s and until now!

Economists now say, despite the initial rebound of the markets in 2003, that we have seen a bubble in the stock market and that the markets, especially technology stocks, won't see new highs for perhaps decades. We couldn't disagree more. This boom has been a bubble boom due to the extreme demographic, globalization, and technological advances driving it. The first bubble occurred from 1985 to 1987, but that was not a technology bubble. The recent one was even greater, from 1995 to 1999, and concentrated largely in the Internet and technology sectors. We see the next and final bubble accelerating from mid-2005 into late 2009 or early 2010. And it is likely to become the greatest intermediate bull market and technology bubble in the last two centuries. This final bubble will likely be followed by the greatest depression in history—at a minimum, the greatest downturn since the Great Depression.

We've been the most bullish forecasters and investment strategists since the late 1980s when we discovered some very simple, but potent new tools for predicting economic trends—tools that economists largely reject because they are too simple and everyday people can understand them. We deal in the basic fundamentals of when we earn and spend money, are most productive as workers, borrow the most, invest the most, and even create inflation due to the expense of raising and educating our youth until their entry into the workforce. These are new statistics that have emerged from the Information Revolution which are highly quantifiable and widely used in consumer marketing—but not in economics. What could be more fundamental to our economy than these basic, easy to understand, highly projectable trends? We find consistently that people readily understand this human, demographic approach to forecasting. Why? Because we all experience similar life cycles as we age!

We're not bullish just because we are optimists by nature. My mother would never tell you that I am an optimistic person! In 1989, we forecasted that the United States would enter a two-year slowdown in 1990 and 1991. We forecasted Japan would then decline versus the United States and Europe for more than a decade. In fact, we thought the stock crash of late 1990 would be worse than what actually occurred. We were also initially forecasting a Dow of 10,000 by the early 2000s, and that was an understatement—although everyone thought we were crazy at the time! In *The Roaring 2000s,* released in April 1998 with final edits in late 1997, we forecasted that the Dow would correct to 7200–7600 by mid- to late 1998 (page 292). The intraday bottom was right in the middle, at 7400. And that's the area we gave for our strongest buy signal again in late September–early October 2002.

In *The Roaring 2000s Investor,* released in October 1999, we forecasted that the Dow was about to hit the top end of our valuation channel by late 1999 to early 2000 and that a sharp correction was due (page 26). On February 1, 2000, we warned in our newsletter that the Internet stocks were approaching a major top. In the April 1, 2000, edition of our newsletter we advised subscribers to start allocating portfolios out of technology and Asia (ex-Japan), more into health care and financial services. Despite the extreme correction that followed, the Dow on September 21, 2001, tested the bottom of our valuation channel and rallied modestly into mid-2002. We gave our first strong buy signal there at 8000–8200 on the Dow. But the Dow Channel was later broken in early July 2002, which gave us targets back to the 1998 lows of around 7400. The Dow finally bottomed at 7286 on October 9. Similarly, we forecasted in late 2000 that the Nasdaq could test its long-term trend line around 2100, and if that broke the next target was the 1998 lows of 1350–1400. That level was also finally broken and we were similarly projecting lows in the 1100 to 1150 range, which occurred at 1114 on October 9, 2002. Hence, we aren't averse to being bearish when called for.

But in our October 1, 2002, newsletter we gave our strongest buy signal ever! The reason we are projecting continued economic and stock advances into 2009 or early 2010 is that our forecasts are based on highly quantifiable demographic and technology trends and they are still pointing very strongly upward. Given the extreme stock crash and political events of 2000–2002, it is amazing that the economy stayed as strong as it did. That was due to continued strong consumer spending while businesses cut back sharply, which only proves how strong demographic trends affect our economy. As Warren Buffett has said, "Markets go up, and they go down." We agree in the short term, and the recent bubble and crash prove that. But we have found that the markets move in very predictable ways over the long term because of these fundamental trends.

Since the beginning we have been forecasting that this great boom would be followed by an extended decline from around 2009 or 2010 into 2022 to 2023, like past bear markets following the peaks in past-generation spending cycles. This occurred from 1930 to 1942 and from 1969 to 1982 in the United States. In the short term, we fully recognize that the stock markets and economy can take strong swings, even in bull markets. Hence, we clearly aren't always bullish! In fact, in Chapter 3 we will demonstrate some cycles that have explained every substantial stock correction over the last four to five decades. And three cycles converged between 2000 and 2002.

The good news again is that the path is clear for stronger advances until mid- to late 2006 before the next minor cycle hits. We then will very likely see a peak in this bull market between early to late 2010. By 2010, all of our critical analysis suggests that we will almost certainly see the beginning of a serious, long-term economic and stock decline that will be worse than the 1970s in the United States or the 1990s in Japan and could rival or exceed the Great Depression in the 1930s. That is the bad news. It is perhaps the most important insight we can give you in this book. There are investing and living strategies that will allow you not only to largely avoid this inevitable calamity, but also to profit from it.

Today we have a very different forecast from Warren Buffett and most experts, as we have since the late 1980s. By sometime in 2010 we still see the Dow hitting 32,000 to 40,000 and the Nasdaq advancing to around 13,000, and potentially higher. Despite the initial strong recovery in late 2003 and early 2004, we see the strongest gains coming between mid-2005 and 2010, especially from mid-2005 into mid-2006 and from late 2006 and 2010. It's clearly not too late to fully participate in the next and greatest bull market in history!

Why do we call this time the investment opportunity of a lifetime? Because the crash and slowdown of 2000–2002 represented an extreme correction and a natural stage in the rapid emergence of new technologies during an ongoing economic boom, much like the extreme 1987 crash and the aftershock in 1990. But this most recent correction was much more like the crash of late 1919 to early 1922 that led into the Roaring Twenties boom and bull market. And that was the greatest investment opportunity of the last century.

Here is an important point we have always stressed for investors. Not every major crash in the stock market is a great buying opportunity, and holding stocks for the long run doesn't always work out in real life. If you had bought the most prominent blue-chip stocks in late 1929, you would have suffered an 87% loss in just three years, still been down 80% thirteen years later, and have just broken even in 1953—twenty-four years later! Even if, much more intelligently, you had bought the Dow right at the bottom of the greatest crash in U.S. history in 1932, you would have seen lower than average returns of about 8% annually into 1942. Only then did the next great bull market start.

If in the next great bull market cycle you had bought the Dow in late 1965, you would have been down 70%, adjusted for inflation, in late 1982, seventeen years later. It would have taken until 1993, twenty-eight years later, to break even. Conversely, if you had waited and bought the Dow right at the bottom of the crash in late 1974, you would have still been down, adjusted for inflation, eight years later in late 1982. That is the harsh reality of real-life investing. Although stock returns average 10% to 11% over most longer-term time horizons, the performance can be very dismal for a decade or more. And these cycles could hit right when you need retirement money the most! Ask the typical couple approaching retirement in Japan in the last decade.

In fact, if you had bought the Nikkei in Japan at the very bottom of the first extended crash in 1992, that would have seemed to be a brilliant move at the time. But you would have been down by another 45%, and more adjusted for inflation, at the recent lows in early 2003, eleven years later. The Nikkei was down by 80% from its top in early 2003, thirteen years later. Why did this occur? Japan did not have a baby boom in the 1950s and early 1960s like most of the major developed countries around the world but had a brief one in the early 1960s to early 1970s instead. So there isn't a new generation to earn and spend more money—until around 2009 to 2020. Then Japan should be growing again while we are busting. In the meantime, Japan's downward slide in demographic spending is coming to an end and there will be modest growth for the rest of this decade.

Only highly predictable demographic trends and technology cycles can tell you whether a major stock crash is just an extreme correction at the worst of overvaluation cycles and short-term political events or the beginning of a long-term decline in the economy and an extended bear market in stocks.

It was the peak in spending and new technology penetration cycles in the late 1920s, the late 1960s, and as we forecast to occur again around 2009–2010, that foreboded the extended economic declines and bear markets in stocks to follow. The Japanese economy hit such a peak, off cycle from the rest of the world, in the late 1980s. That is why Japan has seen a continued decline in the 1990s and early 2000s. We were one of the only forecasters who saw a long-term slide in the Japanese economy when it looked so strong in the late 1980s.

Just as we did in the early 1990s, we offer a unique perspective when the future doesn't look so great. First note that every decade of this boom and most decades in the last century have started off with a slowdown in response to the incredible expansion that occurred in the previous decade. We call this the "Decade Hangover Cycle," and it occurs due to ten-year planning and expansion cycles in large corporations. This cycle is one of

Figure 1.1 Standard & Poor's Home-Building Index, 1989–1991

many we will present in Chapter 3 in forecasting key turning points within this boom and in the bust to follow.

It is only human nature to overexpand when growth sets in and then have to cut back and recalibrate for continued growth in the future. We saw the 1980s begin with a slowdown and then likewise the 1990s. In the early-1990s contraction it was the home-building stocks and S&Ls that were hit the worst (Figure 1.1). They represented one of the strongest sectors in the 1980s, as the baby boomers were peaking in their starter-home buying. Despite not seeing a bubble anywhere near the degree of the tech stocks, home-building stocks crashed 60% in the early 1990s.

In the 1990s it was the technology sector that expanded the most rapidly and was due for a major short-term slowdown and consolidation. Were the early 1990s the end of the boom or simply the end of the housing boom? We are saying that the early 2000s are clearly not the end of the technology boom, nor of the broader economic boom that has been generated by the spending cycle of the massive baby-boom generation. We will tell you how to prepare for that in the coming chapters as well.

The most important points to understand are two, and we explained these concepts in detail in *The Roaring 2000s*. First, since the early 1980s, it has been the rising earning, spending, and productivity cycle of the massive baby-boom generation, here and around most of the world, that has driven this unprecedented economic boom. The Spending Wave in Fig-

FIGURE 1.2 The Spending Wave: Births Lagged for Peak in Family Spending, 1954–2050

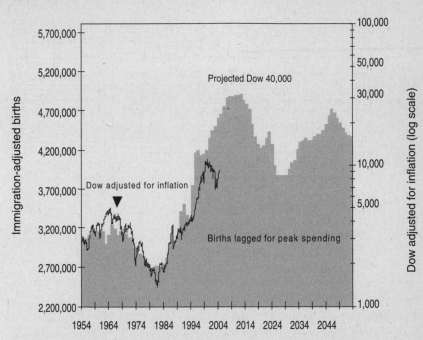

ure 1.2 is simply a lag on the birth index in the United States (adjusted for immigration) for the quantifiable peak in spending of the average household at between age 46 to 50 today, moving forward 1 year every decade. Our recent analysis of the Consumer Expenditure Survey from the U.S. Department of Labor, Bureau of Labor Statistics, shows a double peak in spending at ages 46 and 50. Then spending declines for the rest of the average family's life. Since 1988, when we discovered this indicator, we have been forecasting that this generation would continue spending until 2007 to 2009 and that this boom and bull market in stocks would be much greater than forecast.

As you can see in Figure 1.2, the correlation between the broader stock market and the economy has been very strong, despite major short-term political and economic shocks. Hence, as in the early 1990s, we see a very strong recovery in consumer spending and economic growth with a very strong rebound in the stock markets into at least 2009, and likely into 2010. And then we will see another major long-term decline in our economy set in as there are fewer baby busters to spend money on housing, cars, computers, and so on. New generations create very predictable boom-and-bust

FIGURE 1.3 The Dow Jones Industrial Average, 1900–2025*
The Forty-Year Generation Cycle*

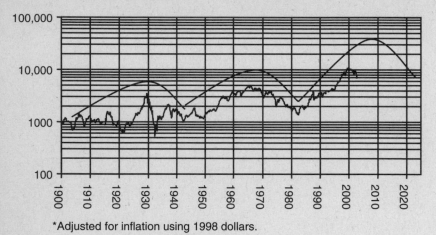

*Adjusted for inflation using 1998 dollars.

cycles in our economy and they occur about every forty years, as we can see by looking at the Dow adjusted for inflation in Figure 1.3.

The first important insight we can give you after the crash of 2000–2002 is that this economic boom is not over. It will be over only after the baby boom finishes its spending and productivity cycles around late 2009 to late 2010.

Another key point made in *The Roaring 2000s* was that every second generation, or about every eighty years, radical new technologies and a new economy emerge, as you can see in Figure 1.4. Since the invention of electricity, cars, telephones, and many other crucial new technologies in the late 1800s, a new economy emerged around the assembly line and the modern corporation, which brought standardized products increasingly into the mass-market price range, along with factory and office jobs and suburban living. The new economy is bringing greater customization of products and services to consumers who increasingly drive a highly bottom-up, network model of more direct marketing and produce-to-order systems that will evolve from real-time production to real-time personalized service in the coming decade and beyond. This new economy will continue to enable a growing shift toward "exurban living" in high-quality smaller towns such as Aspen, Martha's Vineyard, and Hilton Head, and in the outer rings surrounding most urban areas.

At first these new technologies and companies move slowly into niche markets; then, once they hit about 10% adoption by consumers and house-

FIGURE 1.4 The Eighty-Year New Economy Cycle

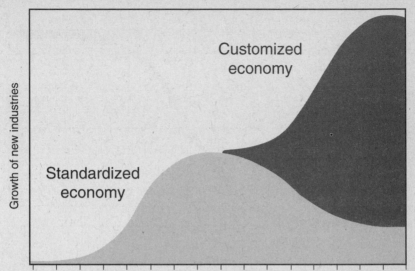

holds, they accelerate rapidly into the mainstream. This is the S-curve principle that we have so consistently stressed in our past books. Figure 1.5 shows that progression of new technologies and products. Cars were adopted by 10% of urban households in 1914, and then suddenly accelerated to 90% by 1928. Cars were invented back in 1886 and took another fourteen years after initial commercialization around 1900 just to penetrate the upscale niche markets. Twenty-eight years after their invention, they suddenly exploded into the mainstream in just fourteen years! We as consumers and experts alike tend to project trends in straight lines into the future. That is not how reality works, any more than average 10% stock returns! And that is why the S-curve is such a powerful forecasting tool.

The Internet, along with cellular phones and home computing, hit 10% between 1994 and early 1996, after the microchip emerged between 1968 and 1971, twenty-eight years earlier. Now these critical technologies are accelerating toward 90% adoption by 2007 to 2009. Just as cars hit 50% penetration in 1921, the Internet and cellular phones hit 50% exactly eighty years later, in 2001. In 1920–1921, as in 2000–2001, we saw a massive consolidation and correction in tech companies and stocks. But this is the critical insight: We still have the 50% to 90% rapid growth and penetration to follow, just as automobiles and other key new consumer technologies did from 1922 to 1928. Hence, the technology sector will continue to lead this

FIGURE 1.5 The S-Curve in Automobiles

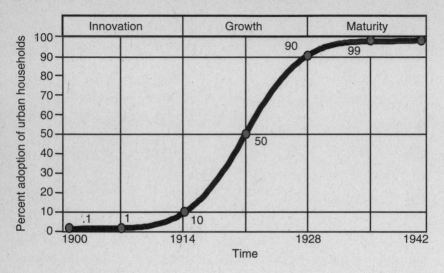

advance, adding continued productivity surges and advances in living standards and lifestyles into the top of this boom around 2008–2009—just as occurred from 1922 to 1929.

The second major insight we can bring you after the crash of 2000–2002 is that this technology revolution is not over. It will peak around late 2009, when most key new consumer technologies have penetrated 90% of their potential markets. Hence, we predict the great boom will resurge into its final and strongest stage, accelerating more fully again by early 2006. This final stage of the boom will last into early to late 2010. The winners of the race for leadership in most of the emerging new industries will be established in the coming decade, not the last decade. The greatest opportunities for investments, business, and career advancement will therefore come in this decade. This is not only the investment opportunity of a lifetime, but the best time to reposition your business and career—including how and where you live—not only for the great boom ahead but for the great bust to follow.

We will examine all of the opportunities for you to personally leverage this last stage of the great boom in the many chapters to come. But first let's look more closely at the crash of late 1919–early 1922 and see why it so closely parallels the crash of 2000–2002. The more critical insight is why we are going to see the greatest bull market in history from late 2002 into at least 2009 and the greatest economic boom in history from late 2003 into

2010. Naturally, you will need some very good reasons for investing aggressively again after the shocking events of the past few years. We will give you those reasons and some very sound strategies for doing so.

THE CRASH OF 1919–1921 AND THE ROARING TWENTIES: UNCANNY PARALLELS TO THE EARLY-2000S CRASH AND THE ROARING 2000S TO FOLLOW

A closer look at the tech wreck of late 1919–early 1922 will give great insights into the incredible tech correction in 2000–2002 and the unprecedented investment opportunity it has created. First let's take a look at another dimension of how the business cycle changes as new technologies or industries emerge on an S-curve progression in Figure 1.6. There are four stages that occur. First there is an Innovation Stage, where many of the new companies emerge as start-ups from a period of radical innovation. Then there is a Growth Boom, wherein those new companies grow rapidly into the mainstream for the first time. That stage is followed by a Shakeout or consolidation as overexpansion meets the first slowing in growth rates as the industry approaches the 50% point in the middle of the acceleration cycle from 10% to 90%. Then fewer surviving companies compete for the final 50% to 90% growth phase in a Maturity Boom. This final boom establishes the leaders for many decades ahead as the industry starts to mature for the first time.

FIGURE 1.6 Four-Stage Industry S-Curve Cycle

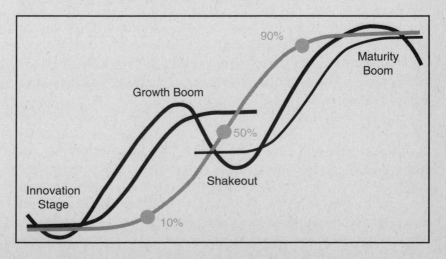

FIGURE 1.7 The Automobile S-Curve

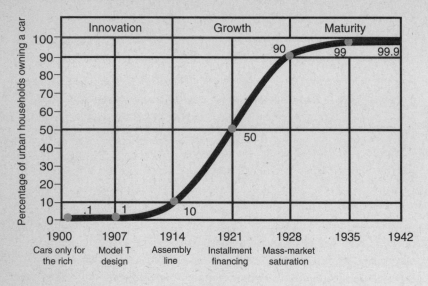

After the invention of the automobile in 1886, car companies first started to commercialize around 1900 (Figure 1.7). There was a start-up boom between 1904 and 1908 that saw the peak of the Innovation Stage. Then the industry started to grow rapidly with many new companies and brands entering, marking the beginning of the Growth Boom. But the biggest breakthrough for accelerating the growth came just as cars were approaching 10% penetration in 1914: the moving assembly line by Henry Ford. With the dramatic drop in prices that resulted, cars suddenly moved to 90% of urban households by 1928. However, the Growth Boom reached its peak in late 1919 and was followed by a very severe Shakeout into early 1922, before the Maturity Boom continued into 1929, spurred on by many further innovations in cars and roads, including installment financing, starting in 1921.

Note that the boom in the stock market during this time of technology acceleration continued up despite World War I and up very strongly for auto stocks (Figure 1.8). In fact, the valuation levels on the Dow and the broader stock indices hit price/earnings (P/E) ratio levels of 26 in late 1919, almost as high as the most extreme P/Es of 28 in the 1929 bubble. We don't have P/E measures for the Auto Index, but I am sure they were much higher than on the Dow, as occurred for the Nasdaq in 1999. From the beginning of 1912 (as far back as we can measure) to the peak of the auto bubble in late 1919, the S&P Auto Index went up about fourteen times. As spectacular as

FIGURE 1.8 Standard & Poor's Auto Index, 1912–1919

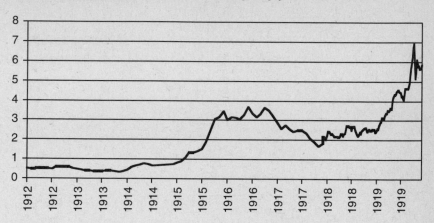

the Nasdaq bubble of the 1990s may seem, it grew only ten times from mid-1992 into the peak—during the same time horizon as the S&P Auto Index in years.

Here is an even more startling correlation: Figure 1.9 shows Intel from mid-1992 versus General Motors from early 1912. The charts are too close for comfort! We saw a similar boom in both leading stocks—and a similar correction to follow. The cycles are almost exactly eighty years apart in line with our New Economy Cycle, which comes every other generation (Figure 1.3). Just ahead we will show how General Motors and the tech indices of the day saw a second great boom and bubble that corresponded with the Maturity Boom stage of the S-curve. But first let's more closely examine the Shakeout Cycle and correction.

Just as the auto and tech bubble looked as irresistible as the Nasdaq market in 1999 and early 2000, a funny thing happened. From late 1919 into 1921 there was an incredible "tech wreck" and shakeout in auto and many other key new-technology industries. As we showed in Figure 1.6, a shakeout occurs as new technologies or industries approach the 50% penetration level. Why? There is an incredible reaction to such rapid growth resulting in overexpansion just as growth rates start to slow at the 50% inflection point. The technologies continue to grow rapidly into mass markets; it's just that the actual rate of growth slows down increasingly. This causes a temporary slowdown and consolidation in the industry to shake out the overexpansion and to create greater efficiencies for further expansion.

Between 1917 and 1922, 24% of car manufacturers and brands went under, as we can see in Figure 1.10. That was only the beginning of the con-

FIGURE 1.9   Tech Bubbles Past and Present
General Motors Versus Intel—Eighty-Year Lag

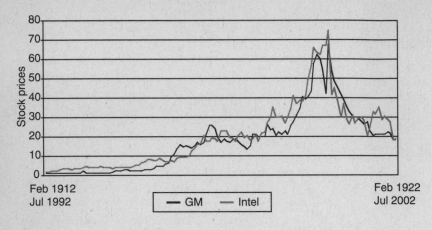

tinued narrowing of companies in the race for leadership into the late 1920s
and early 1930s. By the early 1930s downturn the leaders of the future had
been set. At the bottom of the 1921 recession and stock market crash, General Motors had only 12% of the car market versus Ford's commanding
leadership of 60%. GM not only led the even greater revolution in creating
the new modern corporate organization through Alfred Sloan's stellar leadership in the 1920s, GM also catered to the rising new generation's increasing affluence by offering trade-up brands from the original Chevrolet—to
Pontiac to Oldsmobile to Buick to Cadillac—and was the first to offer in-

FIGURE 1.10   The Auto Shakeout, 1911–1935

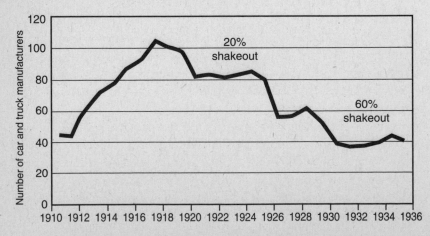

stallment financing. By 1929, at the top of the boom, GM had rivaled Ford's market share, and by the early 1930s it pulled ahead forever. The rest of the story is history. That's why we predict that the leaders in most new emerging technologies, industries, and brands will be established in the coming decade!

This incredible boom ahead will represent the most important time in our lifetimes for creating winning business, career, and investment strategies!

Let's go back to the great crash of late 1919–1921. During this shakeout period, the Dow fell by 45% (Figure 1.11), very similar to the Dow's decline in 2000–2002. The Auto Index (Figure 1.12) crashed 70% into early 1922, very close to the Nasdaq's recent 77% decline. The Tire and Rubber Index fell 72% (Figure 1.13). The leading public stock in the auto sector (Ford was still privately held), General Motors, was down 75% in that correction (Figure 1.14). It is this necessary and violent consolidation in the middle of the rapid growth phase of the S-curve that causes the most violent corrections in the stock market and technology indices during major bull markets. And these extreme corrections, as in 2000–2002, occur only about every eighty years during ongoing bull markets, when radical new technologies are emerging into the mainstream.

From late 1919 into early 1922, the U.S. economy saw a severe fall in consumer and commodity prices as well as 12% unemployment from the shakeout in the rapidly growing tech sectors—much worse than the brief

FIGURE 1.11 The Dow Jones Industrial Average, 1919–1921

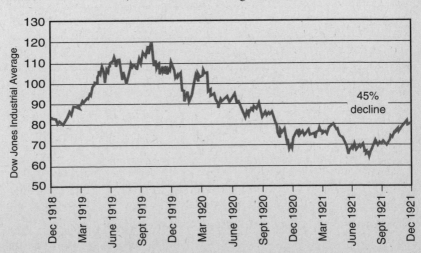

FIGURE 1.12   Standard & Poor's Auto Index, January 1919–January 1923

FIGURE 1.13   Standard & Poor's Tire and Rubber Index,
December 1918–December 1922

recession in mid- to late 2001. The early 1920s looked very much like the beginning of the Great Depression between late 1929 and 1932. But the difference was that this was a shakeout and consolidation in the middle of the
explosive new-technology cycle and was followed by continued spending
and productivity from the rising Henry Ford generation. Only a clear un-

FIGURE 1.14 General Motors Stock Price, December 1918–December 1922

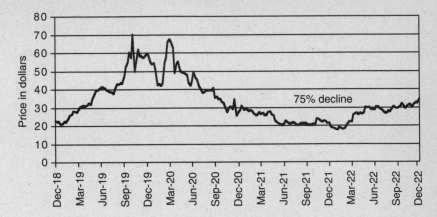

derstanding of demographic and technology cycles would have told you that this was the buy opportunity of a lifetime and for the twentieth century!

THE ROARING TWENTIES,
WHICH FOLLOWED THE GREAT CRASH OF 1920–1921

The rest is history. The United States and most of the world recovered after that extreme correction and we saw the greatest boom and bull market in history up until that time and for the entire last century. Here are the startling facts. The Dow (Figure 1.15), from the bottom in late 1921 to the top of the boom in late 1929, advanced by six times in just eight years, an average annual compound return of 23.87%. The S&P Auto Index (Figure 1.16) advanced twelve times, for an average return of 42.69%, and General Motors (Figure 1.17), one of the leading large-cap stocks, advanced twenty-two times, returning 58.17% to investors who bought in late 1921–early 1922. In how many eight-year periods of history could you have achieved those extraordinary levels of return? None! That's what we mean when we say the buy opportunity of a lifetime!

Now look back at the Intel and General Motors data in Figure 1.9, which are virtually identical going into the shakeout stage eighty years apart. If Intel did as well as General Motors did in the Roaring Twenties boom to follow, Intel would peak around 330, twenty-two times its 2002 low of around $15. That would be four to five times its high in early 2000.

FIGURE 1.15 The Dow Jones Industrial Average, 1919–1929

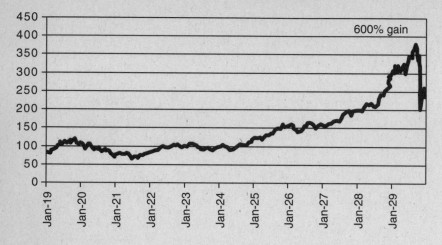

This is our argument for forecasters that say the leading tech stocks will never see their highs again after the recent bubble. We are not specifically forecasting that Intel will reach these levels, but we do feel that the key tech stocks that dominate the coming decade could see similar returns and gains relatively, and Intel is certainly a top candidate for such performance.

In the incredible boom of the 1990s, from the bottom in late 1990 to the top in early 2000, the average annual compound return on the Nasdaq was

FIGURE 1.16 Standard & Poor's Auto Index, 1919–1929

THE INVESTMENT OPPORTUNITY OF A LIFETIME 71

FIGURE 1.17 General Motors Stock Price, 1919–1930

33.02%, 50.03% on Microsoft, and 20.03% on the Dow. The average return from the Dow in the eight-year bull market from August 1982 to July 1990 was 17.34%. The other stellar decade for stocks, the 1950s, saw an average annual compound return of only 13.00% for the Dow. Even if you take the best eight-year period, from March 1948 to March 1956, the average return was only 14.84%.

The average annual compound return on the Dow, 23.87% from September 1921 to August 1929, was greater than any comparable bull market in the last 100 years, making late 1921 the buy opportunity of the last century.

If you look at the projections in Chapter 2, you will see average annual compound returns of 24% on the Dow from the lows of late 2002 into the highs we project in late 2008, and 39% on the Nasdaq if we do see our target of 13,000, and 47% if we see as high as 20,000. That's why we claimed at the beginning of this chapter that investors should see returns as good as or better than in the 1990s in this next and last great stage of the bull market. That is why we published our special report "The Buy Opportunity of a Lifetime" in late 2001 and our second special report, "The Bubble Boom," in late 2002. Given the dramatic long-term market correction and economic slowdown we are forecasting after 2009, we forecast that this will end up being the buy opportunity of the coming century and our lifetimes! And it's not as important that our actual targets get hit, rather that the stock

market enters another strong bull market that you as an investor don't fore-
see until much later in the cycle.

Why was the Roaring Twenties the best decade in United States history
for stock returns? Because we saw the highest productivity rates in United
States history. The only time that such rates have averaged above 3% was
from 1917 to 1929, when the average was close to 4%. High productivity
rates generate earnings that grow much faster than GDP and the stock market simply projects earnings growth many years into the future in valuing
stocks. The reasons productivity rates were so high are twofold. First, the
Henry Ford generation had its peak numbers moving into its peak spending and productivity years. (Back then, with much less education and lower
life expectancies, the peak age would have been in the mid- to late 30s.) Second, radical new technologies were in their peak years of mass-market penetration, moving from 50% to 90% of urban households.

The other period with high productivity rates was the 1960s, wherein
we saw the peak spending and productivity years of the Bob Hope generation and the mass-market saturation of a whole new cluster of less radical
but powerful technologies ranging from home appliances to TVs to jet
travel to synthetic fibers. We are projecting that this decade, the 2000s, will
see similar, and perhaps higher, productivity rates than the near-3% rates in
the late 1990s, more like 4% again. That will generate much more growth in
earnings than will be expected by economists—and much stronger stock
market growth, as occurred in the Roaring Twenties.

It is worth noting that the Roaring Twenties boom was no cakewalk.
We have been warning for over a decade that this 1982–2009 boom would
not be anything like the 1950s and 1960s boom that followed World War II.
That was an orderly time of the maturing of the last revolution in technologies, business models, and lifestyles. This current boom represents the
emergence of radically new trends in these areas and will necessarily be
more gut-wrenching here and around the world. In the early 1920s, Great
Britain saw peak unemployment rates of 18% and was slower to recover
than the United States. Germany's currency started to collapse in 1922 from
the excessive reparation payments from World War I and Germany's economy collapsed from hyperinflation in 1923. So should it be a surprise that
despite this boom there are continued declines in Japan and political crises
around the world from Russia to the Middle East to Asia? And remember,
as mentioned earlier in this chapter, the first modern terrorist event on Wall
Street occurred in late 1920, followed by strong anti-immigration sentiments and ethnic tensions.

THE CURRENT TECHNOLOGY S-CURVE AND SHAKEOUT

Figure 1.18 shows the trend in the Nasdaq back to its inception in 1971. The last major wave of the Nasdaq bull market, from late 1990 into early 2000, saw the technology sectors growing at very high rates since late 1994 and accelerating into a classic bubble after the late 1998 correction, between 1999 and early 2000. We argue that this clearly is not the end of this incredible technology and economic boom—any more than the 1987 bubble and crash was in the Dow and broader markets fourteen years earlier. It takes a few years for such a shakeout in the growth of new technology and business sectors to consolidate as it did from late 1919 through early 1922. But then they boom again!

You can see in this chart how a trend line back to 1994 through the highs and lows of the bubble would project a fair value at the top of this boom of around 10,000. But allowing for another extreme overvaluation cycle, the trend line through the tops would go as high as 20,000. For now, consider that if the Nasdaq simply advanced as much as the Auto Index did in the Roaring Twenties boom, twelve times, that would imply a Nasdaq of approximately 13,000 from the low of 1108 in late 2002. In Chapter 2 we will show a channel technique for projecting the Nasdaq that also points to around 13,000 by the end of this decade.

Our best projection for the Nasdaq is about 13,000 around the end of this decade, but it is possible we could see as high as 20,000.

FIGURE 1.18   The Nasdaq, 1971–2009

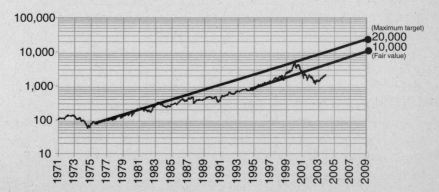

But why do we argue so strongly that a technology boom that so clearly looks to have peaked in a classic bubble is not over? Because the S-curve clearly tells us when a technology boom is over, just as demographics tell us when an economic boom is over. We can see that, in 2000 and 2001, the leading new consumer technologies were at the same point of market penetration on the S-curve as occurred for autos and other key consumer technologies coming into the 1920–1921 crash, eighty years earlier. The Internet hit the key 10% penetration point of U.S. households in early 1996 and has accelerated ever since as we can see in Figure 1.19. The Internet hit 50% penetration in 2001, just as autos did in 1921. Approaching that point you would expect a major shakeout in the industry as has occurred from 2000 through 2002. We were aware of this Shakeout Cycle in the emergence of new products and technologies, but we had no reference for how extreme it could be until we went back and broke out the industry sectors in the 1919–1921 crash when there wasn't a prominent technology index and saw the extreme crash in the Auto Index.

We were aware of that correction as well, but economists and historians had attributed it to the winddown from World War I and the commodity price collapse. But was there a great winddown and collapse in the economy and stock prices after World War II, a much more encompassing war? When we took a closer look at the data, we found that it was the high-tech sectors such as auto stocks that were at the center of that major stock crash and economic downturn.

FIGURE 1.19　The Internet S-Curve, 1986–2016

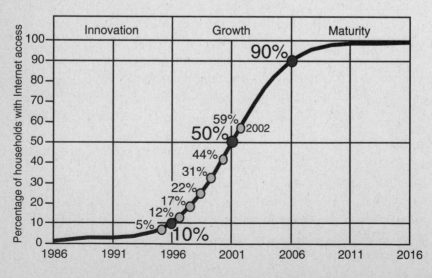

FIGURE 1.20 The Mobile Phone S-Curve, 1980–2022

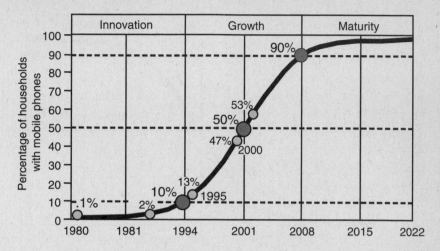

Mobile phones, another key emerging consumer technology, also hit 50% market penetration in 2001 after reaching 10% in 1994 (see Figure 1.20). This technology paralleled cars by exactly eighty years. The point here is simple: once new technologies emerge into the mainstream they continue to grow rapidly, much faster than the economy, until they reach 90% penetration. We are predicting that Internet access will hit 90% penetration by 2006 or 2007 and that mobile phones and wireless technologies will hit 90% by 2008 or so. The terrorist crisis will only increase the impetus toward cellular phones as they proved to be the ultimate emergency response system on 9/11. Not only did they allow many people to communicate with their loved ones at the last minute, but they likely saved the White House from being attacked by the last hijacked airliner.

We also forecasted in *The Roaring 2000s* that the real consumer revolution in new technologies and the Internet would not hit until 2002–2003, when the broadband revolution would accelerate bringing video communications and voice activation to the masses. We never forecasted that a whole new group of dot-com companies would suddenly create new brand names and take over the world. Most of the key technologies and brands that would dominate this revolution were created in the 1960s, 1970s, and early 1980s, much like the last revolution in the 1880s and 1890s and early 1900s. What we forecasted was a radical change in business models and how companies were designed and managed—from the bottom up, not the top down. This is the real impact of the Internet or network revolution, as we will further elaborate in Chapter 8.

FIGURE 1.21 The Broadband S-Curve, 1993–2017

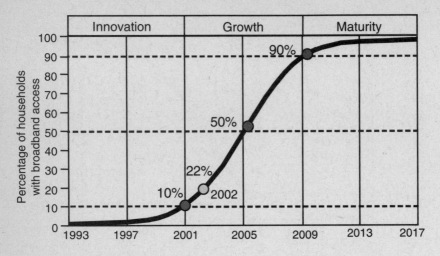

The real revolution is yet to come, as we can see in Figure 1.21. Broadband connections to households, from DSL to cable modems to other applications, hit 10% in late 2001 and are already approaching over 30% in 2004. Digital cameras are following an S-curve similar to that of broadband, and wi-fi is just emerging at rapid rates. Broadband represents the second or incremental S-curve that starts coming into the shakeout stage and accelerates into the Maturity Boom. Hence, the Maturity Boom should formally start in 2003 and accelerate in 2005.

Broadband is growing at twice the rate of the Internet, which has penetrated homes at twice the rate of PCs. We observed this same acceleration of new technologies and S-curves in the early 1900s and Roaring Twenties boom. Key infrastructures such as telephones and home electrification hit the 10% to 90% S-curve acceleration earlier from around 1900 to 1928. But autos and the early home appliances went from 10% to 90% in half the time, from 1914 to 1928. Then radios went mainstream from around 1921 to 1928, twice as fast again.

We are forecasting that the broadband revolution will go mainstream toward 90% penetration of U.S. households by 2009 at a blistering pace that is totally unexpected in the early 2000s. As we forecasted in *The Roaring 2000s,* the broadband revolution will bring the most important stage of the information, computer, and Internet revolutions. Why? It will bring video capability! And that means the ability to communicate face-to-face humanly and to receive real-time personal service over the Internet from companies. This next stage also brings the continuation of massive power in semiconductor chips along Moore's Law and will bring voice activation, which is already beginning to become a reality, as we forecasted. Voice activation means we can increasingly tell computers what we want without a keyboard and complex commands. That will make them more user-friendly as well.

That is why we forecasted in *The Roaring 2000s* that the real revolution, the consumer revolution, would not hit until 2002–2010 (pages 116–117). We continue to think, despite the great crash of 2000–2002, that the coming years will represent not only the greatest stage of the greatest boom in history—but the investment opportunity of a lifetime for investors. But you have to act now—sooner—rather than later. Although the markets have already rebounded substantially since late 2002, the cycles we will present in Chapter 3 strongly suggest that the best years in the markets will come between mid-2005 and mid-2010. But the same cycles suggest caution and a substantial correction into mid- to late 2006, and possibly in late 2007. In Chapter 3, we will also use a variety of technical tools to make our best forecasts for how high the markets could go in the coming boom as well as how far they could fall in the great downturn to follow. We will also present the simplest long-term model ever devised for investing in stocks for the long term, while protecting yourself against the worst corrections.

Get ready for the next and final stage of the greatest boom and bull market in history. We said it profitably in late 1992 and we are saying it again a decade later, in late 2002 and again in late 2004. Don't wait years to see the incredible proof. Use the power of demographics to take advantage of the greatest investment opportunity in history—today!

Chapter 2

THE BUBBLE BOOM

Why the Five Conditions That Create Technology Bubbles Will Continue in This Decade

AS NOTED IN Chapter 1, most experts are strongly suggesting that we have seen a classic bubble and that the stock market boom is over for many years or even decades to come. We couldn't disagree more. This entire boom has been a bubble boom, with the first minor bubble from 1985 to 1987, and the second greater bubble from 1995 into early 2000. These bubbles and crashes have been strongly paralleling the 1902–1929 bull market on an eighty-year lag in line with our New Economy Cycle. That bubble boom set the stage for the greatest advance in mass income in history to follow from the 1930s on, despite the huge crash in the early 1930s. Hence, we also disagree that this technology bubble was a huge mistake and that we will pay a big price for it in the years ahead. Throughout history technology bubbles have instead been a blessing in disguise.

Why? Technology bubbles have created huge investments in radical new infrastructures that have paid off for many decades to follow—investments with a scale and scope that most businesses and governments would not have the capacity to envision or substantiate with quantifiable returns. The crashes and shakeouts that follow only reinforce the companies with viable business models and shift assets and market share to them so that they can lead the next phase of growth and expansion. But the more important near-term insight is that there is another great bubble ahead, just as there were two technology bubbles in the early-1900s bubble boom (which followed an initial smaller bubble into 1907, similar to that of 1987): 1915–1919 and

1925–1929. The next great bubble will likely accelerate between 2005 and 2009 and complete the financing of the Internet, wireless, and broadband infrastructures to create the first affluent/millionaire economy in history into the middle of this century (which we will cover in Chapter 8).

Classic technical analysis for the stock market would reinforce the premise of another great bubble ahead as well. Nearly every major bull market sees three major advances with substantial corrections in between before peaking, also known as Elliott Wave patterns. Since we've seen only two major advances, the first into 1987 and the second into early 2000, there should clearly be one more major advance and another great bubble ahead in the bull market that originally started between late 1974 and late 1982, depending on how you measure the technical patterns. A broader view of the longer-term bull market, which actually began around 1780, shows that the bull wave ahead is likely to represent the final wave and we have seen each wave move up exponentially to a greater degree. This would suggest that the next bubble is likely to be as extreme as the Roaring Twenties bull market from 1922 to 1929, possibly even more so.

We are projecting that investors who have the conviction and courage to buy on pullbacks in mid- to late 2004 are going to see higher average annual compound returns than they would have seen in the last great bull wave from late 1990 into early 2000. In early October 2002 in *The H. S. Dent Forecast,* we gave our strongest buy signal ever based on what we saw in all of our key fundamental trends, cycles, and technical indicators. Even if we are overly optimistic based on very compelling demographic trends, investors should still be rewarded for buying based simply on the compelling Decennial Cycle in stocks, which typically calls for an acceleration between the "5" and "9" years and has been surprisingly consistent back to 1900. We will discuss this powerful cycle and others in Chapter 3 and present the simplest model ever devised for avoiding not only the worst extended bear markets, but also the worst corrections (as in 2000–2002) in bull markets.

TECHNOLOGY BUBBLES ARE DIFFERENT FROM ASSET AND CRISIS BUBBLES

Bubbles are not alike, either in degree or in their basic nature. In August 2002, the *RTW Report* published an issue titled "The Mother of All Chasms" by Paul Philp, based partly on research by Geoffrey Moore, best-selling author of *Crossing the Chasm* and technology marketing consultant.

This report documents how there have historically been three types of bubbles:

1. Asset bubbles
2. Structural instability bubbles
3. Technology bubbles

Asset bubbles would include the Japan Land Bubble of the 1980s and the famous Tulip Bubble of the 1630s, both of which are covered in the next section of this chapter. Such bubbles typically create little or nothing in sustainable value to the economy. Real estate or tulips go up in value, then crash. One could argue that in a real estate bubble new infrastructures are created that can fuel future growth at lower prices after the crash. And that is true. But real estate grows naturally with economic growth, and you wouldn't be creating infrastructures that wouldn't have come into being in a more orderly fashion anyway. The overpriced capacity created during the bubble is merely offset by the lower-priced capacity after the bubble. It is only the investors at the top of the bubble who get burned, not the economy as a whole.

Similarly, structural instability bubbles occur temporarily when there are political or noneconomic shocks to an industry that cannot absorb the shocks. OPEC policies or instability in the Middle East can cause a temporary sharp rise in oil prices without a change in demand from the markets. Prices rise and then crash again when the crisis or threat is over, creating little or no major change in the industry or economy. The oil price hikes in the early 1990s and early 2000s represent this sort of short-term bubble. But this is not to be confused with the more sustained bubble in oil prices that occurred in the 1970s. That represented a long-term scarcity of a key economic resource from the incredible industrial expansion of the last economic revolution. That longer-term rise in prices gave huge incentives to expand oil exploration and alternative fuels that were critical to the next economic revolution. That is actually more similar to the nature of technology bubbles.

Technology bubbles are very different in that they create radical new infrastructures that would not be created by normal economic incentives. Only a few visionaries throughout history have seen the real potential of radical new technologies, such as Henry Ford with cars, or Steve Jobs with PCs, or Marc Andreessen with the Internet. But these visionaries don't have the capital to make the huge investments that these new infrastructures require across the board. The vast majority of governments and exist-

ing businesses simply don't have this vision and don't see the long-term returns on investing in such radical new technologies and infrastructures, especially since the investments are so vast and the returns and benefits so
unclear.

You can see technology bubbles as the economy's way of using our own
predictable human tendencies of greed and fear to seduce us into making
very-long-term investments that create a leap in economic infrastructures
and business models which advance our income and wealth in major, but
largely unpredictable ways, for many decades to come.

That is the basis of our eighty-year New Economy model. The bubbles
will concentrate in the country or region that is leading those new models
and technologies—and those bubbles will tend to come in the first half of
that eighty-year cycle, when the new technologies are rapidly emerging into
the mainstream for the first time. Where have most of the technology bubbles from railroads to automobiles and roads to movies and entertainment
to jet travel to PCs, cellular phones, and the Internet occurred in the last
century? In the United States! Which is the richest and most powerful nation in the world today? The United States! Twelve of fourteen of the technology bubbles since the Industrial Revolution (since the late 1700s) have
occurred in the United States.

The real coup is that the United States largely accomplished this leading and unprecedented standard of living and political power without
being a military aggressor and building a politically controlled empire. It
has instead built a technological and worldwide business franchise. This is
precisely what terrorists and many archaic third-world cultures are reacting
to today. We have not conquered countries militarily, we have only reacted
defensively to protect the free-enterprise system and defend our allies.

Paul Philp identified the five key dynamics that create technology bubbles:

1. The new technology is radical and changes the foundations of the economy and society.

2. No one initially knows how to apply the new technology profitably (re-
   quiring many new entrepreneurial experiments).

3. A shared infrastructure (meaning massive new large-scale investments) is
   required.

4. The economy is healthy (to be able to afford such investments).

5. Inflation is low (favoring equity investments and speculation over low-
   yield bonds).

These bubbles and revolutions have occurred largely in the United States precisely because we have the most prosperous free-market economy in the world. In Europe and Japan, governments retain more power to protect old institutions, which limit entrepreneurial innovations. Their job is to protect the interests of most people, businesses, and institutions in the old economic, social, and political structures. If it were left to major governments or even established corporations, there simply wouldn't be the economic justification for building the shared infrastructure to make the new economy viable and radically more productive. The investment is too great, the risks are too high, and the benefits are not pragmatically clear.

Thank God governments don't drive the modern economy! The best governments, like that of the United States, provide basic infrastructures and a legal system that allows individuals and businesses to drive our economy. This allows the economy to operate more from the bottom up, rather than from the top down. The task of radical innovation is left to the visionary—and more often irrational—instincts of entrepreneurs and individual investors—driven by the natural instincts of greed and improving one's existence. And we will show later in this chapter that for the first time in history, the average person in the United States is becoming an investor and a business owner. That's what is creating the Millionaire Economy, which we will address in Chapter 8.

So here's the real difference in a technology bubble. The irrational speculation creates massive investment in long-term infrastructures, which, unlike real estate, cannot just evolve organically in line with the economy's growth. The revolution can't really take off until such infrastructures evolve suddenly in unison from many different angles. History has clearly shown, as we demonstrated in *The Roaring 2000s,* that it takes a cluster of new technologies to create a revolution, although one or a few may drive and dominate—such as automobiles and electricity or semiconductors and software. Only in the crashes after such bubbles do the real revolutions start to emerge. Here's a quote from Paul Philp:

> Bubbles build the shared infrastructure needed to make radical technologies profitable when there is no economic incentive for any group of investors to build that infrastructure. The economic payback begins at the bottom of the crash, when entrepreneurial businesses start applying the technology and infrastructure to make their businesses' orders of magnitude more productive.

Why? The high investment level creates many innovative attempts at exploiting the new economic and business models. Like tadpoles emerging into a stream, only a few survive. Since no one fully knows how to exploit the new technologies at first, as they are so radical, this massive innovative process is necessary. Yes, so many fail, such as the many dot-coms. But a few companies, such as Dell, eBay, Amazon, AOL, Yahoo!, Cisco, and Google, survive. They become the impetus of the next revolution to be joined and followed by many more companies, new and established, with radical new S-curve accelerations of innovation in products such as broadband and biotech.

Many failed concepts, such as Webvan, become incorporated into existing companies, such as Tesco in the United Kingdom and many grocery store chains in the United States that are now more profitably offering home delivery of groceries without the huge new infrastructure costs that sank Webvan (which had a growing base of satisfied customers). They can simply leverage the radical new technology within existing infrastructures of warehouses and low-cost buying. Wal-Mart may ultimately, decades from now, end up being the biggest single beneficiary of the online ordering and home-delivery revolution. And now it is using Internet-based, low-cost technologies to move into financial services and investing for the everyday household.

But a crash also creates many failing companies that are absorbed by the surviving companies, which thus acquire infrastructures, capacity, and technologies at a very low cost. This allows them to offer much lower prices and better options within proven business models to the many more consumers or business customers who couldn't afford the new technologies or services in the first stage of the revolution. That is how the S-curve progresses after the shakeout stage around 50% penetration (as we described in Chapter 1) into full mainstream penetration in the next boom and bubble to follow. Only once the new markets are near market-share penetration (around 90%) does the technology revolution slow down until the next phase occurs.

Why do existing businesses and governments fail to see the long-term benefits of these new technologies and infrastructures? Because they run contrary to their present and maturing models of existence. When electricity first emerged, who could have seen the emergence of the assembly line and the mass-manufacturing revolution? When the auto first emerged, who could have thought it would launch a revolution in retailing through large department stores such as Sears and a massive migration to suburban living? When the railroad was first built, who would have anticipated that Sears would start selling household goods at the railway stops or that railroads would open up the western part of the United States?

When TVs first emerged, who would have anticipated that they would create a new mass-marketing and advertising-based economy to follow the mass-production revolution around automobiles and the assembly line? When the PC emerged, who would have seen the real-time production and direct-marketing model at Dell—or the Internet? The Internet has leveraged the direct-marketing revolution at Dell and will greatly leverage the broader revolution that only began in the 1970s with direct mail-order firms, not to mention changing the entire organizational structure of corporations, creating a new era wherein nearly every worker becomes a small business instead of an employee.

Now let's look at bubbles throughout history from this very different and more constructive perspective.

A HISTORY OF STOCK MARKET BUBBLES— AND MODERN ECONOMICS AS A WHOLE

Let's review some of the most prominent stock market bubbles in history— and take a longer-term view of modern history to see where we stand today in the evolution of our economy. We have obviously just lived through an extreme bubble in Internet and dot-com stocks and a substantial bubble in technology stocks. The common wisdom is that once a bubble has occurred, the markets don't go to new highs for decades. The truth is that this is sometimes true and sometimes not. First, it is important to note, as Jeremy Siegel (author of *Stocks for the Long Run*) has, that this bubble occurred largely in the tech sectors and not in the broader markets. In 2000, the Dow went to the top of our Dow Channel and has had a correction of 38%, slightly less than it did in 1987, after which the U.S. stock markets kept booming. The S&P 500 corrected by 49% due to its higher concentration of tech stocks. If you were to take the technology stocks out of the S&P 500, you would get a more normal periodic correction within a bull market similar to that of 1990 or 1998. Without the technology sectors, the S&P 500 would have been down only 24% between early 2000 and late 2002.

It was leading large-cap Internet stocks such as AOL that had price/ earnings (P/E) ratios of over 400. It was the new emerging dot-coms that had huge valuations with no earnings in sight and totally unproven busi-

FIGURE 2.1 The Nasdaq, 1990–2002

ness models. This represented a true and extreme stock market bubble and the crash that has followed has been extreme. In late 2002, the Nasdaq was down by 78% (Figure 2.1) and the great majority of dot-coms were gone, with the Internet Index down 93% (Figure 2.2). Substantial portions of the larger technology stocks, such as Lucent, are seriously wounded and may not see new highs. But we are forecasting, against popular opinion, that many of the larger technology companies with leadership positions and strong business models, such as Microsoft, Intel, Yahoo!, eBay, and Cisco, will see major new highs in the coming decade. And there will be new emerging companies that will quickly move into leadership positions in the next phase of the boom.

FIGURE 2.2 The GSTI Internet Index, 1996–2002

Let's start by looking at the history of major stock market bubbles in the past and the psychology that causes them. The truth is, every time we get an extended strong boom in the economy or in strong leading sectors, we get substantial overvaluation. This results from the Human Model of Forecasting (Figure 2.3), which we introduced in *The Great Boom Ahead*. We have a consistent tendency to project recent trends in a straight line into the future, whereas the reality of life is that trends move in a cyclical or curvilinear manner. Hence, we have a grave misperception of reality and risk. The longer the trends go up and the stronger the advances, the more bullish we get about the future and the less risk we perceive. And remember, the stock market values stocks by projecting their earnings many years into the future, exacerbating our straight-line tendencies. When the cycle finally slows and reverses, stocks have excessive valuations and then correct excessively. At the bottom of the slowdown, we project slow growth or decline many years into the future, and here we perceive the greatest risk just when the stock market has allowed for nearly everything that could go wrong in the future and is undervalued. Hence, during the correction we expect very slow growth at best, as we don't anticipate the strong rebound that typically follows.

Our point here is simple. Markets are always overvalued in cycles of growth and undervalued in cycles of slowing. **Bubbles and crashes always**

FIGURE 2.3 The Human Model of Forecasting

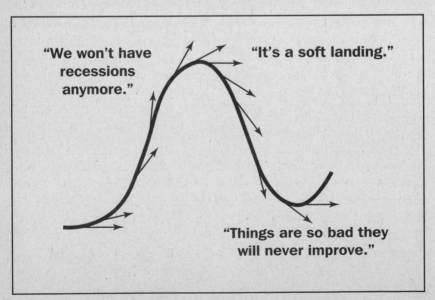

"We won't have recessions anymore."

"It's a soft landing."

"Things are so bad they will never improve."

occur; they are simply a matter of degree. The greatest overvaluation or bubble cycles occur when the economy is accelerating the most strongly, which almost always occurs when demographic trends in spending are pointing strongly up and powerful new technologies and growth industries first enter the mainstream on an S-Curve Cycle. That is why the last major bubble in the U.S. economy occurred in the Roaring Twenties and not in the post–World War II boom in the 1950s and 1960s. Of course, as new technologies accelerated again, starting in the 1990s, we just experienced the next great bubble, but again largely in technology stocks. We have been arguing since mid-2001 that modern-day technology advances see two bubbles, such as those in 1915–1919 and 1925–1929, before peaking and only then see a more extended long-term bear market. The crash of the first auto bubble, the tech stocks of that time, from late 1919 into early 1922 ended up being the greatest investment opportunity for stocks and tech stocks of the last century, whereas the crash of the second bubble from late 1929 into early 1932 represented the end of the great bull market for more than a decade.

The first major bubble in history that was accurately measured was the Dutch Tulip Mania of 1634–1637, graphed in Figure 2.4. The prices of one tulip started at about 1.20 guilders and accelerated in value fifty times in a little over two years, to 60 guilders. Then they crashed 99.8% to .10 guilder in less than a year. That was the most extreme bubble up and down we've seen in measured history. This was clearly not a technology bubble that created critical new infrastructures, just a speculative asset bubble of the most minor degree. Hence, this was perhaps the most ridiculous bubble in modern history. But it is the most quoted bubble in history by bearish historians and stock market analysts and hence very misleading.

The next great bubble was the South Sea Company Bubble into 1720 (Figure 2.5). Here the value of this company's shares (representing the major new technology growth segment of the economy) went up about nine times, from $110 to almost $1,000, in one year, from mid-1719 to mid-1720. It then crashed 93%, to about $70, over the next two years. That bubble was more like the recent Internet Bubble, but even more extreme. The history here is more interesting. There had been a major expansion in population and economic growth in Europe starting in the late 1400s following the invention of the printing press, the last major information revolution. The other major technology revolutions from the mid- to late 1400s included gunpowder and tall sailing ships with navigation advances that allowed them to sail long distances. The sailing revolution allowed not only the discovery of America but also a more lucrative spice and fabric trade

FIGURE 2.4 Gouda Tulip Bulb Prices, December 1, 1634–February 5, 1637

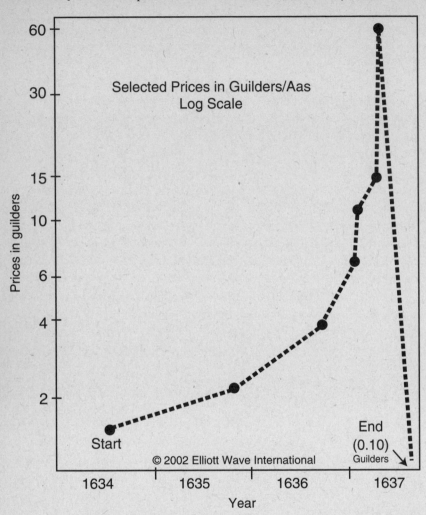

Source: Robert Prechter, *Conquer the Crash*, p. 80.

with the Far East. The success of such trade led to the first publicly owned companies, whose shares were sold to many individual investors in 1607. In essence, this was the raw beginnings of the stock markets. And of course, it was only a matter of time before human nature would generate a stock bubble. We can assume that there were previous, more minor bubbles that are not well known or documented.

By the early 1700s, the population growth that had been leading the

FIGURE 2.5 The South Sea Company, 1719–1722

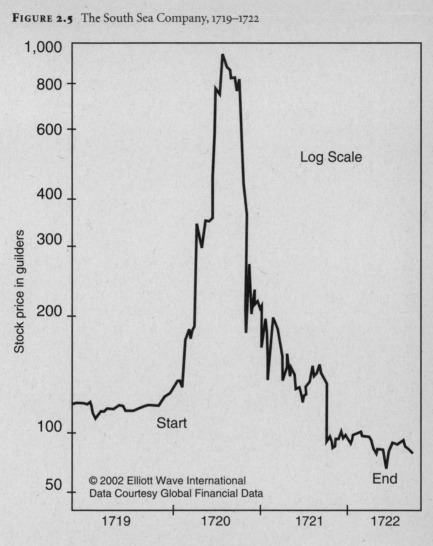

Source: Robert Prechter, *Conquer the Crash*, p. 80.

greatest economic expansion in history started to slow, and that naturally led to a major bear market. Figure 2.6 (which was developed by Robert Prechter at Elliott Wave International, one of our favorite long-term analysts) combines British stock prices as far back as they can be measured (to around 1700) with U.S. stock prices from 1780 on. A 230-year-plus bull market from around 1490 or earlier to 1720 was followed by the crash of the 1720 bubble, representing the beginning of a sixty-nine-year bear market in stocks. We have pointed out in past books that there are greater long-term

FIGURE 2.6 The Grand Supercycle: The Longer-Term Bull Market Since the 1780s

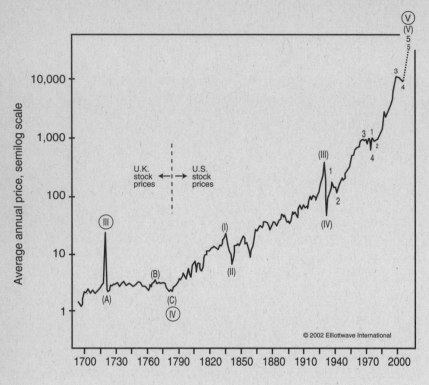

Source: Robert Prechter, *Conquer the Crash*, p. 33, with projections forward by Harry Dent.

bull market cycles, which are followed by more extended bear markets than we are used to seeing in our lifetimes.

The Elliott Wave theory (see www.elliottwave.com), which has been successfully proven and promoted in recent decades by Robert Prechter, author of *Conquer the Crash,* shows that most bull markets evolve in three major advances up with two corrective waves in between. Figure 2.7 shows that pattern of a first wave up, a second-wave pullback (often the sharpest), a third wave up (often the longest and strongest), and a fourth-wave correction (often the deepest), followed by a fifth-wave peak (often the steepest). Then the more extended bear market that follows progresses through three waves: an A wave down, a B-wave bear market rally, then a C wave that completes the downturn before the next bull market begins. This pattern tends to occur in both shorter-term and longer-term market move-

FIGURE 2.7 Elliott Wave Patterns in Nature and Markets

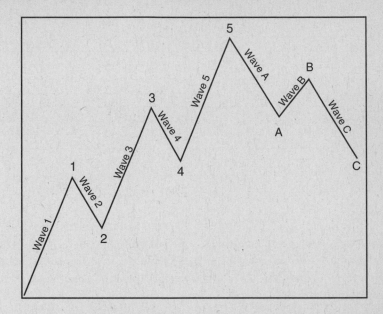

ments. Elliott Wave theory represents the greatest single tool in technical analysis in this century and can help us refine our fundamental demographic and technology cycle forecasts. We can see those patterns in the bull market since 1780 in Figure 2.6, including some of the subpatterns within each major wave.

Let's look back at the larger Elliott Wave pattern of the bull market that started around 1780, as shown in Figure 2.6. The first larger wave up occurred from 1780 to 1832. There was a significant bubble into that peak and a strong second-wave crash that bottomed by 1837. The next or third long-term wave up occurred from 1837 to 1929 with an even stronger bubble at the end. We can see that Roaring Twenties bubble in Figure 2.8. After the bubble peak in late 1919 and the crash into late 1921, the Dow went up six times into late 1929 in eight years and went up four times from mid-1924 to late 1929 in just five years. The market almost doubled in the last year, similarly to the Nasdaq in 1999.

Note that this bubble was nowhere near as extreme as the Dutch Tulip and South Sea bubbles. But the aftermath saw an 87% decline between late 1929 and early 1932. That crash lasted two years and ten months and erased more than all of the gains from the entire bull market from late 1921 to late 1929. That would have told you the stock boom was over for many years to come. Note that the 2000–2002 correction in the Dow lasted nearly as

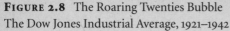

FIGURE 2.8 The Roaring Twenties Bubble
The Dow Jones Industrial Average, 1921–1942

long—two years and ten months—and according to the history of the length of the worst crashes was due to end about when it did. But that crash did not take out anywhere near all of the gains from the previous bull market in the 1990s.

It is important to observe here that the 1920s bubble emerged not only around the peak of a new generation's spending cycle but, more important, around the emergence of a new technology revolution moving into the mainstream. We call this the Automobile/Mass Manufacturing Bubble. Autos, the central new technology, advanced from 10% to 90% penetration of urban households between 1914 and 1928, fueled by the assembly-line revolution in mass manufacturing, as we showed in Chapter 1. By 1929, we would have been due for a major slowdown and consolidation/shakeout in these new growth industries even without a downturn in demographics. But remember that first there was a prominent bubble in technology and auto stocks from 1915 to late 1919, during the Growth Stage of that S-Curve Cycle. This is consistent with our eighty-year New Economy Model, which closely paralleled the most recent tech bubble from 1995 to 1999. Figure 2.9 shows again how General Motors tracked Intel in the 1990s tech bubble almost perfectly eighty years ago.

Most analysts and investors would have looked at the bubble and crash in the tech stocks and General Motors back then and thought, "This bull market is over!" But as you can see in Figure 2.10, repeated from Chapter 1, General Motors went up twenty-two times from 1922 to 1929 for an average annual compound return of 57%. The second bubble into 1929 came at the end of the auto and technology S-curve acceleration during the Maturity Boom stage of the auto S-Curve Cycle and was accompanied by the peak of

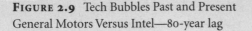

FIGURE 2.9 Tech Bubbles Past and Present
General Motors Versus Intel—80-year lag

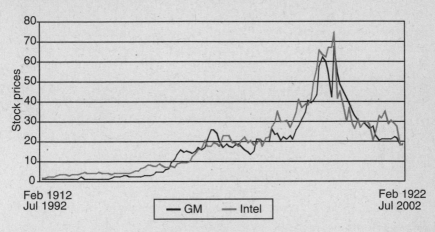

the Henry Ford Generation Spending Cycle. Hence, it initiated a longer-
term bear market and period of consolidation in the economy, unlike the
first bubble into late 1919, which crashed into early 1922 and then went right
into the next great boom and bubble.

We showed in Chapter 1 how, following the crash in early 1922, the Dow
went up by six times, the Auto Index twelve times, and General Motors
twenty-two times into late 1929. There were clearly two bubbles as the new-

FIGURE 2.10 General Motors Stock Price, 1919–1930

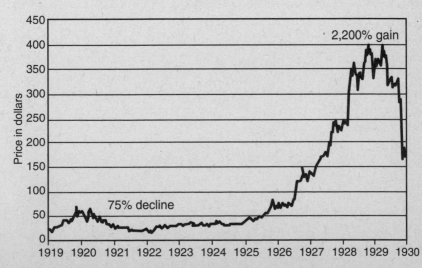

technology revolution emerged and the second bubble saw a greater and more extended decline from late 1929 into 1932. The crash of the first bubble into early 1922 created the greatest buying opportunity for stocks and technology in the last century. Even the crash into mid-1932 created a great intermediate-term buying opportunity into 1937 wherein the Dow advanced by 4.7 times in less than five years (see Figure 2.8). The next major bull market didn't begin until the Bob Hope generation entered its Spending Wave Cycle from 1942 into 1968. That bull market was not as bubble-like since there wasn't the impact of radical new technologies suddenly emerging as only occurs about every eighty years or every other generation. Likewise, the crashes in 1970 and 1973–1974 were strong but not as dramatic.

Another example of a major bubble occurred in Japan in late 1989, as you can see in Figure 2.11. Japan had been emerging as a leading nation since the 1960s, based on a new generation's spending wave, which peaked almost two decades ahead of the U.S. baby boom. In the late 1980s we forecasted that Japan's demographics were not favorable in the 1990s and that it was not leading the key technologies of the future—hence, it would fall rapidly behind in the 1990s boom. Japan's government had rigged its economy to favor key manufacturing industries and to leverage rising real estate prices through low-cost corporate debt, creating both a stock bubble and a more extreme real estate or land bubble than has occurred anywhere else in modern times. Despite those extremes, the advance in the Nikkei from 1982 to 1989 was almost exactly the same as that in the Dow from 1922 to 1929, nearly six times. So this bubble was very similar in the magnitude of gains to the Roaring Twenties bubble in the United States. But this bubble also marked the peaking of a generation's spending cycle and the beginning of a long-term bear market that likely just came to a bottom in early 2003.

FIGURE 2.11 The Nikkei Index, 1982–2003

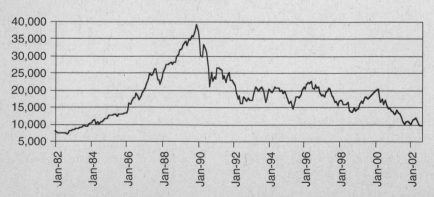

Japan's spending wave points down until 2003 or 2004 and doesn't turn up strongly until 2008 or 2009 into 2020.

If we look back at the 1990s, the first and major crash after the Nikkei bubble peaked in late 1989 lasted two years and four months, into April 1992, and saw a 62% decline. But after a minor "B" wave rally into early 1996, the market declined 80% from its highs in early 2003. Japan's extended bear market was bolstered by the fact that the rest of the world was booming in the 1990s and its strong export industries benefited. Since the echo baby boom to follow is much smaller than the previous generation, and because the world economy will be heading down after 2009 or so, the next bull market is likely to be a larger "B" wave and not make new highs for many decades to come, as mentioned earlier.

Note that the Japanese bubble did not represent a technology bubble. Japan was not the leading country in the world, and radical new technologies were not emerging rapidly into its mainstream economy. It was merely, but very effectively, improving old technologies and business models. The stock bubble in Japan resulted from the leverage of the greater land bubble that the government intentionally created (out of its scarcest resource in a small island infrastructure) to force massive investments in new manufacturing capacity. Hence, even though land and stock prices have collapsed since, Japan has been left with a strong competitive position in many global industries. But it doesn't yet have the capacity to compete in most of the new growth industries and more radical technologies.

The United States is leading the new-technology revolution, which brings us to the latest bubble: the Internet and technology bubble of the late 1990s, which we show again in Figures 2.12 and 2.13. It is important to

FIGURE 2.12 The GSTI Internet Index, 1996–2002

remember, as mentioned previously, that the recent stock bubble and crash
from 2000 to 2002 was centered largely in the technology sectors. The most
extreme bubble obviously came in the Internet sectors. The Internet hit
10% penetration of U.S. households in early 1996, and this sector started to
emerge as a major new growth phenomenon. The real bubble came only
from late 1998 into early 2000. In 1½ years this index went up almost seven
times. Now, that is extreme, more like the South Sea Company Bubble from
1719 to 1720 (Figure 2.5).

The Internet Index crashed 93% from the highs, wiping out more than
all of the gains since 1996. Many of the smaller dot-com stocks have van-
ished or are down by close to 99%. Again, this shows that bubbles are a
matter of degree. Here we had more dramatic gains based on very questionable business models and rare profits to be found—similar to the Tulip
Bubble in the magnitude of the gains and the crash to follow. It is unlikely
that this index will make new highs even though Internet adoption was at
63% as of 2003 and should advance to around 90% by 2006 or 2007. The
driving technologies in this broader revolution are semiconductor chips
and software. The Internet allows computers, communications devices, and
content to be greatly leveraged; hence it represents the most important part
of the shared infrastructure for the new economy. But as is typical of such
infrastructures in the past, it is not a highly profitable product or infrastructure in itself. That's why bubbles are necessary to finance such new infrastructures. And again, when we see a crash wipe out more than all of the
gains from the previous bull market then the market is likely to have

FIGURE 2.13   The Nasdaq, 1990–2002

peaked for a long time, like the Dow and Auto Index from 1929 to 1932 or the South Sea Company crash from 1720 to 1722. On the other hand, the few viable business models that did survive, from eBay to Cisco, will likely see major new highs in the boom ahead.

Now let's look at the Nasdaq bubble in the late 1990s more closely in Figure 2.13. The bubble really started in 1995 and accelerated exponentially from late 1998 to early 2000. From the beginning of 1995 the Nasdaq went up by 6.7 times and advanced by 3.7 times from late 1998 into early 2000. That is stronger than the Dow's advance in the Roaring Twenties or the Nikkei in the 1980s, but still not an extreme bubble—nothing like the Internet, South Sea Company, or tulip bubbles. The crash to follow saw the Nasdaq decline by 78%. But that has taken us only back to levels seen in 1996 and has not erased all of the gains of the last bull wave, which began in late 1990, nor has it taken out the top of the first wave up, which peaked in 1987. That clearly allows for the potential of another wave up in this bull market. We get a better perspective if we look at the Nasdaq (Figure 2.14) over its entire bull market on a logarithmic chart. Logarithmic charts take an exponential trend and convert it to a straight line. In the long term, the growth of any significant percentage increase will compound into an exponential trend. Hence, any technical analyst worth his or her salt uses logarithmic graphs to put long-term trends into perspective. Many of the "world is falling apart" analysts use arithmetic charts when trying to show the extremes of bubbles to scare people into their bear market scenarios.

FIGURE 2.14 The Nasdaq Channel, 1974–2009

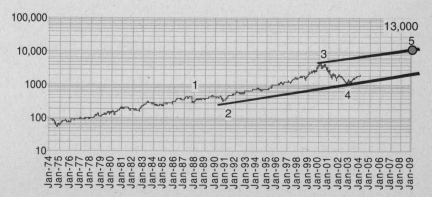

PROJECTIONS FOR THE LAST GREAT BULL MARKET

The strongest emerging innovation in technical analysis, which we have been referring to, is the Elliott Wave (www.elliottwave.com), which was brought into modern interpretation by Robert Prechter. To review, this method says that most bull markets emerge in three major waves up before peaking: a first-wave advance followed by a second-wave correction; then a third-wave advance, which tends to be the longest and largest wave, followed by a fourth-wave correction; then finally a fifth-wave advance before peaking longer term. The Nasdaq in this chart clearly seems to have seen its first wave up into 1987 and then its third wave up into early 2000. If we looked at this chart on technical factors alone, we would assume it has a substantial fifth wave to come, as would broader market gauges such as the Dow or S&P 500. The fourth-wave correction has not taken out the first-wave high. If it had, that would suggest that a peak is already at hand. A fourth-wave correction following the longest and strongest third-wave advance would also be expected to see the deepest correction.

In Figure 1.18 in Chapter 1, we showed a chart of the Nasdaq with a trend line through all of the tops since 1974 pointing to a target of as high as 20,000 by late 2008. There are other ways to project likely targets for tops that we will explore now. One of the best ways to project the fifth-wave, or final, target is to draw a bottom trend line through the second- and fourth-wave lows and then a parallel line through the third-wave peak extending forward. By late 2009, when we roughly project this bull market will end (give or take a year) due to the saturation of new technologies and peak baby-boom spending, this channel would be projecting a Nasdaq of approximately 13,000. That would represent a twelve-times gain from its October 8, 2002, low of 1108, similar to the twelve-times gain of the Auto Index in the Roaring Twenties. Now, the Nasdaq may not go that high—or it might go even higher, like the 20,000 target we will show in Figure 2.18. But a Nasdaq of 13,000 by late 2008 would imply average annual compound gains of 39%. Even if the gains were half that, most investors would be happy campers after the very humbling correction of 2000–2002.

If we go back to the Dow, we can make similar projections and with a higher degree of confidence given the more orderly advances and corrections in the Dow during this bull market. Since 1997 we developed the Dow Channel (Figure 2.15) as our primary valuation tool for the broader markets and to make rough projections for a potential peak target around late 2008. This channel plotted much better than most with the ability to draw

FIGURE 2.15   The Dow Channel, 1982–2010

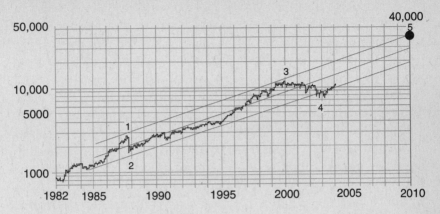

parallel lines through a series of lows and highs to include the first-wave high as well as the third-wave high. It also accurately predicted the rough time frame for a market peak in early 2000 as we hit the top trend line for the first time since 1987. The channel was projecting a Dow of about 35,000 by late 2008, and 40,000 by late 2009. But the channel was marginally broken in July 2002. It first gave an extreme buy signal at around 8,000 in late September 2001 (which still would have been a great place to buy). Then we gave our strongest buy signal ever on October 1, 2002, at a target of around 7,400, based on other technical indicators, including strong support at the late 1998 correction lows.

Channels can be broken slightly on the up- or downside and still remain valid. In fact, just the trend line through the tops can often be a good

FIGURE 2.16   Revised Dow Channel, 1974–2010

indicator of the ultimate topping targets making 32,000 still a viable target by late 2009. Often when a channel is broken on the downside at its fourth-wave low, it will break the channel on the upside to a similar degree when it makes its fifth-wave peak. The best and most reliable channels, like the Dow Channel in Figure 2.15, are drawn through both the first- and third-wave tops as well as the second- and fourth-wave lows. But that is not typical.

Just in case this channel doesn't hold as accurately after the brief break of the lower trend line in July 2002, we have drawn an alternate channel. The good news is that it points nearly as high. Figure 2.16 plots the channel in the more typical way as we did for the Nasdaq in Figure 2.14, with a top trend line from the third wave forward parallel to a bottom trend line through the second and fourth waves. This chart projects a Dow of about 20,000 by late 2008 and 38,000 by late 2009, very similar to the original Dow Channel. Both of the Dow Channels would project average annual compound gains of about 24% from the bottom in late 2002. Those potential returns are higher than investors would have gotten by buying in at the beginning of the 1990s bull market (in late 1990) and holding until the peak in January 2000.

Here's the biggest reason we favor a very strong advance in the Nasdaq and Dow rather than just modest new highs in the last wave of this unprecedented bull market that began in the early 1980s, resulting in the two (and very likely three) best back-to-back decades in U.S. history. If we look at Figure 2.17 (a repeat of Figure 2.6, earlier in this chapter), the Elliott Wave analysis back to the 1700s, it seems clear that we are in the late stages of a larger long-term bull market that began following the sixty-nine-year correction after the collapse of the 1720 South Sea Company Bubble. The first wave peaked in 1832, and the third wave peaked in 1929. It appears we are about to enter the fifth and final wave of the larger fifth wave that started in 1932, both in the Nasdaq (Figure 2.14) and the Dow (Figure 2.15) charts. In fact, there is an alternate and likely more valid wave count for the Dow that we showed in Figure 2.16. Here the first wave up was a short one from late 1974 into mid-1976. Then there was a long sideways second-wave consolidation into late 1982. Then the third massive wave occurred from late 1982 into early 2000. The severe fourth-wave correction hit into late 2002. A final, strong fifth wave would be projected ahead.

But here is the most important point. Notice that since 1780 when this greater bull market began (see Figure 2.17), that the trends have been accelerating in each wave into a larger, longer-term bubble even on a logarithmic graph, which converts a constant exponential trend into a straight-line trend. Each larger wave and each smaller wave within this larger fifth wave

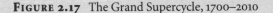

FIGURE 2.17 The Grand Supercycle, 1700–2010

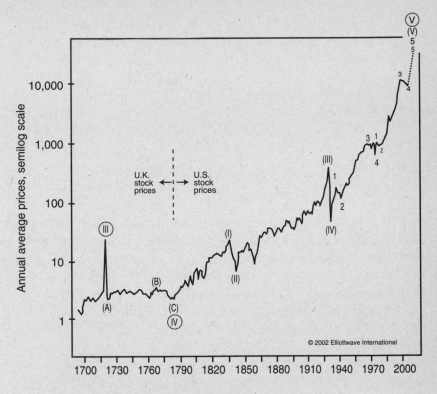

Source: Robert Prechter, *Conquer the Crash*, p. 33,
with projections forward by Harry Dent.

has been more exponential. Would anyone expect that the final wave of
such an accelerating and extreme long-term bubble would not be dramatic? The final advance into the top of the first wave in 1832 was dramatic.
The final advance of the third wave into 1929 was even more dramatic. Because this larger fifth wave since 1932 has already been more exponential
than the previous wave, we find it hard to believe we are not about to enter
at least as great a bubble as occurred in the Roaring Twenties—and likely
even greater as the final wave of this larger fifth wave emerges. Hence, we
feel the most likely scenario for the last stage of this unprecedented baby-
boom spending wave is a great bubble ahead.

What are the more extreme upside targets? The Dow could break above
its original channel (see Figure 2.15) similar to the break below in 2002 and
possibly reach 40,000 by 2010. It is very likely that the bull market could last
into 2010, which could send the Dow to 40,000 or higher. But the real bub-

FIGURE 2.18   The Nasdaq, 1971–2009

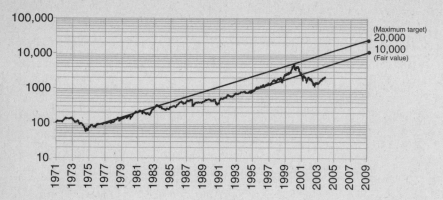

ble is again likely to occur to extremes in the Nasdaq. In Figure 2.18, which we repeat from Figure 1.18 in Chapter 1, we draw a trend line through the tops of the Nasdaq since the bull market there clearly began in 1974. That trend line points to about 20,000 by late 2009 and even higher if the bull market extends into 2010. That would truly be astounding and would represent an eighteen-times gain from the lows in October 2002 and a compound average annual gain of 49%. We still think 13,000 is a much more likely target for a peak.

How could this possibly occur after everyone had just witnessed such a bubble and crash? The truth is that it doesn't take most people long to forget even hard lessons when strong gains stimulate their greed again. If the tech sectors return to very high growth and outperformance after such a crash (as our fundamental indicators strongly suggest), investors could become even more convinced that we are in a new economy and that the economy will boom indefinitely and that technology will keep cranking out strong growth and productivity advances. That bubble is likely to concentrate to the greatest extremes in broadband technologies and biotech, which appear to be the next great frontiers in the Information Revolution. Is that the most likely scenario? Probably not, but we wouldn't rule it out either, and we consider it to be a real possibility.

In the last century we have seen many short-term bubbles and strong corrections occur in various emerging growth sectors and have then seen bull markets follow. First there were the auto bubbles of 1915–1919 and 1925–1929 and the crashes that followed in 1919–1922 and 1930–1932 that we have already covered. Airline stocks crashed by 62% from 1945 to 1948 and 63% from 1990 to 1994 and continued to rally to major new highs until the recent peak in 2000 with no extended bear markets. The dramatic movie industry has also seen crashes of 77% without entering an extended bear market and has rallied strongly ever since, even through the second half of the bear market in the 1970s. The home-building stocks continue to boom but saw a 58% correction in the early 1980s and a 62% correction in the early 1990s. The Hong Kong market has been in a strong bull market since 1974 and has seen two major corrections in excess of 60%, the last of which occurred between late 1997 and 1998.

The point is that strong advances are typically followed by strong corrections even in an ongoing bull market. You don't get high returns without high risks! Forgetting this simple principle causes investors to jump in near the tops of bubbles and then bail out near the bottom and take many years to get the courage to get back in. That's how you lose or make only minimal gains in a great bull market.

WHY A BUBBLE MARKET?

Let's now review the reasons that this unprecedented boom has been characterized by bubbles and will see another ahead. The period 1985–1987 was actually the first bubble in this boom and was followed by the sharpest short-term correction in U.S. history. There was actually a similar peak in 1907 followed by a sharp crash eighty years ago. That 1980s bubble was followed by the tech-led bubble into early 2000 that paralleled the bubble into late 1919, eighty years before. The 2000–2002 correction has been the largest in any leading sector in this boom and lasted only a little longer than the auto crash into early 1922.

Unlike the crashes in 1929–1932, 1973–1974, and 1990–1992 (in Japan), the demographic spending and technology cycles still point up very strongly into 2008–2009. These crashes also saw major deterioration in the economy whereas we experienced only a minor recession in late 2000–early 2001, largely from extreme cutbacks in business capital spending, not by consumers, who kept buying houses in record numbers. The economy has rebounded from there and started to accelerate again in 2003. Hence, we see another strong bubble ahead—the third advance (or fifth wave) to complete a classic Elliott Wave pattern in this boom. Again, the truth about this unprecedented bull market is that each major wave up has turned into a bubble and each bubble has been steeper and more exponential than the previous one.

The first bubble accelerated from 1985 to 1987 and the second from 1995 into early 2000. And we are very clearly forecasting a third and final bubble into late 2009 or early 2010 that could well be even more extreme than the recent bubble. The crash to follow that final bubble will be both more extreme and much longer in duration—more like the Great Depression in degree and the bear market in Japan in length. We are forecasting that the next extended bear market will occur between late 2009 or early 2010 into 2022 with the Dow going down by 70% to 80%–plus and the Nasdaq likely down by 90% or more. We would expect both of these markets, at a minimum, to return to their lows in late 2002. The real reasons for the strong "bubble" nature of this boom are the following:

1. On the eighty-year cycle we are in the Growth Boom stage wherein new technologies emerge rapidly into the mainstream in an S-curve acceleration that creates dramatic growth and a race for leadership in new emerging technologies and industries. Booms such as that in 1902–1929 are always more dramatic and see accelerating bubbles and crashes as the cycle progresses. We saw a clear tech bubble from 1915 to 1919 and then a greater one from 1925 to 1929 after a severe crash into early 1922. We also saw stronger peaks and crashes in 1907 and 1914 (onset of World War I). All of these peaks and crashes that followed were closely parallel on an eighty-year lag to the ones that occurred in 1987, 1993–1994, and 2000–2002. So this boom is very similar to the Growth Boom from 1902 to 1929. The Maturity Booms, such as that in 1942–1968, are more orderly and less dramatic in peaks and crashes.

2. The size of the baby-boom generation here and around the world has further exaggerated both the innovation trends that led to the first real Information Revolution since the printing press and the strength of this boom. This has further exaggerated everything from price-to-earning (P/E) ratios on stocks to debt levels to the bubbles in this bubble-prone Growth Boom.

3. For the first time in history investing in stocks has become a mainstream trend with the advent of discount brokerage and 401(k) plans. Figure 2.19 shows an S-curve in acceleration of equity investing by U.S. households that has mushroomed since 1980. This means many new inexperienced investors entering the markets would clearly add to the formation of bubbles and public manias in the stock market. And many more new households will enter the equity markets in the coming decade to add to the next and perhaps greatest bubble in U.S. and modern history. Note that the worst bubbles in history occurred back in the 1600s and 1700s, when investing was a new phenomenon and most investors were hence inexperienced.

4. As we showed in Figure 2.17, we appear to be heading into the final wave of a much larger bull market that started around 1780. Each wave of the stock

market expansion has gotten more exponential and it is hard to believe that this final wave won't be the greatest. Bubbles are almost impossible to prevent. They start with younger, inexperienced investors who aren't knowledgeable about appropriate ways to value stocks, like the e-traders in the late 1990s. But the strong returns in these accelerating sectors force institutional and mutual fund managers, indeed all investors, to participate or fall far behind in performance. The bubbles finally end when everyone is in and there is no one else to keep buying.

The most important point here should be obvious. Our fundamental indicators clearly forecast that all of the same trends that occurred in the 1990s will continue to advance similarly into 2008 or 2009. The baby-boom Spending Wave still points strongly up into 2009. The key technology S-curves still point up as strongly into 2008. New investors will continue to move into the equity markets over the next two decades. And inflation will remain low, as we will cover in Chapter 6. Hence, all five of the basic conditions covered earlier in this chapter will be in full force in this decade, while technical charts still suggest a strong and final fifth wave ahead. But the best single indicator may simply be that not one credible expert or forecaster expects a great bull market in the years to come.

We say the odds heavily favor another great and perhaps more extreme bubble ahead. Get ready for the most unexpected bull market in history—and a crash to follow that will make the "tech wreck" of 2000–2002 pale in comparison.

FIGURE 2.19   The S-Curve of Stock Investing by the Public, 1900–2009

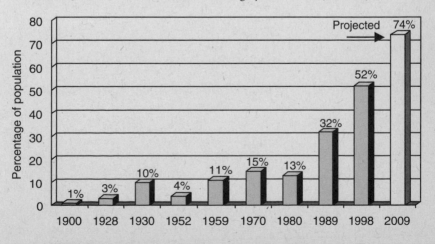

Source: Theodore Caplow, Louis Hicks, and Ben J. Wattenberg, *The First Measured Century.*

The good thing about a bubble boom is that the potential returns are greater. But as we have clearly experienced in 1987 and 2000–2002, the downside risks can be extremely painful. How can you reduce the risks of investing in this more volatile bubble boom and the even greater crash that is sure to follow? In Chapter 3 we are going to look at some very powerful recurring cycles in the stock market that would also suggest reasonable to strong gains in the years ahead without any input from our demographic and technology models. These cycles could also illustrate when you would experience substantial gains and setbacks in the coming years of both extreme boom and bust to help mitigate your risks. We are going to give the most comprehensive forecast ever made for the economy and markets and reveal the simplest long-term model for equity investing ever conceived, one which requires only a few changes every decade.

Chapter 3

TAKING ADVANTAGE OF STRONG RECURRING CYCLES TO REDUCE RISK IN VOLATILE MARKETS

The Most Comprehensive Forecast and Simplest Investing Model Ever

IT IS NOW CLEAR that despite the unprecedented returns in this bull market since late 1982, the volatility and risks are growing. This naturally follows the simple maxim we stress that you don't get higher returns without higher risks. But there are systematic and scientific methods for reducing risk, including diversification of investments, as we will show in Chapter 7. But in this chapter we will look at cycles that can help you reduce your risk in booms and busts, but only if you follow them systematically and take your human emotions out of the equation. Why? They don't work in every year or cycle to the same degree, but they do work over time. In our past books and newsletters we have always stressed a number of recurring cycles with a fundamental base in politics, taxes, and human psychology that repeat themselves in patterns consistent enough over long periods of time and upon which we can base effective investing strategies.

If you look back, you will see that there are clear seasonal cycles in investment markets similar to the seasons in our weather every year as well as long-term cycles. These cycles range from annual to eighty years for practical application, and ultimately over thousands of years. We will look at these cycles beginning with the shorter-term ones and building up to the longer-term patterns. These cycles are the best single means of allowing you to be in equities for most of the best times and out in the worst without having to listen to the day-by-day and month-by-month varied opinions of

Wall Street analysts on "where the markets are headed next." These experts largely have a very poor track record of predicting major changes in market psychology and movements. Even in longer-term bear markets these cycles can allow you to be invested in equities in the best times of opportunities.

Figure 3.1 illustrates a simple analysis of an annual stock cycle by Yale Hirsch *(Stock Trader's Almanac)*, which goes back to 1950 and shows that all of the net gains in the stock market each year tend to be made on average in the six months between November and April. Similarly, an investor would have no gains over time from buying each year only between May and October, when more corrections occur. Why is there a good annual season for stocks? There is tax selling into September–October for reducing tax exposure (selling losers to offset the gains of your winners), which exerts downward pressure on stock prices, and then there is buying back again after that as year-end bonuses, dividends, and tax refunds through April add to investor buying power.

FIGURE 3.1 The Annual Stocks Cycle, 1950–2000

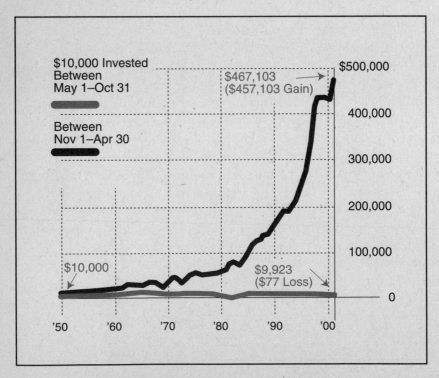

Source: Barron's, September 16, 2002, p. 19; The Hirsch Organization.

This doesn't happen in each year, but there is a clear recurring bias. There have been a number of years where stocks were up from May to October, such as in 1999. There were twenty-one losing periods since 1950 from May to October, but only twelve for November to April. So again, this cycle won't reward you in every year, but over time it is compelling. Figure 3.1 shows that an investor starting with $10,000 in 1950 would have seen it grow to $467,100 by April 2002 if it was invested only between November and April, but would have had a slight loss to $9,923 if it were invested only from May through October each year. This annual seasonal cycle would have suggested that investors should have been moving strongly back into stocks by November 1, 2002, and would also suggest that you be strongly invested by November 1, 2004, if you are still cautious and waiting to get back into stocks again.

Many people think that October is normally the worst month of the year for stocks due to high-profile crashes like those in 1987 and 1929. The market bottoms of 1990 and 1998 also occurred in October. But the truth is that if we go back even further and average the returns in each month since 1896 in Figure 3.2, September is the worst month. September is clearly when

FIGURE 3.2 Good and Bad Months Annually Since 1896

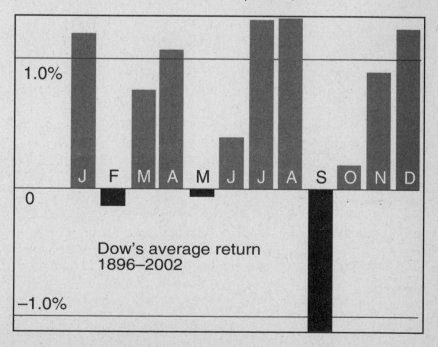

Source: Fortune, September 30, 2002, p.186.

the tax-selling season really hits as professional managers return from summer vacations. Many down years in October have simply been follow-through declines to the downturns that started in September or earlier and have been offset by sharp rises out of such bottoms in October. The other correction months tend to be February (following strong January gains from buying back after tax selling) and May (the beginning of the bad season and vacations in June).

Figure 3.2 shows that on average there is a strong string of good months between November and April, with February being the only exception. That's another reason it tends to be the good season. We also tend to get summer rallies in July and August despite the tendency for the markets to be down more often from May through October following the corrections in May and June. We don't recommend using this for longer-term investors as a trading cycle every year since this cycle is not as consistent as others we will present and the tax (paying every year versus deferring taxes and at ordinary income rates) and transaction costs typically outweigh the benefits. But this cycle is helpful at telling you when to get out and back in when cycles such as the four-year Presidential Cycle hit.

There is a four-year Presidential Cycle that we have also covered in our books and past newsletters that is surprisingly consistent over time. Figure 3.3 shows research by Ned Davis (another of our favorite long-term analysts; see www.ndr.com) that has averaged out performance of the Dow in each year of the Presidential Cycle back to 1900. However, this cycle has been more consistent since World War II. The market tends to be down from late in the first year in office (or in recent decades early to midway in the second year) into late in the second year or midterm elections. In late 2002 we were right at the point where this cycle tends to bottom, another reason we gave such a strong buy signal. Then there is a strong rally from late in the second year until late in the third year. On average, the Dow and S&P 500 are up just over 50% in such a rally.

This cycle hence clearly suggested the strong rally from late 2002 into late 2003 with gains of almost 40%. On average, there is a mild consolidation from late in the third year or early in the fourth year into around the middle of the fourth year. Then we typically see another very strong wave up into the election and the first year of the next term with all of the stimulative fiscal and monetary policies to help ensure re-election and the positive feelings that come with a new president or term. This cycle would suggest that it is highly likely that we will see a strong advance from mid- to late 2004 into early to mid-2006 to follow the initial 2003 rebound. More

FIGURE 3.3 The Four-Year Presidential Cycle

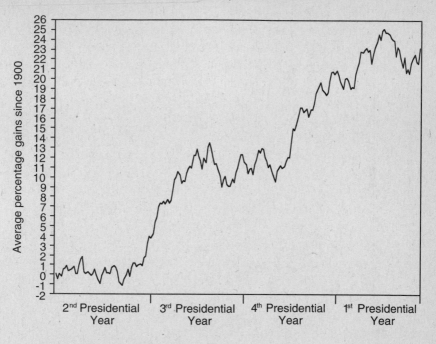

Source: Ned Davis Research, www.ndr.com.

specifically, this cycle would suggest being strongly invested in stocks by late June 2004, or early October 2004 at the very latest.

But every eight years (every other four-year cycle) the pullbacks tend to be much more pronounced. The typical correction in the Dow or S&P 500 have been more like 10% in the four-year cycles but 20% in the eight-year cycles. As we can see in Figure 3.4, the more extreme eight-year cycles include 1974, 1982, 1990, and 1998. In *The Roaring 2000s* (page 292) we used this cycle to predict, several months in advance, that the Dow would correct to 7200 to 7600 by late 1998. The last four-year cycle hit in late 2002. The next major eight-year down cycle is due in mid- to late 2006. This is why we have been forecasting that the rebound from the late 2002 lows in stocks would see a strong recovery and that the next wave should not see any major setbacks on this cycle until mid- to late 2006. That is good news. We should see less volatility in stocks from late 2002 into early to mid-2006, much as we saw from late 1994 into mid-1998—just as investors have such a heightened fear of risk in the years ahead.

This is the most consistent cycle we have observed since World War II.

FIGURE 3.4 Four- and Eight-Year Cycle Corrections
Dow Adjusted for Inflation, 1958–2002

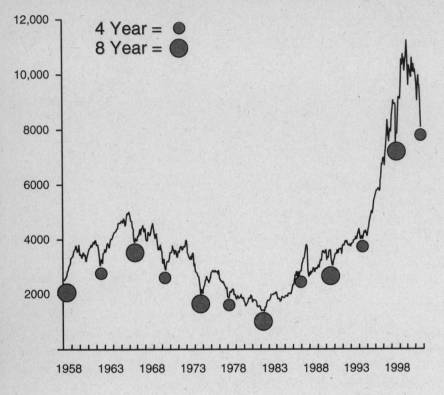

This cycle alone is consistent enough to increase your returns and lower your risks if you follow it systematically over time. Figure 3.5 shows how much better you would have done by simply being out of stocks (S&P 500) and into T-bills in the weak annual season, May through September, of every second year in the Presidential Cycle. Although many of the four-year cycle corrections tend to continue into October, there is also a tendency to have strong initial rallies in that month. Hence, it is better to get out at the end of September than the end of October for testing our model. But if you have the option to time it more precisely, it would probably be best to reinvest after the first week or two in October.

The cumulative returns adjusted for inflation and dividends on $1 invested back from 1952 through 2002, or fifty-one years, would have been $89.29 versus $41.60 on the S&P 500, 2.15 times the wealth. The average annual compound returns vs. the S&P 500 would have been 9.02% versus 7.43%, or 21.4% higher. Your risk level, using standard deviation as a measure of volatility, would have been 13.15 versus 14.70, or 10.5% lower (lower

FIGURE 3.5 Greater Returns from Following the Four-Year Presidential Cycle, 1952–2004

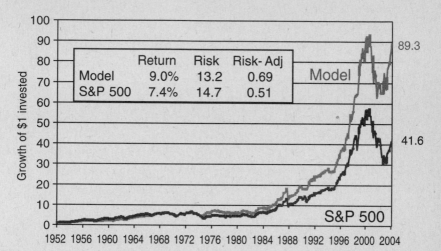

is better when it comes to risk). To get the overall measure of performance, we divide the average return by the average risk to get a risk-adjusted performance index. Here the risk-adjusted performance was .69 versus .51 on the S&P 500, or 35.3% higher, just by following one simple investing rule: getting out from May through September, just five months every four years!

There is another recurring cycle we have noticed in stocks over the last century, the ten-year cycle. As we have already noted, we tend to see economic slowdowns and stock corrections in the early years of every decade to consolidate the overexpansion and overvaluations of the previous decade, especially in the strongest growth sectors. We call it the Decade Hangover Cycle. We already showed how the great auto boom into 1919 ended in a shakeout and correction into 1920 and 1921. The 1930s saw falling markets and the economy into 1930–1932. There was an ultimate bottom after a shakeout and crash in the early 1940s between 1940 and 1942. The 1950s saw the least of this cycle with only a very minor correction in 1950, but there had been a four-year sideways correction in stocks following the winddown from World War II that may have preempted that cycle. Then again, the 1960s saw twin corrections in 1960 and 1962. The 1970s then started off with a sharp correction and recession in 1970.

And then as more of us remember, the early 1980s saw twin stock crashes and recessions in 1980 and 1982. The next decade started with a stock crash and recession in late 1990 into mid-1991. Finally, we have just witnessed a major stock crash and slowdown starting in 2000 that extended into late 2002. Do you get the swing of things here? Almost every decade starts out with a downturn and stock crash and ends up with a strong economy and overvalued stock market that follows that boom into the end of the decade. When the economy booms, and favors certain leading sectors, we overexpand and overinvest. It clearly seems that we have to correct those imbalances in the first year or early years of the next decade before we move on to the next growth stage.

We can see in Figure 3.6 that the first year of every decade has seen at least a minor stock correction and this cycle is more likely to hit earlier in the year, as it did in 1960, 1970, and 1980. The 1970 cycle was stronger than most as the four-year cycle hit along with the beginnings of the downturn of the Bob Hope Generation Spending Wave. The 1990 correction was stronger than average and would have also been signaled by the four/eight-year cycle. But 1960, 1980, and 2000 were not explained by the four-year cycle, only the ten-year cycle.

There is a decennial, or decade-long, pattern in stocks that is actually

FIGURE 3.6 Ten-Year Cycle Corrections (Dow Adjusted for Inflation), 1960–2002

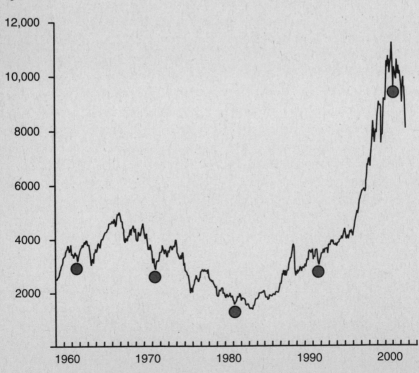

the most powerful for creating effective investment strategies. In Figure 3.7, Ned Davis has gone back to 1900 and averaged out the stock market's gains in each year of every decade, as he did for the four-year Presidential Cycle. The results are very insightful. The summary point here is that basically all of the gains in the stock market come on average in the second half of every decade from the "5" through the "9" years (for example, 1995 to 1999). This is very similar to the fact that all of the gains over time come in November–April, or just half of the annual cycle. This occurs precisely because the advances and economic booms in most decades tend to be followed by consolidations of such gains in the early years of each new decade. And that is what this cycle clearly shows over time. The markets tend to be down from late in the "9" (in the first half of the century) or early in the "0" year (for the second half of the century) into the middle of the "2" year, then rebound modestly into the "3" and "4" years, typically just offsetting the downturns in the "0"–"2" years. Then all of the net gains are made between the "5" and "9" years when the markets tend to accelerate strongly.

Now, just as in the annual and four-year cycles discussed above, every

FIGURE 3.7 The Dow Jones Industrial Average: Decade Pattern
Weekly Data 1/6/1900–12/31/1999

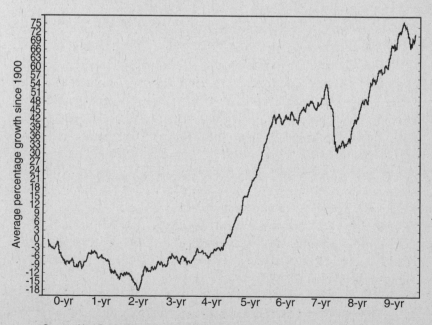

Source: Ned Davis Research, www.ndr.com.

decade obviously doesn't work out exactly in this manner. And there are cycles, like the four/eight-year cycle above, that have their differing impacts in each decade. But the long-term correlation with this cycle in most decades is uncanny. The broader deviations come more from the strength of the fundamental trends in each decade. The 1990s was a very strong decade for trends, from both the Baby Boom Spending Wave and the S-curve acceleration in information technologies. Hence, it had less downward bias in the "0" to "2" years. But even in that decade the markets were down in the "0" year and the gains in the market were more modest through the "4" year in 1994. Then the markets exploded from 1995 through early 2000 with much greater strength than average. Clearly, most of the gains in the 1990s market occurred between 1995 and 1999, the "5" to "9" years.

Conversely, the worst decade for fundamentals in the last century was the 1930s. In that decade the market was down the strongest in the last century during the "0" to "2" years, from 1930 to 1932. Then it advanced strongly again into early 1937 for five years and still held most of those gains until the next crash in 1940–1942, the bad "0" to "2" years of the next decade. Even in the bearish decade of the 1970s, you would have lost a lot between 1970 and 1974 and then seen respectable gains from 1975 to 1979, the "5" to "9" years.

If you knew nothing else, the best times to buy stocks would be midway in the "2" year (the end of June) every decade and you would expect the greatest acceleration of gains between the "5" and "9" years. Then you would sell at the end of the "9" year, and buy back again midway in the "2" year again. There is also a strong tendency for sharp corrections to occur late in the "7" year, as occurred in 1987, 1977, 1947, 1937, 1917, and 1907. That is six out of ten decades! Hence, it would pay over time to be out of the markets from August through October in the "7" years. Figure 3.8 shows how much higher your returns would have been since 1900 versus being fully invested in the S&P 500, by being out from the beginning of the "0" year and reinvesting on June 30 of the "2" year and then being out from August through October of the "7" year, and then being back in until the end of the "9" year. Note that the records that were available back that far weren't adjusted for inflation and dividends weren't added in. So these numbers are a bit different from the ones in the four-year cycle model we tested in Figure 3.5. Just ahead we will look at a similar comparison versus the four-year cycle from 1952 through 2002.

The value of $1 invested would have grown to $6,066.86 versus $148.41, or 44.5 times the wealth over the last 102 years! Note, that although this cycle is more powerful than the four-year Presidential Cycle, the cumulative

FIGURE 3.8   Greater Returns from Following the Decennial Cycle Since 1900

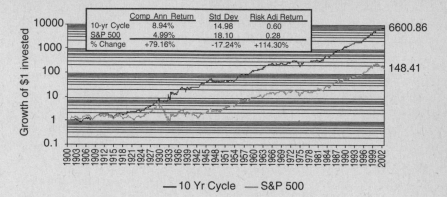

— 10 Yr Cycle   — S&P 500

returns are exaggerated by the compounding over a much longer time period back to 1900. The average annual compound returns would have been 9.88% versus 4.99% on the S&P 500, 79.2% higher! But on top of that your risk level (using standard deviation) would have been 14.98 versus 18.10, 17.2% lower. The risk-adjusted performance would have been .60 versus .28, or 114.3% higher. That is astounding for one simple switching strategy. This cycle is clearly the most powerful if followed systematically over time. But there is another reason the outperformance is greater than from the four-year cycle. The most volatile part of the last eighty-year New Economy Cycle and technology revolution came in the first half of the cycle from 1902 through 1942. Avoiding the more extreme crashes of the early 1920s, early 1930s, and early 1940s would have given an investor greater leverage than in any other time period, and we are in such an era of bubble booms and busts again from 1982 to 2022.

Hence, following this model would have clearly produced much greater returns long term. But you would have also avoided most of the worst stock corrections, including in 1907, 1920–1921, 1930–1932, 1937, 1940–1942, 1960–1962, 1980–1982, 1987, and 2000–2002. Yet you wouldn't have avoided the crash of 1973–1974. The four-year cycle would have saved you part of that downturn. The 1970s is the only decade out of the last ten where you would have been about flat by buying late in the "2" year and holding for the rest of the decade. But remember that even in the 1970s bear market, respectable gains were made from 1975 through 1979–the strong "5" to "9" years. In that decade due to the strong downward bias in demographics and the four/eight-year cycle into 1974, the market was down strongly in the "3" and "4" years.

To get a better feel for this cycle, let's look back at the 1980s. The decade started with two corrections and recessions in 1980 and 1982, recovered strongly into 1983, pulled back briefly in 1984 and then took off from 1985 through 1989 with a brief shock in 1987. That decade was almost a perfect reflection of the decennial cycle. The 1960s saw two corrections in 1960 and 1962 (stronger on the four-year cycle in 1962) and then steady gains through 1968 and only in 1970 was there a major downturn. The 1950s saw steadier gains throughout the decade with minor corrections in 1950, 1954, and 1958 (all on the four-year cycle), as the trends were almost all positive in that decade. The 1950s was the only other decade where you would have been better off not to follow the decennial cycle and just stay in except in the four-year cycles. The 1940s saw strong corrections in 1940–1942 and then gains into 1946 and then was mildly down for most of the rest of the decade. And of course, the Roaring Twenties started out with two very strong down years in 1920 and 1921 and ended up with very strong gains for the rest of the decade that accelerated between 1925 and 1929 on very strong demographic and technology fundamentals.

Over the last century every "5" year has been up. That has typically been the strongest year on average. The next best year has been the "8" year, with eight out of ten up. The "7" and "9" years tend to see sharp rallies and then a falloff late in the year for good positive net gains. The "3," "4," and "6" years also tend to be good years. The "0" year is clearly the worst, followed by the "1" year, with the "2" year down early with a rally late in the year for a slight net loss on average.

Now if we test this Decennial Cycle Model back to 1952 in Figure 3.9 using inflation-adjusted returns and adding in dividends, we can see that this cycle is still more powerful than the 4-year cycle. The cumulative returns on $1 would have been $107.71, 2.6 times the S&P 500 at $41.60 and 21% better than the four-year Presidential Cycle model. The returns would have been 9.42% vs. 7.43% on the S&P 500, 26.8% higher. The risk was 11.86, 19.3% less than the S&P 500 at 14.70. The risk-adjusted return was .79 versus .51, 54.9% higher.

There is another set of longer-term cycles that is worth noting. We have explained how new generations emerge about every forty years. Well, the correlation may be more exact when it comes to the stock market. We have noted major bottoms every forty years in Figure 3.10. The last forty-year lows were in 1982 and 1942. These marked the beginnings of new generation-driven bull markets that typically last 26 to 27 years. Major tops have also come close to forty years apart, in 1929 and 1968 (stocks adjusted for

FIGURE 3.9 Greater Returns from Following the Decennial Cycle Since 1952

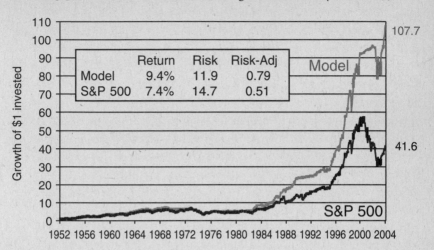

	Return	Risk	Risk-Adj
Model	9.4%	11.9	0.79
S&P 500	7.4%	14.7	0.51

inflation). We are projecting the next top similarly around mid-2010 and the next major bear market bottom in late 2022, which would also correspond with the four/eight-year cycle. Within that forty-year cycle is a twenty-year cycle that hit in early 1922, late 1962, and late 2002. The next twenty-year cycle would correspond to the forty-year cycle low in late 2022. The forty-year cycles then combine every eighty years to mark the emergence of New Economy Cycles. The bottoms would have hit in 1902 and

FIGURE 3.10 Twenty-, Forty-, and Eighty-Year Cycles: The Dow Jones Industrial Average, 1900–2025*

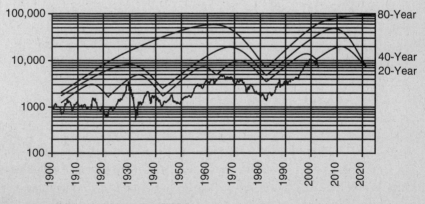

*Adjusted for inflation using 1998 dollars.

1982. The next bottom would hit around 2062, when this technology and economic revolution will have likely run its course.

The very good news is that just when most investors perceived very high risks, following the crash of 2000–2002, there is only one strong four/eight-year cycle pointing down in the coming decade—in mid- to late 2006. There could perhaps be a short, sharp correction in late 2007 on the Decennial Cycle. In the last two decades of intensive research we have never seen such an alignment of fundamental cyclical and technical indicators pointing strongly up for the decade ahead. We said it in late 1992 and we've been saying it since late 2002: Get ready for the next great boom—that is, the next great bubble ahead! If you missed the first great buying opportunity between late July and early October 2002, there should be another great entry point between September and December of 2004.

A COMPREHENSIVE FORECAST FOR THE GREAT BOOM AND THE GREAT BUST AHEAD

Here's the best picture of how we see the coming two very dynamic decades playing out by combining our demographic, technology, and cyclical indicators covered thus far and utilizing other indicators, such as our Inflation Indicator, which we will present in Chapter 6.

The Initial Recovery: 2003 to 2004

In the October 2002 issue of *The H. S. Dent Forecast* we gave our strongest buy signal ever for stocks and foresaw the strong initial rebound for the economy and stocks into 2003. The first wave up in this final fifth-wave finale to the boom that began in 1982 (and longer term in the broader boom that began back in the 1780s) peaked in January 2004. The Dow traded sideways between 4,700 and 10,900 into mid-2005. The third wave up is likely to begin by August of 2004, just before this book will be published. The final great buy opportunity at 10,000 occurred in late April of 2005. On our cycles the best time to buy would likely be by mid-October of 2005. We also forecast that inflation rates would remain low, and by mid- to late 2005 ten-year Treasury bond yields would start to fall from near 5% back down to below 4%. By late 2005, we think, the markets are likely to start accelerating again with more leadership from technology stocks. However, the economy is not likely to show strong growth again until early 2006 onwards.

The Acceleration Phase: 2005 to Mid-2006

We expect a stronger rally in the stock market by mid-2005 and stronger economic growth by early 2006 due to a strong resurgence in business capital spending. The Dow will hit new highs in the first half of 2006, ending "The bubble has burst and the bull market is over" theories. Mid-2005 to early 2006 will likely see the lowest inflation rates yet and be the best time between 2005 and 2010 to refinance your home or business real estate or to borrow long term for your business. Technology companies will be leading in growth and earnings, and their stocks will be clearly outperforming again from 2005 on, much as they did from 1995 to 1999. Then we could see some initial signs of mildly rising inflation in 2006 and the Fed will likely start to tighten more significantly than it did beginning in 2004. Stocks will likely continue strongly up at first, ignoring this change in short-term trends. Why? Earnings will still be soaring due to rising productivity trends. But stocks are likely to complete their third wave up somewhere between July and August 2006. We could see the Nasdaq at 3,000 by then.

Then we will see the first major setback in the markets on the four/eight-year cycle, likely to be over by October 2006. We would expect a 10% to 20% correction in the Dow and stronger for leading sectors like the Nasdaq and financial services. The threat of political factors and terrorist events are very likely to rise in 2006 and the president's ratings are likely to fall. We will very likely be issuing sell signals in stocks and/or recommending more defensive portfolio allocations between July and August, and likely strong buy signals again around mid-October. The economy may slow a bit in the latter part of 2006, but we shouldn't get even close to a recession.

The Next Great Bubble: 2007 to 2009–2010

We should see the fifth wave of this final wave since late 2002, the next real bubble phase, a very strong tech-led rally from late 2006 into late 2009 that could extend into mid- to late 2010. We should see a sharp rally in stocks in 2007 in the best year of the four-year Presidential Cycle. Inflation could start to rise mildly again. There could be a brief and even sharp setback in late 2007, especially if the Federal Reserve adopts a tightening bias as an attempt to stop the next bubble in stocks. But we think that cycle is less likely to kick in significantly after a substantial correction in late 2006. If we do see such a correction, that would represent another strong buy signal for stocks. Technology stocks will start to lead even more strongly from 2007 into 2008 as the boom and bubble rages on, despite a likely continued inching up in inflation rates and Fed tightening. The Republican party elected in November 2004 will likely win the White House again in November 2008, despite problems in the Bush administration in 2005.

Here's where the scenario gets more tricky and variable. The demographic trends in baby-boom spending are likely to hold up into 2010. But the technology S-Curve Cycles are likely to peak and start slowing between mid-2009 and late 2009. The Decennial Cycle generally points up into late 2009, and the ten-year and four-year minor cycles will hit in 2010. It is likely that the technology markets will start to peak first, around late 2009, and cause some volatility on the downside at first. Tech markets are likely to slow before broader spending and investors will start to remember the last bubble and get more cautious on tech and growth stocks first. But they will not sell out of stocks in such a strong market. They are likely to gravitate toward broader Dow-like stocks. Hence, the broader markets are likely to peak between mid-2010 and late 2010, or September 2010 at the very latest. Early September 2010 would be our best guess. The record federal budget deficits of 2004 will near disappear by 2010. Let's briefly review the indicators we will be watching to gauge approximately when the next bubble will peak.

INDICATORS FOR SPOTTING THE
TOP OF THE GREAT BUBBLE AHEAD

We will first be monitoring our Dow and Nasdaq channels. If we hit the top of those channels for the first time since early 2000, then that would be the first sign of a correction. If the Nasdaq punches above our first channel that points to around 13,000 (Figure 2.14) by late 2009, while the Dow does not hit or push through the top of its channel (Figures 2.15 and 2.16), that could be a sign that the Nasdaq is heading into an even greater bubble than in the late 1990s and could approach close to the 20,000 mark (Figure 2.18). In that case we would give the market more leeway and not get defensive until the Dow also hit the top of its channel. If the Nasdaq does not hit the top of its most bullish channel pointing toward 20,000 and the Dow starts to punch over its channel, then that would be a sign that we are nearing the final stages of the bubble. We would start getting cautious and then certainly issue a sell signal if the Nasdaq hit 20,000, the top of its more bullish channel in Figure 2.18—although a target that high is unlikely.

Figure 3.11 summarizes the most likely scenario for the Dow by super-

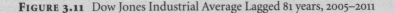

FIGURE 3.11 Dow Jones Industrial Average Lagged 81 years, 2005–2011

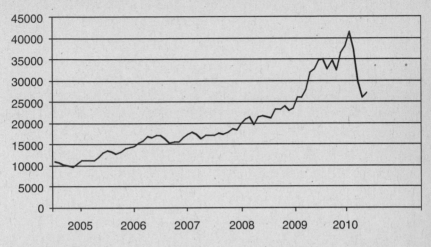

Source: Yahoo Finance

imposing the performance of the Dow in the Roaring Twenties on an 81-year lag starting in early 2005. This chart would suggest a new high in the Dow of 12,000 by early 2006. The Dow could hit 14,000 to 15,000 before the four-year cycle correction back to as low as 12,000 into late 2006. The Dow is likely to first hit 20,000 by late 2008, then zoom to 30,000 to 32,000 by late 2009, and finally reach 38,000 to 40,000 by mid- to late 2010.

There are key divergences we would also look for as we approach a top. In the 1929 bubble top, small caps peaked in October 1928, almost a year before the large caps did, and headed down into 1929 (Figure 3.12). In fact, small-cap growth stocks peaked in April 1928, six months before the overall peak in small caps (Figure 3.13). Since the race for leadership in this Growth Boom stage favored larger-cap stocks, we saw an environment where investors in the last year of the bubble gave up diversification and focused increasingly on the hottest sector of large-cap growth. Similarly, in the early 2000 bubble, the Dow peaked in January 2000 and then started to decline, while the technology stocks continued to soar into March. Investors again shunned all stocks except for the hottest technology large caps. We would look for both of these types of divergences again, with a small-cap divergence likely giving us a much longer lead time.

The most significant divergence came as technology stocks peaked ahead of the broader markets, the opposite of what occurred in the recent

FIGURE 3.12 Small-Cap Versus Large-Cap Stocks, 1926–1932

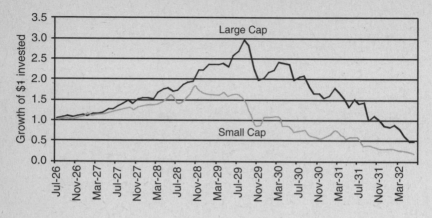

FIGURE 3.13 Small-Cap Growth Versus Small-Cap Value, 1926–1932

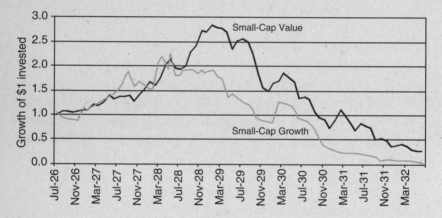

bubble top. The Automotive Index, along with GM, peaked in March 1929, six months ahead of the Dow in September 1929, and declined rather sharply while the Dow and the broader large-cap market continued to climb (Figure 3.14). There are two factors that likely caused this divergence. First, investors could have started remembering the previous auto and tech bubble into 1919 and started getting more cautious on that sector ahead of time, switching more to nontech large-cap stocks. Second, the S-curve for automobile penetration had hit its 90% mark by late 1928, and that would mean a slowing in growth despite a still-booming economy from demographic trends.

Hence, it is quite possible, and in fact likely, that the Nasdaq or some

FIGURE 3.14 The Dow Jones Industrial Average Versus Automotive Stocks, 1925–1932

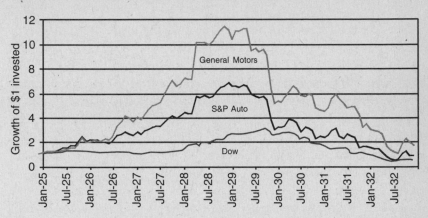

key sectors of technology will peak several months before the Dow around late 2009. That would be a very important divergence. For example, we could see the Nasdaq peak around late 2009 and see the Dow continue to advance well into 2010. We will obviously be looking at the next bubble as it develops and incorporate technical indicators to measure excessive bullishness and valuations in our newsletter. Missing the crash that follows this coming bubble may be the most important thing you can do for your net worth in the coming decade. The first stage of the next crash is likely to be much steeper than the crash of 2000–2002. But you also don't want to get out too early as the greatest gains are typically made in the last six to twelve months of the bubble. Now we will shift back to how the great downturn is likely to unfold between 2010 and 2022.

The First Great Deflationary Crash: Late 2010 into Early 2013 or 2014

Somewhere between mid- to late 2010 we expect the next great bubble to burst and for us to see another crash that will look much like the 2000–2002 crash, only worse and steeper at first. The difference is that this will usher in a deeper and longer-term bear market and depression, similar to the last shakeout stage on the eighty-year cycle that hit in the 1930s and the bear market in Japan in the 1990s and early 2000s. Whether the tech stocks peak first around mid- to late 2009 or whether the broader markets peak in early to mid-2010, we expect the first major shock to the markets to hit by mid- to late 2010. This is when the ten-year cycle will hit (along with the downward phase of the Decennial Cycle from late 2009 into mid-2012), and it will be followed by the four-year cycle from May to October 2010 and then followed by the stronger four/eight-year cycle from May to October 2014.

Hence, we can expect the first sharp decline in the stock market to begin, especially between May and September 2010. Technology spending should start to slow by sometime in late 2009 and then fall off somewhat into 2010. General consumer spending should start to slow sometime in 2010 and drop off more sharply into 2011. We should fall into an official recession by early to mid-2011, but this recession will last much longer and go much, much deeper. The biggest surprise will be that we are likely to see the first signs of deflation, or an actual fall in consumer prices between 2011 and 2013. Between 2011 and 2014, we will see housing prices start to decline substantially, especially in high-end urban, suburban, and resort areas. But the worst news is likely to come from escalating terrorist activities, especially in major cities in the United States, just when we may feel we have largely won the war on terrorism.

While the stock market and especially tech stocks are crashing, high-quality corporate and government bonds will be appreciating in a classic "flight to quality" due to the economic slowdown. By late 2010 we should see the first decent rebound in the stock market, but the economy and the stock market will very likely continue to worsen dramatically into 2011 to 2013 despite strong stimulus by the Fed and Congress. The president at that time will not be reelected in late 2012 and an FDR-type president will win a landslide victory. Sometime in 2011 the slide in the economy will cause even high-quality bonds to get lower credit ratings, and even bonds will fall temporarily in value with rising yields, but the worst falls in value will come in the riskier, higher-yield bonds. From early to mid-2011 into mid- to late 2012, investors are likely to do better in short-term T-bills and money market accounts than in bonds.

We should see the bottom of this first crash by late 2012 to early 2013. But after another possible bear market rally into 2013, we are likely to see the markets down again on the four/eight-year cycle back near the 2012 lows or we could see a slight new low by late 2014. The Dow could drop as low as 7,000 to 7,400. The economy is likely to continue to weaken into at least early 2015 with unemployment levels reaching at least 15% between early 2013 and early 2015 while more deflationary forces are likely to set in. But there will be very strong reductions in interest rates by the Fed and strong fiscal stimulus by the new president that will lead to a modest rebound by sometime in 2015 and lessening deflationary pressures. Government deficits will hit unprecedented levels relative to GDP between 2013 and 2015 from dramatically falling tax revenues and rising social costs. Then a more sustainable bear market rally is likely to begin by late 2014.

The Bubble Bear Market Rally: 2015 to 2019

The years 2015 to 2019 will be a very confusing, but more positive time with hopes for a sustainable recovery amid strong moves by the government to stimulate the economy. It worked in the early 2000s, but it won't work as well in this downward demographic environment—any more than it did in Japan in the 1990s. But there should be some strong signs of economic recovery and a bubble bear market valley. Enough to likely keep the new president in power in the 2016 elections. After all, we are in a huge economic crisis and we need consistent leadership. The market will likely rally strongly after falling to such low levels. We should see the strongest bear market rallies in 2015 and 2017–2018 and then a setback on the four-year cycle into late 2018. By sometime in 2017 the economy will pick up more momentum from the short-term rising trends in demographics. But by late 2019 or early 2020, those demographic trends will wane again and the Decennial Cycle will turn downward. There will continue to be at least mild deflationary trends despite government stimulus from 2015 into 2019, which will be good for high-quality long-term bonds. The marked rise in terrorist, political, and social unrest in urban areas will cause more people to decide to move to higher-quality resort and exurban living areas. These areas could start to appreciate again as home values continue to drop or remain weak in most urban/suburban areas.

The Second Great Crash: 2020 to 2022

Between late 2019 and late 2022, we should see a final crash in the stock markets that should wipe out most or all of the gains of the 2015–2019 period, and we are likely to see a double bottom or new lows of around 5,000 to 7,400 on the Dow and around 1,100 on the Nasdaq. Deflationary forces should be at their strongest and the economy should continue to decline despite stimulative measures by the government as the Spending Wave will continue down again along with the family-formation cycle of the new echo boomers. This will represent a time period when the greatest threats from the Middle East in large-scale terrorism and the Far East militarily (North Korea and/or China) could come to the United States and Europe. The seeds of World War III, if it is to occur, are most likely to emerge here, if not sooner! Unemployment will resurge in this period, perhaps to as high or higher levels than in 2013 to 2015 unless an actual large-scale war results to offset them.

The Next Long-Term Bull Market Begins: 2023 On

The economy is likely to end its slide by sometime in 2023, or 2024 at the latest, along with an end to the deflationary forces. The stock market is likely to bottom and turn up ahead of the economy by late 2022 and perhaps as early as late 2020. International warfare and the first long-term rise in the Spending Wave of the echo boom should cause upward trends again. Interest rates as well as bond yields will begin to rise, signaling an end to the long boom in bonds and the beginning of the next bull market in stocks. That bull market should last into 2040 or longer, but not be nearly as strong in the United States as the great bull market from 1982 into 2010. The demographic and technology trends will simply not be as strong and even growth in strong areas like China will start to wane by then. In fact, it is likely that such a bull market in the United States will only rally back toward the highs of 2010 and not exceed them for the rest of most of our lifetimes.

THE SIMPLEST STRATEGY FOR LONG-TERM INVESTING IN VOLATILE TIMES

If we are right then our predictions for the great bust and rising terrorist and war threats should scare the hell out of you! The crash of 2000–2002 was a wake-up call for all of us to the volatile nature of this boom and these times altogether, especially given the new terrorist threat. The first wake-up call was in 1987, but after more than a decade of strong markets with only minor corrections most financial advisers and long-term investors felt very comfortable with a simple "buy-and-hold" strategy. "Buying on dips" became an increasingly popular strategy in the 1990s. But 2000–2002 was much more than a dip, it was comparable to the 1973–1974 crash that occured in a longer-term bear market and lasted longer than most buy-and-hold investors could bear.

Although we expect much less volatility for the next five years, we do expect even more volatility after 2009. But most important, we're getting clearer on the simple fact that for the first half of the eighty-year cycle there is much greater volatility both in the booms and in the busts. Hence, what we have now developed is a very simple model that allows you to largely be invested (to the degree appropriate for your risk tolerance and income

needs) in stocks, but to be able to protect your portfolio from the times
when downside volatility is most likely to occur.

There are three simple recurring cycles in the stock market that can be
documented and systematically built into your investment strategy to give
you the best chances of avoiding these extreme risks while still capturing
the lion's share of the extraordinary gains ahead. The first we covered in
Chapter 1. The stock market does best and is generally up when increasing
numbers of people are moving into their peak spending years, as in
1983–2009. It does worse about every forty years and generally heads down
for longer periods when fewer people are moving into their peak spending
years, such as in 1969–1982 or 1930–1942.

We can look back at the Spending Wave chart and its high correlation
to long-term stock prices adjusted for inflation in Figure 3.15. We have
always recommended being invested strongly in large-cap stocks when
the Spending Wave is pointing up and getting more into bonds, foreign
markets, or defensive sectors when the Spending Wave is pointing down.
Remember, we are forecasting as high as 40,000 on the Dow by late 2009 or
early 2010. It will be pointing down strongly from late 2009–2010 to 2020/
2022, and our best forecast is that the Dow will return to at least its late-.

FIGURE 3.15 The Spending Wave: Births Lagged for Peak in Family Spending

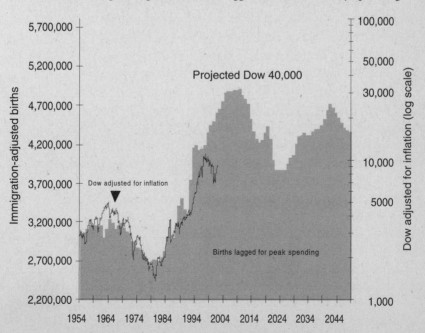

2002 lows of 7286. And in the deflationary downturns, such as in 1930–1942 and 2010–2022, this model will save you much more than in the inflationary downturns, such as in 1969–1982.

The second recurring cycle was the four-year Presidential Cycle we covered in this chapter in Figure 3.3. We showed in Figure 3.5 that an investment strategy that pulled out in the weak annual season in the second year of each presidential term would have increased your wealth by 2.3 times (since 1952) with 22.6% higher average annual compound returns and 10.7% less volatility.

The third and most powerful recurring cycle was the Decennial Cycle, shown in Figure 3.7. This cycle is the most powerful of the three and is documented back to 1900. Figure 3.8 showed how over the last fifty-one years your wealth would have become 44.5 times greater by following this model than by just being in the S&P 500. The returns on average were 79.2% higher and the risk was 17.2% lower, for a risk-adjusted return 114.3% better. If we go back to 1952 as with the other models, in less volatile times, the wealth grew by 2.6 times with average returns 28.3% higher and risk 19.6% lower.

What if we were to combine all three models? That's what we do in Figure 3.16. We are out of stocks and into T-bills when the Spending Wave is pointing down and when the Decennial and Presidential cycles are pointing down. There's one exception. We still move into stocks for the powerful "5" to "9" years of the Decennial Cycle even when the Spending Wave is pointing down, except when the other cycles are pointing down. If we back-

FIGURE 3.16 The Composite Cycle Model, 1952–2003

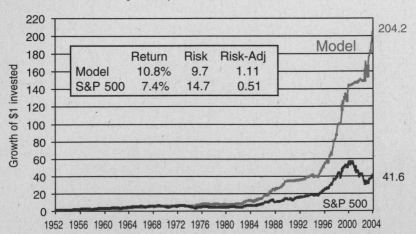

test this combined model back to 1952, when we have the first measurable data for the Spending Wave, we get even more compelling results from a very simple model that would have you invested the majority of the time over the last five decades. The growth of $1 to $204.25 versus the S&P 500 at $41.60 was 4.9 times. That is truly astounding! The average annual compound returns at 10.77% versus 7.43% on the S&P 500 would have been 45.0% higher and the risk or volatility at 9.69 versus 14.70 would have been 34.1% lower. The risk-adjusted performance at 1.11 versus .51 would have been a whopping 117.6% better annually.

An even better way of gauging the performance is to look at the portion of the upside gains captured versus the downside losses avoided. This model would have captured 95.5% (or missed only 4.5% of the upside gains) while experiencing only 62.0% of the downside losses (or avoiding 38.0% of the downside losses). That is a great trade-off. Yet the greatest pain and temptation to sell come in the most extreme downturns. The worst extended downside loss in this model would have been only 16.4% versus 51.9% on the S&P 500, 68.4% less risk! That represents a huge advantage. But most important, this model would have you out of the markets in the greatest times of potential risk in the future according to our detailed forecast in Chapter 2: from 2010 to 2014 and from 2020 to 2022. It would also have you out from May to October 2006 and August through October 2007. Otherwise, you would be invested largely from October 2002 through 2009, a time period where there are huge potential gains in the stock market that can build your wealth to the point that you have the ability to continue to prosper afterward with safer investments in what should be the worst period in U.S. history.

This model would represent the best simple strategy for equity investing for everyday people who want to minimize their risks and volatility but still take advantage of the long-term returns in equities. In Chapter 7 we will present a slightly more complex model that focuses on the best sectors of equities in each season of the economy and gets dramatically better returns at slightly lower risk levels than the S&P 500. That would represent the best simple model for more aggressive investors.

Here we have a simple, systematic model that would, on average, more than double your risk-adjusted performance annually with only a few major changes per decade and without your constantly having to listen to the news and trying to decide whether this or that expert is right and when to pull out of the markets.

Summary

Despite the very difficult and enduring crash of 2000–2002 we are more bullish than at any time in the last two decades of our forecasting work. We have been calling late 2002 to late 2005 "the investment opportunity of a lifetime." All of our fundamental and cycle work suggests that investors are likely to see the highest average annual compound returns in history from late 2002 into early to late 2010, both in broader indices like the Dow and S&P 500, and more so in the strongest sectors, such as technology, biotech, financial services, health care, and Asia apart from Japan. In Chapters 6 and 7 we will look at how you can better refine your portfolios to focus on the best sectors in the great boom and great bust ahead. In Chapter 7 we show much greater returns from our Composite Cycle model in Figure 3.16 by simply adding the ability to focus in large- or small-cap stocks and long-term or short-term bonds according to our models for forecasting when those sectors will do best as tracked and forecast in Chapter 6.

But first, in Chapter 4, the prospects for real estate and your home appreciation in the boom and bust ahead—they are not as great as you might think. Then, in Chapter 5, we will look at how demographics, technology, and these recurring cycles will affect your key life decisions, from when to sell your business and your house to the best time to send your kids to college and the best places to live in the downturn.

As bullish as we are for the coming decade, we are also forecasting that this will be the last great bull market for decades to come. This is your last chance to make extraordinary gains in your wealth. Those gains will allow you to sail through the next great winter and with our strategies you can continue to grow your wealth more modestly rather than lose most of it. But you have to have the guts and insights to buy when most people are still cautious after the crash of 2000–2002 and the slow recovery into 2005.

Chapter 4

DEMOGRAPHICS AND THE OUTLOOK FOR REAL ESTATE

Home Prices Will Continue to Underperform Stock Prices and the Economy for the Rest of This Decade

THE TYPICAL HOUSEHOLD has around 50% of its net worth invested in personal or investment real estate. Hence, making the right decisions here can have as major an impact on your long-term wealth as your investment portfolio. The period 2000–2002 saw stocks go down and home prices go up, and home prices generally kept going up into mid-2005. So naturally most investors were thinking real estate is the better place to be for the coming years. But then housing prices started to slow and decline in some upscale areas starting in late 2005, which could be a warning of changing trends.

We will show in this chapter that the average home price has seen nowhere near the appreciation of stocks in the past three decades and that housing prices are likely to continue to grow slower at best and may even weaken while the stock market sees its next great bull market and bubble into at least late 2009. While many experts were forecasting a crash in the housing market in 2002 and 2003, we were forecasting in a special edition of our July 2003 newsletter that the strongest demographic trends in home buying had clearly passed and that housing growth and prices would slow substantially by 2005 to 2006.

We argued that there wouldn't be a major crash since the economy and mortgage rates would be too favorable. But we warned that the upscale markets were more vulnerable on the downside. After more modest growth at best again into 2010 or 2011, most real estate markets are likely to take their first major decline since the Great Depression from around 2011 into 2014, when the baby boomers have completed their spending cycle and are starting to downsize their housing. Then we will see a real crash in housing prices, and that will affect your real estate and your life. There will be continued weakness into around 2023, as the baby-boom downturn finally bottoms, similar to what occurred in Japan from the early 1990s to the early 2000s and to what occurred in the United States during the Great Depression.

This is our most comprehensive analysis on the real estate markets as the annual Consumer Expenditure Survey by the U.S. Bureau of Labor Statistics now has more data on primary home and vacation home purchasing patterns. Our analysis here is based on the surveys from 1996 to 2000 that we have analyzed in greater detail. In this chapter we are going to take a comprehensive look at the hard demographic trends in home buying (as well as commercial real estate) and how they change by age and income level.

Conversely, we have projected a strong appreciation in stock prices similar to the 1990s bull market based on the continued rise in spending by the baby-boom generation over the rest of this decade. In addition, the acceleration of new technologies such as home computing, cell phones, and the Internet into the mainstream of our economy from 1994 into 2008 or 2009, after the shakeout of 2000–2002 in the middle of this cycle, will also bring a second surge in major technology and growth industries as well as higher productivity rates, as occurred from 1914 to 1928 in the new economy emerging with autos and electricity into the Roaring Twenties. However, despite these strong fundamental trends in the economy into at least 2009, home prices are likely to grow much slower and possibly even decline a bit according to the more specific demographic spending patterns on housing that were at their peak levels between 1998 and 2003.

The first and larger part of this chapter will focus on the trends in primary residences and vacation homes, the homes most of us own for personal use. Real estate represents a large part of most people's net worth and although it is not just an investment for most of us, it still affects our financial well-being and borrowing power. In Chapter 5 on life planning, we will also look at how you can use new demographic databases to gauge overvaluation and undervaluation in the areas where you own homes or are looking to buy or relocate.

THE FACTORS DRIVING HOME-PRICE APPRECIATION

In this chapter we will look at all of the key cycles that shape home demand and pricing at each stage of the demographic cycles that affect housing and real estate. There are four fundamental trends that affect housing growth and prices:

1. **Predictable spending trends by age and income in housing:** Demographic spending trends are obviously the largest factor driving home building and home appreciation rates over time and that is the primary focus of this chapter. As people and households age they spend more on housing up to a point, but the patterns of spending are highly affected by their income level, as well. The demographic trends we examine have been projecting a marked slowing in growth after 2003 and a broader peak in housing demand by 2011 with a much larger drop to follow in demand and prices.

2. **Mortgage rates and affordability:** The lower inflation rates are, the lower mortgage rates will be. More people can afford larger houses and can qualify for home purchases and mortgages as mortgage rates fall. Since late 2002 and early 2003, we have been predicting that interest and mortgage rates would rise a bit with a stronger economic recovery. But our inflation indicators in Chapter 3 also have been predicting that inflation and interest rates are likely to settle down and fall modestly again from mid- to late 2004 into late 2005 or early 2006. From 2006 on, we should see very modest rises in inflation rates. Hence, inflation should remain in the .5% to 3.0% range for the rest of this decade. Continued low inflation and mortgage rates into 2005 should cushion the demographic weakness we forecast over the coming years.

3. **Overbuilding cycles:** There are clear overbuilding cycles by developers in response to growing demand, which tend to create overcapacity, causing prices to decline often in advance of such a peak. The excess inventories of housing created into 2004 will likely be worked off early into mid- to late 2005. Then prices and building will grow at a much more modest rate into the rest of this decade at best. It is clear to us that the strong housing cycle in the last several years has resulted in overbuilding, especially in the mid- to upper-end housing segments. This will add to the slowing and/or weakness in prices that began in 2004 and will likely continue into much of 2005.

4. **The overall economic trends:** When the overall economy is growing and employment is increasing, incomes grow and the propensity to buy hous-

ing or trade up to a better house grows to a degree, in addition to the effects of demographic trends and mortgage rates. When the economy declines in general, future expectations of consumers decline and major durable goods, especially housing, are affected to a degree, likewise. Our demographic forecasts for the overall economy were forecasting a stronger recovery from late 2003 on and a very strong overall economy with low inflation from 2005 into 2009 or 2010. Such strong economic trends will help to keep housing demand and prices stronger than they would otherwise be due to demographic trends alone. But after 2010, the overall demographic rise in spending by the massive baby-boom generation will be turning down much as it did in Japan from 1990 into 2004. In addition, our long-term inflation indicator is projecting deflation after 2010. A weak economy and deflation in prices will cause the first major decline in home and real estate prices since the early 1930s and many segments of the market will stay weak for many years, as has occurred in Japan since 1990.

TRENDS IN HOME PRICES

We will start by looking at the home price trends since the recession of 1974. Home prices have been rising steadily for most of this boom since 1975 with the slight exception of the early 1990s, as we show in Figure 4.1. As impressive as such trends appear, since 1975 the average house price has gone up by 4.4 times while the Dow has been up more than twenty times from 1975 to 1999, and was still up eighteen times in 2004! The reason house appreciation feels so substantial is the leverage from the mortgage.

Of course, house prices are generally less volatile than stock prices—rising more steadily over time and falling less in down markets. But stocks are easier to sell at will and real estate is not so easy when the markets finally get overbuilt or demand weakens rapidly, as occurred in the early 1930s and the early 1990s. That is when housing felt like a trap and was a riskier investment than most people assumed from the otherwise steady appreciation that was typical. And remember that most houses have a substantial mortgage, which increases the leverage both on the way up and on the way down. We have been forecasting since July 2003 that we could see a flattening and more likely a minor decline in house prices between late 2003 and 2005, and that there will be a major decline between 2011 and 2014 and likely beyond.

The first insight from demographic demand trends is that house prices will grow more slowly over the rest of this decade and may even decline modestly, especially between 2004 and 2005. But the more critical insight from this report—for developers, mortgage lenders, home buyers, and

FIGURE 4.1 Average and Median Home Prices, 1975–2002

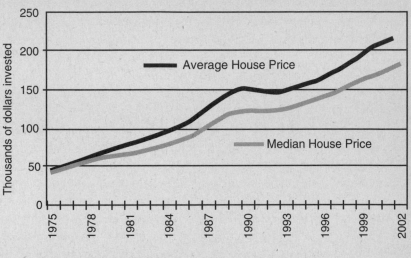

Source: Milken Institute, September 2002.

investors—is that housing is not just a simple rise-and-fall phenomenon driven by age like many other categories of spending we analyze. There are many surges in house buying over the consumer life cycle and great differences between purchasing patterns between higher- and lower-income consumers and different sectors of real estate ranging from offices, retail, and hotels (commercial)—to apartments, primary homes, and vacation/retirement homes (residential) as new generations of consumers age and move through predictable cycles of spending and needs.

THE GREAT CRASH IN HOUSING? NOT YET! ECONOMIC CONDITIONS WILL BE TOO FAVORABLE

There was much talk between 2002 and 2003 about a housing bubble, and there was a book published titled *The Coming Crash in the Housing Market.* Author John Talbott (and many other forecasters) has been predicting a crash in real estate on a lag to the crash in the stock markets between 2000 and 2002. The argument, among much data on rising debt and home price trends, is that consumers feel reality in their home values a few years after they do in their stock wealth, much as occurred in the early 1930s in the United States and the early 1990s in Japan after major stock crashes. But those stock market crashes occurred when the overall demographic trends had already turned down long term for the corresponding economies. We showed in Chapter 1 that the recent stock crash in the United States is much like the great shakeout and bubble burst in high-technology growth that occurred in the early 1920s and resulted in an even greater boom and technology bubble into late 1929 in the Roaring Twenties. We have not been predicting a crash in housing prices, as the economy will be strong due to broader demographic spending trends and mortgage rates remaining very favorable.

There will be greater strength in the multifamily, vacation/retirement, and exurban segments of the residential market as well as in the hotel and retail sectors of commercial real estate over the coming decade. Most sectors are likely to decline substantially as the baby boom Spending Wave peaks by early in the next decade and overbuilding cycles occur again into that peak. The next bubble in the stock market that we are forecasting for late 2005 into 2010 should eventually add to the weakness in the economy and the housing markets when we see a stock collapse and business/technology shakeout between 2010 and 2014 that is even stronger than what occurred between 2000 and 2002.

THE DEMOGRAPHICS OF HOME BUYING

We will look at home buying from four different angles to get the most complete view: total home purchases (net of sales) by age, average purchase price by age, average home value by age, and mortgage interest by age. Then we will look at these four dimensions by three different income levels: the top 20%, the middle 40%, and the bottom 40%. First note that home buying is different from other areas of consumer spending as homes last a very long time and new buying adds to the total stock of homes, putting pressure on land availability and environmental capacity. Rising demand against such limitations creates a trend of generally rising prices. Most homes are also mortgaged and paid for over time. Hence, a large expenditure comes up front, but most of the expenditures from mortgage interest to maintenance and property taxes are spent more evenly over time. Hence, we do have to look at a number of dimensions of home buying to get a clear picture of how it grows in volume and in value.

The most primary data we now track from the Consumer Expenditure Survey by the U.S. Bureau of Labor Statistics is the total home purchases of the sample by age in Figure 4.2 from 1996 to 2000. This chart is the best proxy for the overall size of the new-home market annually as the baby-

FIGURE 4.2 Total Home Purchases, by Age

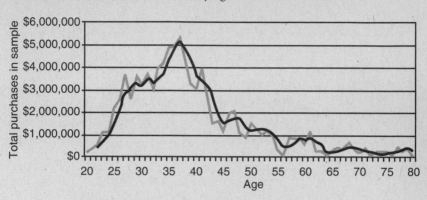

Source: Consumer Expenditure Survey, 2000; U.S. Bureau of Labor Statistics.

boom generation ages. Note that in all of the charts we present there are two lines. The lighter line represents the actual survey data and the darker line represents a three-year moving average to smooth the trends a bit since the survey sample is rather small. The summary insight from Figure 4.2 is that the greatest home-buying years fall between age 26 (when the average person gets married and peaks in his or her rental cycle) and age 42.

Here we can see that house buying surges strongly into age 37. There is a starter-home surge into age 28–31 and a trade-up surge into age 37. Then the growth begins to slow after age 37 and slows more markedly after age 42. The peak baby boomers born in 1961 would have hit the primary peak in home buying in 1998 and the secondary peak at age 42 in 2003. Obviously that doesn't mean that the total market has peaked as we continue to add smaller levels of purchases on top of the present stock of homes. But the momentum clearly began to slow in 2004 and will continue to do so. There are secondary surges on the way down at around age 47 (peak in 2008 for peak baby boomers born in 1961) and from age 57 to 61 (peak in 2022).

Figure 4.3 shows the average home price paid for those who purchased, by age. This chart gives a better insight into the trade-up cycle, price points for various age ranges, and trends in appreciation. Homes will tend to grow in line with the peak prices of homes purchased by age and income, plus the general inflation rate, except to the degree there is overbuilding, which was certainly the case into 2003. The starter homes bought between ages 24 and 31 move up from around $100,000 to almost $140,000. Then there is peak trade-up buying into the age 37 peak and another surge into 41 (2002) around $170,000. There are two further trade-up surges, one from 44–49

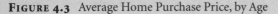

FIGURE 4.3 Average Home Purchase Price, by Age

Source: U.S. Bureau of Labor Statistics, Consumer Expenditure Survey, 2000.

(2005–2010) at $175,000 and a peak trade-up cycle from ages 57–62 (2018–2012) up to about $220,000. Despite the fact that the momentum in house buying has peaked, pricing trends are likely to continue to move up very modestly over the rest of this decade (after declining a bit into 2005) as we approach the peak in purchase price trends at around age 49 in 2010.

Figure 4.4 shows the average value of homes as people age, further illustrating the trade-up cycle but also showing when they start to downsize. The value of homes rises steadily into age 39 and peaks at about $145,000. Then there is a second rise from around age 47 to 56 up to $156,000. After age 56 (2017 for peak baby boomers) some households start downsizing

FIGURE 4.4 Average Value of Home, by Age

Source: U.S. Bureau of Labor Statistics, Consumer Expenditure Survey, 2000.

and that would create selling pressure especially on mid- to upper-end homes. Figure 4.3 shows the average purchase price is the highest in the late 50s and early 60s, but that represents a small percentage of the population purchasing. The divergence between falling average home values (Figure 4.4) and rising average purchase prices (Figure 4.3) would strongly suggest that rising homeowners in their late 50s and 60s are often inheriting homes, not buying them. These inherited homes are more modest on average, but for the smaller percentage of people who do purchase in their late 50s and early 60s, this represents their largest home purchase on average and the ultimate trade-up cycle for the everyday household.

One of the most fundamental trends in the home market is that higher percentages of households qualify for mortgages and own homes as they age and can afford to. Figure 4.5 shows that the percentage of households that owns homes rises steeply into the early 40s, when it hits 70%, and then more gradually into the late 60s, when it peaks at 83%. The average overall today is 68% and will clearly continue to move up in the coming years adding more lower to midpriced demand than upper price. Upper-income households buy their largest homes earlier, as we will show later in this chapter, and more and more lower-income households buy homes or inherit them over time.

Figure 4.6 shows mortgage interest rising steadily into age 41 and then falling off for the rest of the life cycle. This graph also suggests a peak in overall buying momentum by age 41, which would have occurred in 2002 for the baby boomers, versus age 37 in Figure 4.2. It is the more affluent households that are dropping off after age 37, as we will show later in this

FIGURE 4.5 Percentage of Population Who Own a Home, by Age

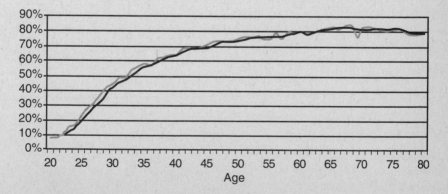

Source: U.S. Bureau of Labor Statistics, Consumer Expenditure Survey, 2000.

FIGURE 4.6 Average Mortgage Interest Paid Annually, by Age

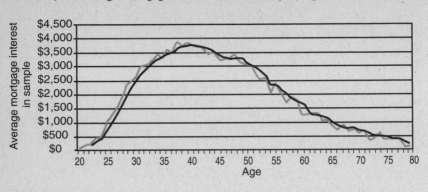

Source: U.S. Bureau of Labor Statistics, Consumer Expenditure Survey, 2000.

FIGURE 4.7 Percentage of Population Who Have a Mortgage, by Age

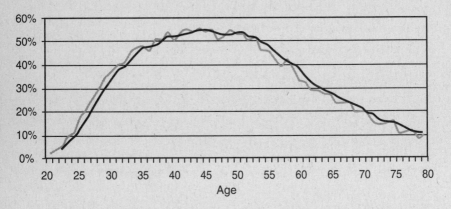

Source: U.S. Bureau of Labor Statistics, Consumer Expenditure Survey, 2000.

chapter. Most households mortgage their home purchases at first and pay down that mortgage slowly over time. But more pay cash out of their savings or past house equity as they get older, and others inherit houses, which have already been paid for by their parents. Figure 4.7 shows the percentage of households that have mortgages, which rises into the mid-40s, peaking at 55%, plateaus, and then drops off steadily after age 56, when average home values peak and downsizing begins.

We can get a more in-depth look at the primary start-up and trade-up buying cycles in Figure 4.8, which shows the percentage of households that are first-time or starter-home buyers and repeat buyers or trade-up, according to Realtor surveys. The greatest numbers of first-time buyers occur

FIGURE 4.8 First-Time Versus Repeat Home Buyers

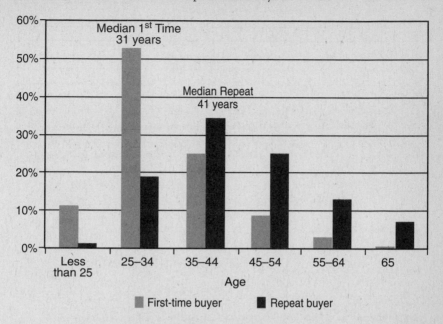

Source: National Association of Realtors.

between ages 25 and 34. Our interpolation of these statistics would suggest a peak around ages 31–32. The median or typical first-time buyer is age 31, confirming a peak around that age. Repeat buyers peak between ages 35 and 44, with an interpolated peak around ages 40–41. The median repeat buyer is 41, confirming a peak around that age, as does the peak in mortgage interest at age 41.

Figure 4.9 shows the number of purchasers at each age from the Consumer Expenditure Survey. This graph shows a peak in the total volume of buyers at age 38 and a secondary peak at age 42. From this graph we can again see that the prime time for volume of home buyers is between age 26 and 42. The peak numbers of baby boomers would have been progressing through that cycle from 1986 to 2003. Note that there is a very steep dropoff in the volume of buyers after age 42 (2003 for the peak baby boomers) into age 49 (2011). This strongly suggests that developers overbuilt into 2003 and that the demand for new homes will continue to slow over the rest of this decade. The overbuilding is likely to be worked off by late 2005, when there can be the potential for modest price appreciation again. But the appreciation is likely to only be modest as average purchase prices and home values don't appreciate much after age 42.

FIGURE 4.9   Home Purchasers, by Age

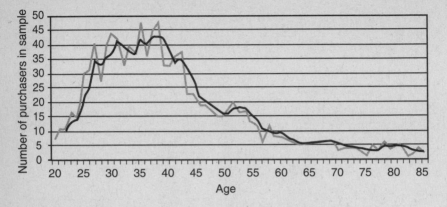

Source: Consumer Expenditure Survey, 2000; U.S. Bureau of Labor Statistics.

SUMMARY OF OVERALL DEMOGRAPHIC TRENDS

The clear peaks in the momentum in housing growth clearly occur from mortgage interest to trade-up buying around age 41 or age 42 at the latest. The peak in total home purchases at age 37 is more influenced by the top 20% of affluent home buyers. Hence, the peak in growth due to demographic trends should have clearly peaked by late 2003. Dramatic drops in mortgage rates also kept housing markets and prices strong into mid-2003, but that trend is largely over. Housing prices should continue to flatten or weaken into 2005. By late 2005 or 2006, further trade-up buying cycles and the general demographic trend toward rising average purchases and home values should cause modest growth and appreciation into 2010 or 2011. But the best of the growth in housing markets and prices is clearly behind us and we would expect housing as an industry to underperform the economy for the rest of this decade. We will show later in this chapter that the vacation/resort and apartment markets will be where the growth is for residential builders and developers.

AFFLUENT HOUSEHOLDS' HOME-BUYING PATTERNS

It is critical to understand that home-buying patterns are very different for different income households. The upper-income households buy their starter and trade-up homes earlier and represent the largest part of the market in dollar value due to higher home prices. Figure 4.10 shows the total home purchases by age for the top 20% of income households at each

FIGURE 4.10 Total Home Purchases by Top 20% of Population, by Age

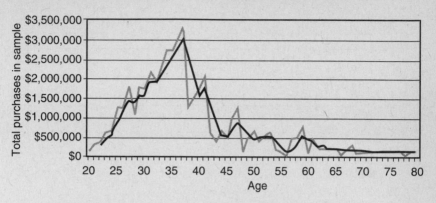

Source: U.S. Bureau of Labor Statistics, Consumer Expenditure Survey, 2000.

age. The rise and fall in the volume of purchases is very steep for this group. There is a starter surge into age 27 and then a trade-up surge into age 37. Hence, the largest buying surges by the affluent would have peaked for the baby boomers by 1998. There are two significant secondary surges after that peak into age 41 (peak in 2002) and 47 (peak in 2008). There is continued buying at lower levels between ages 49 and 59 (between 2010 and 2020), but downsizing sets in for this segment after age 54 to offset that from 2016 on.

Figure 4.11 shows the average home purchase price for those who bought. It steadily rises toward $400,000 by age 39 (peak in 2000), with brief peak surges toward $500,000 around age 46 (peak in 2007) and age 57

FIGURE 4.11 Average Home Purchase Price by Top 20% of Population, by Age

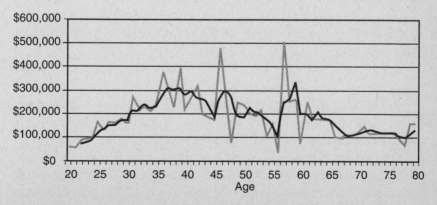

Source: U.S. Bureau of Labor Statistics, Consumer Expenditure Survey, 2000.

Figure 4.12 Average Value of Home Owned by Top 20% of Population, by Age

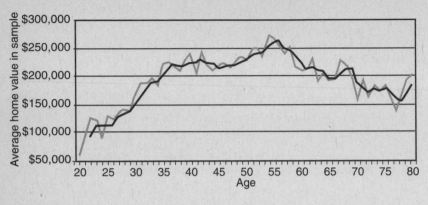

Source: U.S. Bureau of Labor Statistics, Consumer Expenditure Survey, 2000.

Figure 4.13 Average Mortgage Interest Paid Annually by Top 20% of Population, by Age

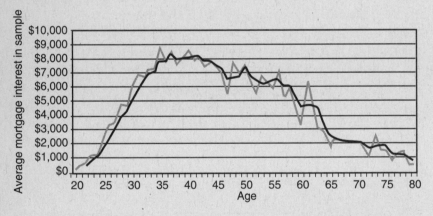

Source: U.S. Bureau of Labor Statistics, Consumer Expenditure Survey, 2000.

(peak in 2018). Figure 4.12 shows that the average home value peaks by age 54 and downsizing starts to set in after the children are gone. Mortgage interest (Figure 4.13) for this group peaks early at age 35 and then drops off substantially after age 40. Mortgage lenders should expect declines in this market for many years to come, except occasional refinancing surges.

For this affluent group the momentum in growth rate has already passed, between 1998 and 2002. Very low mortgage rates kept this and all markets strong in pricing into 2003. This market, after performing so strongly into 2002 and 2003, has declined the strongest in 2004 and should continue to into mid- to late 2005. There may be modest appreciation in this market again into 2008 or 2009 due to the last spike in buying around age 47, coinciding with the likely bubble in the stock market. When the economy turns down by 2011 this sector of residential real estate will be hit the hardest again.

Upscale Markets Have Both the Greatest Upside and Greatest Downside

Have you ever wondered why mortgage rates are higher for "jumbo" loans on higher-priced houses even though the income and credit ratings of such buyers are typically stronger? It is because the banks understand the fact that upper-end homes tend to appreciate more rapidly in a growing market but then tend to decline more dramatically in down markets. There is more risk in such homes, just as in growth and tech stocks versus the S&P 500. During the housing downturn in the early 1990s, the price of an average home was down less than 10%, while that of some of the most upscale homes declined by 40% to 50%. Figure 4.14 shows the price trends in the higher-priced metropolitan areas in the East. This chart and the next three come from Fidelity National Information Solutions (FNIS). You can access a number of useful articles for free on its Web site (www.fnis.com), and there also is a wealth of information that you can access for a fee.

FIGURE 4.14 Home Price Trends in Selected Northeastern Cities

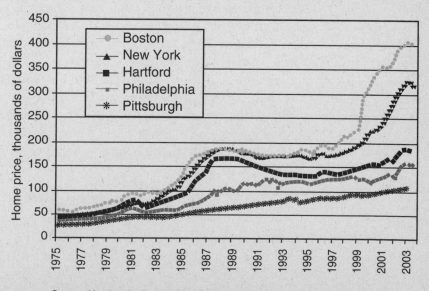

FIGURE 4.15 Home Price Trends in Major California Markets

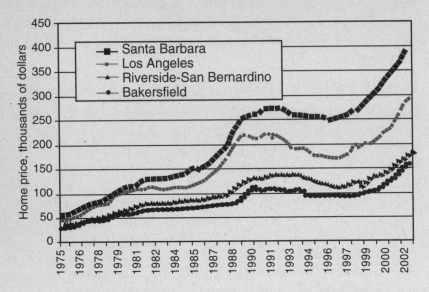

In Figure 4.14 we can see that Boston had the highest median home prices of any large metro area on the East Coast at $400,000 in 2003. New York follows at $300,000, and prices go as low as $110,000 in Pittsburgh. The point here is simply that the higher-priced the market, the more it rises in boom times. When prices start to crest and slow, as has started to occur in 2004, there is typically more downside risk in such markets.

Figure 4.15 shows a range of markets in southern California ranging from the highest-priced, Santa Barbara, to the lowest-priced, Bakersfield. Here again we can see that during the recent boom the prices accelerated the fastest in the highest-priced markets, such as Santa Barbara (up to $400,000) and Los Angeles (up to $300,000). Riverside home prices reached only $180,000, closer to the national average, and it is one of the few affordable places in the greater L.A. area. Bakersfield, way out in the valley, has seen the smallest appreciation acceleration and has the lowest prices at about $165,000.

In Figure 4.16 we get the best view of how the more upscale and exclusive homes in a high-priced market accelerate more to the upside in a housing boom, creating more of a bubble. This chart shows different-size homes in Greenwich, Connecticut, one of the most upscale neighborhoods outside New York City. The prices of the largest homes in the 5,000–7,500-

FIGURE 4.16 Home Price Trends by House Size in Greenwich, Connecticut

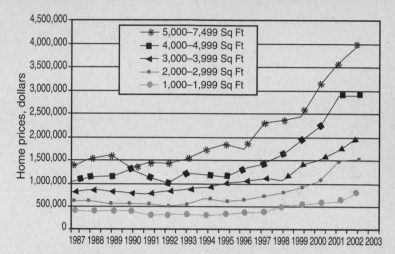

square-feet range average $4 million and have accelerated the fastest. The prices of the largest homes in the 4,000–5,000-square-feet range average $2.9 million and have accelerated nearly as dramatically. But as we go down the size and price range, the acceleration is less dramatic.

It shouldn't be surprising that as house prices have slowed in 2004 the upscale markets are tending to see prices begin to fall substantially in some areas. First, the dropoff in buying after the peak at age 37 and the secondary peak around age 41–42 is steeper for the top-20% income group, as we showed in Figure 4.10. Second, where there is greater acceleration to the upside there is likely to be a greater downside risk when prices fall. FNIS has two indicators that can help you determine when such a fall is likely to occur in your local metropolitan market. The first is its Real Estate Leading Index, which it has created for each of 316 metropolitan markets in the United States. Figure 4.17 shows that index for San Francisco, the most overpriced market in the West. This index has been warning of a slowing in prices ahead since early 2000 and is now just starting to turn up mildly again.

FNIS also has a shorter-term indicator it calls the Buy/Sell Indicator. This indicator measures the momentum in buying and selling and gauges likely turning points in real estate markets, just as "oscillators" do for stock and commodity markets. If we look at the index for San Francisco we see that it was very close to giving a sell signal at the end of 2003 and home

FIGURE 4.17 FNIS Real Estate Leading Index: San Francisco, 1986–2004

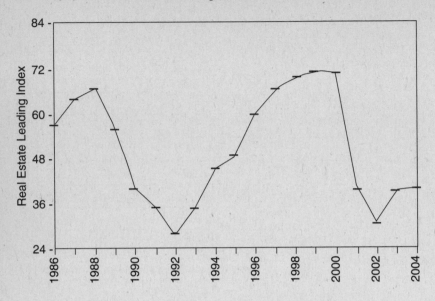

prices have clearly slowed since then with many upscale areas down 10% to 20%. We will look at how to apply these indicators as well as others in your local area in Chapter 5, when we look at innovative approaches to using demographics for life planning beyond just your investment portfolios.

MIDDLE-INCOME HOUSEHOLDS' BUYING PATTERNS

The middle-income market is the next 40% of incomes, from the 20% quintile to the 60% quintile. This would represent middle- to upper-middle-income households. At its peak the total home-buying power of this market is only 64% of the upper-income market even though there are twice as many households. This group has also peaked in its buying momentum. Total home purchases in Figure 4.18 show a starter-home cycle into age 31 and a trade-up cycle into age 39. The trade-up cycle for this group would have peaked in 2000. The dropoff in buying after that point is strong from age 40 into age 42; then there are significant smaller continued trade-up spikes into around ages 43, 52, and 56.

Figure 4.19 shows the average purchase price, which rises steadily into

FIGURE 4.18 Total Home Purchases by Middle 40% of Population, by Age

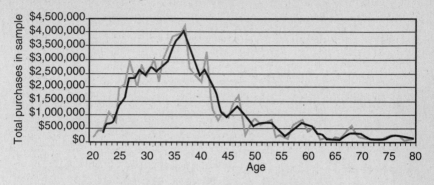

Source: U.S. Bureau of Labor Statistics, Consumer Expenditure Survey, 2000.

FIGURE 4.19 Average Home Purchase Price by Middle 40% of Population, by Age

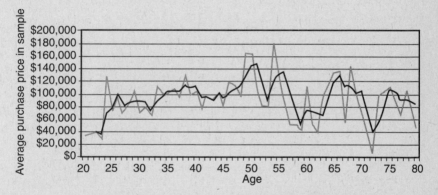

Source: U.S. Bureau of Labor Statistics, Consumer Expenditure Survey, 2000.

age 38 to about $130,000. Note that at a similar age, the top 20% are paying more than three times the price at $400,000. Then the strongest trade-up occurs from age 46 to 54 and hits peak prices of almost $190,000. To summarize, the greatest volume of buying comes around age 39 and the highest prices paid appear around age 54. Figure 4.20 shows that the peak home values occur around age 56, at around $135,000, and then home values tend to flatten out. This group does not see as strong a downsizing trend as the upper-income households. They seem to trade up to a better house, typically by their late 30s, and then stay in it into retirement. Mortgage interest (Figure 4.21) for this group similarly plateaus between ages 40 and 47 (in

FIGURE 4.20 Average Value of Home by Middle 40% of Population, by Age

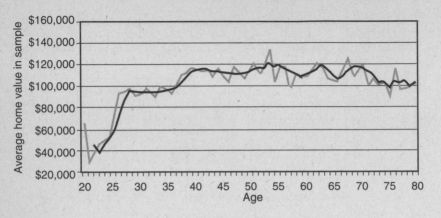

Source: U.S. Bureau of Labor Statistics, Consumer Expenditure Survey, 2000.

FIGURE 4.21 Average Mortgage Interest Paid Annually by Middle 40% of Population, by Age

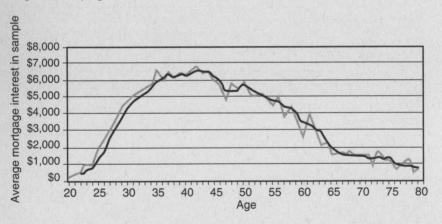

Source: U.S. Bureau of Labor Statistics, Consumer Expenditure Survey, 2000.

2001 and 2008 for the peak baby boomers) before dropping off. Mortgage lending will stay more buoyant for this group but will continue to weaken a bit in the year ahead.

The demographic trends for this segment would also suggest a substantial slowing in the market over the coming years, but that prices and mortgage lending will hold up better here in the housing correction of 2004–2005 and for the rest of the decade than in the upper-income market.

Lower-Income Households' Buying Patterns

This market is obviously the smallest in dollar volume and the most different. These households keep steadily qualifying for mortgages and house affordability into retirement. This market at its peak home purchasing in dollars is only 38% of the middle-income market. Their peak purchases (Figure 4.22) see a starter surge into age 33 and a peak trade-up surge into age 39 (peak in 2000), much like the middle-income home buyers. But there are more significant continued trade-up surges into around age 44 (in 2005), 49 (in 2010), and 55 (in 2016). The largest subsequent trade-up surge occurs into age 62, much later than other segments. The average purchase price (Figure 4.23) gets up to about $125,000 by age 35, similarly to the middle-income buyers, but the highest average prices are paid at age 62 up to $200,000. Hence, there is a lot of overlap between the middle 40% and bottom 40% in price points. It's just that more of the bottom 40% buy later in their life cycle.

The average home value in Figure 4.24 climbs steadily into age 67, showing the greatest difference in this market. They just keep trading up into retirement as their discretionary income increases and they receive inheritances. People in this segment demonstrate a stronger motivation to improve their living standards over their life cycle and become "middle-class" with a lot of rising immigrants and ethnic groups. Their mortgage interest (Figure 4.25) has a dual peak at ages 41 and 48 before falling off.

Although this is the smallest and lowest-price-point market and would

Figure 4.22 Total Home Purchases by Bottom 40% of Population, by Age

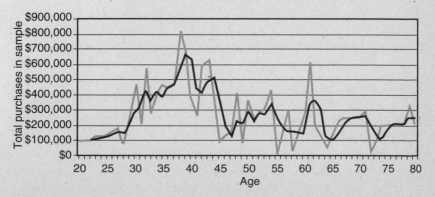

Source: U.S. Bureau of Labor Statistics, Consumer Expenditure Survey, 2000.

FIGURE 4.23 Average Home Purchase Price by Bottom 40% of Population, by Age

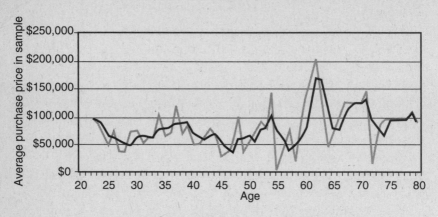

Source: U.S. Bureau of Labor Statistics, Consumer Expenditure Survey, 2000.

FIGURE 4.24 Average Value of Home Owned by Bottom 40% of Population, by Age

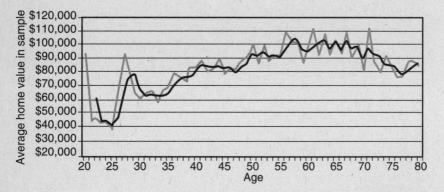

Source: U.S. Bureau of Labor Statistics, Consumer Expenditure Survey, 2000.

have peaked in growth momentum between 2000 and 2003, this market grows the most as new generations age and will represent better growth and price appreciation than the middle and upper segments looking ahead. This segment will keep the lower-to-middle end of the housing market stronger in the coming years. This market coupled with the rising tide of starter-home buying by the echo boom will represent the strongest and most buoyant market in the downturn after 2010 or 2011 as well.

FIGURE 4.25 Average Mortgage Interest Paid Annually by Bottom 40% of Population, by Age

Source: U.S. Bureau of Labor Statistics, Consumer Expenditure Survey, 2000.

ARE CONSUMERS' DEBT LEVELS SUSTAINABLE?

We have clearly shown that the demand forces from demographic trends will not be as strong for housing after 2003. But again, we have not been forecasting a deep crash, but merely a slowing and modest declines, with stronger declines in the upscale markets and most overvalued areas. Remember that we are in a bubble boom. It's just that the housing market is not nearly as volatile as the stock market on either the upside or the downside. The experts who have been predicting a crash focus much on the fact that consumers have borrowed excessively, induced by lower mortgage rates, and can't sustain their spending on housing. That is not going to be the case over the rest of this decade, nor was it the recent reason for the slowing of the housing market.

The fact that mortgage interest, which is by far the largest component of consumer debt, peaks at age 41 suggests strongly that overall consumer debt and mortgage lending will grow much slower than the economy into the future just when most economists are so worried that consumer debt is excessive and could cause the level of consumer spending not to be sustainable in the future. The gap between income and spending widens between age 25 and age 50 in Figure 4.26. Rising marginal tax rates take a greater amount of this excess in income over spending into the late 30s;

FIGURE 4.26 Pretax Income, After-Tax Income, and Expenditures, by Age

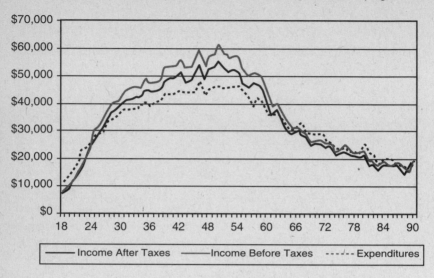

Source: U.S. Bureau of Labor Statistics, Consumer Expenditure Survey, 2000.

then savings and investments grow from the late 30s into the early to mid-50s. As the baby boomers continue to age over the decade ahead, the trends are likely to be toward slower rates of growth in debt, not rising levels of indebtedness relative to income and assets.

Contrary to popular opinion, most homeowners have much more equity in their homes than most experts believe. The equity in their home of the average household has declined since the late 1970s, when it was at 70%. At that point in time the Bob Hope generation had peaked in the home-buying cycle by the mid-1960s and had largely paid down their mortgages as they aged. The baby boomers were coming into their new home-buying cycle, and these younger buyers borrowed more against their newer homes. In addition, mortgage rates have declined from as high as 16% in 1981 to as low as 5% in 2003. That makes mortgage borrowing more attractive and more affordable. But despite these trends, the average household who owns a home has 57% equity and only 43% in mortgage debt. And mortgage debt represents 77% of total household debt. In fact, after declining in the early and mid-1990s with the housing decline, household equity has risen to new highs as of 2002. So the American consumer is not about to run out of spending power on housing or in general due to excessive indebtedness (except for a small minority of marginal households).

Figure 4.27 gives the clearest picture of why housing markets have continued to rise in this boom beyond the steady rise in demographic trends that represent the primary trend, and despite rising overall debt levels as baby boomers both spend more and borrow more (at least up until recently at peak mortgage interest levels around age 41 in 2002) as they age. Falling mortgage rates since the early 1980s have caused the percentage of after-tax income required for mortgage payments to fall from 61% in 1982 to 30% in recent years. This again means that the average household can increasingly afford to qualify for a mortgage and afford a larger house at the same income level.

This trend should remain low over the rest of this decade with continued low mortgage rates and rising average income levels as the boom in spending continues into 2009 or 2010. Again, we don't see a problem with households affording modestly rising home prices ahead, and mortgage debt levels should actually decrease as a percentage of household income in the coming years. Installment debt on car and furnishings will likely rise a bit as a percentage of income, but that represents a much more minor percentage of overall household debt.

FIGURE 4.27   Housing Affordability and New-Home Sales, 1975–2002

Source: Milken Institute, September 2002.

CONTINUING MEGATREND:
CONSUMERS WILL CONTINUE TO FLEE TO THE EXURBS

In Chapters 9, 10, and 11 of *The Roaring 2000s*, we covered in depth the long-term shift in population (Figure 4.28) wherein information technologies are allowing more people to live in higher-quality resort and exurban areas outside of today's urban and suburban areas. Lower-priced homes, less congestion, and more recreation are the drawing cards. The areas just outside of major cities as well as vacation, resort, and college towns should continue to grow faster than suburban areas and attract more households as telecommuting through broadband Internet increases and home prices continue to be more attractive in many of these areas. This trend is a broad trend like the shift from cities to suburbs, starting in the early 1900s, but accelerating for many decades into the 1970s. These trends, along with the stronger demographics of vacation and retirement home buying, will make these areas more attractive for developers and buyers/investors as home buying and price trends start to slow in the coming years. These areas will be even more attractive as havens of escape during the great downturn from 2010 into around 2023.

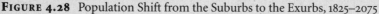

FIGURE 4.28 Population Shift from the Suburbs to the Exurbs, 1825–2075

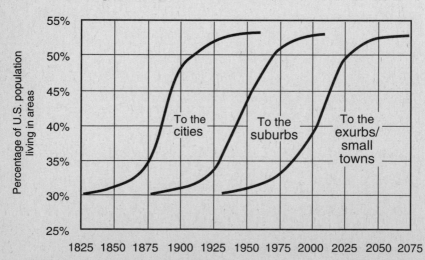

CAN HOUSING AND REAL ESTATE
PEAK AHEAD OF THE ECONOMY?

A peak in housing starts and housing prices occurred midway into the Roaring Twenties boom likely for the same reasons as today: the momentum in house buying peaks demographically ahead of overall spending. The number of housing starts (Figure 4.29) peaked in 1925, five years ahead of the downturn in the overall economy in 1930, and declined into 1933. House prices drifted down mildly from 1925 into 1929 while the economy was strong and then fell more dramatically into the worst years of the Depression, from 1930 to 1933. We don't have very good data on national housing prices back then, but the most reliable data are in Figure 4.30, which shows the asking price of houses in Washington, D.C., from 1918 to 1941.

After peaking in 1925, prices fell modestly, by about 7%, into 1929, and then fell by another 21% from 1929 into 1933, or 26% from the peak in 1925. Note that this chart represents asking prices. Selling prices could have been substantially lower in such a horrific downturn. And if the median or typical house fell by 26% from 1925 to 1933, you can be sure that high-end homes fell by closer to 40% to 60%! By the end of the Great Depression in early 1942, home prices had still not recovered to levels seen at the top of the boom in 1929 or 1930 and were still well below the peak prices in 1925. Average home prices fell 40% in Japan from 1992 to 2004.

FIGURE 4.29 Housing Starts, 1918–1941

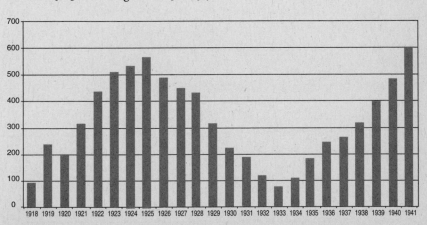

Source: "Historical Statistics of the U.S.: Colonial Times to 1970," U.S. Bureau of the Census, 1975.

Figure 4.30 Median Asking Price for Existing Houses in Washington, D.C., 1918–1941

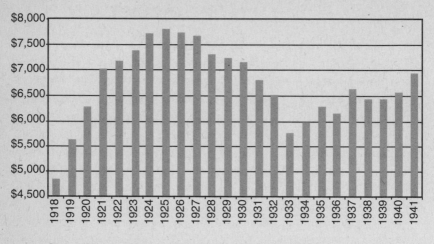

Source: "Historical Statistics of the U.S.: Colonial Times to 1970," U.S. Bureau of the Census, 1975.

We don't have demographic data on the peak in spending or on home buying back in the early 1900s or even into the 1960s. But it is clear that the average life expectancy and average peak in spending was much earlier back then. It is also clear that the momentum in home buying and building peaked about five years ahead of overall spending and economic activity. And current demographic data show that the momentum peaks around age 41, but that the peak in overall house pricing and demand occurs more around age 49 or 50 in line with the peak in overall spending. Hence, it is likely that home prices could start to flatten or fall a bit in the next few years and even decline modestly overall for the rest of this decade, despite a booming economy.

But it is perhaps more likely that housing prices will flatten or fall a bit in the next two years or so and then rise modestly, especially at the very high and low ends of the markets, after 2005 according to the demographic trends we have presented in this chapter. Since 1994 the rate of home ownership has risen from 64% to 68%. It could easily rise another 2% to 4% to 70% to 72% by the end of this decade, adding 2 to 4 million in new home demand over the next six years or so as the continued, but lower-volume, trade up buying cycles for lower-income households in this report would suggest. But this will tend to bolster the low-income end of the market more than the middle-income market, which should remain more flat.

Upper-end homes should decline the most between late 2005 and 2007, but should get a modest boost from the bubble in stock prices from 2005 to 2009 and a resurgence in vacation home buying into ages 48 and 65.

Summary of Single-Family Housing Prices: Taking into account the general economic trends, it appears likely that price gains for residential home prices will at a minimum grow much slower in the coming years and could even fall modestly. The strongest momentum should be in the lower end of the market, and the greatest slowing and/or decline is likely to occur in the higher-end markets in urban and suburban areas. The upper-end markets may make a modest comeback in the bubble stage of the economy between late 2007 and 2010, when affluent households feel more flush. The vacation, retirement, and exurban home markets are likely to fare better and represent the only healthy part of the overall residential home market.

But always remember that real estate markets are very local as well. Areas that are attracting large migration due to quality of life or affordability, or that have a limited amount of land available for development, are likely to continue to appreciate despite slowing national trends in demographics. But the appreciation in hotter markets, such as Las Vegas, Phoenix, Myrtle Beach, and southern Florida, are still likely to be less robust due to the slowing demographic trends, after declines from 2006 on.

If you are thinking about selling your home in the coming years, certainly do so by 2010 or early 2011 at the very latest.

Large, upscale urban/suburban homes will be hit the worst between 2011 and 2014, and they won't see a substantial rise again for years as the demographic trends in trade-up homes will be pointing down into around 2016 and the economy will continue to be weak into 2023 or so due to broad demographic trends in spending.

Continuing Hot Spots: Vacation, Resort, and Retirement Areas

Six percent of all homes and a growing percentage of home sales are of second or vacation homes. New data from the Consumer Expenditure Survey strongly suggest that instead of simply peaking in the early 50s (as rough statistics we have collected in the past would suggest), there is a dual surge in vacation home buying with a first peak in the late 40s and a second higher peak in the late 50s and early 60s. Hence, this market has much stronger de-mographic growth in the coming years. The survey also shows that vacation home buyers are not largely an affluent market but are spread across the in-come spectrum. This is probably due to the popularity of time-shares.

Figure 4.31 shows total purchases of vacation homes. Note that the data here are very scant due to the small percentage of buyers. There is a first major surge that peaks around age 48 (in 2009 for the peak baby boomers) and a second set of surges that peaks between ages 58 and 65 (in 2016 to 2026). Hence, the vacation home market should remain strong into the end of this decade, suffer some decline with overall economic and housing trends beginning around 2010, and pick up again by 2015 or 2016. The best time to buy a vacation home would either be now, when mortgage rates are very low, or after the crash and downturn, around 2013 to 2014, after which prices are likely to appreciate again.

Figure 4.32 shows the average purchase for the entire population and gives us a better idea of the size of the market over time. Figure 4.33 is skewed a bit by the larger number of peak baby boomers in their late 30s and early 40s. The largest volume of overall buying occurs in the late 50s and early 60s, as do the highest prices. The market size in the late 50s to early 60s is about double the size as the late 40s. Hence, this market clearly has the greatest difference in demographics looking forward. Assuming age 63 to be the peak, a lag on the rising baby-boom birth trends from 1937 to 1961 would show a rising wave of peak vacation-home buyers from 2000 into 2024. And prices in this market have been accelerating since 2000.

FIGURE 4.31 Total Vacation-Home Purchases, by Age

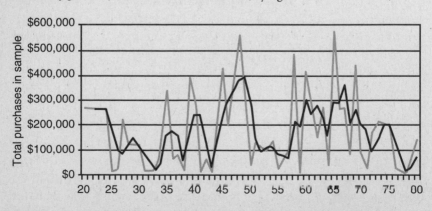

Source: U.S. Bureau of Labor Statistics, Consumer Expenditure Survey, 2000.

Figure 4.32 Average Vacation-Home Purchase Price, by Age

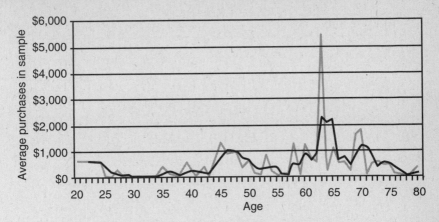

Source: U.S. Bureau of Labor Statistics, Consumer Expenditure Survey, 2000.

Mortgage interest on vacation homes (Figure 4.33) has two peaks, at age 41 and at ages 56–58. Only 52% of vacation-home buyers use mortgages versus 94% for recent primary residence buyers, and the older buyers at the peak of the vacation-home cycle in the late 50s are even less likely to finance such a purchase as they receive inheritances and gain higher discretionary income and savings. Hence, the mortgage interest chart understates the relative size of the vacation-home market and especially understates the magnitude of the peak spending trend into the late 50s and mid-60s, which is clearest in Figure 4.33.

The median age of vacation-home owners is 61, which would also confirm a much later peak in buying, but that is also reflective of the fact that most people keep these homes well into retirement even if they buy them earlier in the cycle. Baby boomers will also be retiring in increasing numbers between 2000 and 2024. There is an exact overlap in the rising cycle of vacation-home buying and retirement as well as between attractive areas for vacation homes and retirement. Hence, the retirement trends will only bolster the resort and vacation markets. And retirement communities and developments will offer strong growth for developers for decades to come.

Figure 4.34 shows the median prices of vacation homes since 1989. After recovering from the 1991 recession and real estate crunch into 1993, vacation-home prices have been advancing more rapidly since 1995 and have gone up dramatically from 2000 to 2005 despite the economic slowdown and stock crash, which is in line with the beginning of the vacation-home spending wave from 2000 into 2024 on a sixty-three-year lag in

FIGURE 4.33   Mortgage Interest Paid Annually on Vacation Homes, by Age

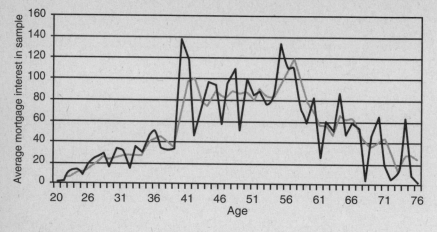

Source: U.S. Bureau of Labor Statistics, Consumer Expenditure Survey, 2000.

births. We have been forecasting for years that the vacation-home market would be stronger than the trade-up home market in this decade, and that clearly seems to be the case thus far.

Prices in the vacation- and retirement-home markets have also weakened in many areas in response to the overall slowing in home markets that we anticipate from 2006 to 2007, but there is likely to be a wider divergence between growth and appreciation in vacation markets than in primary

FIGURE 4.34   Median Price of Vacation Homes, 1989–2001

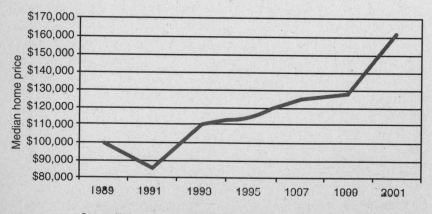

Source: National Association of Realtors.

homes after 2007. The stock market bubble we are projecting for 2005 to 2010 will also strengthen the demand for vacation homes in particular, as people will feel wealthier and more able to make such discretionary purchases. The states with the highest percentage of vacation homes (which should mean stronger home-price trends in those states in the coming years) are, in order: Maine, Vermont, New Hampshire, Alaska, Delaware, Florida, Arizona, Wisconsin, Montana, and Hawaii.

Figure 4.35 shows the number of people who will turn age 62 in the next two decades. This lag on the birth index is the best proxy for the growth in vacation- and retirement-home buying which will be the strongest market looking forward since baby boomers passed their peak in family-home buying by late 2003. As you can see, the demand for these types of homes and the growth of vacation, resort, and retirement areas will continue even in the great downturn we forecast to come after 2010. In Chapter 5 we will look at how you can use local demographic data to determine the best areas for investing in vacation and retirement homes and which local markets will benefit from these trends. We will even show you how you can scout out areas that have people with lifestyles similar to yours for greater compatibility.

FIGURE 4.35 Growth in Number of Retirees, 1980–2020: Immigration-Adjusted Births Lagged 62 Years

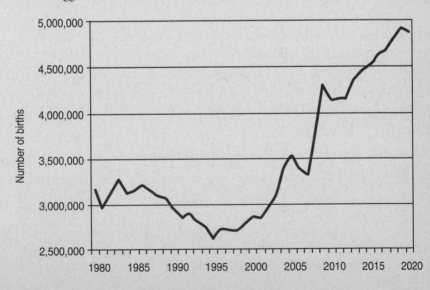

Summary of Vacation, Resort, and Retirement Home Trends: The vacation-home market will continue to grow faster than primary residences, especially after 2003, when the demographic demand for primary homes slows in the face of rising mortgage rates and overbuilding. There should be a near-term slowing in vacation-home prices as well in 2006. There is likely to be a stronger resurgence in demand from late 2007 to 2010 as the economy enters another bubble stage in the stock market and the third and largest wave of baby boomers peaks in its first major vacation-home buying surge. If you have a vacation home you are thinking of selling, 2010 would be the optimum time for allowing appreciation but dodging the early and severe stages of the next economic downturn. The projected bubble burst and demographic decline in overall spending that should hit between late 2010 or 2011 and 2012 or 2014 should at first hit discretionary vacation-home markets hard, especially on the upper end. The best time to buy or invest in a vacation home would be during any weakness into 2007, well ahead of the peak of the boom—or around late 2013 to 2014, when prices are down but there are still many years of rising demand into the second major set of surges that should occur especially between 2016 and 2024 or 2026.

TRENDS IN INVESTMENT AND COMMERCIAL REAL ESTATE

We will now briefly look at the areas of real estate that many of us look to more for pure investment in our investment portfolios, as opposed to living purposes. We will look at how demographics drive residential rental properties; office, industrial, and retail space; and hotels. Note that these areas are more of a business, which requires a more sophisticated level of local supply and demand and market segmentation analysis that is outside the scope of this book. But you can be aware of which sectors are most favored by general demographic trends if you are involved in these sectors of real estate or include them in your investment portfolio.

The Next Hot Spot: Multifamily and Rental Properties

The echo baby boom is moving into its family formation and marriage cycle, which correlates with the peak in rental expenditures for apartments and multifamily housing. Figure 4.36 shows spending on rental housing, which peaks between ages 24 and 26. Figure 4.37 shows how multifamily housing peaked in 1985 and then declined despite a booming economy and falling mortgage rates. The peak in the baby-boom cycle would have hit by

FIGURE 4.36 Average Annual Rental Expenditure, by Age

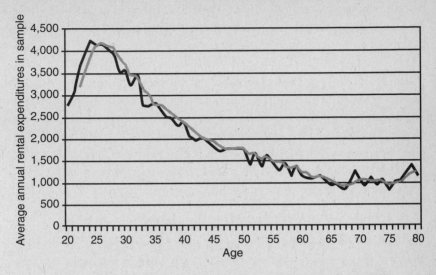

Source: U.S. Bureau of Labor Statistics, Consumer Expenditure Survey, 2000.

FIGURE 4.37 The Multifamily Housing Cycle, 1969–2001

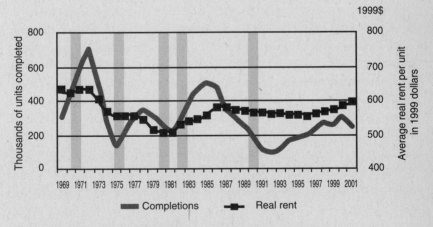

Source: Torto Wheaton Research, an independent research unit of
CB Richard Ellis. www.tortowheatonresearch.com.

1986 on a twenty-five-year lag to the peak births in 1961. The trends have
been modestly up in recent years but should be stronger ahead. A twenty-
six-year lag today to account for the rising average age of marriage would
project rising demand from the echo-baby-boom generation between 2003

and 2016 or 2017. The rising affordability of homes may cut into this growth a bit during the boom but will conversely accelerate the demand for rental apartments in the downturn, when people tend to feel less confident about buying a home.

Summary Trends for Apartments and Multifamily Housing: This market should be stronger than residential home sales and prices for the rest of the boom into 2009 and should fare substantially better than general home sales and prices in the downturn from 2010 to 2017. Taking over or building low-cost rental properties after 2012 could be a good opportunity in the downturn, as well as buying failing low-end housing developments and offering them for rent between 2013 and 2017.

The Outlook for Office and Industrial Properties

The market for offices and commercial and industrial real estate tends to correlate with the size of the workforce it houses and secondarily with the strength of the economy and employment rates. The average age of workforce entry today is 20.5. A lag on the birth index for the average age of workforce entry would project a peak of the baby-boom office and industrial trend around 1980 to 1981, then slowing trends into 1995 or 1996 and then rising trends again with the echo baby boom into around 2010 to 2011. Figure 4.38 shows the office cycle and Figure 4.39 shows the industrial cycle, both of which peaked in 1985. That's a few years later than the demographic cycles would have projected. But that can be explained by the severe unemployment that occurred in the twin recessions of 1980 and 1982. These markets were slowed by that downturn, but the sharp rise in employment that followed in the recovery from 1983 to 1985 would have caused them to peak later, as they both did in 1985. They then declined in line with the demographic trends despite a strengthening economy.

Although both of these cycles are pointing up into 2010 or 2011 with rising echo-boom entry into the workforce, there are three factors that will affect them, causing lower growth than would be expected, especially in such a booming economy. First, the baby-boom generation is starting to retire in rising numbers and is increasingly offsetting the echo-baby-boomer entry rates. Our Long-Term Inflation Forecast, covered in Chapter 6, projects the percentage growth of the workforce for 20-year-olds entering (on a three-year lag) and 63-year-olds exiting and is a better proxy for the office and industrial markets than a mere lag for workforce entry. We have made one change here in Figure 4.41 to reflect the potential for commercial real estate markets; we take out the three-year lag for expenditures on new

Figure 4.38   The Office Cycle, 1967–2001

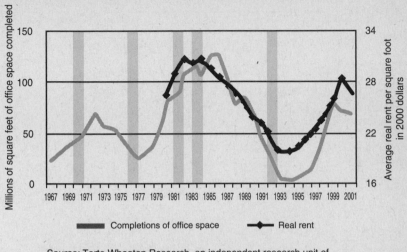

Completions of office space   ◆ Real rent

Source: Torto Wheaton Research, an independent research unit of
CB Richard Ellis. www.tortowheatonresearch.com.

Figure 4.39   The Industrial Cycle, 1967–2001

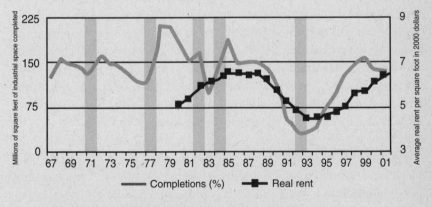

Completions (%)   ■ Real rent

Source: Torto Wheaton Research, an independent research unit of
CB Richard Ellis. www.tortowheatonresearch.com.

workers before they become productive that we use to correlate with inflation in the Inflation Indicator. Figure 4.40 would suggest that office and industrial markets, after rising more strongly with the jobs recovery in late
2003 and 2004, should then grow slower than the economy.

The second factor is the steady shift to part-time and full-time home-

FIGURE 4.40   Workforce Growth Forecast, 1950–2030

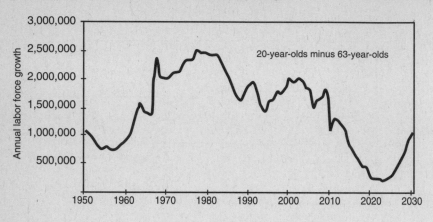

Source: U.S. Census Bureau and U.S. Bureau of Labor Statistics.

based employment that is a by-product of the technology revolution and the new economy. This trend is allowing businesses to expand with less office space than in past booms. The third factor hits in the downturn from 2010 to 2023 due to the sharp rise in unemployment that will accompany this mega-shakeout in the business sectors, similar to what occurred in the 1930s. Unemployment hit a peak of 25% in 1933, at the lowest point of the Great Depression. Although we don't expect unemployment to get that high, we will surely see unemployment rates worse than in the recession of 1982, and we would expect at least 15% unemployment in the downturn after 2009. Hence, the office and industrial real estate markets are likely to be among the worst hit in the downturn after 2009 or 2010.

Retail and Shopping Centers

The retail and shopping center markets are very similar to the apartment and multifamily markets, as they have to expand to meet the shopping needs of new households as we get married around age 25 to 26. As with the office and industrial markets, both of which benefit from rising employment levels in a strong economy, the retail market benefits from higher spending when there is continued growth in broader demographic spending trends, as we are forecasting into at least 2009. In Figure 4.41 we show a twenty-six-year lag for new-household formation as a general proxy for the more specific demographic trends driving the need for retail stores and malls. The echo baby boom should cause accelerating trends from 2002 into 2016 or 2017 (by then the average age of marriage is likely to be closer to 27).

FIGURE 4.41 Twenty-six-Year Lag for Peak Trends in Retail, 1937–2027

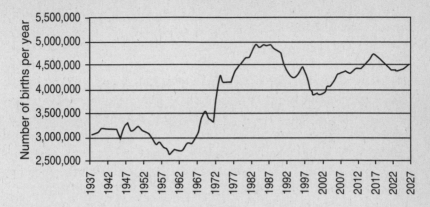

Again the downturn will impact this trend after 2009 or 2010. But the general spending and economic trends continue to point up into at least 2009, while the economy is still booming. Figure 4.42 shows the trends in retail real estate growth. The cycle first peaked in 1986, twenty-five years after the peak of the baby-boom birth index for the average age of marriage back then. The one caveat here—and this might explain why the growth in the retail market has underperformed the rising rental trends in recent years—is that new technologies continue to improve the efficiency of retail

FIGURE 4.42 The Retail Cycle, 1969–2001

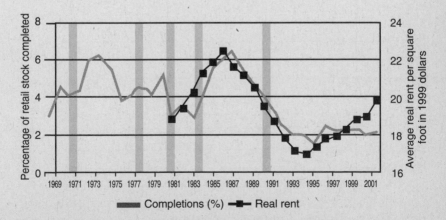

Source: Torto Wheaton Research, an independent research unit of CB Richard Ellis. www.tortowheatonresearch.com.

space and Internet commerce is slowly but surely replacing some of the bricks and mortar, and that should continue and even accelerate in the coming years and decades.

Hotels

Hotels, not including those in resort areas, which tend to follow more closely the vacation travel trends that peak around age 54, tend to simply correlate with the economy and the Spending Wave for peak spending. The hotel cycle in Figure 4.43 first peaked in 1987 along with the stock market peak but quickly bottomed in 1988 and has turned up ever since. This trend should peak around 2009 or 2010 and then turn down with the Spending Wave into 2023 or so.

Resort areas and hotels should grow more dramatically over the rest of this decade as the economy booms and travel comes back due to decreasing fear of terrorism. The peak in leisure travel at around age 54 (Figure 4.44) should keep this sector stronger than average into around 2015 or 2016. This sector stays buoyant into around age 62, so there should not be a sharp downturn after 2016. But the broader economic downturn after 2009 or 2010 will certainly affect this sector, especially in the early stages from 2011 to 2014. Terrorist threats, which are likely to increase again in a deteriorating worldwide economic environment, are likely to hurt this sector even more from 2011 to 2023.

FIGURE 4.43 The Hotel Cycle, 1971–2001

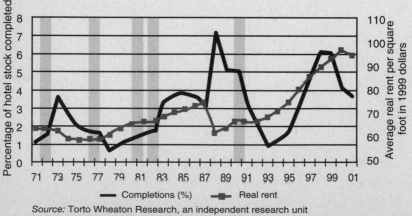

Source: Torto Wheaton Research, an independent research unit of CB Richard Ellis. www.tortowheatonresearch.com.

FIGURE 4.44 Leisure Travel Expenditures, by Age

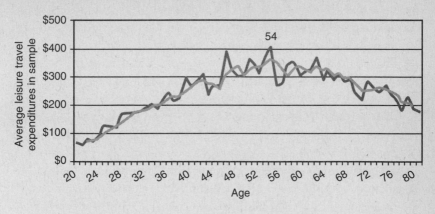

Source: U.S. Bureau of Labor Statistics, Consumer Expenditure Survey, 2000.

BRIEF SUMMARY OF ALL REAL ESTATE MARKETS

Into 2005 the vacation/retirement-home markets have generally fared the best, followed by apartments and multifamily housing and the lower end of the residential markets. The upper-end residential market should slow the most in 2006 and will likely continue to slow the most into 2007. But the luxury-home markets could see another minibubble into 2010, and these homes should be sold between late 2009 and 2010 as they will fare the worst in the great downturn. In the commercial arena, hotels should fare the best followed by retail. Office and industrial space should fare well at first in the recovery in 2004 and 2005 and then underperform for the rest of the decade but remain buoyant. The office and industrial sectors should not be a major focus for investment looking forward and should also be sold by late 2009 as they will be hit hard by the ensuing unemployment trends.

During the downturn from around 2011 to 2023, upper-end residential, office, and industrial real estate should see the strongest declines. Affordable apartments and low-end single-family housing should be the most buoyant. The vacation, resort, and retirement sectors will be hit hard at first but show the greatest potential for recovery after around 2014. The two best strategies for the downturn would be to buy distressed real estate in vacation/resort/retirement areas and apartment/low-end housing sectors and refinance such properties at lower mortgage rates to play the rebound in the stronger demographic sectors once the worst of the downturn and crash are over by late 2014. And finally, exurban areas and resort areas will continue to grow despite the demise of many suburban/urban markets, during the final stages of this boom and especially in the great downturn. But they will also get hit in the general downturn at first. Developers and households would do well to target these areas rather than the overbuilt urban/suburban areas that will continue to slow due to demographic trends.

Now that we've looked at the factors that will impact your real estate holdings, in Chapter 5 we will extend our demographic forecasting tools to looking at how your business, your life, your children, your philanthropic interests, and your retirement will be affected by the trends ahead. Although you have your own life cycle and plans, the economy has its life cycle and plans—and it will affect your life in major ways. In the next chapter we will look at a new dimension in financial planning.

Chapter 5

LIFE PLANNING

How the Economy's Life Cycle Will Intersect with Your Own

How the Economic Cycle Will Affect Your Life and Your Business— Over the Rest of Your Lifetime

In Chapters 1 through 3 we showed how long-term trends, including in the stock market, are far more predictable than we have been led to believe by economists. In Chapter 4 we showed how those trends will affect your home and real estate investments for decades to come. In Chapters 6 and 7 we will show how demographic trends will affect different sectors of your investment portfolios and retirement plans and we will have some very critical insights there. But here is the most important question: How will these trends affect your life: your business, your career, where and how you retire, the value of your house, where you live, your children's education and career choices, your hobbies, whether you are starting, buying, or selling a business, your estate and tax planning, and even your charitable giving?

The whole point of building wealth is to give you more choices in life and create a better quality of life. The point of this chapter is to show you that you can't just consider your own life cycle and needs when planning for the key events of your life as most good financial planners already do. Why? The economic life cycle can and will have a major impact on those decisions.

Let me give just one example. Say you are 46 in 2004 and are planning to sell your business when you turn 54 so that you can move to southern

Colorado, where you would do part-time business consulting and spend more time skiing, thus creating a greater incentive for your post-college-age kids to come visit more often. The problem with that natural life goal is that you would be 54 in 2012. The economy and the stock market are very likely to be in a strong downward trend from 2010 into 2023 with the worst part of the crash in stock prices and real estate values setting in by 2012. You could probably get much more for your business if you sell it in 2008 or 2009, four years earlier than your planned date, near the top of the boom. You could probably get 30% to 50% more for your urban/suburban home by 2009. In fact, you may not even be able to sell your home at any reasonable price in 2012.

You could sell the business in 2009 or 2010 and then decide whether to move to Colorado then or to wait a few years. The best bet, taking into account the economic cycle, would be to sell your house by 2009 and either move then or begin searching for a new home in Colorado. It might be best to rent for a few years until you find where you really prefer to live by spending more time "hanging out." Then buy your new house when home prices are likely falling strongly into 2012 to 2014. Waiting until 2013 to 2014 will probably bring you the best price on your new resort home with much lower mortgage rates to boot. Why? Our inflation forecast (in Chapter 6) is calling for deflation in prices and falling interest rates starting in 2010, and especially from 2014 on. Combining your life goals with the economic cycle could allow you to semiretire with two to four times the assets and to buy that dream home for as much as 50% less and finance it at mortgage rates you would not dream of today!

THE ECONOMY'S LIFE CYCLE IS ABOUT THE SAME AS OUR OWN: EIGHTY YEARS

If we look back at Chapter 1, new economies emerge every other generation, or about every eighty years. That is about the same as the average human life cycle today. And the economy has four very distinct seasons, as we show in Figure 5.1: Innovation Stage (with inflation), Growth Boom, Shakeout (with deflation), and Maturity Boom—much like youth, adulthood, midlife, and retirement for human beings or like spring, summer, fall, and winter in terms of seasons. These long-term seasons and the demographic-driven trends within them that cause innovation, technology adoption, GDP growth, inflation, stock market booms and busts, borrowing, investing, and home buying, have the capacity to have a great impact on your life

FIGURE 5.1 The Four Seasons of the Eighty-Year Economic Cycle

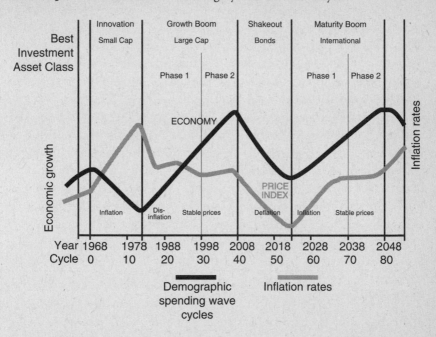

decisions. The worst time to sell a house or a business would be during the Shakeout Stage from about 2010 to 2023, especially toward the end. Conversely, that would be one of the best times to buy a house or a business. 2010 to 2023 would also be the worst time for your kids to be graduating from college and entering their careers. That would also be the worst time to rely on the stock market to grow your investment or retirement accounts. Bonds, Asian equities, defensive stocks, and low-cost real estate rental properties would be much better.

The models for forecasting the economy, inflation, large-cap stocks (adoption of new brands and technologies), and small-cap stocks (innovation of new brands and technologies) are great tools for looking ahead to better plan key life events and changes as we will cover in more depth in Chapters 6 and 7. But we will introduce tools and principles for planning your life in this chapter since clarifying your life goals and personal assets and income needs over time is the first and most important step in effective financial planning. Getting a realistic view of your personal future requires having a clear overview of the different seasons and when they approximately will begin and end, as shown in Figure 5.1.

The Innovation Stage is characterized by radical innovation of new technologies, products and lifestyles as well as rising inflation and worsening recessions in the economy. The last such season occurred from 1969 into 1982. The Growth Boom sees the mainstream adoption of those innovations with a race for leadership to see which companies will dominate the new industries. This season is characterized by rising productivity, a booming economy and stock market, and falling inflation rates. The last such season occurred from 1902 into 1929. The present Growth Boom started in late 1982 and will likely end between late 2009 and early 2010.

The Shakeout Stage is the worst, like the Great Depression from 1930 into 1942. It sees dramatic business failures and layoffs with deflation in prices and a more dramatically declining economy. The next depression season will hit from early to late 2010 into 2022–2023. Given the fact that we may be peaking demographically from an even longer-term economic and stock boom that started back in the late 1700s (as we showed in Chapter 2), this Shakeout Stage could be the worst in our history and we may not see new highs in the stock market in our lifetimes.

> The most important thing you can do today is to leverage this boom to prepare for this very difficult downturn ahead in your career and investment strategies and then sell most of your growth investments and real estate by 2010.

The Maturity Boom is the last season and the most stable and rewarding for most people. You get a less chaotic boom with incremental innovations increasingly adopted from the Shakeout Stage. There is mildly rising inflation and the full flowering of the technologies, lifestyles, and business models that emerged with the new economic cycle. These are like the "happy days" of the 1950s and 1960s. The last Maturity Boom occurred from late 1942 through 1968. Note that it started with rising inflation and World War II, but then mellowed out into the greatest decades of mainstream prosperity and shared values in U.S. history.

The next Maturity Boom should occur from 2023 or 2024 into at least 2042 and likely into the late 2040s or early 2050s. That will be our kids' boom in which all of the new technologies, lifestyles, and business models emerging in recent decades will be commonly accepted and well integrated into our society and lifestyles. Our kids grew up with computers and the Internet as we grew up driving cars and watching TV. But that boom is not likely to rival the baby-boom-driven bull market in stocks from 1982 to 2009 either in economic growth rates or stock returns. The best opportunities will come from the new leading countries and population centers in

Southeast Asia and India, where migration to cities and demographics will be stronger.

The most important point here is that each of these long-term seasons has very different trends in innovation, economic growth, and inflation. They favor very different investments and have a huge impact on our life-styles, careers, and businesses. Nothing is more critical to our long-term life and investment planning, not even our own life cycles, as the economic life cycle is much bigger in the whole scheme of things.

LEARNING TO "THINK DEMOGRAPHICS"

Before we look at all of the impacts of the economic life cycle on your life, let's start by teaching two simple tools for learning to "think demographics" when looking at your life and future from all angles: investment, career planning, personal real estate, business strategy, children, and life goals. There are two things you need to understand to quickly and simply calcu-late the economic impacts on any future events you are considering once you have a basic understanding of the four seasons. The first is that you need to know the key birth surges and declines that have occurred in the past decades that will cause rising or falling trends in different economic and human activities in the future. We show the key cycles in Table 5.1. If you are a financial planner and you work with clients often, you should memorize these key cycles in births. Others can simply refer to this chart when making future projections.

The second tool is to know the key demographic life events that drive the most important economic trends summarized in Table 5.2. Workforce entry (on a three-year lag) drives inflation, and innovation follows a simi-

TABLE 5.1 Key Surges and Declines in Births

	UPTRENDS	DOWNTRENDS
Bob Hope generation	1909–1914	1917–1919
	1920–1921	1924–1933/36
Baby boomers	1937–1943	1944–1945
	1946–1947	1948–1950
	1951–1957/61	1962–1968
	1969–1970	1971–1973/76
Echo baby boomers	1977–1990	1991–1996

TABLE 5.2 Key Lags for Major Economic Impacts*

LIFE EVENT	AVERAGE AGE
Workforce entry	20
Inflation (three-year lag on workforce entry)	23
Innovation	23
Family formation	26
Starter-home purchase	31
Peak rate of borrowing	32
Peak housing expenditure	42
Peak debt levels	42
Peak spending	48
Peak rate of investment	54
Peak of power in business and politics	58
Retirement (disinflation)	63
Peak net worth	64
Peak of philanthropy	65

*Note: Most of these ages are moving forward about one year every decade.

lar twenty-three-year lag, or what we call "the yuppie factor," as our most educated and innovative people enter their life and career cycles after college. Marriage at age 26 accelerates economic spending at the greatest rate and drives apartment rentals and purchases of low-end durable goods. Having children, typically in our late 20s, greatly changes our life and spending priorities, as well as our "family values." Consumer-trend chronicler Faith Popcorn became famous for tracking and forecasting the "cocooning" trend among baby boomers in the 1980s and 1990s—the hiding out from overwhelming changes in the world. We attribute that trend more simply to baby boomers having children and becoming more family-oriented in that time period.

At age 31 the average person buys his or her first house and debt grows at the fastest rate as he or she furnishes that house. By age 42 we have the highest overall debt levels just after we purchase our largest house between age 37 and 42 and furnish it. The peak in spending that drives overall economic growth is at age 46 to 50 today, or about 48 on average. The peak rate of investing annually is around age 54 and the peak of our cumulative net worth is at around age 64. In between we see the peak of our career and power cycles to change institutions, business models, and work at around age 58. And at age 63 the average person retires today. We expect the average retirement age to move forward at least a year every decade into the future and perhaps faster as baby boomers realize that they will live longer than their parents and decide to be more active in retirement through longer careers, part-time work, and philanthropic activities.

In addition to these key summary trends, you can approximate the peak spending in any product area that your business may be involved in and similarly lag forward from the key birth surges to see when the growth of your business will be strongest and weakest in addition to seeing the broader economic cycles. You can access spending by age on 190 product categories from the Consumer Expenditure Survey at www.bls.gov/cex/#data. We summarize the key spending trends by age in greater detail for most major products and services on our Web site at www.hsdent.com. Click on "Key Concepts" and then "Consumer Product Trends." However, we advise businesses to survey their customers directly to get the most accurate read on what age represents the peak in buying of your products as well as how that varies by different income and market segments, which can be different than the average statistics. It is also important to note that these trends are typically moving forward about a year every decade as a general rule. Hence, the peak in spending will be around age 49 in 2010, 50 in 2020, and so on.

To summarize: You can take the peak age for any major economic trend and lag the birth index forward to see approximately when such trends will be rising or falling decades ahead. Then you can see how those trends will affect the times in your own life cycle when you are planning to make major decisions or changes and see how changing economic trends will affect those decisions.

How Demographics and the Economic Cycle Affect Your Business and Career

Let's look at another brief example to show how powerful these simple tools can be. Let's say your business is managing apartment complexes for young couples. To see when your business would boom or bust, you would lag the recent birth surge for the echo boom from 1977–1990 (from Table 5.1) for rising trends in family formation (from Table 5.2) and peak real estate rentals at age 26 (from Figure 5.2). That would project a growing market for your properties and rising rentals from 2003 to 2017. You would use age 27 for family formation for projections a decade out given that the average age of marriage is moving forward about a year every decade. So the very simple calculation would be 1977 + 26 to get 2003 for the beginning of that growth market, and 1990 + 27 to get 2017 for the approximate peak.

But then you would logically consider that if the overall economy is

FIGURE 5.2   Annual Apartment Rental Expenditures, by Age

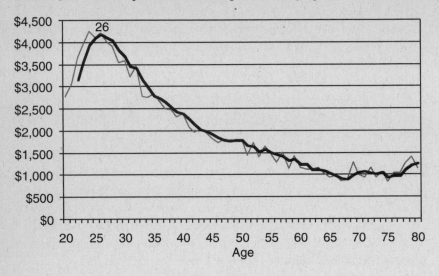

scheduled to decline from late 2009 or 2010 into around 2023 due to the peak spending cycle for the overall economy, that should inevitably cause weaker than anticipated growth from 2010 to 2017 even in an upward cycle for rental properties. The truth is that there may be rising demand for rentals with rising unemployment causing fewer people to be able to buy a home, but rents on your properties would certainly fall. With both a bad economy and a slowing of household formations, the apartment market should be downright horrible from 2018 into 2023. So it's time to expand and prepare for growth, as well as anticipate higher income in your business, from 2003 to 2009. But your business could face substantial challenges from 2010 on and major declines from 2018 on. On the other hand, if you were to offer low-cost rental properties in the downturn after 2009 or 2010, when fewer young families will be able to afford to buy a house, you might prosper even in the downturn. You could even expand your business and market share in that time period by using your successful strategy and cash flow to buy out competitors at bargain-basement prices.

But you would also want to look at the outlook for inflation and interest rates, as your mortgage costs are one of the key expenses in your business. The Inflation Forecast, which we will cover in Chapter 6, predicts continued falling inflation and long-term mortgage rates from 2005 into early 2006, mildly rising inflation and mortgage rates from early 2006 into 2009, then dramatically falling rates again from 2010 on. That means you would be better off keeping your present mortgage from late 2004 into early 2006, and then refinancing to lock in a lower fixed rate from early 2006 into 2009 or 2010. You could then consider switching back to a variable-rate mortgage in late 2009 or paying off your mortgage out of your profits to enhance your ability to lower your fixed costs and sustain your business in the downturn.

But here's the best strategy: don't expand your investment in properties in the latter years of this decade. In fact, sell off some of your properties by 2009 to create excess cash and a very liquid balance sheet. Then you could have both cash and borrowing power during the early stages of the downturn to buy rental properties or properties that could be converted to rental properties at greatly depreciated costs and then offer very-low-rent apartments to echo boomers and other people struggling in the downturn. Then you could start selling off those properties when the rental market is likely to weaken again after 2018. As much as the banks will tighten up on credit in the downturn, they would prefer to have you take over a failing company with your solid financial position than have it go bankrupt. So opportunities will abound!

If you were looking to sell your business, 2008 or 2009 would likely be the best time. But even if you decided to keep your apartment-rental business into the downturn because you thought you could continue to prosper with a low-cost rental strategy in a rising demographic market for rentals, you should again strongly consider selling the business by 2018, when rental demands are likely to start falling and the economy is likely to remain weak and get even weaker into 2023.

Let's take another brief example. Let's say you own and have built up a camping equipment business that has expanded to three stores in your metropolitan area over the last ten years. You now have a business that is not just a mom-and-pop operation but you have already started to prove that you can expand this business into similar demographic areas of consumer demand, both in your area and into other potential areas in your region and even potentially into other areas around the country. How will demographic cycles affect your business? Demographic cycles in Figure 5.3 clearly suggest that camping equipment sales have two major surges, the first into ages 23–24 for young people before they settle into their career and family cycles, and the second into around ages 54–55, the peak years of leisure travel for maturing adults.

Your business will be heavily affected by both generation spending cycles—the baby boom and the echo baby boom—in the coming years and decades. If we take the overall peak at around age 54, baby boomers would be in a rising tide of spending from 1991 (1937 + 54) to 2015. The rising tide

FIGURE 5.3 Purchases of Camping Equipment, by Age

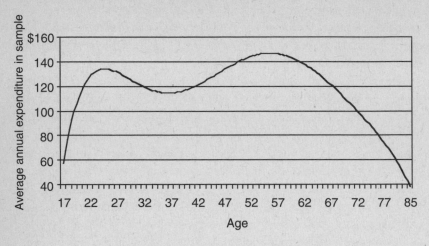

of the echo baby boomers would be moving into the first strong surge in spending from 2000 (1977 + 23) into 2013 (1990 + 23). After 2015, both of these cycles would be pointing down, as would the general economy. Up until 2009 or 2010, the economy will be rising as well. So sometime between 2009 and 2015 would be the time to sell this business, or at least brace for a major downturn in your industry.

Let's say that you are getting older and your children don't have any interest in your business. Your best bet would be to sell by late 2009 while the economy is still strong and your business sector is very strong. Cash out and plan where you want to relocate for retirement, or perhaps consider if you want to open a store in one of the mountain areas farther out where you plan to retire. That area is more likely to be growing in the downturn, when more baby boomers retreat to exurban areas, as they get older and buy vacation homes or retire.

On the other hand, let's assume that you have children who have been involved in the business and you would like to see them carry on the tradition. First, they can expect the business to do much better than most in the early years of the downturn. But after 2015, look at the slide from the decline in baby-boom buyers! You and they will have to make a hard decision about whether to carry on the business through the downturn or to sell it toward the end of the upturn and then start a new business (or buy that business back) in the downturn.

As in the apartment-rental business, you would have to adjust for the fact that the broader downturn in the economy after 2009 would adversely affect your sales to some degree. Hence, the best time to sell your business would still likely be in 2008 or 2009. But if you decided to keep your business for the long haul, the downturn would, likewise to the previous example, give you the opportunity to expand by buying other camping stores at lower prices in the downturn. Since the camping equipment business would be faring better than most other businesses due to the second surge in buying into the mid-50s, you could still have the option of selling your business as late as 2015 at a reasonable price, albeit probably substantially less than if you sold in 2008 or 2009.

YOUR CHILDREN AND GRANDCHILDREN: HOW WILL THE ECONOMIC LIFE CYCLE AFFECT THEIR EDUCATION, CAREERS, AND FINANCIAL WELL-BEING?

Now let's start to consider the most important factor in our lives: our children and grandchildren! Let's say, for simplicity's sake, you have only one child and at the end of 2004 he is about to turn sixteen and will apply for his driver's learning permit in the coming year, which is scary enough. He will graduate from high school in mid-2007. If he were to go on to college as many kids do, he would be scheduled to graduate in mid-2011. The economic cycle suggests strongly that he would be entering the job market after the beginning of the next great downturn and depression. That means it could be very difficult to find a job and to sustain employment even if he did initially find a job. Businesses will be in the strongest layoff and consolidation cycle since the early 1930s, much worse than the crash in 1974 or the dot-com and technology bust of 2000 to 2002.

Knowing this would give you and your son (or daughter) some different options to pursue. The best could simply be this. Encourage and give incentives for your son to enter college at first part-time or at night and to find a job with an up-and-coming growth company, large or small, when he gets out of high school. A smaller company is likely to be more receptive to hiring a high school graduate with strong skills and motivation than a larger company is, especially if you as parents have local contacts, or own a family business. It could be best to have your son enter a business and make inroads as he takes some college courses at night. He could grow in that business and become a more valued employee into 2009 or 2010. Then when the economy starts to turn down and layoffs are likely, he might be able to go back to college full-time and focus on the areas of education that he has found to be most critical to his advancement in the company, after having some real experience of his strengths and weaknesses and the areas he is most interested in. After 2008, his chances of getting into a good college will rise as college enrollments from the echo-baby-boom generation will be declining due to demographic trends, as you can see in Figure 5.4.

Your college costs as parents are likely to go down and your son's prospects of getting into a better school are likely to go up in the downturn that follows after 2009. His greater knowledge of the company and his interests from working in the real world for a few years are likely to hone his focus and his motivation for excelling in college. Work experience is another factor for increasing his odds of getting into a better college. All of these trends would suggest that the best time to enter college would be after the fall of 2009 and even better into 2012. Then as the economy continues to slow as he finally graduates between 2012 and 2015 (assuming he took some courses before entering) this strategy would allow him greater leverage with the company if he chooses to come back in a difficult period. And the economy should start to pick up on a more sustainable basis for the first time in 2015.

Even better, he could choose to pursue a graduate degree in his field of interest at even lower cost and with greater company and/or scholarship funding into 2014–2015. By the time he gets his graduate degree, the economy should have passed its worse consolidation and downturn since 1932 or 1933 and there should be the first real bounce in economic activity into

FIGURE 5.4 Eighteen-year Lag for College Enrollments, 2003–2018

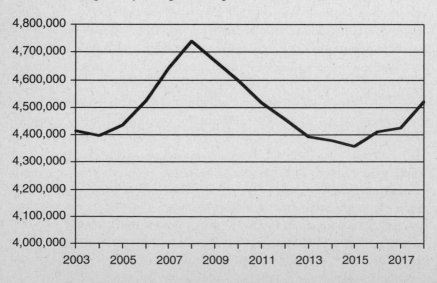

2019 or early 2020. That would be a much better time to re-enter the company, or even start a new company in the same field, and develop a new or expanded career strategy before the final downturn hits between 2020 and 2023. When looking for employment in the downturn after college, the best prospects would shift toward innovative small companies rather than large, established companies as the Innovation Stage of the echo-baby-boom generation will be rising into 2013 or 2014 and remain buoyant into 2025 or so with the final stage of a lower number of births in the echo-baby-boom cycle. Industries like health care would have the strongest demographic demand in this otherwise weaker economic period.

By entering a company and going back for greater education at the most appropriate stages of the economic life cycle, your son could optimize his education and career opportunities and with major savings to you as parents or grandparents. Those savings could foster higher education potentials than planned at substantially lower cost to you and/or your son. And again, since entrepreneurship opportunities tend to flower in downturns, your son could even have the opportunity to start his own business or a consulting relationship in the industry he first entered in 2006 to 2009. Up until recently, the greatest numbers of millionaires per capita were created in the 1930s in a similar Shakeout Season of the economy.

If you have younger children or grandchildren, obviously the best time for them to go to college or graduate school will be between 2010 and 2023. The best time to enter the workforce or a new career would be from 2015 to 2017 or 2023 on. Given that demographic growth trends will be much stronger during the next boom in emerging Asian and South American countries, it would make a lot of sense for your children to learn Chinese or Spanish and to consider working in multinational companies whose focus is overseas in newly industrialized economies.

PLANNING THE SEASONS OF YOUR CAREER

The same logic applies to your own career planning. Let's assume you are 39 years old and an information systems analyst in a larger company. First make sure that your company is going to be one of the leaders in your industry in the intense race for leadership that will ensue into 2009. Otherwise you might get a pink slip even in a booming economy. If your company survived the crash of 2000–2002 without losing market share, that would be the first good sign. Second, question whether your company is in an industry that will be leveraged by the growth of information technologies and especially broadband Internet connections in the coming decade. Will video communications and voice activation increase or personalize the level of service your company can deliver at lower costs?

Will your company's products or services benefit from the aging of the baby boom into their late 40s, 50s, and 60s? Industries such as financial services, health care, leisure and travel, retirement homes and services, convenience services, and upscale foods and restaurants are examples of sectors that will benefit. Other industries will benefit from the family-formation cycle of the echo baby boom: apartment rentals; discount retailers such as Wal-Mart, IKEA, and Target; stereo equipment; and so on. You will have to do some research and/or survey your customers and determine who are the peak buyers of your product. Then you can simply lag that peak spending age from the birth index and determine when the growth markets will be the strongest.

Then figure in the economic cycle. If you are 39 in late 2004, the economy will peak around 2009 when you are age 44. You will likely be near the peak of your career cycle and due for the midlife crisis that hits the average American between the mid-40s and early 50s. This is when most people consider changing their lives and entering a second career or starting their own business or buying a vacation home or even moving to a resort area. If such a move requires additional education, after 2009 would be a good time to take a leave of absence to do so. As mentioned earlier, downturns can be a great time to start a new business as the larger companies are in great disarray and are too busy consolidating to take advantage of new, smaller markets that are emerging. In the downturn your company may see an advantage to subcontracting your services part-time to cut costs while retaining your experience and skills. This would give you a reasonable cash flow as well as some spare time to start your own business or to offer similar subcontract services to other companies in your industry.

By 2009 or so, your children will likely be leaving the nest. Maybe that vacation home would be the best way for you to attract them to see you regularly once they get involved in their own education, careers, and family. Who doesn't want to go skiing or to the beach once a year? And of course, that means attracting the grandchildren so they come along as well. Of course, if you are going to make such a transition the economy will have a great impact. If you instead own your own business, try to sell it before the downturn. If you work for a company negotiate the consulting contract part-time near the top or in the early stages of the downturn. If you need further education, do that in the downturn. If you want to move, sell your house by 2008 or 2009 before the downturn hits. If you want to buy a new home or vacation home, wait until the downturn sets in strongly, between 2012 and 2014. You may have to rent for a while, but you should save a lot of money and get a chance to better evaluate the new area you are moving into before buying for the long term.

RETIREMENT PLANNING

For most people, retirement can be the most important phase of financial and life planning. It is here that you have the greatest risks of health complications, your desire to work hard tends to fade, and you want and need the greatest comforts in life. If we continue with the same example, assuming you are 40 years old in 2004, the normal time for retirement would be somewhere between age 63 and 65, probably closer to age 65 by then. By the time you are looking to retire in 25–26 years, or between 2028 and 2029, the economy should be booming again from the spending of the echo-baby-boom generation with a strong recovery from the great bust of 2010–2023. That boom should start to manifest strongly around 2023, or at the latest by 2025–2026. There are many things you must consider to maximize your retirement.

The first is your investment strategies between now and then. With another five to six years of a strong bull market and given that you will be moving into your late 40s, there is no reason for you not to have a very strong but diversified equity portfolio concentrated in growth stocks and areas such as technology, financial services, health care, Asia, travel and leisure, and real estate (especially resort or exurban). But even though you would still be of the age to take equitylike risks, when the downturn hits after 2009 you should have the bulk of your portfolio in high-quality long-term corporate bonds either for the whole downturn; or after the worst of the first crash hits between 2012 and 2014, you could shift more into Asian and drug/health care stocks and mutual funds or rental real estate and defensive stocks such as utilities. Most stock and equity markets will deteriorate between 2009 and 2022, much as occurred in Japan between 1990 and the early 2000s. Only this will be worse due to stronger demographic downtrends in the United States and a downturn in Europe and many countries.

Then starting around late 2022 you could actually allocate more of your portfolio to mutual funds, stocks, and real estate again, in U.S. and international sectors, even though most people your age would prefer to be in bonds or fixed annuities. Why would you do this? Because the economic cycle would strongly suggest a consistently rising market for equities and real estate and moderately rising inflation trends that would devalue the principle of your bonds. At that point you should decide what you really need to insure income needs and have that portion of your portfolio locked into a fixed annuity or in shorter-term bonds or CDs that will not be adversely affected by rising inflation trends. As you get older you can reallocate more of your equity gains into fixed annuities to secure your income, but it is better to wait as long as you reasonably can to allow for higher gains in the equity portion of your portfolio.

As mentioned earlier, it doesn't make sense to own real estate in most areas after 2009. It would be better to sell your house in the city or suburbs and rent if you have to for several years. Then you can either buy a vacation home that you convert to a retirement home during the downturn, or simply wait and buy your dream retirement home around 2022 to 2023 when you will likely get the very best price and lowest mortgage of your lifetime. Then that home can appreciate through your retirement and add to your assets and net worth as you age. You should be able to sell that home at a higher price until at least 2040.

If you prefer to have a part-time occupation during retirement, you could buy a small business very cheaply, perhaps for nothing down and a payout over time, between 2014 and 2023. Then that business could grow in income and value, again adding to your assets as you retire and age. If you play it right with your investments, your home, and your part-time business, you should be able to retire with more income than you need and have a greater net worth at death than you started with at retirement to pass on to your children, grandchildren, and other loved ones.

Estate and Tax Planning

Let's say you are in your late 50s, when people with higher incomes do the greatest estate planning. How do we know that? Through demographic statistics, of course! For the households with the top 20% of income, the greatest amount of life insurance is purchased in the late 50s. That is when more affluent households still have high discretionary income and are starting to clearly see retirement just over the horizon. That is when they need to shelter the most income and assets for tax and estate tax purposes, as Figure 5.5 shows.

Now, you may be thinking that marginal tax rates are going down with the Bush administration and that estate taxes are also being curtailed, so

FIGURE 5.5 Annual Life Insurance Premiums Paid, by Age and Income Level

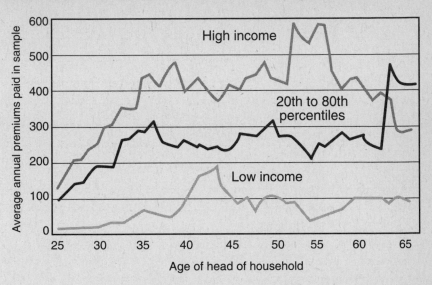

that tax planning may not be as critical in the future as it has been in the past for more affluent households. The eighty-year economic cycle would suggest differently. In the Roaring Twenties boom, eighty years before the coming boom in our New Economy Cycle, tax rates also declined as the economy boomed and the government had increasing surpluses as a result of the rising tax revenues. But when the Great Depression or Shakeout Season hit in the 1930s, marginal tax rates began their sharpest rise in history for two decades. Why? In a strong downturn the government's tax revenues fall even more dramatically and social and welfare costs rise exponentially. The government simply can't raise taxes on the average person when wages are falling and layoffs are rising. So it has to come from the more affluent. In addition, World War II, which hit in the early 1940s, at the end of the Great Depression, required even greater government expenditures. We predict that a similar military or political crisis will hit again around 2018 to 2025, as we will cover just ahead.

In Figure 5.6 you can see that the greatest government spending relative to GDP and hence the greatest relative deficits hit from the early 1930s into the mid-1940s. That is when marginal tax rates soared the most in U.S. history to as high as 90%, as Figure 5.7 demonstrates. Hence, we would forecast that marginal tax rates would continue to decrease at least according to plan into 2009 or 2010, but that shortly after that they would rise strongly again. That also means that estate taxes may increase and other tax deduc-

FIGURE 5.6 U.S. Federal Budget Deficit/Surplus as a Percentage of GDP, 1900–2004

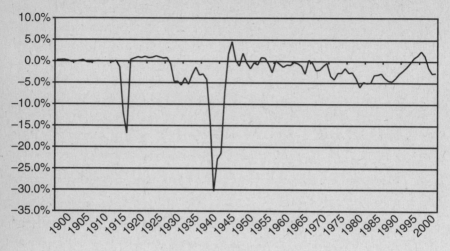

Source: Office of Management and Budget, Budget of the U.S. Government.

FIGURE 5.7 Marginal Tax Rates, 1913–1999

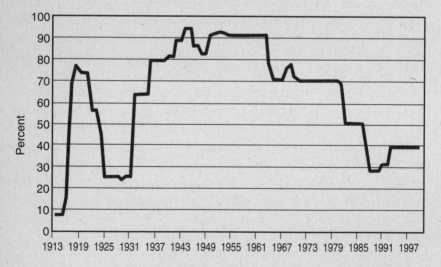

tions for the affluent, such as charitable donations, may be more restricted. If you are 40 today, you should be planning in advance for rising taxes and lock in your estate and tax-deferred investments and insurance policies before 2010 so that the government cannot reverse them easily. This is a very compelling reason to be talking with a competent financial adviser who will focus on estate and tax planning today!

For these reasons we continue to advise more affluent families to max-imize tax-deferred and tax-sheltered investments in the coming decade. And remember that we are forecasting that there will be substantially rising numbers of $100,000-plus annual income and $500,000 to $1 million plus net worth households by the top of this boom. More of us will have to deal with these issues in the future. So how should you look at your estate and tax planning over the rest of your life?

Regardless of your age, taxes should continue to be more favorable into 2009 to 2010 with only minor rises if John Kerry is elected in 2004. Then tax rates are bound to rise, perhaps sharply from 2011 or 2013 into 2025 or be-yond.

Then tax rates should moderate and ultimately begin to fall into the boom from 2023 into the early 2040s or beyond. Let's go back to the 39-year-old life example. You should be more in equity-oriented invest-ments to leverage the boom into 2009 or 2010, and tax rates should continue to fall moderately with continued favorable treatment on capital gains on those equity investments. You should obviously maximize your—and/or your employer's—contributions to your 401(k) plan or your IRA or self-employed plan. These plans bring the greatest tax shelter since the por-tion of your earnings that go in are not taxed to begin with and they con-tinue to grow tax-free until you withdraw them for retirement.

Even though the limits of such contributions are rising, there are clear limits. To the degree that you have additional income you can invest, you can purchase a variable annuity or a variable universal life policy. These in-vestments combine life insurance with a full range of investments includ-ing equity mutual funds. The life insurance gives you tax deferral on the gains of such investments and the "variable" feature allows you to invest in mutual funds that don't have a fixed return like fixed annuities that invest in long-term bonds. These vehicles do have extra costs that must be con-sidered, but they will allow you to participate in the boom in the coming years with much higher potential returns than bonds or fixed annuities and to shelter those gains from income taxes. In addition, when the economy starts to turn down after 2010, when most equity mutual funds will go down in value, you can switch from equity to bond funds and benefit from the declining economy and deflation trends.

This is the real secret that most people don't understand about variable annuities: You can make major changes in your investment strategies when the economy changes seasons without paying taxes on the gains from your past strategy! Most investment strategists will tell you that you don't need to bear the greater insurance costs of a variable annuity as you can simply invest in large-cap stocks, hold them until retirement, and pay capital gains taxes only when you sell them. Try holding those stocks from 2010 to 2022!

The real cost of such a strategy is twofold. First, some of those stocks (remember Enron?) could become losers even in the boom and you may be forced to sell them or suffer strong losses or pay taxes on whatever gains you may still have. Second, the eighty-year economic cycle and demographic spending trends strongly suggest that such blue-chip, large-cap stocks will decline dramatically for more than a decade as they did in the United States from late 1929–1942, from late 1968–late 1982, and in Japan from late 1989 into early 2003. If you sold such stocks in 2008 or 2009 to avoid such a downturn you would have to pay 20% in capital gains taxes to the federal government, plus your full state income tax rate, which can be as high as 9% to 10% in states such as California and New York. Saving 20% to 25% on average in taxes could be worth far more than the marginal insurance fees you paid for the variable annuity.

Then, when the stock market turns back up again for the long term around late 2022, you can switch your investments back toward equity mutual funds and keep the portion you need for income or withdrawals in bonds—again without tax consequences for making such major changes in your portfolio. In this way you will be able to maximize your portfolio returns in the great boom, protect your gains, continue to grow your portfolio through bond investments in the great bust, and then move to the degree you can back into equities in 2023 or beyond. You would have sheltered your investment income entirely against taxes until you needed to withdraw income, just as with a 401(k) plan. But there is a step beyond that in tax planning.

That's where variable universal life policies come into the picture. To make a long story short, these policies allow you not only to defer gains on investment income until you withdraw them for income in retirement but also to borrow against the cash value of the life insurance policy to draw most of your income tax-free even in retirement. Note that variable universal life and variable annuities are more complex investment vehicles and entail costs that may be 1% or more annually for the extra benefits that you can derive, but we think that for the appropriate investors with high marginal tax rates and a long-term time horizon those costs are well worth it.

From our analysis the greatest risk is not the slightly higher fees, assuming you have a high enough marginal tax rate and are going to hold the annuity long enough to benefit from the tax deferral, but potential under-performance of the equity mutual funds in variable annuities for long down cycles like 2010 to 2022. In variable annuities this can cause you to have less retirement benefits than anticipated. But in variable universal life policies such underperformance can cause you to have to cough up more premiums to maintain the policy just when you are in the worst financial position in a downturn. We obviously recommend consulting a competent financial adviser with experience in this area to help evaluate your risks, costs, and benefits. Don't enter such an investment without getting clear answers to these issues. Most important, have your financial adviser design an investment strategy long term that takes into account the changing seasons and investment environment in line with our portfolio strategies in Chapter 7.

CHARITABLE DONATIONS

Most of us want to give something back to society or our community, es-pecially as we age and have more assets and fewer everyday financial obli-gations. Very few financial experts would consider how the boom-and-bust cycles in our economy would affect charitable giving beyond the obvious point that most people would feel pinched in their income and assets by a downturn and would be more generous in an upturn. Just as we can predict when most people peak in their estate and tax planning through demo-graphic statistics, we can predict when most people will peak in their char-itable giving (Figure 5.8). Around age 65 is the peak for the average person. That means we will see the greatest rise in philanthropy in history from 2002 (1937 + 65) to 2026 (1961 + 65) as the massive baby-boom generation ages.

Let's say you are 60 in 2004 and already have been starting to give to your favorite charity, now that your expenses for raising your kids are well behind you and you have more income than you can spend and an invest-ment portfolio that is well on track for meeting your retirement needs. In fact, you find that this has been your greatest joy, second only to providing for your family. You could already anticipate that you would typically have your highest urge to give to charities around 2009, when you turn 65, as you retire and start to need more of your investment income to live on. This may come as a shock at first, but the economic cycle would advise that you

FIGURE 5.8 Annual Charitable Donations, by Age

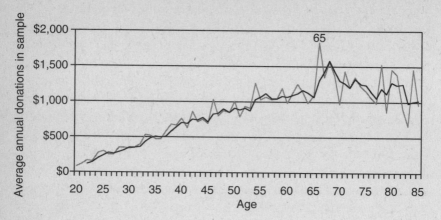

not give as much money to charity now, but instead invest it for the next five to six years and give more to such charities after 2010 when they will need it the most.

Before charities send somebody to bind and gag us, let us explain why this could be of much greater benefit to your designated charity as well as for your tax planning. First ask yourself this question: Do most charities have greater needs for funding and their work in good times or bad times? Everything from poverty to family abuse to the exploitation of the environment in third-world countries will grow in a downturn as in 2010 to 2023 with rising unemployment. Wouldn't it be better to give more when your charity most needs it to fight the greatest injustices? And wouldn't you expect that their sources of donations could dry up even more severely in the downturn we are projecting after 2010, similar to when we saw charities starving for funding in the short, severe stock market crash of 2000–2002?

Now ask yourself a second question: During this great boom, how will most charities invest your donations? In bonds, CDs, or at best in very conservative stock portfolios? The fiduciary responsibilities and regulations they face make it likely that they may earn only 3%–10% at most. You can earn substantially more than that on your investments into 2009 given the strong economic cycle we project and contribute much more several years down the road when the downturn sets in and your charity has greater needs and less funding sources. They, as well as the beneficiaries, will appreciate your donations more.

Now ask yourself a third question: Is your charity more likely to keep down costs and spend your donations more efficiently in a boom or in a bust? Just like businesses and even more so, charities are likely to be running at top efficiency in a downturn when less funds are available from donors and their demands to contribute to their causes grow. So we would suggest that you allocate your charitable donations into an investment fund or a charitable remainder trust or a donor-advised fund over the coming years and then distribute the greater proceeds from those investments to your charity after 2009, when they will need it the most. This way you contribute more when it is most needed and can optimize your impact on the causes you most value. This obviously doesn't mean that you wouldn't give anything in the coming boom years.

But there is still a fourth issue to address: When will you get the most benefit from the tax deductions from your donations? As we addressed in the estate and tax planning section of this chapter, taxes tend to fall during the boom and rise, often dramatically, during the bust. If you are a more affluent household, you are likely to get more effective tax deductions from your donations when tax rates start to rise again in the downturn for many years to come. And finally, your potential returns from continuing to invest your money will go down during the downturn even if you switch to corporate bonds and investments that will prevent your net worth from declining as we advise. Hence, 2010 to 2023 will be the optimum time for most people to donate to their favorite charities unless there is a very compelling need for projects you value now. But at least you can weigh your options in light of the economic cycles ahead that could clearly have a major impact for your charity and for your tax planning.

In recent years, new entities called donor-advised charitable trusts have emerged that allow you to invest with a tax deduction now and have a percentage go to the types of charities you favor. There are also charitable remainder trusts that allow you to set up an irrevocable trust that holds assets you donate, gives you a fixed return for income until you die, and then the remainder of the assets go to the charities of your choice at your death. Finally, more people are starting their own public or private nonprofit foundations where you get tax deductions for donating assets (especially appreciated stock) into the organization. Then you as a foundation can direct both the investments and where and when the donations go. This is the ideal way to make a difference if you have enough assets to be able to afford the minor costs of setting up (typically, $3,000–$10,000) and running such an organization.

The best time to set up one of these charitable vehicles will be in the coming years when you have stocks and investments that have appreciated a lot in the great boom ahead. Hence, we would advise talking to a financial

adviser about your options in this area. But in the next part of this chapter
we will address the most critical issue we see for life planning ahead: Where
do you want to be living in the next great downturn, a period when not
only economic and social instability will inevitably rise, but when the terrorist threat that strongly emerged in late 2001 is likely to become worse
than ever?

THE IMPLICATIONS FOR LIFE PLANNING FROM THE
TERRORIST THREAT AND INCREASING POLITICAL
INSTABILITY IN THE COMING DEPRESSION

In late 2001 we put out a special report called "The Terrorist Attack." In that
report, which you can read on our Web site, www.hsdent.com, we presented
a very contrary view of this very serious crisis. In the near term we commented that the terrorists seem to strike the hardest when we are the most
complacent and not expecting it. There was a cycle of threats ranging from
the Persian Gulf War to the bombing of the World Trade Center in 1993.
Then terrorist threats subsided until 2001. Since then we have, again, been
on total alert and the terrorists have been unable to strike again in a major
way despite plots to do so. In short, we are certain to see further terrorist attacks in coming years, but not likely as dramatic since we seem to be winning
the war on terrorism rather than losing it. Such events are likely to cause
short-term pullbacks in the stock market that will represent buying, not selling, opportunities for the smart investor who understands our cycles.

We don't see the terrorist threat offsetting the fundamental economic
and market trends over the coming boom years any more than similar circumstances did in the Roaring Twenties boom on our eighty-year cycle.
Eighty years ago we saw the first modern terrorist threat in the U.S., a bomb
on Wall Street at J. P. Morgan during the technology wreck of 1920–1921.
That set off an anti-immigration trend and saw the rise of the Ku Klux Klan
to its highest relative membership in history by 1924. In addition we saw the
boom of many growth industries alternating with the decline of many old
companies as well as Prohibition and "gangsters in the streets." The income
disparities between the rich and poor continued to widen.

These very volatile social and political trends did not prevent the economic and stock boom of the Roaring Twenties, nor did the terrorist attacks on September 11, 2001, stop this boom. Unless there is an extreme
terrorist event that greatly weakens our technological infrastructures, we
don't see the terrorist threat stopping this incredible boom ahead. And we

don't think such an event is as likely to occur in the coming years now that we are on full alert and are much more powerful than these small, but very creative terrorist organizations. This cycle of terrorist threats is much like the cycle of large- and small-cap stocks. New innovative companies attack the market shares of very powerful, established companies just as they are peaking in the Spending Wave Cycle and are very complacent, and when new innovative cycles rise from the next young generation.

The third world is now beginning to rise just as the developed world, epitomized by the United States, is at its greatest peak since the Roman Empire—just before its fall and the Dark Ages set in for many centuries after the 400s A.D. So just as we have been forecasting that the terrorist threat that reared its head in late 2001 would have less impact than feared in the coming years, we do clearly feel that this is a long-term trend that will impact our economy and lifestyles for decades to come. We see the greatest threats naturally coming in the downturn from 2010 to 2023 when economic conditions deteriorate here and even more so in most third-world countries. We will be more complacent again at the top of this boom, as we were in the early 2000s after another decade of a booming economy and likely progress on the war against terrorism.

This backlash against American culture and capitalism should not be that surprising. We, and many parts of the world, have made incredible progress in living standards in the last century, while a majority of the world's population is still living below our poverty standards and many nations are falling further behind. But the biggest issue is that our more democratic, free-market, and liberal lifestyles are a direct threat to many very fundamentalist cultures around the world. These cultures live by very restrictive and moralistic codes. They cannot easily defend these codes against the TV and consumer franchise world of the West, which is seen as a temptation to their culture and especially their children. In addition, they don't understand why we are so prosperous and they are not. It just doesn't make sense to them.

That's why there is a holy war against American capitalism. We are the enemy to many fundamentalist cultures around the world and to the most radical factions and people, such as Al Qaeda and Osama bin Laden, who believe we must be totally destroyed for the highest religious principles. With the rise of the larger third world and the maturing of the more prosperous developed world, this conflict was inevitable from historical perspectives. In addition, as we mentioned in Chapter 3, Southeast Asia and China are rising as the newly developed economies with greater demographic trends for the future. History would also suggest that as new major

economic, political, and military powers rise, they inevitably come into conflict with the established powers. Hence, we see the strong likelihood of economic and/or military conflict with countries like China in the coming
decades. Our eighty-year cycle would strongly suggest that this would occur
on an eighty-year lag to World War II, around 2018 to 2025.

Given the peak of this great Growth Boom cycle and the Shakeout Season to follow, as well as the longer-term potential peaking of the broader
Western civilization boom that began between the Crusades and the Re-
naissance, this terrorist threat from declining third-world countries and the
potential military threat from rising industrialized countries suggests that
the downturn could bring lifestyle threats greater than imagined by most.
Even if they are less, such a downturn should bring you to consider the ultimate question in lifestyle strategies:

WHERE DO I WANT TO BE LIVING IN THE GREAT BUST AHEAD?

From 2010 into around 2023 we see the economy declining, first in the
United States, and then around the world, with some exceptions, such as
Southeast Asia and India. But even those areas that are highly export-
oriented will suffer some declines in growth and prosperity. The world is
clearly likely to become a more difficult place. That's when the seeds tend to
grow for dissatisfaction, terrorism, and dissent. In the Roaring Twenties
everyone loved business and capitalism, and then in the 1930s everyone
hated them. That's when antibusiness policies and the New Deal developed
to protect the average person from the swings in the economy, and when
Social Security was established.

We will not only see such sentiments occur domestically a decade from
now, but the reaction from the third-world fundamentalist cultures will also
rise. They will be saying: look at how free-market capitalism and globalization caused this great economic bubble that threatened our cultures and
then caused the greatest downturn in history! These people will be suffer-
ing even worse economic conditions than they are now and will have more
reason to revolt against the United States and its culture and economic/
military policies.

So think for a moment about a world where domestic unrest is increasing as a result of accelerating unemployment and international unrest
and increasing terrorist attacks, just when we thought that we were finally
winning the war on terrorism. And in the final stages of the downturn we

could be facing some type of military or political confrontation not only with Middle Eastern countries but also with major Asian nations, such as North Korea, Indonesia, or even China. Where do you want to be living? Our answer is simple: in a high-quality exurban area outside of the major urban areas that will be the most threatened, and even outside of very-high-profile resort areas such as Aspen and Palm Beach!

If we stop for a moment and put ourselves in the mind of a terrorist organization or nation that wants to attack the very foundations of Western society, where would the most likely targets be in the United States? We would list them in this approximate order of priority:

1. New York City and surrounding areas

2. Washington, D.C.

3. Los Angeles and Hollywood

4. San Francisco and Silicon Valley

5. Houston/New Orleans (oil centers)

6. Las Vegas (the epitome of American leisure)

7. Southeast Florida (high-affluent urban area with a high Jewish concentration)

8. Chicago (midwestern center and skyscrapers)

Buying your dream vacation home or retirement home, either now or in the early stages of the downturn, could be the most important decision of your life. You could increasingly do business and communicate from a high-quality area outside major cities with greater recreation and nicer weather due to continued advances in Internet and broadband technologies. Since these areas will attract more people, and especially more affluent people, there will be growing restaurant and entertainment options. And where do you want your children living? Even if you can't convince them to move to such an area because they are in their family and career cycles, at least your home could be a place they could come to if life in the major urban/suburban areas becomes threatening. But how do you decide when to sell and move—and where?

There is another long-term cycle that will cause many people to consider relocating to high-quality exurban and resort areas. We covered this cycle in depth in Chapters 9 and 10 of *The Roaring 2000s*. Every economic revolution brings technologies that open up new lower-cost, higher-quality-of-life living areas, as we show in Figure 5.9. Railroads, power plants,

FIGURE 5.9 Three Waves of Migration, 1825–2075

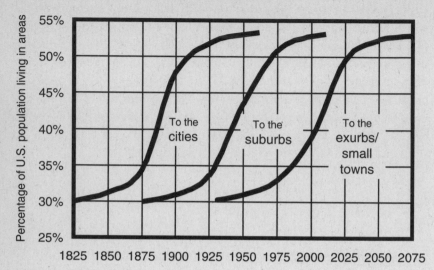

and telegraphs allowed us to migrate from rural areas to cities. Then the automobile, telephone, and electricity revolution allowed us to shift from cities to suburban areas. Now the Information Revolution—being accelerated by the Internet, home PCs and entertainment devices, cellular smart phones, and broadband (wired and wireless)—will allow more people to live, do business, and communicate from exurban areas just outside of the suburban fringes and high-quality-of-life resort areas and college towns.

Rural areas are finally becoming hip again! Where is the highest-priced real estate in the United States? In San Francisco? New York? No, it's in Aspen, Colorado, and Jupiter, Florida! This is a long-term trend that will grow over the rest of most of our lifetimes and represents the greatest long-term trend in real estate.

The summary insights here are the following: If you are considering buying a vacation or retirement home in the near term, it should be a good investment into 2009 or so. You could either opt to sell it by 2009–2010 or keep it through the downturn, especially if this is a home or property that you plan to keep long-term or retire in. Your appreciation in the coming years should offset the potential declines after 2009. Then we feel there is a rising potential for appreciation after the early years of the downturn from around late 2014 on as more people migrate into these areas, despite the poor overall economic conditions.

If you do elect to sell a vacation or resort property by 2009, you should strongly consider repurchasing between mid-2012 and late 2014 in a desirable exurban area after prices have fallen or at least stagnated. The highest-quality areas should do the best after the initial decline in prices for a few years, but even nice, safe middle-class small towns increasingly should become havens, in the downturn. If you are considering buying a vacation home later in the boom cycle, for instance after 2005, it would be better to wait and buy around 2012 to 2014 or so and rent a great place in the meantime.

FOR INFORMATION ON LOCAL REAL ESTATE MARKETS

In addition to the demographic cycles we presented in Chapter 4 to help you gauge when to buy and sell real estate, there are two new Web sites that can help you to gauge growth and valuation trends in your local markets. Mike Sklarz of Fidelity National Information Solutions has developed models for analyzing home prices in 316 local markets at www.fins.com/products. Click on "Value Your Home." John Burns Real Estate Consulting has demographic models for determining which states and counties are attracting the age 45–64 vacation and retirement-home buyers and will be the best markets in the years ahead. Burns's Web site is at www.realestate consulting.com. You can buy local reports for as low as $95 and his entire national database for $4,995. We offer a special report, "Demographic Trends in Real Estate," at our Web site, www.hsdent.com, at the online store, which includes a section on how to use databases like the ones above to analyze whether home prices are likely to continue to grow in your area or are getting overheated.

In Chapter 6 we will take an in-depth look at how demographic indicators can allow us to project which types of financial investments, from bonds to large-cap stocks to small-cap stocks to international stocks, will do well in the years and decades ahead. We will also look at how to project inflation and interest rate trends. In Chapter 7 we will look at how risks and returns will change in the different seasons of our eighty-year economic cycle and how to design the best-diversified portfolios for the boom ahead and the more extended decline to follow.

Chapter 6

THE OUTLOOK FOR INVESTMENT MARKETS

Large-Cap, Small-Cap, and International Stocks; Long- and Short-Term Bonds

WHICH INVESTMENT SECTORS WILL DO THE BEST IN THE COMING BOOM YEARS?

Now that we have introduced you to the realities of the next great downturn, let's get back to the brighter picture we see for the next five to six years. As we go into the next great boom, what sectors will do best? Will they be technology, biotech, financial services, health care, travel and leisure, energy, multinational, Asia, or Europe? Should you be in large-cap or small-cap stocks? Small caps trounced large caps from 1958 to 1983, while large caps increasingly outperformed from 1984 to 1999. Will small caps handily beat large caps again now, after large caps hit extreme valuations in early 2000 and then underwent a shakeout phase? When should you be in growth stocks and when in value stocks?

Do the early 2000s mark a new era in value stocks, as Warren Buffett and many others are forecasting? When will long-term bonds be better in price and yields and when should you be in short-term bonds? Long-term bonds have handily beaten short-term bonds since 1981. But short-term bonds beat long-term in the 1970s. How do you make sense out of these very confusing times of change for long-term investment strategies? Just when one investment sector seems to be doing the best, another suddenly starts to do better. Most of us buy into whatever has done the best for the last several years, just in time to see those sectors decline. How can we reverse this "perverse" investment outlook, which always seems to get us to do the wrong things at the wrong times?

As we continue to study the implications of demographic trends, we find that we can predict all of the key trends that will affect your investments for many decades to come, as we summarized in the introduction to this book. Most economists find this to be incomprehensible, yet most financial advisers and investors we make presentations to find demographic trends easy to understand and highly reliable in projecting such long-term trends. How can you be comfortable as an investor not having a clue when the next major shift in trends will occur and destroy your net worth or render your present investment strategies ineffective? We will start this chapter by looking at the prospects for the preferred and best risk-adjusted long-term investment sector for most investors: large-cap stocks.

LARGE-CAP STOCKS ARE A LEVERAGED PLAY ON ECONOMIC GROWTH

Now that we have established that we are very likely to see another great boom ahead, the most important question is obviously, When will it be the strongest, and where will the best opportunities for investing be? You must remember that this decade will be a volatile one, much like the Roaring Twenties, with much social change and many disruptive political events. Though we can predict that it is highly likely that we will see such volatility, we can't always anticipate exactly what political and social events will hit or when except through the cycle analysis we presented in the previous chapter. The terrorist events starting in late 2001 and the confrontations with unscrupulous dictators in 2003 will likely have many repercussions in the years and decades to come. So keep that in mind while we look at the predictable trends that are very likely to occur over the coming years and decades. We feel that the terrorist threats will be less than many expect for the next several years. The greater threats will come in the downturn to follow this boom.

The most important point for investments is that large-cap stocks follow the economy and the Spending Wave. That is our large-cap indicator and forecasting tool. In fact, over time large-cap stocks are a leveraged play on economic growth. Since 1900, GDP growth, led by consumer spending, has averaged 5.5% and adjusted for inflation 3.4%. Large-cap stocks (S&P 500) have grown 9.9% or 6.6% adjusted for inflation, roughly twice the growth rate of the GDP, both nominal and real. In the recent boom period of 1982–2000, the stock market grew at 2.7 times the GDP rate, 16.5% versus 6.2%. When adjusted for inflation, stocks grew 12.7% versus the

GDP's 3.2%, or four times the rate. Hence, stocks tend to naturally do even better in extended boom periods and grow exponentially compared to GDP growth in boom periods. They correlate in the long term with the economic growth and earnings growth of corporations that follow.

Hence they are inherently a leveraged play on the economy and rising consumer spending. When consumer spending is rising, stocks grow exponentially as they project that growth years into the future and are overvalued at the tops of economic growth periods. Then, conversely, they drop exponentially when growth declines with consumer spending, as in the 1930s in the United States and the 1990s in Japan. The Spending Wave (here in Figure 6.1 repeated from Figure 1.2) shows when the economy will boom and bust five decades ahead. But an important point here is that large-cap stocks follow that trend very closely when adjusted for inflation and on a logarithmic or exponential scale, as we use in the Spending Wave. Hence, we can see the trends in large-cap markets such as Dow and S&P 500 five decades in advance.

That's astounding, when you think about it! This is not a new indicator. We have been using it since 1988, and the economy and stock markets

FIGURE 6.1 The Spending Wave: Births Lagged for Peak in Family Spending, 1954–2050

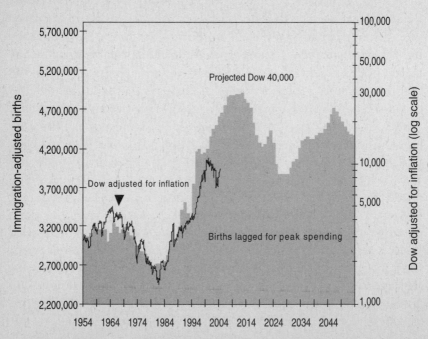

FIGURE 6.2 The Japan Crash of 1990–2003: The Nikkei Versus the Decline in Consumer Spending, 1987–2003

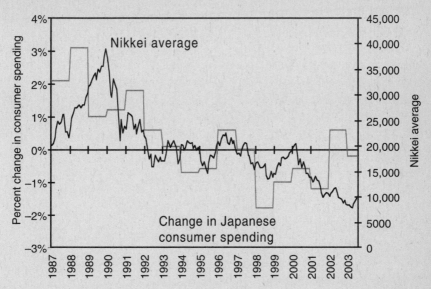

have continued to follow it despite temporary periods of overvaluation and major stock crashes such as those in 1987 and 2000–2002. But first, if you think stocks won't decline when our economy declines after 2009, consider the plight of Japan after late 1989. Figure 6.2 shows the decline in consumer spending that led and correlated with the decline in the Japanese stock market from 1990 into 2002. We predicted the decline of Japan in the late 1980s based on its declining demographics of consumer spending into the early 2000s.

There are actually two components to the U.S. Spending Wave that give greater insights into the economic growth ahead. The dominant one is the lag on births (adjusted for immigration) for the average peak in spending around age 48 today, moving forward a year every decade toward age 49 by 2010. We also adjust this indicator to a lesser degree for the acceleration in spending that comes as we get married around age 26 today, also moving forward about a year every decade. The greatest increase in spending comes as we form families in the mid- to late 20s. Figure 6.3 shows the changes and impacts of these two factors. The massive baby-boom generation has been the primary impetus behind this incredible boom since late 1982, including the large-cap-stock surge, as we can see with the lag for peak spending. But if we look at the second trend in Figure 6.3 we see that the lag for family for-

FIGURE 6.3 Family Formation and Peak Spending Cycles, 1954–2050

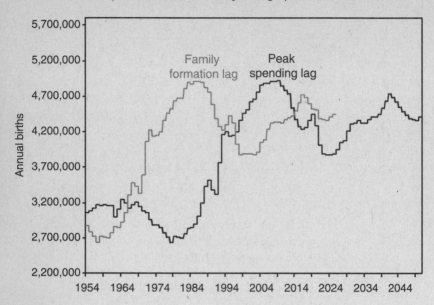

mation had a positive trend on the economy from the late 1950s into 1986 and will again from 2003 into 2017. This was another reason we expected the economy to rebound more strongly than forecast in 2003.

The peak spending of the Bob Hope generation was starting to slow and plateau from the late 1950s into 1965. Note that the Dow, which more purely represents the large-cap stocks of that era, actually peaked adjusted for inflation in late 1965. But the beginnings of the large baby-boom family formation cycle added to the growth in the economy and gave small to midcaps a very big boost from the late 1950s onward. The downturn from the late 1960s into the early 1980s would have been substantially worse if the family formation cycle had not continued to rise so strongly. But from 1987 into 1998 the family formation cycle from the baby bust was trending downward against the broader baby-boom trend. And we saw a number of substantial corrections in that time frame despite the ongoing boom.

The fact that the economy went into a period of worsening recession in the 1970s and early 1980s and the broader large-cap stock market continued to decline (adjusted for inflation) shows that the peak spending cycle is clearly the more dominant and primary cycle. Similarly, the economy and stock markets continued to advance after the family formation cycle turned sharply down after 1986. But the good news is that the family formation cycle started to turn up very slowly in 2002 and accelerated again starting in 2003.

Why is that so important? Both cycles kicked in more strongly in 2003 and we saw a stronger recovery from the 2000–2002 slowdown. 2003 will turn out to have been one of the stronger years for economic growth in the coming decade and one of the top three or four years for gains in the stock market. But more important, the baby-boom peak spending cycle will begin to plateau and slow from late 2005 or early 2006 into late 2009 or early 2010, just as the Bob Hope Generation Spending Cycle did in the late 1950s and mid-1960s. The echo-baby-boom stimulus will add economic growth in the last years of this boom, just when the economy will need it most. That means we should expect stronger economic growth from 2005–2006 into 2009–2010 than would occur based on baby-boom trends alone, especially between mid-2007 and mid-2009, when both cycles should experience stronger upward trends again.

The family formation lag will continue to add to the economy's strength even after the baby boomers peak around mid-2009. This trend will soften the strong downturn into around 2018 before it then turns down again from 2019 into 2023 or 2024. But if past history is a guide, it will clearly not stop us from seeing a major economic and stock decline starting by 2010, especially since the echo-baby-boom generation is substantially smaller than the baby-boom generation and the end of the great technology explosion will see its bubble burst with strong downward implications for the stock market and the economy.

The crash of 2000–2002 saw only a very minor recession precisely because the baby-boom spending trends were still pointing up so strongly and the downtrend in the family formation cycle was bottoming. After all, $7 trillion in wealth was destroyed by the stock crash, and we had some of the worst political events in many decades. But consumers still needed to spend and buy houses and cars—and they did with the help of falling interest rates. Hence, we still expect a very strong stock crash between 2010 and 2012, likely continuing into late 2014, as forecast in Chapter 3. There will be sharply rising unemployment from the shakeout in business that will follow, much as in the early 1930s. But then we also clearly expect that very slow or even slower economic growth could reoccur when both indicators are pointing down, from 2020 into 2023.

So we still see the trends heading down into 2010 and beyond despite the adjustments for echo-baby-boom family formation into the Spending Wave. The more important impact will be on the business sectors that benefit. Upscale spending in the retail sectors will boom more into 2005, but the discount sectors—firms ranging from Wal-Mart to IKEA—should fare better from 2003 into 2017 as these new families buy the basics upon moving into their first apartments—and the downturn after 2009 makes consumers more price-sensitive.

If we combine these two indicators the result is a better composite gauge on economic growth from 2002 into 2009. The baby boomers and the echo baby boomers drove stronger spending starting in mid-2003. That's when we began to see a more robust recovery in the economy after the initial rebound from the slowdown of 2000–2002. The second half of 2003 should represent one of the strongest periods for growth. The year 2004 should continue to see a solid recovery, but with little improvement until a stronger acceleration from mid-2005 on. In 2006 we could see slower growth in the first quarter, followed by a stronger surge from sometime in 2007 into around late 2009 to mid-2010, driven in part by a very strong stock market after late 2006.

There is another reason that growth should be stronger than the Spending Wave would forecast for the latter part of the boom with its plateau in growth between 2005 and 2010. In 2000 the census gave us current data on the age distribution of every age in the United States. We were then able to re-create a birth wave that would include all immigrants and then converted that into a new version of the Spending Wave. What we saw from this revised model is that there is a larger tail of baby boomers at the end of the birth cycle than the original birth numbers would suggest. That would imply a continued strong uptrend rather than a slowing of growth. This is due to immigration. In 1997 we started adjusting the Spending Wave for immigration. We did that by developing an average age curve for immigration by analyzing the age distributions in past years. We took the immigration numbers each year and then redistributed these people back to when they were born to get an immigration-adjusted birth index, as discussed in Chapter 1 of *The Roaring 2000s*.

Figure 6.4 shows a slightly different spending wave that we constructed from the 2000 census data that should have more accurately calculated in the immigrants by age than our computer model. There was a onetime anomaly that model didn't take into account. Between 1986 and 1989, the U.S. government issued a onetime amnesty offer to illegal immigrants. If they would declare, they could become legal immigrants. This program caused a sharp spike in declared immigration, especially into 1991, as you can see in Figure 6.5. This spike was due to existing illegal immigrants declaring, but also attracted a new surge of young immigrants to take ad-

FIGURE 6.4 Census 2000 Spending Wave, 1982–2050

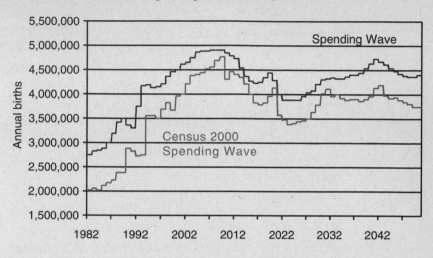

FIGURE 6.5 Immigration, 1820–2002

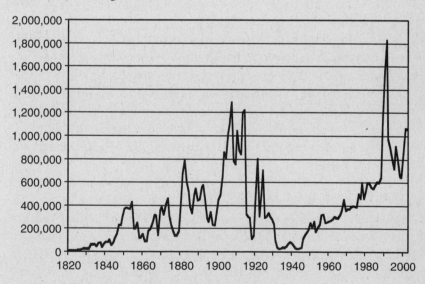

vantage of the program in a short period of time. This brief burst of new immigrants was highly concentrated in the latter birth years of the baby boom, especially between 1960 and 1961, causing the sharper uptrend in the Census 2000 Spending Wave in the latest years of the boom compared to the Spending Wave in Figure 6.1 where the trends are flatter.

To summarize: both the amnesty immigration spike and the echo-baby-boom family formation cycle will cause the latter years of this boom to be stronger than the baby-boom birth and spending patterns alone would suggest. But this logic works in reverse as well. Figure 6.4 shows a steeper dropoff in spending likely after 2009, as the sharper rise turns to a sharper falloff after the effects of the amnesty immigration surge. This would imply, in addition to the final burst of the tech and stock bubble, that the initial downturn from 2010 on is likely to be severe.

The strongest time for GDP growth should be from mid-2003 to mid-2006 and 2007 through 2010. After early to late 2010 growth should begin to decline, and sharply at first, for many years into at least early 2015 with the rapid decline of baby-boom spending. The years 2010–2012 and 2014–early 2015 are likely to see the strongest downturns and recession years in the first stage of the decline. Unemployment rates should hit their first bottom between early 2013 and early 2015. There could be some reprieve in 2017 and then a more robust rebound into 2018 or 2019 with the last minor wave of baby-boom spending kicking in along with much stimulus from the Fed and government public works programs. We should then see another very strong downturn from early 2020 to 2023 when both sectors are pointing down strongly at the same time. Thus late 2010–2012 and 2020–2022 will likely be the worst years for the stock market. And 2011–2013 and 2021–2023 will likely go down as the worst periods for our economy since 1930–1933. This is where we are likely to see the highest unemployment levels—15% or possibly higher in the United States. Unemployment levels should bottom by early 2023 if we enter a major war or adverse political cycle in the early 2020s, which history strongly suggests is likely. The only sustainable positive period for the stock market and economy is likely to be between late 2014 and late 2019.

To summarize: The strongest years ahead for economic growth and large-cap stocks should be mid-2005 to mid-2006 and then again from late 2006 into early to late 2010. Then there should be a strong decline from late 2010 into at least late 2012 and possibly into late 2014, and then a significant rally into 2019. Then we should see another very strong downturn from 2020 into late 2022 before the next, less dramatic and more orderly long-term boom and stock market advance begin.

SMALL CAPS FOLLOW THE INNOVATIONS
OF YOUNGER PEOPLE

In Jeremy Siegel's book *Stocks for the Long Run,* he showed that small-cap stocks have outperformed large-cap stocks from 1926 to 1997 with average returns of 12.5% versus 11.0%. Does this mean that you are better off in small-cap stocks? We will show in Chapter 7 that as a general rule the risks and volatility of small-cap stocks greatly outweigh their slightly higher returns. But the more important insight here is that there are long periods of time when large-cap stocks do better and when small-cap stocks do better, and of course, these different periods are driven by demographic trends. Jeremy Siegel notes that most of the outperformance of small caps came in just eight short years, from 1975 to 1983.

So the real question should be: Why did small caps outperform large caps so strongly from 1975 to 1983? There must be a reason for this. Is there any way we could have known to be in small caps for that astounding period? First, how astounding was it? Small-cap average annual returns were 35.3% and outperformed large caps by four times in cumulative returns and 2.2 times in average annual returns from 1975 to 1983. But it wasn't just those eight years. In *The Roaring 2000s Investor,* we showed that small caps, for the twenty-five-year period from 1958 to 1983, had cumulative returns almost seven times greater than large caps (Figure 6.6).

That was a twenty-five-year period when you would have been much better off in small caps. The average annual returns for small caps from 1958 to 1983 were 17.31% versus 9.56% for large caps, or 81% higher. The annual risk was 56% higher at a standard deviation of 23.60 versus 15.12 for large

FIGURE 6.6   Small-Cap Stocks Versus Large-Cap Stocks, 1958–1983

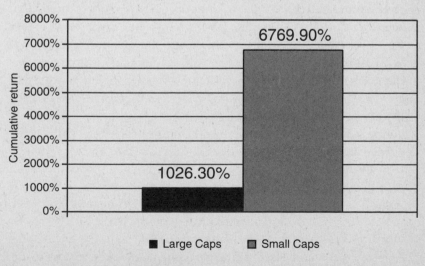

Source: Ibbotson & Associates.

caps. That is still a very favorable risk/return tradeoff for aggressive investors. Only in that unique time period would the higher risks of small-cap stocks have made that investment worthy. What was the reason for this? It was the massive baby-boom generation moving into its youthful Innovation Stage.

Small-cap stocks move in very different cycles from large caps. They are both driven by economic growth, of course, and that is a matter of the Spending Wave and the lag on the birth index for the peak spending by consumers (Figure 6.1). In addition, small caps benefit from innovation and the emergence of new products into niche markets where smaller companies have the competitive edge over larger companies. It is young people who drive such innovation. We call it the "yuppie effect." As new upscale people enter the workforce after college, they are the key drivers of new trends in technologies, products, and lifestyles.

The period 1958–1983 is simply a twenty-two-year lag (graduating from college) on the baby-boom birth index for the largest Innovation Stage in history. In that period we saw everything from Elvis to the Beatles to Jimi Hendrix in new music, the sexual revolution and new yuppie lifestyles, and the entire evolution of semiconductors to microchips to PCs to operating systems. And we saw new products ranging from Starbucks to Armani and new retailers from Sharper Image to Wal-Mart to Charles Schwab. We saw the rise of BMW, Mercedes, and Lexus and the fall of Cadillac and Lincoln.

We have since found that the best overall correlation for the performance of small-cap stocks is a twenty-three-year lag on the birth index (adjusted for immigration) as most of our peak ages are moving forward on average over time. This gives these new yuppies a year to get out of college and get fully established in their new careers and spending patterns. We have developed a simple, but effective model for projecting the performance of small caps that tells you when to be invested in those stocks. This model simply combines the Spending Wave to reflect when the economy will be growing or declining on a 100% weighting, with a twenty-three-year lag for peak innovation on a 75% weighting. Figure 6.7 shows the correlation since the early 1950s with the Small-Cap Indicator and a commonly used small-cap index that represents the smallest 20% (or ninth and tenth deciles) of NYSE stocks. Note that the Russell 2000 is the most commonly used small-cap index today, but it does not go back before 1980.

There were only two significant divergences from the Small-Cap Indicator's forecast. The first was between 1969 and 1974. We have always commented that the small-cap stocks do poorly in the early years of an extended downturn. When the largest companies were hit severely in the

FIGURE 6.7   Small-Cap Indicator, January 1954–January 1999

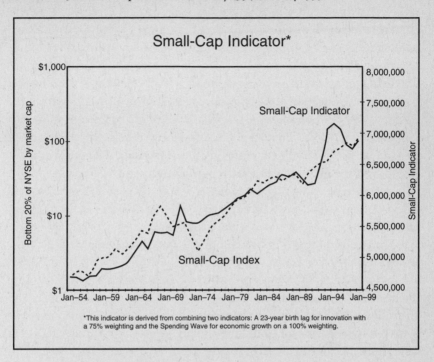

stock crashes of 1970 and 1973–1974, small caps were hit even harder despite the fact that they were in a positive cycle of innovation on a twenty-three-year lag. This also occurred in the early 1930s during that extreme crash that ushered in the Great Depression. When the largest companies look very shaky, investors get even more worried about smaller companies.

Small caps had been outperforming large caps since 1958 and had a bit of a bubble into their top in late 1968, as the best sectors always do at the crescendo of a major bull market. Note that 1968 was the peak of the last long-term bull market as measured by the broader S&P 500 index adjusted for inflation that peaked due to small-cap strength three years after the Dow in 1965. But then small caps did get hit harder than the indicator would have suggested when the twin crashes of 1970 and 1973–1974 set in.

The other divergence was in the mid-1990s. There was a very short but steep rise in births just after World War II. That brief rise was not reflected as sharply in the economy, nor in the large-cap or small-cap stock indices, as it was such a short-term anomaly that it quickly reversed itself. We have noticed in the past that very short-term swings in the Spending Wave or demographic indicators do not have a substantial impact in the short term. It is the long-term trends in spending and the stock market that are more critical. Otherwise, this indicator has been very accurate in predicting when and how well small caps will perform just as the Spending Wave does for the large-cap stocks. And the greatest two periods were 1958–1968 and 1975–1983.

We will not see such stellar performance from small caps in the future even though the echo baby boom has been entering its Innovation Stage on a twenty-three-year lag since 1999. But small caps will do much better than they did in the 1990s. Small caps underperformed large caps from 1984 through 1998 as the baby bust was taking the wind out of their sails with declining innovation trends. But since 1999, they outperformed through 2002. Many experts are taking this as a sign of a new era of small-cap dominance and large-cap decline, as occurred in the 1970s. And of course, we disagree due to the very different stage in the demographic and technology cycles ahead versus the 1970s (although when in doubt, disagreeing with the "experts" is usually profitable).

Our indicators show that small caps will do better from 1999 into 2009 than they did into 1998, but large caps will still have the edge, especially when adjusted for risk and volatility from late 2002 into 2009 or early 2010. Why? We are still in a continuing boom, unlike the 1970s, and a race for leadership to see which large companies are going to dominate the key industries of the future on the S-Curve Cycle (as occurred in the 1920s). Large caps naturally have the edge during the 10% to 90% acceleration of new technologies, except for the shakeout phase in the middle that we just saw between 2000 and 2002.

Small caps came into the crash of 2000–2002 very undervalued, as their performance had been suboptimal for many years. Large caps came in very highly valued, the most overvalued in history, precisely because they performed so well especially from 1995 into early 2000. So it was natural that the large caps would take a much bigger hit in such an extreme valuation-oriented correction. But remember that the echo baby boom is not as large a generation on a relative scale as the baby boom. That's why we won't see the same stellar performance we saw in the 1960s and 1970s for small caps. But the performance will be much closer to that of the large caps in the coming decade, but as we will discuss in Chapter 7, the risks will be higher.

Large caps, again, follow a different drummer. They simply correlate with the overall growth of the economy and the peak spending of new generations that drive it. As these new generations age, they adopt the innovations of their youth (dominated initially by small caps) increasingly into mass markets when they spend the most around age 48, resulting in increasing dominance by large-cap stocks. Hence, as we showed in Figure 6.1, large-cap indices like the Dow or S&P 500, adjusted for inflation, closely follow a forty-eight-year lag on the birth index (adjusted for immigration), moving toward a forty-nine-year peak in the coming decade. That has always been our leading indicator for large-cap stock investing, where most investors tend to concentrate and where the best risk/return ratios are. The large size of the baby-boom generation, combined with the greater under-valuation of large caps following the crash of 2000–2002, suggests that large caps will do better than small caps from late 2002 into late 2009 when adjusted for risk. But the good news is that they both will do well and small caps won't underperform as much as they did in the 1990s. Hence, small-cap stocks can be added to your portfolio for diversification, but we still recommend leaning more strongly toward the large caps or focusing on large caps exclusively.

In Figure 6.8 we show the difference between our models for large- and small-cap stocks both past and future. We can see that these models would have forecasted that small caps would greatly outperform large caps from 1958 to 1983, dead on for the optimum time to be in small-cap stocks. Then the model would have suggested that large caps would have increasingly outperformed from 1984 to 1998 as they clearly did. Small caps did indeed outperform from 1999 into 2002. But the model now forecasts that large caps should perform slightly better from 2003 into 2009 or 2010, and very

FIGURE 6.8 Large-Cap Indicator Versus Small-Cap Indicator, January 1954–January 2029

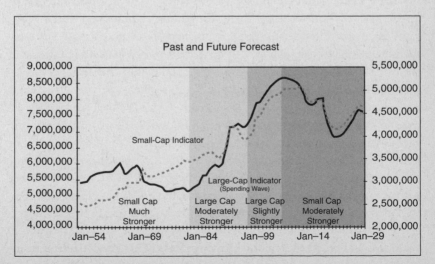

FIGURE 6.9   Large-Cap Valuations: The Dow Channel, 1982–2010

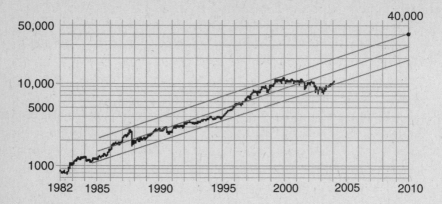

likely at lower risk levels. And again, the undervaluation of large caps coming out of the 2000–2002 crash would make their performance even better in the years to come.

Our best gauge for the valuation levels of large-cap stocks is the Dow Channel in Figure 6.9. Similarly to 1987, we hit the top of the valuation range between mid-1999 and early 2000. In *The Roaring 2000s Investor* we forecasted that we were due to hit the top of this channel between the fourth quarter of 1999 and the first quarter of 2000 and that a sharp correction would likely follow (pages 26–27). But in late 2002 we tested the bottom of that channel sooner than we would have originally anticipated from past trends, just after the panic selloff from the terrorist attacks. This test clearly signaled extreme undervaluation and the greatest buy opportunity since late 1994, when the Dow tested the bottom of this channel after the 1987 top.

We gave an ultimate buy signal in late September 2001 for 8100 to 8300 on the Dow in our newsletter, *The H. S. Dent Forecast*. We then tested the bottom of the Dow Channel again in July 2002, but this time we broke below it and we gave strong buy signals for around 7400, the next strong level of support from the 1998 lows in early October 2002. And again, we were calling this the buy opportunity of this century as we outlined in our special report "The Buy Opportunity of a Lifetime." Note that we continue to project a Dow of 20,000 by late 2008 and as high as 40,000 by late 2010, similar to our forecasts in *The Roaring 2000s*, despite the temporary break of the Dow Channel in 2002. Hence, the sharp correction of 2000–2002 has created the opportunity for much more attractive returns in this next stage of the greatest bull market in history!

On the other hand, small-cap valuations (Figure 6.10) have steadily

FIGURE 6.10 Small-Cap Valuations: T. Rowe Price Indicator, 1990–2000

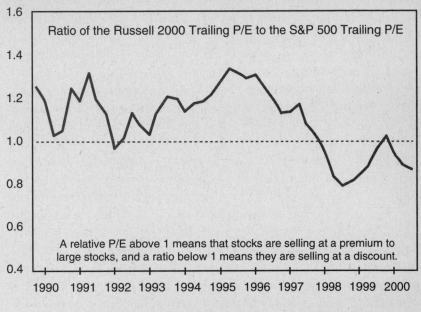

Sources: T. Rowe Price Associates, data Standard & Poor's, Frank Russell Company.

risen from very low levels in 1998 back closer toward fair value in 2003, according to the indicator developed by T. Rowe Price that measures the P/E ratios of small-cap versus large-cap stocks. Hence, not only do large caps have a slight edge in performance according to our large-cap and small-cap indicators, large caps are also at slightly more attractive valuation levels—but this is not likely to last for long. Therefore, our advice is to continue to focus entirely or largely in large-cap stocks and mutual funds. They are easier to find, track, and evaluate—and the risk levels tend to be lower with higher risk-adjusted returns, as history has shown. (We will discuss this further in Chapter 7.)

We see late 2005 to mid- to late 2010 being similar to late 1994–early 2000 due to the continued S-curve acceleration of new technologies and the race for domination of new emerging markets that began in 1994 and should continue at least into 2009. In the first rapid growth phase before the shakeout, from 1994 to 1999, large-cap stocks trounced small caps. The average annual returns were 23.46% versus 15.61%. In Chapter 7 we will show that large-cap growth stocks did even better. But it wasn't just the higher returns. The annual risk was extremely low for the level of returns and less than half that of small caps, at only 7.79 standard deviation versus

16.36. There simply wasn't a better place to be invested from 1994 through 1999. We expect a replay of that scenario from late 2004 into 2009–early 2010 as the second great S-curve growth stage, from 50% to 90% penetration, sets in.

The large-cap concentration will be even greater toward the top of this boom just as it was in the late 1920s. We have data on large caps versus small caps back to 1926. From 1926 to 1929, $1.00 invested in large caps would have grown to $2.08 versus a decline to 82¢ in small caps, with risk levels of 12.18% and 25.34%, respectively. Small-cap stocks peaked in late 1928 and began turning down a year before large caps as the race for leadership intensified and investors herded toward the large caps in the final bubble just as they did toward tech stocks in late 1999 and early 2000. But farther out into the future, small caps will have a moderate edge into the next major downturn after 2009, as shown in Figure 6.8, due to the continued Innovation Stage of the echo baby boom into around 2013.

Small-cap value should clearly be the best equity sector in that extreme downturn. But the fact that the echo baby boom's birth cycle is smaller and shorter than the baby boom's means that this will be the first down cycle where the Innovation Stage of the next generation does not create a boom in small-cap stocks while large caps decline. The coming downturn from 2010 to 2023 will therefore see declining trends in both large caps and small caps, unlike in the 1930s and 1970s downturns wherein small caps performed well after the initial crash.

And if you are going to look at small caps, we always advise waiting until we've seen a major crash in the large caps before investing in small-cap stocks once we enter an extended decline due to demographic forces. That is an ironclad rule that we add to our Small-Cap Indicator. Our models in Chapter 7 will be recommending that aggressive investors start looking at the best sectors of stocks after 2012, and that growth investors do so from late 2014 on. Then you could look at small caps in addition to large caps into 2019. As we showed in *The Roaring 2000s Investor,* small caps also outperformed large caps six times in cumulative gains from 1932–1946 when the Bob Hope generation was in its peak Innovation Stage—but only after the crash of 1929–1932, when they not only peaked a year earlier than large caps in 1928 but declined to a greater degree! Similarly, the greatest outperformance in history of small over large caps came after the 1974 crash, from 1975 into 1983.

Despite the brief resurgence of small-cap stocks from 1999 to 2003, we still see large caps having the edge from late 2004 into 2009 or early 2010, especially when adjusted for risk. But small caps will still perform better than they did in the 1990s and can be used, to a degree, for diversification in a portfolio without penalizing returns as much as they did in the 1990s. In the great downturn from 2010 to at least 2022, both sectors will decline, but small-cap value should be the best place to look for selective opportunities after major crashes in the broader markets, as well as in Asia.

INTERNATIONAL EQUITIES

The other broad sector of opportunity for investing in stocks and mutual funds is the international sector. In Chapters 3 and 4 of *The Roaring 2000s Investor* we looked at the demographic trends in most countries, developed and emerging, around the world. We are not going to repeat that extensive analysis here, but we included the summary charts of demographic growth prospects for fifty-two countries in Chapters 3 and 4 of *The Roaring 2000s Investor*. To make a long story short, the greatest growth trends are in China, Southeast Asia, and India. Europe is a mixed bag, but the growth trends are generally positive into 2009–2011, with countries such as Spain and Portugal showing stronger growth lasting into around 2020. South America has strong trends but suffers from the emerging-world paradox that we covered in Chapter 4 of *The Roaring 2000s Investor*.

The key insight there was that until you develop the political and economic infrastructures to support an industrialized and middle-class economy, demographic trends from consumer spending and free-market business are not the primary drivers of the economy. Hence, we don't recommend investing in countries that have not clearly achieved the newly industrialized stage with reasonable political stability. This includes most of South America and Central America and Asian countries like Indonesia, Malaysia, and the Philippines, as well as India and Pakistan. Most of Africa is out of the question.

Hence, we recommend investing in the more developed economies of Southeast Asia, including Hong Kong, Taiwan, South Korea, Singapore, and urban China—and, further out into the future, India. We don't recommend Japan as strongly, as its Spending Wave (after declining for thirteen years after 1990) doesn't turn up strongly until 2008 or 2009. Asia, including Japan, will be a great place to diversify equity investments after the great boom peaks in the United States and most of Europe.

We are forecasting that from mid-2005 into 2010, large-cap growth stocks will again have the best risk/return performance for investors, much as in 1994–1999. Then their time will be over for more than a decade to fol-

low, from late 2010 into at least 2022. Very-high-quality bonds, CDs, and
T-bills will be king after late 2010, and so may the best sectors of small-cap
value and late-stage spending sectors like health care, to the degree you invest in U.S. stocks after 2010—but wait for a major crash between late
2012/early 2013 and late 2014. Many parts of Asia, including Japan, China,
and South Korea will still be growing after 2010 and will represent the best
opportunities for large-cap equities. It would be best to wait at least for the
first major corrections in world markets into late 2012 or late 2014 to invest
in Asia. Between early and late 2010 it should be best to scale back from
U.S. equities, both large-cap and small-cap, into high-quality corporate
bonds.

PREDICTING INFLATION AND THE BOND MARKETS

Siegel's book also clearly shows, as you would expect, that stocks greatly
outperform bonds over the long term. From 1926 to 2000, large-cap stocks
had average annual returns of 10.91% with annual risk levels (standard deviation) of 20.73%, versus long-term bonds at 5.34% returns and risks of
8.07%. Stocks have delivered roughly double the returns of long-term
bonds over the last century, but at a little more than double the risk. That
would only be fair and expected. But it would also say that bonds are a
slightly better risk-adjusted investment. And of course, stocks have less predictable returns for meeting near-term life goals. So many investors need
bonds to secure approaching needs for college or retirement. In addition,
bonds can be used in a portfolio simply to bring down the risks and volatility even when the income is not needed in the near term.

It is important to understand that there is a very wide choice both in
maturities of bonds and the risk level of the loan that underlies them, which
creates many different investment advantages and disadvantages. Changes
in economic trends, higher or lower inflation rates, and stronger or weaker
growth can make a big difference in the relative performance of short-term
or long-term bonds or high-yield (junk) and lower-yield (high-grade)
bonds. For example, during this boom from 1982 to 1997, long-term government bonds outperformed short-term bonds in inflation-adjusted returns,
9.6% versus 2.9%. That is very substantial and resulted from the fact that inflation rates were falling for most of this boom and longer-term bonds benefit both from higher yields as well as the capital appreciation from falling
interest rates.

The simplest insight into bond investing is that long-term bonds do

better when inflation is falling and short-term bonds do better when inflation is rising. Demographic trends will forecast approximately when inflation will rise or fall two decades in advance! The second insight is that
higher-risk or higher-yield bonds do better when the economy is strong
and lower-risk or lower-yield bonds do better when the economy is weak.
The Spending Wave will predict when the economy will be stronger or
weaker for almost five decades into the future.

Figure 6.11 is an update of our Inflation Indicator in past books. We
have updated it with more years of data, and, based on this longer time
frame, we have recalibrated back to our original three-year lag on labor
force growth (when we first discovered this indicator in 1989) from a two-
year lag in past years. Our view of inflation is very different from economists'. We don't see it as a "monetary phenomenon"—too many dollars
chasing too few goods. That is merely the symptom. We see it as the very
fundamental cost of raising and educating young people and then incorporating them into the workforce. Every major period of rising inflation in
history has seen higher expenses either to fight a war or to incorporate
young people into the economy, and, conversely, lower productivity (from
such younger people) and/or lower production of consumer goods (in war
periods).

The only reliable indicator outside of major war periods that we

FIGURE 6.11 Inflation Indicator, 1959–2006

have been able to find to project inflation trends is labor force growth on a three-year lag. Note the incredible correlation of this long-term indicator with changes in inflation trends, despite the fact that so many individual variables—from oil prices to commodity prices to growth surges and down-turns, government deficits, trade deficits, and currency exchange rates—can change so dramatically over time. In fact, the only major divergence from this indicator came when the more extreme 1974–1975 downturn caused demand pressures to turn down sharply enough ahead of the indicator's prediction of falling inflation rates. Likewise, the rapid recovery caused de-mand pressures to turn up more quickly. But again, that was only a short-term divergence. This indicator basically predicted when inflation rates would be falling and when they would be rising, and captured almost all the key turning points.

This brings us to the basic seasons in inflation trends and when to be in long-term or short-term bonds for your portfolio strategies. With strong rising trends in inflation from the late 1960s into the late 1970s, short-term bonds were best. And since the Spending Wave was forecasting increasing recessions in the economy, the highest-quality short-term bonds—T-bills and high-grade corporate CDs—were better. Those investments at least kept you slightly ahead of inflation and gave you very predictable income streams. On the other hand, if you had bought thirty-year government or twenty-year corporate bonds, you would have been constantly locking in lower yields that would have not only penalized you in your income stream into the future but would have devalued the principal of your bonds as in-flation rates and interest rates continued to rise into 1980 to 1981.

The trends changed dramatically as the baby bust was entering the labor force at slower rates and the new baby boomers were rising in their productivity as workers; inflation fell—dramatically at first, from 1980 into 1986, and then again from early 1991 into late 1998. During that period long-term bonds would have had the advantage of locking in higher yields, whereas shorter-term bonds would have given you lower yields into the fu-ture, as well as returning substantial appreciation on the value of your bonds. That's what occurred for most of the 1980s and 1990s as the baby bust entered the workforce. That's why we were predicting near-zero infla-tion rates by the mid- to late 1990s in the late 1980s and early 1990s in *The Great Boom Ahead*.

In the early to mid-1980s bonds did almost as well as large-cap stocks, despite their lower risk. In fact, 1981 to 1986 were the best five years in his-tory for long-term bonds. The advantage of bonds versus stocks waned in the 1990s as stocks did much better and disinflation was much milder, but that period was still one of the better in history for long-term bonds. In the next decade stocks will beat bonds to an even greater degree. It will be the downturn of 2010–2023 that will see long-term bonds as the best risk/return investment again, much as in the 1930s and 1980s. But between now and then there will be some interesting plays in the bond market for investors who need fixed income for near-term life goals or for reducing the risk and volatility in their portfolios.

Again, we have been able to get a more accurate forecast for near-term inflation trends by using monthly labor force growth on a three-year lag (Figure 6.11). Even though we can roughly forecast the entry and exit of new generations, as we will discuss just ahead, we can get actual labor force growth numbers that affect short-term swings in the economy, like the slowdown of 2000–2002, which was not due to demographic trends, but to the tech shakeout and business overexpansion of the late 1990s. If we look at Figure 6.11 we can see that inflation trends were rising above trend in 1999 when inflation started to resurface. The slowdown in 2000 to 2002 helped to reduce the slightly rising inflation potential into 2002. Due to the slower economy in 2000, and especially in late 2001–2002, inflation pressures were already low in 2003 and early 2004 in the recovery and should continue to fall a bit or remain flat into around early 2006. The Inflation Indicator in Figure 6.11 also suggested a substantial drop in inflation rates after 2002 into 2003.

This means that inflation rates would start falling again by late 2005, after the Fed raises short-term interest rates when it sees the economy and stock market recovering more strongly from late 2003 on. Mid-2005 to early 2006 will represent a great time to lock in long-term government and corporate bond yields again and benefit from appreciation as interest rates fall. After rising a bit into mid-2004, mortgage rates are likely to start falling again into mid-2005 or early 2006, and then start rising again mildly between 2006 and 2010. We have developed a new indicator for better projecting inflation trends past the three-year lag on monthly labor force growth. The Long-Term Inflation Forecasting Model in Figure 6.12 looks at the predictable intended entry of new workers and the exit of retiring workers over the next two decades.

In the past we have used government forecasts of labor force growth that incorporate demographic projections, but a lot of other stuff clouds the real picture—just as most economic models do. Demographic research shows that the average person enters the workforce today at around age 20 and retires at age 63. The entry age seems to be rising very slowly, but the retirement age may grow to later ages as baby boomers look at living longer

FIGURE 6.12 Long-Term Inflation Forecasting Model, 1950–2030

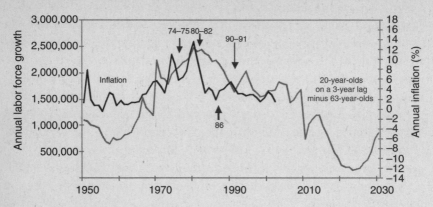

and being more active in retirement, but that hasn't occurred yet and the leading edge of the baby-boom generation was just entering retirement starting in 2000. The impact of new workers' entering is the traditional three-year lag of rising office-space investments and expenditures for equipment and training before higher productivity starts to offset those investments. But the impact of people retiring has an immediate impact from freeing up office space and equipment. Hence, our new model forecasts labor force growth by adding a twenty-year lag on the immigration-adjusted birth index with an additional three-year lag for rising productivity, and then subtracting a sixty-three-year lag for retirement with no lag.

What this indicator forecasts is that the first wave of baby boomers will start to exit the workforce faster than echo baby boomers will enter, especially from 2003 into 2005. Then the second wave will exit, making a steep drop to 2010. The third and largest wave will exit from about 2014 or 2015 into 2026. This means we are likely to see continued disinflation, not only as a result of our more accurate three-year lag on monthly labor force growth into mid-2005 or early 2006 but also due to the accelerated baby-boom retirements into 2005. We could see lower interest rates between mid-2005 and early 2006.

We see long-term bonds doing much better than short-term bonds between mid- and late 2004 and mid-2005. Stocks will do better in that time frame, but to the degree you have fixed income in your portfolio, long-term bonds will be the place to shift. And you can afford to move into higher-yield or higher risk bonds due to the stronger economy. Then short-term bonds would be a better bet from early 2006 into 2010, when inflationary pressures should rise again mildly before falling dramatically in the years to follow. From late 2010 on, high-quality long-term corporate bonds should be the best overall risk/return investment into 2022–2023, with one caveat: T-bills or CDs will be better during the first real shocks to economic growth likely around 2011 to 2012, when bonds will very likely be downgraded due to the sharp deterioration in earnings of companies as occurred between mid-1931 and mid-1932 in the last deflationary downturn (Figure 6.13).

Figure 6.13 shows how the price of corporate bonds dropped an average of almost 30% from late 1928 into mid-1932. The sharpest drop came between mid-1931 and mid-1932, when the stock market was in its steepest decline and bottoming process. Figure 6.14 shows how the decline was much worse in lower-quality bonds. When the yield goes up, the value of the bond goes down. Bond yields went from around 4.2% to about 5.7% on Aaa twenty-year corporate bonds between mid-1931 and mid-1932, while Baa bonds went from around 5.8% up to almost 13% between mid-1930 and mid-1932—a much more dramatic change in yields and prices. By the end of 1932, Aaa bonds had already recovered most of their price drop. So, the first lesson is that you want to be in the highest-quality corporate bonds possible. The second is that even in such high-quality bonds, there will be a temporary panic when the crash is at its worst, and in that brief one-year or so period, T-bills or short-term, high-quality CDs would be the best place to have your money—or cash.

We could see the first real bout of deflation in prices since the early 1930s begin in 2011, and then we will see a major wave of deflation from 2014 into 2020 to 2023. That will wreak havoc on earnings and unemployment, in addition to the already strong downturn in spending from 2010 on. The worst corrections in the stock market are likely to coincide with the years that bring both the strongest downturns in spending and the greatest deflation. Those years would be 2011–2012, 2014, and 2020–2022. The worst phase of the first great crash from 2010 into 2012 is likely to come between mid- to late 2011 and mid- to late 2012. T-bills and high-quality CDs will be the best defense against those most ominous periods, while high-quality corporate bonds should fare the best for the rest of the period from 2010 into 2022 or 2023 that will very closely parallel the 1930s and early 1940s. Why do we not recommend long-term U.S. Treasuries? Because the immense pressures from rising unemployment and Social Security demands, along with much lower personal and corporate tax revenues, will put the U.S. government in a position of unbelievable mushrooming deficits and higher bond offerings to finance those deficits that will make their bonds less attractive than the most stable and surviving large corporations.

To summarize: We are generally recommending long-term corporate

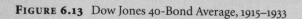

FIGURE 6.13 Dow Jones 40-Bond Average, 1915–1933

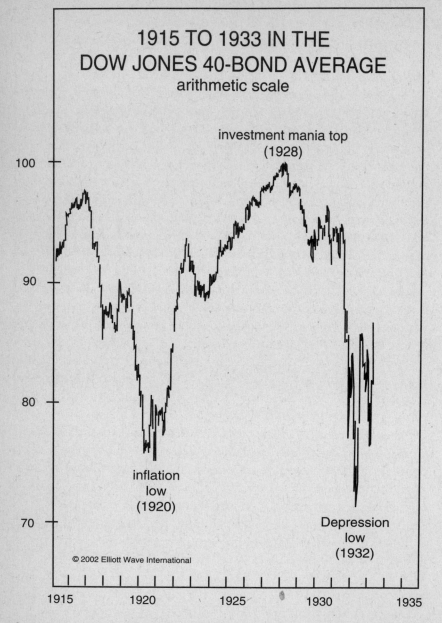

1915 TO 1933 IN THE
DOW JONES 40-BOND AVERAGE
arithmetic scale

investment mania top
(1928)

inflation
low
(1920)

Depression
low
(1932)

© 2002 Elliott Wave International

Source: Robert Prechter, *Conquer the Crash,* 2002, p. 146.

FIGURE 6.14 Moody's Corporate Bond Yields, 1929–1932, inverted, log scale

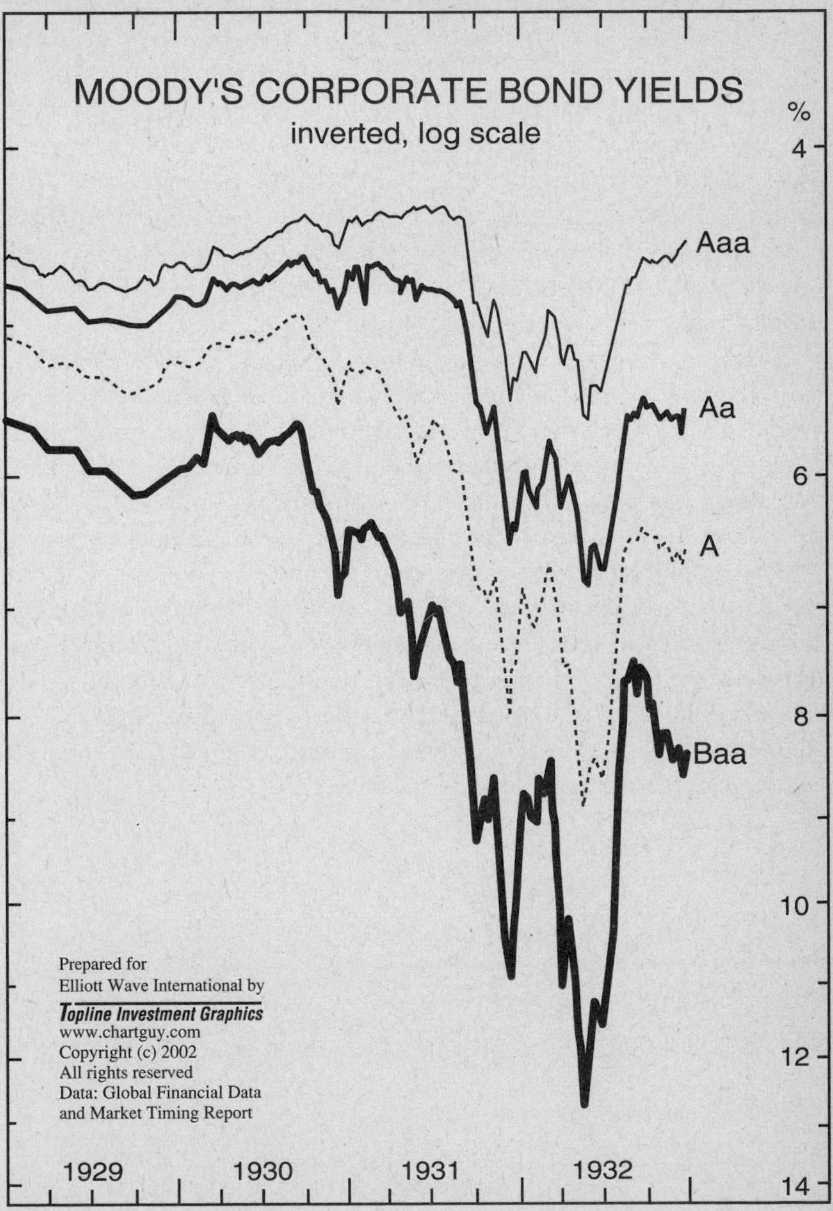

MOODY'S CORPORATE BOND YIELDS
inverted, log scale

%
4

Aaa

Aa

A

6

Baa

8

10

Prepared for
Elliott Wave International by
Topline Investment Graphics
www.chartguy.com
Copyright (c) 2002
All rights reserved
Data: Global Financial Data
and Market Timing Report

12

1929   1930   1931   1932

14

Source: Robert Prechter, *Conquer the Crash,* 2002, p. 144. Elliott Wave International, Global Financial Data and Market Timing Report.

and government bonds from mid-2004 into mid-2005–early 2006. Then short-term CDs and T-bills from early 2006 into late 2010 for the portion of your portfolio that needs to be in fixed income. Then from late 2010 on we are recommending very-high-quality long-term corporate bonds with the option of switching into T-bills and high-quality CDs from mid-2011 into late 2012. Long-term corporate bonds should be best again from 2013 into 2020. Then we recommend T-bills and CDs again from 2020 into 2022. After 2022 or early 2023, long-term bonds should be out of favor for decades as we see mildly rising inflation trends as we did from the early 1940s into the 1950s and 1960s. Use CDs and other very-short-term debt instruments for the fixed-income portion of your portfolio after 2022.

Now that we have looked at the broader sectors of investments and when they will be most favored or disfavored, in Chapter 7 we will show how the risks and returns of different investments vary dramatically in the different seasons of our economy that are created by demographic and technological trends. We will look at how to build diversified portfolios in the best sectors of investments, while avoiding sectors that are not favored by demographic trends. We will also look at the best sectors within large-cap growth stocks that we see as the best area to focus in for the great boom ahead. We will also outline basic strategies for playing the greatest downturn since the Great Depression. Finally, we will develop a more focused version of the simple equity model that we presented in Figure 3.16 in Chapter 3 that gives more than double the returns of the S&P 500 over the last five decades with risks that are still lower.

Chapter 7

OPTIMUM PORTFOLIO STRATEGIES FOR THE GREAT BOOM AHEAD AND THE GREAT BUST TO FOLLOW

Understanding Risks and Returns in the Different Seasons of Our Economy

THE CORE PRINCIPLES OF INVESTING

Perhaps the greatest lesson from the 2000–2002 crash was not to concentrate in only the hottest sectors of the market, abandoning systematic and diversified investment strategies. Most investors have a grave misunderstanding of risk. We tend to think that the longer an investment goes up or outperforms, the more likely it will do so in the future. Conversely, we think the longer it goes down the more likely it is to do so in the future. This point of view is dead wrong most of the time and represents the foundation for the oldest principle of successful investing: *contrary thinking.*

Let's quickly review the Human Model of Forecasting in Figure 7.1, repeated from Chapter 2. We tend to forecast trends as a straight-line extrapolation from the past when reality is clearly such that trends move in a curvilinear or cyclical manner. This tendency causes us to be the most optimistic and risk-accepting at the top of a cycle when there is actually the greatest risk and negative returns likely ahead. And then we become the most pessimistic and risk-averse at the bottom, when the markets have washed out and discounted the worst of risks and the longest periods of high returns typically lie ahead.

This tendency to project the recent past into the future is what makes most of us terrible investors, and it causes bubbles to develop near the tops

FIGURE 7.1 The Human Model of Forecasting

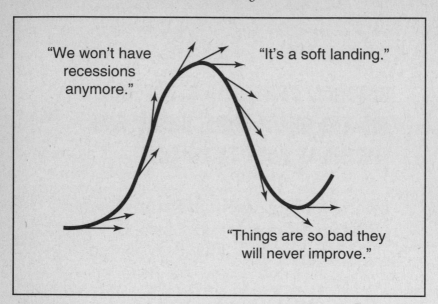

of very robust markets as occurred in 1987 and 1999. The bubbles with un-realistic valuations, of course, develop to the greatest degree in the strongest sectors during the uptrend in the cycle. Most investors buy more and more of the hottest sectors and less and less of sectors they may have previously included in their portfolio for diversification of risk. Hence, we abandon the principle of diversification that actually represents the best single way of reducing our risk while aiming for strong long-term returns. As a result, we get ourselves into the highest-risk positions just before a major correction, so that we suffer the worst of the downturn, and then put ourselves in the lowest-risk position by selling out just in time to miss the stellar returns of the next rebound.

The principle of diversification is the most critical. If you diversify in several sectors (typically four to five), in the long run you will get the cumulative returns of those sectors, but in short-term corrections you will typically experience less volatility or risk. Why? Different sectors go up and down at different times and to different degrees. So the different cycles tend to offset one another to a significant degree. This also means that you need to choose good, long-term sectors that have low correlation and move in different patterns over time, as we will cover later in this chapter.

So let's stop here to summarize the realities of human tendencies and the core principles of investing required to counter those tendencies.

THE SEVEN HUMAN REALITIES OF INVESTING

1. The nature of the markets is that they move in a cyclical and progressive (or exponential) manner.

2. We project in a linear manner, hence we have a grave misunderstanding of reality and risk.

3. Our human tendencies cause us to perceive low risk (near tops) when risk is greatest and high risk (near bottoms) when it is lowest.

4. We tend to chase the hottest sectors, funds, and stocks and perceive such a strategy to be the way to achieve the highest returns, even though that has proven not to be effective precisely because we tend to buy into those sectors when they are hot and to sell out when they are not—hence, we don't realize those great gains—or, at worse, we even lose money.

5. Even in extended bull markets, there are substantial corrections, and especially in this "bubble boom."

6. You don't get higher returns without taking higher risks. The strongest sectors in the most recent upturn typically suffer the greatest setbacks in the correction to follow. Only systematic investment strategies can offset these inherent risks to a substantial degree.

7. The market is not your friend. "I believe in the markets, I believe in me." It is constantly trying to talk you into buying near the top and selling near the bottom, which reduces your long-term returns while increasing your long-term risks. Smart investors buy low and sell high by following a system.

THE SEVEN CORE PRINCIPLES OF INVESTING
(TO COUNTER OUR HUMAN TENDENCIES)

1. Always follow a system, despite your emotions.

2. Use an objective financial adviser or coach to keep you on that system.

3. Learn to think contrarily; don't buy more high and sell more low.

4. Don't chase the hottest investments based on performance alone. Understand the past risks associated with the returns of each investment and how they differ in varying economic cycles.

5. Always diversify among at least four different investment sectors that have relatively low correlation in both up and down markets.

6. Understand your risk tolerance and income needs, and don't commit to a portfolio strategy that is likely to violate your personal limits in risk.

7. Focus on diversified sectors that are favored by projectable mid- to long-term trends within your time horizon.

We covered these principles in more depth in both *The Roaring 2000s* and *The Roaring 2000s Investor,* and most of them have been espoused by the most successful investment strategists and experts of the past century. But there is one principle—and perhaps the most important—that we have been able to leverage to a high degree with our research. That is Principle 7: Focus on diversified sectors that are favored by projectable mid- to long-term trends within your time horizon. The unique advantage of our forecasting tools is that the demographic and technology/product/industry/new economy life cycle (S-curve) trends we covered in Chapter 1 are highly quantifiable and projectable. What we have found in our research is that it is actually the short-term trends in the market that are highly susceptible to political events and swings in investor psychology (greed and fear) that are very hard to predict. Most experts focus on such trends and perceive that long-term trends are impossible to predict, precisely because their experience with short-term trends is so sporadic.

The truth is that long-term trends are very fundamental, and hence cause-and-effect-driven, which actually makes them highly projectable decades out with a relatively high degree of accuracy. The indicators and forecasts we have given thus far in this book can help you clearly determine which sectors of our economy and investments are the best places to be for many years to come as well as when they will not. Hence, you can develop a portfolio that is both diversified (Principle 5) and focused in all winning segments (Principle 7). This is the greatest advantage for long-term portfolio design precisely because the commonly accepted strategies for diversification spread a portfolio randomly among very different investment sectors and half of those sectors tend to underperform substantially for long periods of time and bring your returns down more than required to lower your risk.

Our approach allows you to still be in all high or favorable return sectors while lowering your risk by choosing the outperforming sectors that move in different patterns—the best of both worlds! How do we do this?

THE SECRET OF ASSET ALLOCATION

One of the greatest innovations in investment management in this Information Revolution since the invention of computers in 1946 has been the practice of asset allocation that brings a scientific and quantifiable approach for achieving effective diversification in investment portfolios. Harry Markowitz first developed the theory behind this practice in the early 1950s (for which he won a Nobel Prize in economics in 1990). The principle again is actually quite simple. If you diversify into several different investment sectors, you will achieve the same cumulative returns of those sectors in the long run, but the volatility and risks in short-term swings in the markets can be reduced substantially to the degree that those sectors inherently move up and down in different patterns over time. So the critical insight was to historically analyze different sectors and compare their patterns of volatility to determine which sectors had the least correlation in movement short term and long term.

To summarize: by putting four to five or so of such low-correlation sectors in a portfolio, the extremes in highs and lows in short-term fluctuations of the market would be lower than if you were only in one sector, while you could still target the cumulative or average returns to meet your investment needs and risk tolerance. This is the best single method of reducing risk in investments. Yet most investors think the best method is buying the sectors that have been the strongest and seem to be indestructible and then jumping out of the markets every time a correction looks possible. The great majority of investors, using these methods, end up losing as their own fear and greed works against them—and they are not based on a realistic understanding of risk, as we pointed out earlier.

It is very hard to tell exactly when a bull market run will finally end. Most people get out substantially too early or too late. Then it is equally hard to pick a bottom, and then again, investors tend to get back in too early or too late. Most people lose by trying to time the market short term and end up with higher tax bills to boot. We recommend largely staying invested except when strong recurring cycles such as the Decennial and Four-Year Presidential cycles hit. And, of course, you generally don't want to be in stocks when the demographic trends turn down, as they did in Japan in the 1990s or the United States in the 1930s and 1970s.

However, there is a serious flaw in modern asset allocation practice. It's not that it doesn't work or isn't quantifiable and scientific. It is the time frame that the academics and experts have used to measure the average risk and returns of such investments. They used the longest time frame possible, back to 1926, where there was adequate data on major sectors such as large-cap and small-cap stocks, and short-term and long-term bonds—which would naturally seem to make the most sense. Yet it doesn't make that much sense when you realize that a seventy-plus-year time frame does not match the investment time frame of virtually any investor (which is typically five to ten years or thirty years at most). And it makes no sense whatsoever if you understand the very different stages our economy goes through due to demographic booms and busts and new technology/new economy cycles.

To make a long story short, what the experts have done is to average out some of the most extreme economic cycles that occurred in the real life of investors since 1926: the Roaring Twenties, the Great Depression, World War II, the postwar boom of the 1950s and 1960s, the inflationary recession of the 1970s, and the incredible boom of the 1980s and 1990s. As we showed in Chapter 1, there is an approximately eighty-year cycle in which new economies emerge and mature every other generation. Figure 7.2 shows how this occurs in four distinct stages, just as we showed in the S-curve progression in Chapter 1. These create what we call the "four seasons" of our economy. There are two very different booms and two very different busts that follow the same four-stage life cycle that new products and technologies do. In addition there are two substages in the boom periods, with rising, falling, or moderate inflation trends. These four "seasons" represent

FIGURE 7.2   The Four Seasons of Our Economy, 1968–2048

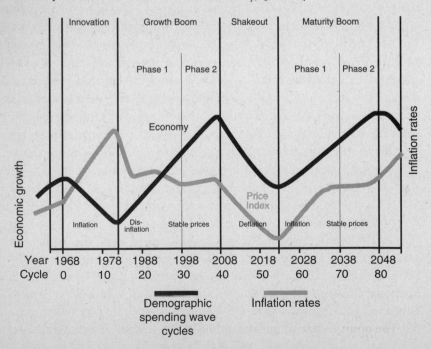

long periods of time wherein the fundamental economic trends will generally go in one direction.

The most important insight here is that these seasonal trends clearly
favor some sectors of investments and disfavor others. Why diversify into
investments that have long-term downward trends?

The last economic season was the first season in the cycle, the Innovation Stage, with rising inflation and worsening recessions from late 1968
into late 1982. It was in this stage that the most important new innovations,
from microchips to PCs, emerged for generating the next technology and
economic revolution. Large-cap stocks and long-term bonds were crucified, while small-cap stocks, real estate, and many international sectors did
well. Small caps were the best single sector, as small companies benefit from
innovations that come earlier in the new generation's life cycle. In the
Growth Boom Stage, the new generation is moving into its family and career cycle and adopting the new products it innovated in the Innovation
Stage. Hence, there is strong, sustained growth in the economy, a rising
stock market, and falling inflation rates from rising productivity and falling
workforce entry. The trends all reversed from the 1970s and the trends again
largely went in one direction favoring certain types of investments and dis-
favoring others. In our current Growth Boom Stage since 1982, large-cap
stocks and long-term bonds have been the heroes, while international,
small-cap and real estate sectors have lagged in returns to different degrees.

The Shakeout Stage follows and was represented in the last economic
cycle by the Great Depression, which followed the Roaring Twenties (top of
the Growth Boom). Deflation, massive unemployment, extreme stock
crashes, falling real estate prices, and the more incremental technology innovations that extend the growth of the new industries are the trends in
that phase. High-quality corporate bonds are the best sector in that season.
Most equity and real estate sectors get hammered the worst in this stage,
with the exception of international areas with growing demographic trends
such as China, Japan, and South Korea from 2010 to 2020.

Then finally the new technologies and industries enter a Maturity
Boom Stage with a growing economy from the next generation's innovations, with mildly rising inflation trends (coming out of the deflation era)
that moderate as the generation increases its productivity, and a few large
companies dominating most maturing growth industries. In the next Maturity Boom from 2023 into the 2040s, international growth stocks should
be the best sector, along with large caps and small caps, while long-term
bonds will be the worst sector.

The point is that an understanding of the seasons of our economy is critical to focusing in the sectors that will be favored mid- to long term. The secret to asset allocation is to choose strong sectors that are favored by the season and to then identify which sectors or subsectors have low correlation and can create effective diversification. This will allow you to achieve the highest returns possible at lower risks. Do not just randomly pick sectors that have low correlation over very long periods of time. The classic approach to asset allocation gives investors more moderate returns in exchange for lower risks precisely because very-long-term research shows low correlation. However, our research has shown that the actual returns, correlations, and risks can vary enormously within each season and we will comment more on that later in this chapter.

By averaging out all of these extreme seasons over the last seventy-plus years, the experts came to the conclusion that the best risk/return portfolios would come from diversifying equally among the four broadest investment sectors: large-cap stocks, small-cap stocks, international stocks, and bonds. These sectors do have low correlations, but much of their low correlation is because they perform so differently in these long-term seasons, but not always in the short-term corrections, when the rubber meets the road and you are tempted to buy or sell. Again, we have found that in most seasons, two of these sectors will do well and two will lag in the booms—and worse, do very poorly in the busts. This classic approach is still a "good" way to invest, as it does achieve a reasonable degree of diversification and lower risks versus returns. But it is clearly not the optimal way to invest since it causes the investor to give up more returns than are necessary to achieve those lower risks in each season.

We are also told, by the experts, that we should simply hold stocks and equity investments for the long run. Why? Because they deliver the highest long-term returns and they always come back if you have a long enough time horizon. They typically say a ten-year time horizon is sufficient and that would fit many of our investment objectives. But we would argue again that it makes a huge difference where you are in the seasons and economic cycle. Let us give you a few examples of reality and see how you feel about the proposition of holding stocks for the long run. If you had bought blue-chip stocks in 1929, you would have suffered an 89% loss by mid-1932 and, despite a strong short-term rally into 1937, you would have still been down by almost 80% adjusted for inflation in 1942 when the next boom season started. You would have had to then wait twenty-four years, until 1953, to break even! Ouch!!!

Similarly, if you had bought the Dow in 1965 you would have been down by 70%, adjusted for inflation, fourteen years later, in late 1982, and would have finally broken even in 1993, twenty-eight years later. Or internationally, if you had bought the Nikkei in Japan in 1989 you would have been down by 67% by 1992 and down by 80% in early 2003, thirteen years later. Our demographic trends suggest a rally in the Nikkei from around 2003–2004 into 2020, but the trends aren't likely to be strong enough to see a new high back above the 1989 high for many decades. So you might not see positive returns in your entire lifetime if you happened to buy stocks for the long run in Japan! And the terrible but real truth is that most investors buy more toward the tops of markets due to their emotional approach to investing.

Why do the experts take such a long-term approach, which is so at odds with our time horizons and the reality of long-term economic cycles? It is precisely because they don't have proven tools for forecasting long-term trends, and hence, they see the world as a "random walk." They believe that short-term political and random trends are more important than long-term trends, which as we show are highly projectable. Hence, they are left with a reality that anything could happen in the future and that changes in short-term trends could significantly alter the long-term trends, while our research shows that the long-term trends manifest despite the short-term fluctuations. Hence, they feel the best way to project the future is the long-term average of what has happened in the past. And that would bring you back to a very moderate return portfolio in this decade.

And why do they believe this random walk theory of reality? Because, outside of a few less reliable and quantifiable long-term cycles such as the Kondratieff Wave (over fifty-five- to sixty-year cycles), there exists in economic theory and history no way of projecting fundamental trends—that is, until the 1980s. It was in the early eighties that the U.S. government started tracking demographic trends in economic activity and spending with the ability to use computers to analyze them. Such demographic data has been used mainly in consumer marketing to better identify the best segments for focusing and advertising consumer products and services.

Our research, from my practical experience in strategic planning and marketing, has simply allowed us to extend this new technology of demographics into longer-range forecasting. What we are saying, as we did in the introduction, is that this new methodology is simply a part of the new Information Revolution and brings business and investment strategy to a new level of effectiveness that simply was not possible before, like air or space travel before this century. And the truth is, like on the S-curve progression of any new technology or idea, it will take many decades for most people to realize the potential of such new research and practices. That is why it represents a huge advantage to you today!

We are simply trying to convince you to take advantage of these new but very scientific and quantifiable economic insights before the greatest boom in history is over. Many businesspeople, financial advisers, and investors have already reaped huge gains from these insights since the late 1980s when we first established them.

What we will do now is take a new look at the long-term performance of different investment sectors and see just how much the risks and returns vary in each season, and why it makes no sense to base your projections for the next decade or more on the average risks and returns of the last seventy years or more. We recommend comparing risks and returns either with performance in the present economic season or in similar seasons in the past. It makes no sense to compare investment performance today with the inflationary/recession era of the 1970s, or even the boom of the 1950s and 1960s, and certainly not with the Great Depression of the 1930s.

A clear understanding of quantifiable and projectable fundamental demographic and new technology/new economy cycles is your greatest advantage for leveraging the final stage of the greatest boom in history into 2009 or early 2010, and for preserving your wealth in potentially the greatest downturn we will see from 2010 into around 2022. We are recommending the opposite of what the experts have been recommending recently, and we will be recommending the opposite of what they will be saying in late 2009. This represents the ultimate in strategy for long-term timing and contrary thinking.

A New Look at Long-Term Investment Trends

We'll start again with the most important trend: equity investing. And we will start from the best present long-term analysis and work into the new insights from our economic models. Long-term studies have shown that stocks greatly outperform bonds and other major investments, and that small-cap stocks substantially outperform large-cap stocks. That would make sense given that stocks are more risky than bonds and small caps are more risky than large caps. Remember Principle 6 from "The Seven Human Realities of Investing," presented earlier in this chapter: You don't get higher returns without taking higher risks. In Table 7.1 we show the difference in large-cap stocks versus small-cap from 1926 to 1996 from Jeremy Siegel's excellent book *Stocks for the Long Run*. First note that the smallest stocks, the tenth decile or lowest 10% in size, had average annual returns of 13.83%, 40.5% higher than the largest, or first decile (top 10%) of stocks at

TABLE 7.1 Risks and Returns of Stocks by Size

Size Decile	Compound Annual Return	Annual Risk	Risk-Adjusted Performance Index
1st (largest)	9.84%	18.9%	.52
2nd	11.05%	22.4%	.49
3rd	11.49%	24.2%	.47
4th	11.63%	26.7%	.44
5th	12.16%	27.5%	.44
6th	11.82%	28.5%	.41
7th	11.88%	31.0%	.38
8th	12.15%	34.8%	.35
9th	12.25%	27.3%	.45
10th (smallest)	13.83%	46.5%	.30

Source: Jeremy J. Siegel, *Stocks for the Long Run* (New York: McGraw-Hill, 1998).

9.84%. So why shouldn't you just hold small-cap stocks for the long run? The real story comes when you look at the difference in annual risk, which measures how much up-and-down volatility you have to stomach as an investor.

The smallest-company stock risk of 46.5% was almost 2.5 times that of the largest-company stock risk at 18.9%. 150% higher risk for 40% higher gains? It doesn't take a genius to tell you that's not a good deal! You'd spend all those extra gains on Pepto-Bismol and likely find yourself selling near bottoms far more often and missing most of those gains anyway.

To make the overall picture clearer, we added the last column of this table by dividing the average annual returns by the annual risk to create a simple risk-adjusted performance index. The real secret in this chart is that the largest 10% of stocks actually have the best risk/return ratio at an index of .52. It goes down only as you go to smaller companies. But there is one exception. The ratio rises back up to .45 for the smaller stocks just above the bottom 10%—at the ninth decile. The reason is that the annual risk was much lower for those stocks compared to the smaller or larger companies just above it.

That would suggest that the small-growth companies that make it through the highly competitive growth race in new markets have established a more dominant and sustainable competitive position in their maturing niche markets. So to the degree you do decide you want the higher returns of small-cap stocks, history would suggest that it is much better to go for the larger companies in that investment class. Small-cap companies are most typically defined as the bottom 20% of NYSE listed stocks (or the ninth and tenth deciles in Table 7.1). The ninth decile or larger 10% are clearly more attractive for long-term investment. But note that the risk/ return ratio is still more favorable for the largest company stocks in the top 30% or three deciles, especially the first decile or top 10%.

There is another important point that Siegel makes about small-cap stocks. Most of the outperformance came in just eight years, from 1975 to 1983. We will explain that more fully just ahead. But if you take out those eight years, small-cap stocks would have actually underperformed large caps over the last seventy-one years with much higher risks to boot. This would make a nearly ironclad case that large-cap stocks are a much better long-term investment for the vast majority of investors over most time periods.

EQUITIES: GROWTH VERSUS VALUE AND HOW IT DIFFERS IN LARGE- AND SMALL-CAP STOCKS

The other major clear choice for investors is whether and when to concentrate more in the value or growth sectors of large- or small-cap stocks. Over time growth and value go through different cycles and perform better or worse at different times. Hence, they have their midterm and long-term seasons as well. Over time value has a clear edge due to our human propensity as investors to overreact in boom and bust cycles. Over the last century the greatest long-term investors, from Graham and Dodd to Templeton to Buffett, have tended to be value investors. It sounds great to follow such proven strategies, but that unfortunately takes more guts than most of us have in reality. The famous maxim is "Buy when there is blood in the streets." Very few investors will buy stocks or real estate when their prospects look so dismal. We are programmed to buy high and sell low, as we covered earlier.

Here again is where demographic cycles can be so helpful. The effects of the different seasons in our economy driven by demographic cycles create huge differences in the returns and risks of small- and large-cap stocks, as well as growth and value. But most important, it is much easier to buy when there is "blood in the streets" when you know the fundamental growth trends are still very favorable! But even when they aren't, as in 1930–1942 and 1969–1982, value stocks will obviously do much better, as often will small caps due to the Innovation Stages of the next young generation. But in extended booms such as in 1902–1929, 1943–1968, and

1983–2009, large caps and growth stocks will tend to do better. For instance, from 1983 to 1999 growth stocks averaged 19.54% annual returns versus 17.34% for value stocks and large caps averaged 13.93% versus small caps at 9.97%. By using this strategy you can at least be leaning your portfolio in the right direction even if you don't always buy near bottoms when the news is at its worst.

There are very clear cycles even in booms like this one. There are the Decade Hangover Cycle and Decennial Cycle, which we covered in Chapter 3. The practical implications here are that in the early years of most decades, when stocks tend to be down, value stocks do better. In the 1980s, we had a series of slowdowns and stock corrections that favored value stocks. For most of the 1980s, value did better than growth. This is typical of the earlier years of a long-term boom, as occurred in the 1940s. Investors are slow at first to embrace the very stocks that got so hammered in the extended downturn before. Growth started to show itself in the late 1980s, until the Decade Hangover Cycle of the early 1990s set in.

Similarly, after the Decade Hangover Cycle of the early 1990s, value stocks outperformed for two years in 1992 and 1993. But for the rest of the 1990s—eight out of ten years—growth outperformed, as you can see in Figure 7.3. The average annual returns in the 1990s for growth stocks were 21.56% versus 15.53% for value. This meant 38.8% higher returns with risk levels only 29.9% higher. Hence, growth stocks had better returns even when adjusted for risk. Just as the S-curve acceleration increasingly favored large caps in the 1990s, it also favored growth stocks, especially from 1994

FIGURE 7.3 Growth Versus Value, 1990–1999

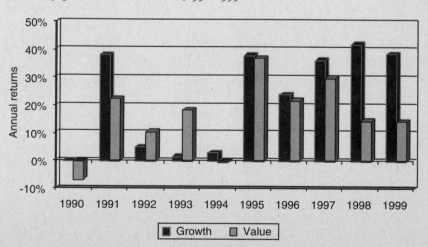

on, when the S-curve started to kick in with consumer technologies such as cellular phones.

Once again value outperformed in 2000 through 2002, while growth and value performed similarly in 2003. But by mid- to late 2004 into 2009–early 2010 we expect growth stocks to lead strongly again as they did from 1994 to 1999. Since we slightly favor large caps over small caps in our models for the coming decade, the best sector for the coming years should be large-cap growth stocks, just as occurred from 1994 to 1999. Large-cap growth stocks tend to dominate increasingly into the 10% to 90% penetration cycle on the S-curve, except in the three-year shakeout in the middle as we approach the 50% S-curve penetration level, as from late 1919–early 1922 or early 2000–late 2002.

GROWTH VERSUS VALUE IN LARGE AND SMALL CAPS

The growth-versus-value issue becomes much more interesting when we look at the differences between large-cap and small-cap stocks over the long run. In small caps there is a much wider divergence. Value is clearly far superior over time, and growth is actually very unattractive. We call these small-cap growth stocks the "gold rush stocks." In large caps, value has a moderate edge over time, but in boom periods, growth is slightly better. Large caps clearly don't vary as much over time in the risk-adjusted performance of growth versus value. Note in Table 7.2 that small caps in the last seventy-three years have seen the most value-oriented stocks outperform the most growth-oriented with average annual returns of 16.28% vs. 0.59%. That is truly astounding! To add insult to injury, the risk levels of small-cap growth were higher by 21%, 40.37 versus 33.35. When it comes to small-cap stocks, value is clearly better, as are the larger half of those companies in that arena as we showed earlier in this chapter.

The reason for this at the simplest level is that there is such a growth struggle for many "tadpoles" to make it when new markets first emerge, yet most of these start-up companies ultimately go under in the innovation or small-cap shakeout to follow, just as we saw in the dot-com crash. This shakeout occurs about midway between the .1% and 10% innovation stage of a new S-curve, just as we get a large-cap shakeout in the middle of the 10%-to-90% growth stage. When these companies take off, they initially have very high growth rates, resulting in very high P/E (price to earnings) ratios. But few will survive, making small-cap growth stocks a very bloody battlefield, as we saw after the e-commerce bubble burst in 2002. On the

TABLE 7.2 Summary of Growth Versus Value, Large- and Small-Cap Stocks, 1926–2000

	AVERAGE ANNUAL RETURN	STANDARD DEVIATION	RISK-ADJUSTED PERFORMANCE INDEX
Small-cap growth	0.59%	40.37%	.01
Small-cap value	16.28%	33.35%	.49
Large-cap growth	10.39%	20.66%	.50
Large-cap value	13.76%	26.81%	.51

other hand, the great battle and volatility of small-cap stocks create opportunities to buy greatly beaten-down firms that do survive or turn around and make strong profits. This is why small-cap value investing pays off so well.

When we look at large caps, they do better in value over time, with average annual returns of 13.76% in value from 1926 to 2000 versus 10.39% in growth. But the risk in the growth stocks was a surprising 33% less at a standard deviation of 20.66 versus 26.81. The reason again is simple: value stocks tend to perform better in downturns, which occur less of the time. But in those downturns the volatility level is much greater, especially with stocks that look very questionable and then turn around. Growth stocks do better in sustained expansions, when risks are actually lower. When you adjust for risk, the index of performance was .502 for large-cap growth and .513 for large-cap value—very close, with only a very slight edge to large-cap value.

To summarize, over the long term, large-cap growth and value stocks perform about the same when adjusted for risk. The real truth is that large-cap value stocks do better in extended downturns such as in 1930–1942 and 1969–1982, and in the early years of most decades or long-term growth booms. When our Spending Wave indicator points down, it's better to be in large-cap value. But our strategies in a downturn clearly prefer not to be in large-cap stocks at all, as they follow the growth of the economy and do the best in boom periods and the worst in bust periods. We tend to prefer bonds, small-cap value, or demographically favored international stocks or late-stage spending sectors such as health care in such extended downturns.

Why is there such a small variation in large-cap growth and value performance? Most very large companies have already made it through the race for leadership and don't have as great a chance of suddenly failing. But they do fall out of favor for shorter periods of time due to complacency in management and market shifts, and can be better buys when they are undervalued and are turning back around. This gives the slight edge to value. It's much harder to kill a large company! But these companies also have to keep growing to initially establish and then maintain their dominance. That's why large-cap growth stocks do better in periods of strong technological expansion, such as late 1914 to 1928 or late 1994 to 2008–2009.

Hence, we have the paradox that over longer periods of time value investing tends to be only very slightly better for large caps, but unbelievably better for small-cap stocks. But in extended booms, and particularly in the latter part of such booms, where larger firms are increasingly competing in a race for leadership to see who will dominate the emerging mass markets, growth tends to have the clear edge, concentrated in large caps, with only brief periods of real strength for small-cap growth. Small-cap growth is clearly by far the worst overall sector for investing over time, with much lower returns and much higher risks. They are the gamblers' or fools' stocks. But there are times in the beginning stages of new innovation surges and S-curves that small-cap growth does very well, as in 1958–1968 (first wave of baby-boom innovation) and 1975–1980 (peak wave of baby-boom innovation). We are projecting that small-cap growth will do well from 2003–2008, but still not quite as well as large-cap growth when adjusted for risk.

We get even greater insights if we dig down into the cycles of large-cap growth, large-cap value, small-cap growth, and small-cap value in greater detail in Table 7.3. For this table we used the groundbreaking research of Kenneth R. French (professor of finance, Tuck School of Business, Dartmouth) and Eugene F. Fama (professor of finance, University of Chicago), which estimated average annual returns for growth and value in both large- and small-cap stocks farther back than anyone else has. These data are not as accurate and reliable as the Ibbotson Associates studies, but Ibbotson is now using these data as well since they are the best available.

This is a long, detailed table, so we will just give you the summary insights. From 1927 to 1929, large-cap growth had the strongest returns. In the crash of 1930 to 1932, large-cap value did the best. From 1933 to 1946, small-cap value excelled with the exception of a brief period from 1938 to 1940, when large-cap growth did the best. From 1947 to 1957, both large-cap growth and large-cap value did the best, with the edge going to large-cap value. From 1958 to 1968, small-cap value and small-cap growth did the best, with the edge again toward value as the baby-boom Innovation Stage kicked in. From 1969 to 1972, large-cap growth was strongest. In the crash of 1973 to 1974, as is typical in a major crash, large-cap value held up the best and small-cap growth was crucified the worst.

TABLE 7.3 Average Value-Weighted Annual Returns: Small-Cap Growth, Small-Cap Value, Large-Cap Growth, Large-Cap Value, 1927–2000

	SCG	SCV	LCG	LCV
1927	53.39	39.16	46.52	29.53
1928	10.39	79.54	48.4	56.41
1929	−51.41	−45.38	−22.13	7.41
1930	−51.78	−49.81	−26.38	NA
1931	−79.18	−50.4	−35.48	NA
1932	−3.98	17.52	−9.98	120.85
1933	5.57	138.25	42.78	43.63
1934	24.46	19.2	12.77	−20.96
1935	53.65	80.01	43.56	90.84
1936	27.83	67.19	27.05	36.74
1937	−65.31	−53.79	−33.64	−41.31
1938	25.39	0.94	34.13	28.66
1939	−13.16	−3.3	4.61	−18.75
1940	−26.88	−10.6	−10	−10.46
1941	−52.61	−5.02	−11.55	−5.1
1942	14.64	36.58	15.48	47.54
1943	14.5	120.57	18.41	41.14
1944	71.79	64.07	16.72	59.73
1945	80.49	91.21	30.17	40.45
1946	−11.68	−12.92	−8.12	−11.43
1947	−7.28	8.53	5.68	8.24
1948	−8.76	−0.3	4.33	6.15
1949	14.48	22.89	25.98	14.65
1950	22.3	54.91	24.64	48.7
1951	14.53	7.23	20.43	16.81
1952	−14.95	5.51	12.72	24.56
1953	−15.15	−5.55	3.84	13.04
1954	29.83	70.41	48.36	72.64
1955	10.17	27.5	30.09	23.82
1956	−5.65	8.54	5.07	−3.64
1957	−14.31	−14.77	−8.87	−22.64
1958	78.76	70.41	40.33	76.95
1959	7.96	20.46	16.48	7.4
1960	−24.51	−6.43	−2.89	−7.8
1961	31.58	26.65	23.2	20.38
1962	−8.64	−9.85	−14.33	2.02
1963	32.07	31.36	23.66	34.03
1964	14.88	26.91	17.61	17.34
1965	31.23	47.7	16.4	15.26
1966	−4.56	−5.91	−11.58	−12.84
1967	134.89	88.03	30.76	25.95

(continued on next page)

	SCG	SCV	LCG	LCV
1968	39.06	59.16	2.37	25.08
1969	−33.64	−32.6	7.98	−18.11
1970	−32.74	−0.22	−8.32	9.21
1971	21.71	15.07	23.19	20.62
1972	−6.26	10.65	24.61	10.12
1973	−52.35	−31.15	−18.84	2.19
1974	−31.68	−17.82	−30.6	−32.54
1975	63.74	61.37	30.61	38.63
1976	44.29	56.61	12.47	44.11
1977	23.2	30.93	−11.49	−2.39
1978	25.19	26.12	7	−1.48
1979	54.67	38.29	7.99	17.16
1980	64.4	25.6	32.49	16.47
1981	−25.96	14.81	−6.89	16.58
1982	17.73	39.23	22.33	20.58
1983	12.59	57.29	16.94	23.39
1984	−24.96	5.56	0.56	26.08
1985	19.03	23.4	31.89	32.53
1986	−3.53	7.48	14.55	26.96
1987	−25.44	−2.59	9.02	−0.51
1988	9.92	25.28	11.11	27.29
1989	7.69	10.91	37.5	28.25
1990	−28.46	−30.1	6.9	−14.02
1991	60.87	42.77	48.78	19.41
1992	−5.5	38.8	2.52	35.96
1993	0.04	39.68	−4.76	31.04
1994	−22.01	2.14	4.35	0.81
1995	32.82	35.32	37.53	44.17
1996	−0.31	24.97	23.44	15.74
1997	2	38.5	33.85	28.2
1998	−9.1	−4.27	47.85	15.59
1999	67.08	24.15	25.08	−12.71
2000	−36.2	3.41	−14.25	21.98

Source: Kenneth R. French and Eugene F. Fama, mba.tuck.dartmouth.edu/pages/faculty/ken.french/

But from 1975 to 1980 small-cap growth saw one of its rare great out-performances, followed by small-cap value leading from 1981 to 1983 as the baby-boom innovation tide was moving into its peak years. Into the new boom, large-cap value first showed the greatest returns from 1984 to 1988, then large-cap growth again from 1989 to 1990. Then small-cap value led again from 1991 to 1993, only to be followed by one of the greatest large-cap growth runs in history, from 1994 to 1999. This was the beginning of the greatest S-curve acceleration of new technologies into the mainstream since 1914 to 1928. The shakeout in the middle of that cycle then favored small-cap value from 2000 into 2002 as a new cycle of innovation from the echo baby boomers kicked in, while the large caps saw their very high growth valuations severely tested. And now our models favor large-cap growth and, to a lesser degree, small-cap growth from 2003 into 2008 or 2009.

In Table 7.4 we can see the differences in returns and risks since the crash of 1974 (a time period that comprises most of our investing experience) and the advantage to investors of having been in the best asset classes when they were leading. Note that not only are the average annual returns very high when a sector is leading, but the risks are relatively low and sometimes very low. This violates the basic principle that higher returns entail higher risks. Over time that is true, but when an investment sector is in its "sweet spot" you get the highest returns and the lowest risks. But these periods typically last only three to six years.

Let's look at the strongest examples from Table 7.4. When small-cap

TABLE 7.4 Best Asset Classes, 1975–2001—The Advantages of Investing in the Best Sectors Since the Crash of 1974

	AVERAGE ANNUAL RETURN	STANDARD DEVIATION	RISK-ADJUSTED PERFORMANCE INDEX
1975–1980 Small-cap growth	43.12%	11.45%	3.77
1981–1986 Small-cap value	31.81%	13.41%	2.37
1987–1990 Large-cap growth	13.11%	16.00%	0.82
1991–1993 Small-cap growth	27.94%	11.21%	2.49
1994–1999 Large-cap growth	29.40%	7.90%	3.72
2000–2001 Small-cap value	8.34%	7.62%	1.09
Best-choice portfolio	25.61%	17.66%	1.45
S&P 500	14.64%	13.59%	1.08

growth was in its sweet spot from 1975 to 1980, the returns were an astounding 43.12% per year with very low risk levels of 11.45. Small-cap
growth continued to do very well into 1983, and it was eclipsed just a bit by
small-cap value. Why did this stellar outperformance occur? Small caps
were at the peak years of the Innovation Stage on a twenty-two-year lag to
the massive baby-boom birth index. In addition, we had just come out of
the panic crash in the early years of a long-term demographic downturn,
when small caps had been crucified and our rule says it is the best time to
buy small-cap stocks.

The second stellar period of extreme returns with very low risk was 1994
to 1999. Large-cap growth delivered returns of 29.40% with extremely low
risk of 7.90. The risk-adjusted performance index of 3.72 was about as high
as it gets and nearly as high as the 3.77 index for small-cap growth in 1975 to
1980. Why did this occur? We were, and still are, in the Growth Boom season, which most favors large-cap growth stocks, and the S-curve acceleration cycle in new technologies, starting in 1994, which has created a race for
leadership that particularly favors large-cap growth stocks. In Table 7.5 we
look at the huge differences in performance between the different sectors of
the stock market in this strong period of advance from 1994 to 1999.

Large caps outperformed small caps by 50% in returns, but at less than
half the risk level. Yet it was clearly large-cap growth doing so well. Large-
cap value did only slightly better than small caps but had much lower risk
levels. Also note that small-cap growth did 62% better than small-cap
value. If we compare the best segment, large-cap growth, to the worst segment, small-cap value, the outperformance was almost three times in returns at 45% lower risks. The risk-adjusted index for large-cap growth was
3.9 times that of small-cap value. That is truly astounding! Again, we are
just trying to demonstrate how different the returns and risks can be in different seasons and subseasons that our indicators can largely forecast.

TABLE 7.5 Performance by Asset Classes, 1994–1999

	AVERAGE ANNUAL RETURN	STANDARD DEVIATION	RISK-ADJUSTED PERFORMANCE INDEX
Large-cap	23.46%	7.79%	3.01
Large-cap value	16.33%	10.36%	1.58
Large-cap growth	29.40%	7.90%	3.72
Small-cap	15.61%	16.36%	0.06
Small-cap value	9.98%	14.33%	0.70
Small-cap growth	16.16%	17.48%	0.92

We expect a similar period of continued large-cap growth dominance after the shakeout period of 2000–2002 from mid-2005 to 2010, as we are still in the Growth Boom Stage, which favors large caps, and the S-curve acceleration will continue from 50% to 90% favoring growth. More important, the leaders in most new technologies and growth industries will be established in the coming decade. We will discuss the business strategies that can give your business a sustainable competitive advantage in Chapter 8.

We are strongly recommending that investors concentrate and diversify among large-cap growth sectors, such as technology, financial services, biotech, health care, and Asia ex-Japan, from late 2002 into 2010. These are the same sectors that outperformed from 1994 to 1999 but then got hit hard in the 2000–2002 crash and shakeout. That makes them even more attractive now.

The second-best sector in equities for the coming years is likely to be small-cap growth, then large-cap value, then small-cap value. But why not concentrate more or entirely in the large-cap growth area? We will show later in this chapter that you can get very effective diversification from different sectors within large-cap growth. You can also bring in degrees of small-cap or international or real estate, as well as bonds to reduce risk and provide income. But our cycles and indicators strongly suggest that the highest returns and the lowest risks will be in large-cap growth—the very sector investors have been shunning like the plague in recent years.

The reason for leading you briefly through this rather complex performance maze was not to confuse you, but to show that these four different choices in equity investments have clear patterns of better and worse performance in time periods ranging from a few to several years. Our different models would give good indications of when to lean in each direction. Again, our Decennial Cycle suggests that the early years of each decade will favor value and large-cap or small-cap, depending on which generation cycle is being favored at the time. Our simple model in Chapter 3 would have you in bonds or money markets during those periods, or you could choose to switch to large-cap or small-cap value if you prefer always to be in equities. But some investors may find that the stress and difficulty of changing their portfolios for these one- to three-year cycles may be more than they are willing to keep up with, plus there are the minor trading expenses and more significant tax impacts from moving into and out of investment sectors more often. So we present another simple model as an option. You can get substantially greater returns than the S&P 500, with more attractive risks, by simply focusing on more critical longer-term changes in trends.

LONGER-TERM INVESTMENT TRENDS WITHIN
THE FOUR SEASONS OF THE ECONOMY

Let's look again at the four seasons that our economy goes through every eighty years in Figure 7.4. Each major asset class or broad investment category that experts use to design portfolios tends to dominate each different season. Small caps do the best in the Innovation Stage, and if you had to choose for the whole season, it would be better to be in small-cap value. International stocks are usually the next best category, with large caps and bonds doing poorly. Large caps dominate the Growth Boom Stage, and if you had to choose, large-cap growth would be best. Bonds do well due to disinflation, especially in the first half, when small caps and international lag but do all right because of the strength of the economy.

Bonds do best in the Shakeout Stage and long-term corporate bonds are the best single category. Small-cap value tends to be the next best category as well as select international stocks where there is demographic strength. But most investments do poorly in this stage. Preservation of capital is the key goal with modest gains, and high-quality bonds are the easiest way to accomplish that. International stocks and multinational

FIGURE 7.4 Economic Cycles and Investment Strategies, 1968–2048

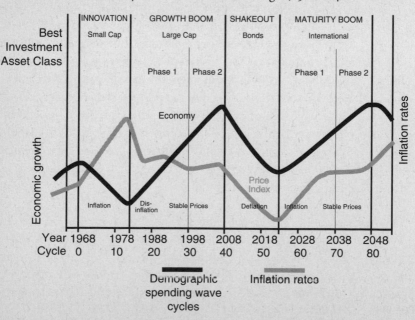

companies should fare the best in the Maturity Boom Stage of this cycle, from the early 2020s to the early 2040s as demographic trends are less strong in the United States and the industrial and information revolutions spread to emerging countries with much larger markets.

In each season, one investment class dominates and another does well. But the other two lag and often seriously underperform. Hence, it doesn't make sense to diversify into sectors that are bound to underperform for long periods of times when our simple indicators tell you that.

Table 7.6 gives the statistics on how these four broad investment classes have fared in the different seasons including the two subseasons of the boom periods when inflation rates tend to moderate and new technologies tend to accelerate. The top part of the table shows cumulative returns during each season. The bottom part shows the average annual compound returns and the average risk level.

Since sufficient data exist only back to 1926, we can capture only the last four years of the last Growth Boom Stage, which started around 1902 and peaked in 1929. Note that represents an almost exactly eighty-year lag to the present Growth Boom from late 1982 into 2009. In Table 7.6 we can see that large-cap stocks clearly did the best, as would be suggested by that cycle. The very poor performance of small-cap stocks is exaggerated by the fact that they peaked in late 1928, one year ahead of large caps, and dropped

TABLE 7.6 Asset Classes in Each Season, 1926–1999

	LARGE CAP	SMALL CAP	LT BONDS	INT'L
1926–1929	108.40%	−13.20%	31.99%	NA
1930–1941	−11.10%	11.56%	127.28%	NA
1942–1957	482.01%	893.03%	−25.71%	NA
1958–1968	195.08%	724.93%	−4.03%	NA
1969–1982	−3.00%	67.10%	−17.84%	−3.03%
1983–1999	817.86%	403.05%	210.73%	643.75%

	Large Cap		Small Cap		LT Bonds		International	
	AVG. ANN. RETURN	STD. DEV.	AVG. ANN. RETURN	STD. DEV.	AVG. ANN. RETURN	STD. DEV.	AVG. ANN. RETURN	STD. DEV.
1926–1929	20.15%	19.89	−3.48%	24.82	7.18%	2.93		
1930–1941	−.98%	35.51	.92%	57.76	7.08%	5.32		
1942–1957	11.64%	13.76	15.43%	19.92	−1.84%	4.61		
1958–1968	10.34%	11.59	21.15%	16.28	−0.37%	4.52		
1969–1982	−0.22%	16.13	3.74%	25.58	−1.39%	11.18	−0.22%	16.39
1983–1999	13.93%	14.86	9.97%	17.70	6.90%	7.94	12.53%	17.43

substantially in 1929. But even if we look just at 1926 to 1928, large caps had a cumulative return of 120.69% versus small caps at 69.78%. The risk level for large caps was 19% lower as well. Bonds did well due to favorable inflation trends but certainly saw nowhere near the performance of stocks, as we are forecasting for the coming decade.

Then came the Shakeout Stage from 1930 to 1941 (the markets actually bottomed in early 1942) with a sharply falling economy and deflation in prices. This was the worst season for most investments except bonds. Here we can see that bonds were clearly the best investment and with extremely low risks in the bottom half of the chart. Returns of 5.94% would have looked like heaven when stocks and real estate were taking their largest falls in history. Small caps did better than large caps but at even more extreme risks. Again, note here that not only did stocks have low or negative returns, but their risks were also extremely high in this season. This is the opposite of what occurs in the boom seasons when returns are high and risks are low.

Clearly, the risks and returns in these different seasons have little resemblance to the averages that investment experts and academicians quote over time. They look so moderate because they average out these extreme boom and bust periods. But the patterns of risk and return couldn't be more different.

The first stage of the Maturity Boom Stage sees rising inflation trends coming out of a deflationary period and, of course, a booming economy. Bonds obviously wouldn't do very well, and stocks clearly outperform. In the last such period from 1942 to 1957 bonds actually lost a bit while both large- and small-cap stocks did well. Small-cap stocks had 33% higher average annual returns, but the risk was 45% higher. So risk-adjusted large-cap stocks were still the best place to be. In the second stage of the Maturity Boom (1958–1968 in the last cycle) the Innovation Stage of the next generation kicks in, giving an increasing edge to small caps. The cumulative returns for small caps were 3.7 times those of large caps, with annual returns averaging 105% higher from 1958 to 1968. Since their risks were only 40% higher, the clear edge in this period shifted to small caps. Bonds were just slightly negative and did only a little better than in the first stage of the Maturity Boom, as inflation rates were edging up modestly. Note that bonds have poor performance in the Maturity Boom Stage due to a consistent, modest rise in inflation trends. But they do even worse in the Innovation Stage to follow.

The Innovation Stage started just after the peak of the Bob Hope generation's Spending Wave Cycle and saw not only worsening recessions, but also an acceleration of the mild inflation trends and a falling stock market (especially when adjusted for inflation). This is obviously the worst season for bonds, and the negative returns increased. The worst for the bond markets hit in the second half of the 1970s, when inflation was the most extreme. Large-cap stocks had very slight negative returns for the period with very substantial risks (especially in the crashes of 1970 and 1973–1974), higher than in the boom. Real estate had its best relative outperformance ever. Real estate is a leveraged hedge against inflation because of mortgage lending. And in this particular period, a much larger generation was starting to move into offices, apartments, and starter homes, driving up demand despite a generally falling economy. Small caps clearly performed the best but with even higher risks than large caps.

As we commented earlier, one of our strong rules for small caps is that we don't buy them in the early stages of a long-term downturn since they get crucified in the early stages even if they are in a positive Innovation Stage. Buying small caps after 1974 would have given investors the highest stock returns in the last century with very reasonable risk levels. International stocks did about the same as U.S. large caps, but certain sectors such as Japan and third world did much better. Overall, like the Shakeout Stage, the Innovation Stage represents a difficult economy that is challenging for most investments. Small caps, real estate, and international were the places to selectively focus. The safest place was short-term securities, such as T-bills and CDs. Large-cap stocks and long-term bonds were the worst place to be.

In the first phase of this Growth Boom Stage, with falling inflation trends and strong economic growth, the heroes of the boom have been large-cap stocks and bonds. Large-cap stocks have seen substantially higher average annual returns than in the boom from 1942 to 1968. Bonds saw almost as good a return on average as in the deflationary 1930s. When adjusted for the very low risk levels, bonds would rate second to large caps as the best risk-adjusted investment. International had both lower returns and higher risks than large caps. Hence, they lagged significantly, especially in risk-adjusted performance. The biggest laggards were small caps. They had both the lowest returns and the highest risks—the worst of both worlds! Again, it shows that within a good or bad season for a sector, higher returns don't always come with higher risks and vice versa.

The second and last stage of the Growth Boom Stage, similar to the Roaring Twenties with relatively flat inflation trends and the crescendo of the "race for leadership," should continue to most favor large-cap stocks and large-cap growth in particular. But as we showed earlier, small caps will do much better and could have returns close to or even slightly higher than large caps until the last year of the bubble. But the risks are likely to be substantially higher. So we still give the clear edge to large-cap growth stocks from 2003 to

2009. Bonds will have very low yields and mixed performance with mild appreciation from falling rates into mid-2005 or early 2006 and then some depreciation from mildly rising inflation from 2006 into 2010. Bonds will be the worst place to be in this last phase of this great boom. International will do well but will lag U.S. large and small caps as a general rule, except possibly for Asia ex-Japan, where the demographic trends are the strongest in the world.

We showed the advantages of being in the best sectors, including growth and value, from 1975 to 2001 in Table 7.4. In Table 7.7 we show the impacts of simply being in the best broad sectors during these longer-term seasons and subseasons that are easier to identify and require switching investment strategies less often. Here we simply go into bonds for the terrible Shakeout Stage and switch between large-cap and small-cap stocks when our large-cap and small-cap indicators are more favorable. This strategy would have gotten you average returns of 13.42%, 69.2% higher than that of the S&P 500 at 7.93%—with risks of 17.94, 8.8% lower than the 19.67 risk

TABLE 7.7 Optimum Asset-Class Strategy No. 1, 1926–1999

	COMPOUND ANNUALIZED RETURN*	STANDARD DEVIATION
1926–1929 Large cap	20.15%	19.89
1930–1942 Long-term bonds	5.94%	5.24
1943–1946 Small cap	35.76%	28.89
1947–1957 Large cap	12.37%	12.97
1958–1983 Small cap	11.88%	21.82
1984–1999 Large cap	13.76%	15.11

	CUMULATIVE RETURN*	COMPOUND ANNUALIZED RETURN*	STANDARD DEVIATION
Optimum strategy	787,786.65%	12.89%	17.73
S&P 500	28,227.97%	7.93%	19.67

*Real returns, adjusted for inflation.

level for the S&P 500. The risk-adjusted performance of .73 was an impressive 87.5% better. That represents a huge advantage long term and resulted in cumulative returns that would have created 39.6 times the cumulative wealth over seventy-four years! Note also that a risk-adjusted performance of .40 for the S&P 500 is very low and would suggest that merely holding stocks for the long term is not a very good strategy at all.

We do even better if we allow ourselves to include small caps in the off-seasons, when they are in a positive cycle on our 22–23-year lag for innovation. But we should do this only according to our rule that says to wait until we see a major crash in the stock market in the early years of a long-term bear market. For this strategy, in the 1930s Shakeout Stage we would have held bonds from 1930 to 1931, then switched to small caps from 1932, when the market bottomed, to 1946 when the Small-Cap Indicator and Bob Hope Generation Innovation Stage peaked. Similarly, we would have moved into T-bills from 1969 through 1974, as long-term bonds were fighting rising inflation trends. Then we would have switched to small caps from 1975 after the crash through 1983, when the Small-Cap Indicator peaked for the baby-boom generation.

The returns in Table 7.8 are astronomical compared with that of the S&P 500, but the risks obviously explode as well. Here the average annual returns go up to 16.12%, which creates cumulative returns or wealth that would have been 224.5 times that of the S&P 500 over seventy-four years. Whereas strategy no. 1 reduced risks by 8.8%, this strategy increased the risks by 36.8%. That came from more time in the small-cap sectors in volatile off-periods versus being in bonds. The risk-adjusted returns still came in at a respectable 50% better than that of the S&P 500. Strategy no. 2 obviously entails switching a little more often and higher risk levels. Either could be appropriate depending on your need for returns and your risk tolerance as an investor. Both strategies result in huge differences in your wealth due to the power of compounding higher returns over long periods of time. But risk-adjusted, strategy no. 1 in Table 7.7 is better.

We can go another step simpler for investors who desire to make the fewest changes in their portfolio and focus on equities for the long term. The most powerful single insight is that for stock investing, large-cap growth stocks generally do the best, risk-adjusted, in extended boom periods and small-cap value does the best in off-periods, which tend to see innovation by the next young generation. Small-cap growth only rarely outperforms small-cap value, and large-cap value doesn't outperform for long enough periods or by substantial enough margins when it is better than large-cap growth and has higher risks associated with it. Our models

TABLE 7.8 Optimum Asset-Class Strategy No. 2, 1926–1999

	COMPOUND ANNUALIZED RETURN*	STANDARD DEVIATION
1926–1929 Large cap	20.15%	19.89
1930–1932 Long-term bonds	15.49%	6.03
1933–1946 Small cap	20.01%	46.07
1947–1957 Large cap	12.37%	12.97
1958–1983 Small cap	11.88%	21.82
1984–1999 Large cap	13.76%	15.11

	CUMULATIVE RETURN*	COMPOUND ANNUALIZED RETURN*	STANDARD DEVIATION
Optimum strategy	2,169,536.07%	14.45%	25.80
S&P 500	28,227.97%	7.93%	19.67

*Real returns, adjusted for inflation.

can most clearly indicate when large caps and small caps will do the best and for more prolonged periods. Hence, the simplest strategy for investors and financial advisers is to alternate between small-cap value and large-cap growth when our generation cycles suggest that innovation or mainstream growth will dominate on lags of 22–23 and 47–48 years, respectively.

Table 7.9 shows how different the performance is in both the risk and returns of large caps and small caps when they are in their seasons. From 1958 to 1983, when the Small-Cap Indicator was stronger, small caps outperformed large caps by 7.5 times in cumulative returns, with 2.5 times the average annual returns and only 53% higher risk. That is a huge advantage that was accentuated by the massive size of the new baby-boom Innovation Stage. Then, when the Large-Cap Indicator was stronger from 1984 to 1999, large caps outperformed 2.5 times in cumulative returns with 60% higher average annual returns and 15% lower risks. That is also a substantial advantage.

TABLE 7.9   Small Caps Versus Large Caps: Performance in Their Best Seasons

	CUMULATIVE RETURN	COMPOUND ANNUALIZED ROR	STANDARD DEVIATION
1958–1983			
Small cap	1,752.02%	11.88%	21.82
Large cap	233.93%	4.75%	14.22
1984–1999			
Small cap	274.42%	8.60%	17.80
Large cap	686.75%	13.76%	15.11

If we go back in history and simply alternate between large-cap growth when that indicator is stronger and small-cap value when that indicator is stronger, we get very substantial performance advantages with only four changes since the Great Depression. In Table 7.10, we start in 1932 due to our rule of not being in small caps or any equities in the early years of a major bear market. From 1932 to 1946, we would have been in small-cap value, then, from 1947 to 1957, in large-cap growth. Then, from 1958 to 1983, it would have been back to small-cap value, and then large-cap growth again from 1984 to 1999.

The simple truth is that the two great long-term sectors for equity investing occur at both extremes of the spectrum, small-cap value and large-cap growth. These two sectors can be alternated in the changing innovation and peak spending seasons.

From 1932 to 1946, small-cap value had almost three times the annual returns but a little over double the risk. That still resulted in 22% better risk-adjusted returns. From 1947 to 1957, large-cap growth had 1.4% better returns at 30.5% lower risk for a risk-adjusted return of 31% better. From 1958 to 1983, small-cap value had almost three times the returns again, but at 40% higher risk, for a risk-adjusted performance 81% better. Then, from 1984 to 1999, large-cap growth had returns 23% higher but a risk level 18% lower. That meant 53% better risk-adjusted returns.

If you had invested in these two different sectors in the time periods, our models would have shown your compounded average annual returns over the last sixty-eight years to be 20.55% versus that of the S&P 500 at 12.52%. That is 64.1% higher returns from this one simple investment-switching strategy, which would have entailed only three changes in your equity investment strategies over the last seven decades—no going to cash or bonds. But the bad news is that risk was 78.4% higher than that of the S&P 500, largely resulting from the fact that small caps are so crucified in

TABLE 7.10 Simplest Long-Term Switching Model for Equities, 1932–1999

	Small-Cap Value			Large-Cap Growth		
	Average Annual Return	Standard Deviation	Risk-Adjusted Performance Index	Average Annual Return	Standard Deviation	Risk-Adjusted Performance Index
1932–1946	25.24%	50.49%	0.50	9.22%	22.53%	0.41
1947–1957	14.46%	17.94%	0.81	14.66%	12.47%	1.18
1958–1983	20.74%	23.74%	0.87	8.12%	16.76%	0.48
1984–1999	15.78%	16.93%	0.93	19.47%	13.75%	1.42

Best Choice in Each Season Versus S&P 500

1932–1999   20.55%   versus   12.52%

the early stages of extended bear markets such as in 1970–1974. The greatest part of the higher risk came from the very volatile 1932–1946 period. Although the returns were much higher from this strategy, the risks were greater than the returns, resulting in a risk-adjusted performance 9.0% lower.

In this post–World War II era from 1947 on, this strategy would have seen returns of 19.07% versus 13.20% in the S&P 500, or 44.7% better. The risk level was 18.63 versus 14.09, 32.2% higher. This resulted in a risk-adjusted performance of 1.02 versus .94, or 8.5% better. This strategy is much simpler and clearly delivers much higher returns over time, but the higher potential risks make it substantially less optimal than strategies nos. 1 and 2. Although we generally prefer strategy no. 1, different investors have different risk profiles and different capacities to monitor their portfolios and make changes. Hence, in this more complex chapter we are trying to give you as much understanding and as many credible choices as possible to find the strategy that fits you or your clients.

All three of these strategies would continue to have you in large-cap growth stocks into early to late 2010 since the continued boom and S-curve progression favor that sector the most. After 2010 our models would suggest being not in U.S. equities at all, but in T-bills, CDs, high-quality corporate bonds, and Asia. Normally we would be recommending small-cap value after the first major crash into the next Shakeout Season. But for the first time in history, the echo-baby-boom generation to follow will be smaller than the baby boom, and hence, the innovation trends will not be strong enough to warrant investing in small caps. So for an equity-only strategy we would be recommending Asia, including Japan, from 2010 to 2022. Yet it would also be better to wait for the first major worldwide crash, into around mid-2012 or late 2014, to start buying Asian stocks.

THE ULTIMATE INVESTMENT STRATEGY: COMBINING OUR CYCLICAL COMPOSITE MODEL WITH OUR BEST ASSET-CLASS MODEL

After all of this rather complex analysis of risk and return and the advantages of different investments in different seasons and cycles, we can return to the simplicity of our composite equity investment model in Chapter 3 (see Figure 3.16). But we can add just a few simple but powerful twists from the insights of this chapter. That model had you either in the S&P 500 (large caps) when our three key recurring cycles told you to be, or then in T-bills when the cycles weren't favorable. Now, in Figure 7.5 (starting from 1952, in line with our Composite Cycle Model) we simply use the best overall sector of equities—large caps or small caps—when we are invested, depending on which one is more favorable according to our large-cap and small-cap models.

That would mean that when we were invested in equities we would be in large caps from 1952 to 1957, then small caps from 1958 to 1968, then small caps from 1975 to 1979, then large caps from 1983 to 1999, then large caps

FIGURE 7.5 The Optimum Composite Cycle Model, 1952–2004

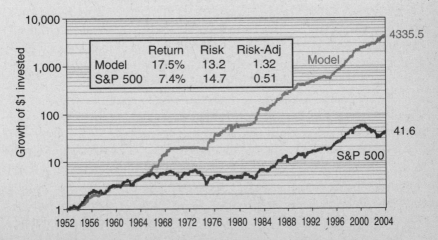

from 2003 on. Then, when we switch out of equities due to our cycles, we switch into long-term bonds in the Growth Boom and Shakeout Stages, when inflationary trends are generally down, and into T-bills in the Maturity Boom and Innovation Stages, when inflation trends are generally up. But also note that our Inflation Indicator Model can forecast if inflation trends will be generally upward or downward at least three years in advance.

The performance here is even more astounding. The inflation-adjusted value of $1 invested in 1952 would have been $4,335.54 versus $41.60 in the S&P 500, or 104.2 times the cumulative wealth. The average annual compound returns were 17.47%, or 135.1% higher than the S&P 500 at 7.43%. And the risk or standard deviation was 13.23 versus 14.70, or 10.0% lower. In addition to the overall volatility being lower, this model captured 132.6% of the upside volatility while capturing only 86.0% of the downside volatility. The maximum drawdown or loss that an investor would have had to endure was only 25.75% versus 51.86% on the S&P 500.

This model represents an incredible performance advantage with only simple and occasional switching rules that don't depend on short-term or technical indicators that change. You can program this model today for the rest of your life. It offers the potential for 135% better gain at 10% less risk. This is the general model we recommend for more aggressive investors—and in the next part of this chapter we look at how you can focus on the best-diversified sectors within this model in the coming years to improve performance even more.

But before we move on, we would like to make one simple change to the simpler Composite Cycle Model we presented in Figure 3.16 at the end of Chapter 3. That model had annual returns 45.0% better than the S&P 500 with risks 34.1% lower. If we just add one simple twist, we can improve the performance of this model while offering a risk level that would be suitable to more equity investors. Here in Figure 7.6 we simply add the rule of switching to T-bills (when we move out of the S&P 500) in the rising inflation seasons of the Maturity Boom (1942–1968) and the Innovation Stage (1969–1981). Then we switch into long-term bonds in the Growth Boom and Shakeout Stages, which tend toward disinflation. But we stay in the less volatile large-cap stocks instead of allowing switching to small caps, as we did in the Optimum Composite Cycle in Figure 7.5.

With this one simple change, we increase the cumulative growth of $1 to $372.40 versus $204.25 on the previous model and $41.60 on the S&P 500, or 9.0 times the wealth versus 4.9 times before. The returns now at 12.06% were 62.3% better than that of the S&P 500 at 7.43%, and the risk

FIGURE 7.6 The Composite Cycle Model, Using T-Bills or Bonds, 1952–2004

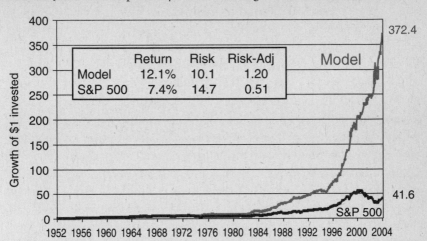

	Return	Risk	Risk-Adj
Model	12.1%	10.1	1.20
S&P 500	7.4%	14.7	0.51

level was 31.95% lower at 10.07 versus 14.70 for a risk-adjusted improvement in performance 135.3% better.

We see this equity model in Figure 7.6 as the best simple strategy for moderate growth and risk investors, while the Optimum Composite Cycle in Figure 7.5 is the best for more aggressive growth investors. Both models can be improved by our analysis of the best, most diversified sectors to focus on in the next great boom ahead as we will in the next section.

To summarize this chapter thus far, the performance of different investment asset classes and/or sectors that you can choose from is very different in the alternating long-term seasons of our economy and in specific rising seasons for different investments based on their own lags on the birth and generation cycles. Hence, we recommend that you concentrate only in investment classes and sectors that are favored in any time horizon and build diversified portfolio strategies within those demographically favored sectors.

We will now turn our focus to the next key issue for refining your strategies: How should your portfolio be positioned for the next and final wave of the greatest boom in history? The best strategy is to be diversified in four to five different sectors, beyond what we have covered thus far in the interest of explaining how risk and returns vary in different seasons and time periods and offering the simpler strategies for investors and clients that prefer that. But what are the best sectors of equities to focus in for the great boom and bubble ahead into 2008–2009? Then we will look at more

staged strategies for playing the extreme downturn that is likely to follow—
and that is the trickiest stage of the eighty-year economic cycle.

THE ULTIMATE PORTFOLIO STRATEGY
FOR THE ROARING 2000S

Let's start by reviewing our fundamental forecasts for the years ahead into the
peak of this boom around early to late 2010. We see continued low inflation
rates, falling substantially from mid-2004 into mid-2005 or early 2006 and
rising slightly from 2006 into 2010. Risk-adjusted, we see large caps doing the
best and roaring out of the correction phase that came to an end in early October 2002, especially from mid-2005 into 2010. We also see small caps doing
better than in the 1990s boom, which was dominated by large caps. But the
most critical forecast is that large-cap growth will be the best sector, not likely
in returns but certainly on a risk-adjusted basis, as we kick back into the re-
sumption of the powerful S-curve progression in new technologies and
growth industries and see a race for leadership that will determine the large
companies that will dominate these industries for decades to come.

We recommend concentrating largely in large-cap growth for the equity portion of your portfolio as well as tilting your portfolio toward equities as strongly as your risk tolerance will allow you. You can use large-cap
value and small-cap growth and value for greater diversification, as our
small-cap model is also very bullish into the end of this decade. But the key
issue becomes: How can you achieve effective diversification while focusing
to the maximum in large-cap growth and/or other equity sectors?

In The Roaring 2000s Investor (Chapter 2) we outlined an entire array of
portfolios from aggressive to conservative that had achieved superior returns in the 1990s boom while focusing in large-cap growth sectors that
achieved effective diversification. We used the best-outperforming sectors
of large-cap stocks, given the S-curve acceleration in technologies and the
sectors with the strongest demographic. This leads us to the best four sectors: technology, financial services, health care, and Asia ex-Japan. But these
sectors also provide effective diversification as well. We get the strongest returns from the technology and financial services sectors and the best diversification from different patterns of movement from the health care and
Asia sectors. Most investors would assume that the risk/return performance
of our portfolios has weakened due to the 2000–2002 crash, because the
large-cap growth sectors we favor were hit so hard.

The truth is that our portfolios from 1990, updated through December

2003, still have better risk/return performance ratios than those of the S&P 500 and the Classic Asset-Allocation Model—even after the greatest large-cap crash in decades.

What we are going to do now is update the performance of those portfolios through the incredible crash of 2000–2002, as summarized in Table 7.11. We will further analyze the trends to come with the most optimal portfolios we can recommend into 2010, taking into account the minor changes in trends in inflation and small-cap forecasts for the coming decade. We will start by updating our aggressive growth portfolio from *The Roaring 2000s Investor* in Figure 7.7.

In this portfolio we concentrate fully in large-cap growth sectors that demographic trends are favoring: technology, financial services, health care, and Asia ex-Japan (as we explained in greater detail in *The Roaring 2000s Investor*). We chose these sectors not only because they had already proven to outperform the S&P 500 on average in the 1990s, but also because they had relatively low correlation for effective diversification. Up through March 1999 in *The Roaring 2000s Investor,* this portfolio had outperformed the S&P 500 by 26.4% in average annual returns with only 2.1% higher risks.

When we update the portfolio through the bubble into early 2000 and through the crash of 2002 into the beginning of the recovery into late 2003, we get even better results. The portfolio had average annual compound returns of 15.3% versus 10.9% for that of the S&P 500, with average risks of 18.4 and 16.4. That meant 40.4% higher returns with only 12.2% higher risk for a risk-adjusted performance of .83 versus .66, or 25.8% higher. The returns are much higher, and the risk-adjusted performance is slightly higher than the performance of the S&P 500 through March 1999 since the S&P 500 also got hit hard in the 2000–2002 crash. Hence, even our most aggres-

TABLE 7.11 Dent Portfolios: Return Versus Risk, January 1990–December 2003

	RETURN	RISK	DIFFERENCE IN RETURN VERSUS S&P 500	DIFFERENCE IN RISK VERSUS S&P 500
S&P 500	10.9%	16.4		
Classic Markowitz portfolio	8.6%	10.9	−21.1%	−33.5%
Aggressive growth portfolio	15.3%	18.4	40.4%	12.2%
Growth portfolio	14.4%	15.7	32.1%	−4.3%
Growth and income portfolio	12.8%	13.4	17.4%	−18.3%
Conservative portfolio	11.7%	10.1	7.3%	−38.4%
Very conservative portfolio	10.6%	5.3	−2.75%	−67.7%

FIGURE 7.7   Aggressive Growth Portfolio, January 1990–December 2003

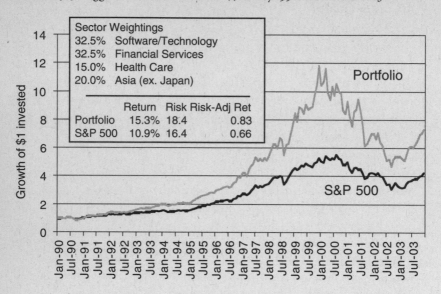

sive portfolio strategy works over time, even through strong corrections if you stick with it.

This portfolio clearly outperformed the Classic Asset-Allocation Model, which suggests being equally in all four major asset classes: large cap, small cap, international, and bonds. As of March 1999 in *The Roaring 2000s Investor,* our aggressive growth portfolio had outperformed the classic model (Markowitz portfolio) in Figure 7.8 by much greater margins in returns than the S&P 500. That model underperformed the S&P 500 by 39.2% even though it reduced the risk level by 24.5%. That still represented an unfavorable risk/return alternative to the S&P 500. But the crash of 2000–2002 temporarily brought out the broader diversification advantage of that model.

Despite that near-term advantage, our aggressive growth model is still superior when updated through the end of 2003. It delivered 77.9% higher returns at 68.8% higher risk for a risk-adjusted return 5.1% higher. And this is after most of our large-cap growth sectors took the greatest beating of this entire boom! We forecast an environment into 2009 that will favor our aggressive portfolio and other portfolios by increasingly wider margins, as occurred in the 1990s, and disfavor again this classic model for many years to come. So the statistics should look much more favorable for our portfolios versus the Classic Asset-Allocation Model by the end of this decade.

Figure 7.8 Classic Asset-Allocation Model, January 1990–December 2003

Our growth portfolio (Figure 7.9) had outperformed the S&P 500 as of March 1999 by 18.0% with risks only 1.0% higher. This portfolio tilted more toward less volatile "Dow-like" multinational stocks and included 10% in short-term prime rate fixed-income funds. When we update this portfolio through the end of 2003, we get even greater results despite the crash. The

Figure 7.9 Growth Portfolio, January 1990–December 2003

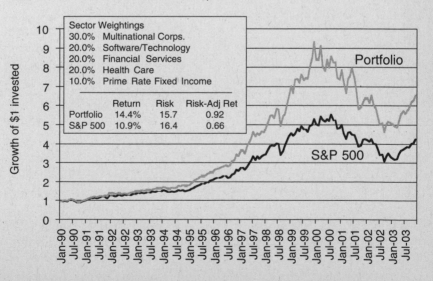

average returns of 14.4% were 32.1% higher than that of the S&P 500 with risks at 15.7 versus 16.4, or 4.3% lower, resulting in a risk-adjusted return of .92 versus .66, or 39.4% higher. The returns in this portfolio were 67.4% higher than the classic model with risks 44.0% higher, for a risk-adjusted return 16.5% higher. Note that the risk-adjusted performance of this port-folio at .92 has been 10.8% higher than that of the aggressive portfolio at .83. For most equity-oriented investors this is the superior strategy all the way around, unless you desire higher returns and are willing to take the slightly higher risks of the aggressive portfolio. Those risks obviously caused more pain between early 2000 and late 2002. But our fundamental and cycle fore-casts suggest much less pain in the years ahead and greater outperformance by the aggressive model.

Our growth and income portfolio (Figure 7.10) is our middle portfolio for risk tolerance and best for investors who are approaching retirement and need more income and less risk but still want to lean more toward equities. And again, our forecasts predict much better returns at lower risk levels than in the recent past for equities and especially large-cap growth stocks and funds. This portfolio had underperformed the S&P 500 as of March 1999 by only 1.1% in returns with risks 27.1% lower while concentrating 40% of the portfolio in fixed income. Ten percent was in convertible bonds to benefit from the equity trends, and 30% was in short-term prime rate trusts. If we update this portfolio, we get risk-adjusted results of .96 versus .92 in

FIGURE 7.10   Growth and Income Portfolio, January 1990–December 2003

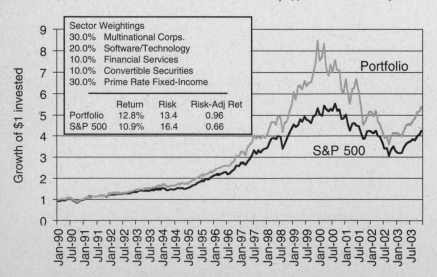

the growth portfolio in Figure 7.9. The returns of 12.8% were 17.4% higher than that of the S&P 500 at 10.9%, with risks at 13.4 versus 16.4, or 18.3% lower, for a risk-adjusted advantage of .96 versus .66, or 45.4% higher.

Our conservative portfolio (Figure 7.11) was designed for the investor in the early stages of retirement, with 55% fixed-income and equities focused largely in less volatile multinational stocks but with a 10% kicker in technology. That portfolio had underperformed the S&P 500 by only 15.9% in returns with risks 38.5% lower as of March 1999. As of the end of 2003, this portfolio actually had returns of 11.7% versus 10.9% on the S&P 500, or 7.3% higher, with risks of 10.1 versus 16.4, or 38.4% lower—despite having 55% in reliable fixed-income sectors. The risk-adjusted return advantage of 1.16 versus .66 was even higher and represented a 75.8% improvement! Who could argue with that for a conservative or retired investor? This truly represents the best of both worlds achieved through scientific portfolio design and demographic trends.

Finally we come to our most conservative portfolio (Figure 7.12), designed for the investor who needs to rely almost totally on fixed income or just doesn't believe that stocks will ever go up again. This portfolio has only 20% in equities, but it is concentrated in the top two performing sectors. In reality, very few investors need 100% income in the near term. This portfolio had underperformed the S&P 500 33.9% as of March 2000 with risks 70.1% lower. Updated to the end of 2003, it continues to have the highest

FIGURE 7.11 Conservative Portfolio, January 1990–December 2003

FIGURE 7.12 Very Conservative Portfolio, January 1990–December 2003

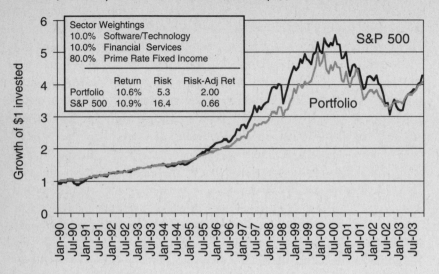

risk-adjusted performance of any of our portfolios, at an astounding 2.00 index. The returns at 10.6% have now been only 2.8% lower than that of the S&P 500, with risk at 5.3, or 67.7% lower, slightly better than before the crash. This portfolio proves that even at the lowest risk levels, including a very small portion in the best equity sectors during a boom like this, it can enhance risk-adjusted returns remarkably.

POSITIONING FOR THE GREAT BOOM AND BUBBLE AHEAD

Since we are forecasting a boom period of slightly less duration but with as high or higher average annual compound returns for late 2002 into late 2009, as occurred in the incredible bull market from late 1990 into early 2000, it would make more sense to compare the returns and risks of that period to the future rather than incorporating the extreme crash of 2000–2002. It's not that we don't expect future corrections, but they will be more like those in 1990 and 1998, at worst, rather than those in 1987 or 2000–2002. And remember, we have only one serious cycle, the four/eight-year cycle, hitting in mid- to late 2006 between 2003 and 2009. And then there is a minor potential cycle to hit in late 2007 on the Decennial Cycle.

First we will look at performance from November 1990, just after the correction that bottomed in October 1990, into the peak in March 2000, which comprises the entire last bull market wave. Then we will narrow down even further to the more astounding performance from the beginning of 1995 into March 2000, when the S-curve progression kicked in, which we see resuming again from sometime in 2005 to 2009.

Table 7.12 shows the returns, risks, and risk-adjusted performance of our portfolios versus the S&P 500 and the classic model exclusively in the last great bull market before the great crash of 2000–2002. The aggressive portfolio beat the pants off the S&P 500, delivering double the returns and slightly lower risks! Here the average annual returns are almost double across the board, yet the risks are substantially lower. The risk-adjusted performance is two to three times better as a result. This again represents the power of focusing in a strong sector such as large-cap growth when it's in its sweet spot. Note that the aggressive growth portfolio does better in risk-adjusted performance versus the growth and growth-and-income portfolios, better than it did in Figure 7.8 with the crash of 2000–2002. This was the equity-oriented portfolio best positioned for the sweet spot of that incredible bull market.

Again, the reason we focus on this chart for looking at risks and returns is that we are projecting similar to slightly higher average annual returns and a slightly better economic environment from late 2002 into late 2008 or 2009. We are projecting an average return for the Dow of about 21% or higher, in line with the S&P 500 returns from November 1990–March 2000. But the Dow's returns in that period were only 17%. Therefore our portfolio strategies should be based around this period and could do approximately as well and likely better—but only if we are positioned in similar sectors that will benefit. This chart should give you something to be very excited about when everyone has been assuming much lower returns in the years ahead.

If we narrow down to the best years in the market following the

TABLE 7.12 Summary of Portfolios, November 1990–March 2000

PORTFOLIO	ANNUAL RATE OF RETURN	STANDARD DEVIATION	RISK-ADJUSTED PERFORMANCE
Markowitz	16.24%	6.65%	2.44
S&P	21.26%	9.24%	2.30
Aggressive	32.70%	9.02%	3.63
Growth	28.82%	9.36%	3.08
Growth and income	27.56%	6.48%	4.25
Conservative	22.88%	5.54%	4.13
Very conservative	20.31%	2.66%	7.64

TABLE 7.13   Summary of Portfolios, January 1995–March 2000

PORTFOLIO	ANNUAL RATE OF RETURN	STANDARD DEVIATION	RISK-ADJUSTED PERFORMANCE
Markowitz	17.90%	6.46%	2.77
S&P	27.54%	6.72%	4.10
Aggressive	37.14%	8.69%	4.27
Growth	33.36%	7.45%	4.48
Growth and income	30.70%	5.46%	5.62
Conservative	24.69%	5.01%	4.93
Very conservative	20.16%	1.93%	10.45

S-curve acceleration, the returns are even higher (Table 7.13). But note that the S&P 500 had a very large jump in performance. This is because the S-curve acceleration and race for leadership created the greatest advantage for the largest growth companies that dominate the capitalization-weighted S&P 500 index. (The top fifty stocks tend to drive that index since each stock in the index is weighted by its total stock market valuation, greatly skewing the value of the index toward the largest stocks.) Hence, in this period, despite even higher returns and lower risks, our portfolios had a bit less advantage versus the S&P 500. But they still beat it handily when most mutual fund managers and investment strategists could not. Why? Because we were concentrated in the same strong large-cap growth sector but focused even more in the very best subsectors.

In summary, the returns that we expect from late 2002 into late 2009/early 2010 should be at least as strong as in Table 7.12 and could approach that of Table 7.13, if we are right about the economic environment into 2010. The real question now is how specifically you should position yourself for the next great bull market, especially as it starts to show itself in 2004 as this book is published. Since late 2002, we have been recommending that investors skew their portfolios even higher, toward the more aggressive sectors, such as technology, financial services, and biotech. Why? That brings us to another key principle we covered in *The Roaring 2000s Investor* called dynamic rebalancing.

DYNAMIC REBALANCING

Normally, when you or an adviser sets a portfolio strategy, similar to the portfolios we reviewed above, part of the system of investment is to periodically rebalance your portfolio back to its original targets. This typically occurs once a year but can occur from once a quarter to once every two years. We favor doing it once every year or two to minimize tax impacts and trading costs. As different sectors perform differently, it is natural for your portfolio to stray from the intended percentages in each sector. So it would make sense to sell some of the sectors that have done best and buy some of the sectors that have done worse to get you back on track.

There is an added advantage to doing this. This tactic brings in a long-term tendency toward buying low and selling high. If one sector has outperformed substantially, it is more likely to take a correction and underperform in the future. By selling a bit of that sector and buying in an underperforming sector, you create a systematic tendency to buy low/sell high that tends to improve your risk/return ratio marginally over time. And that is what systematic investing is all about. Building in automatic allocations and reallocations gives you greater odds of better performance without allowing your natural human emotions and reactions to set in and get the best of you.

Dynamic rebalancing employs the same principle, but more powerfully at extreme times in the markets. Instead of rebalancing at random, say once a year, you instead rebalance, and to greater extremes, when the markets go to extremes or when certain sectors outperform or underperform by wide enough margins. A typical parameter that could be used is that you sell down a sector back to its original target when its percentage of the portfolio exceeds its target by 30%, or, conversely, you buy more when it falls 30% below its target. Using our aggressive portfolio as an example, the tech sector is weighted at 32.5%. That means you would rebalance when the tech percentage hits 42.25%, which is 30% higher than 32.5%. Then that excess from selling would be put first into the sector that had fallen the most as a percentage of the portfolio until it reached its target, and then into the next weaker sector if there was still money left over. Or if technology fell to 22.75% (30% lower than 32.5%), you would buy more technology back up to 32.5% and sell the sector or sectors that had outperformed to create the cash to buy more technology.

There are alternative methods to employ. We also try to plot each sector into channels of growth, drawing trend lines through the highs and lows around the longer-term trend line up, as we did with the Dow Channel (Figure 2.15 in Chapter 2). When a sector gets to the top of its range, you sell some of that sector; when it gets to the bottom of its channel you buy more. But the most important tool we deploy is to rebalance the portfolio in the most dynamic fashion when the market gets to extremes like when we hit the top of the Dow Channel between late 1999 and early 2000 and the bottom in late 2002. This is where we concentrate our dynamic rebalancing to get the greatest increase in returns and reduction of risk long term. Although we have used the Dow Channel as our main guide for doing this, we also try to chart individual sectors in channels, such as technology, financial services, health care, and Asia ex-Japan.

In the April 1, 2000, issue of *The H. S. Dent Forecast*, we recommended rebalancing out of tech and Asia, which had the strongest performance in the 1999 bubble, and increasingly into health care, financial services, and multinationals. That was just after we had hit the top of the Dow Channel for the first time since 1987 and after the Internet (we warned in February of that top) and tech sectors looked as though they were cresting. Then, conversely, when we hit the bottom of the Dow Channel in late 2001 and again in late 2002, we recommended allocating back strongly into tech and financial services, and to a lesser degree into Asia, while selling off the health care sector, which had done so well for most of the correction. We ended up breaking the Dow Channel temporarily and falling toward the next level of strong support, around 7400 to 7600 (the 1998 correction lows). Then, in early October, we gave our strongest buy signals and reallocations. Since then we have been recommending overweighting technology in our aggressive portfolio to 35% to 40% and will be recommending 40% by mid- to late 2004, with Asia at 10%–20%, financial services at 25%–30%, health care at 10%, and biotech at 5%–15%.

The next likely time for dynamic rebalancing should come around May 2006, when the four/eight-year cycle kicks in. Then we would be looking at cutting back the tech and other outperforming sectors, such as financial services and perhaps Asia, and adding to health care and/or Asia if it had underperformed into that time period. But of course, these decisions would depend on how much these sectors had outperformed or underperformed by that time. Employing our cyclical Composite Cycle Model, we would also be looking at reducing risk by moving into bonds exclusively, or to some degree, between May and October 2006 and August and September 2007.

We see the greatest buy opportunity for stocks in your lifetime starting back to late 2002 and again between May and October (or December at the latest) 2004—the last great chance to invest ahead of the next bubble! We see the greatest performance to come in the large-cap growth sectors, which have been so out of favor in the crash of 2000–2002. The best sectors ahead are likely to continue to be technology, financial services, biotech, health care, and Asia ex-Japan. Take the time to thoroughly consider the evidence in this book and make perhaps the most important decision for your financial future.

But most important, make sure you get on and maintain a system of investment that keeps you from repeating the mistakes of most investors over the last several years. Our experience is clearly that having a good financial adviser or mentor is the best way to do that. And remember that we are forecasting that the next great bubble, which is likely to occur between 2005 and 2009, will be the last. You must be planning today for how you will shift your portfolio and investment strategy more radically when this great boom finally comes to an end by 2009 to 2010 and the season changes dramatically toward deflation and slowing economic growth.

A PREVIEW OF INVESTMENT STRATEGIES FOR THE GREAT BUST AHEAD, 2010–2022

In our next major book we will cover in more detail the best strategies for preserving and expanding your wealth in the deflationary downturn from around 2010 to 2022, which could rival or exceed the Great Depression. But here we will give you a clear preview of how you can turn an adverse cycle into continued growth in your wealth. Most investors will lose most or all of their gains from the great boom in the great bust ahead.

The first principle that you need to understand is that there will be "no place to hide" in most stock and real estate sectors in the early years of the downturn, when the bubble bursts again. In addition to the 2000–2002 crash, we reviewed the crash of late 1929–early 1942 and found that most sectors of the broader markets did poorly, even utilities, telephones, and movies. The time period when the first great crash is likely to occur is between early 2010 and mid-2012. The longest and greatest crashes in the last century (Figure 7.13) have been limited to thirty-four months in the early 1930s and have more typically been closer to thirty months (2½ years), including those in late 1919–early 1922, late 1929–early 1932, early 2000–late 2002, and 1990–early 1992 in Japan. The great lesson of the crash of 2000–2002 was that in that 2½-year cycle, almost all sectors of the stock market (including most international sectors) were hit strongly as the crash went on, even more defensive sectors like health care. This wasn't like the normal corrections we get every four years or so on the Presidential Cycle, where if you are diversified you suffer only minor losses and hence it's best just to ride through those corrections.

FIGURE 7.13 Four Great Crashes of the Last Century

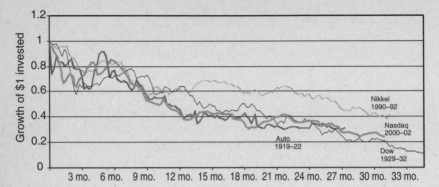

When you hit the end of a demographic cycle of spending, a
technology bubble, or the first 2½ years of the Decennial Cycle,
it's simply best to be in high-quality long-term or short-term fixed
income to weather the potential storm.

Hence, from early to late 2010 into late 2012 we highly recommend that
you switch your portfolio entirely or nearly entirely into high-quality long-
term corporate bonds or short-term fixed income (such as T-bills, CDs,
and one-year Treasuries) to preserve your wealth and grow it modestly at
first. Our two long-term models earlier in this chapter, in Figures 7.5 and
7.6, which combine the three recurring cycles—the Four-Year Cycle, the
Decennial Cycle, and the Spending Wave—would have you out of the stock
market into long-term bonds from 2010 into late 2022, except for the
strongest part of the Decennial Cycle, from late 2014 into late 2019.

Figure 7.14 looks back at the great crash from late 1929 into early 1932
(when the Dow lost 89%) and shows how you could have preserved your assets with very modest gains by being in long-term corporate bonds, long-
term government bonds, one-year government bonds, and T-bills. This
chart includes interest and any capital appreciation or loss. You can see in
this chart that there was a short-term panic in longer-term bonds when the
Depression started to get severe, from mid-1931 into early 1932. During the
crash, the safest T-bills would have seen around 5% gains, long-term corporate bonds around 9%, one-year government bonds around 12%, and long-
term government bonds around 14%—while the stock market fell by 89%.

But for the longer Shakeout Season and difficult economy from late

FIGURE 7.14 Total Return on Bonds During the Great Crash, September 1929–June 1932

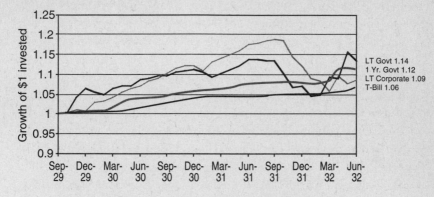

1929 through early 1942 (when the Dow was still down almost 80% from the top) high-quality long-term corporate bonds were the best place for secure returns, as you can see in Figure 7.15, with long-term government bonds being the next best. When there is a period of deflationary trends, you want to lock in higher yields while they fall, which gives you capital appreciation on your bonds in addition to your interest. Corporate bonds not only have higher yields than government bonds, but the strongest corporations actually weathered the Great Depression a bit better than the U.S. government, which saw mushrooming deficits from falling tax revenues and rising social costs.

While the stock market was very volatile and alternating between being down 89% in 1932 and still down 76% from the top in 1942, you could have

FIGURE 7.15 Total Return on Bonds, September 1929–April 1942

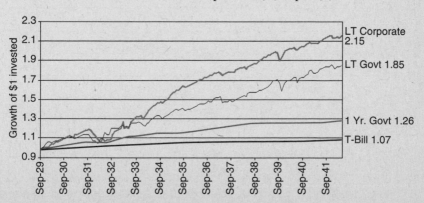

grown your wealth to 2.15 times (or 115% gains) in high-quality corporate bonds (twenty-year Aaa), 1.85 times (85% gains) in long-term government bonds (ten-year Treasuries), 1.26 times in one-year government bonds (26% gains), but only 1.07 times or 7% gains in T-bills.

But there should be a significant bubble-like bear market rally between around late 2012/early 2013 or late 2014 at the latest, into as late as the end of 2019 (as there was from early 1932 into early 1937). More aggressive investors could start buying stocks around late 2012 or early 2013, when a bottom looks near. Growth investors would probably be better to wait until the Four-Year Cycle bottoms by early October 2014 and play the strong five-year portion of the Decennial Cycle as our long-term models would suggest. More conservative investors would do best simply to ride out the downturn in safer long-term high-quality corporate bonds from late 2010 into late 2022. We will outline those three strategies just ahead. But first let's look at the sectors of our economy and globally that will have demographic trends behind them in the downturn—after the first great crash.

In the United States and other maturing economies, such as those in Europe, the strongest major sector in the demographic downturn will be health care. Figure 7.16 shows the total spending on health care from twenty-six categories of the Consumer Expenditure Survey. This is the only large category of spending that rises into the mid- to late seventies. And the strongest sector is prescription drugs (Figure 7.17), which peak around age 77. Hence, the health care industries will continue to grow with the baby-boom spending cycle through the downturn and into around 2038. Hence,

FIGURE 7.16 Average Annual Health Care Spending, by Age

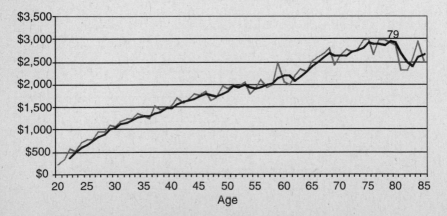

Source: U.S. Bureau of Labor Statistics, Consumer Expenditure Survey, 2000.

FIGURE 7.17 Average Annual Prescription Drug Spending, by Age

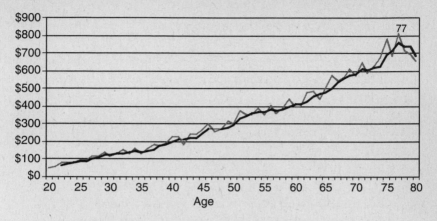

Source: U.S. Bureau of Labor Statistics, Consumer Expenditure Survey, 2000.

investors can focus on buying health care, drug and pharmaceutical, bio-tech, and health insurance stocks—or of course U.S. and global health care mutual and index funds—after the crash.

Another sector with rising trends and less volatility is newspapers and magazines, as shown in Figure 7.18. This sector grows until around age 68. The lowest-risk industry with moderate returns is likely to be utilities, wastewater, trash collection, etc., as shown in Figure 7.19, where we look at

FIGURE 7.18 Average Annual Spending on Newspapers and Magazines, by Age

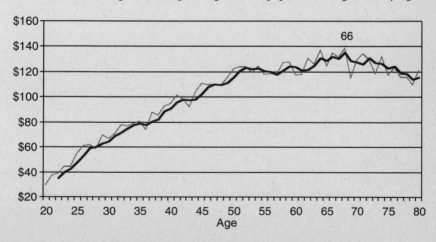

Source: U.S. Bureau of Labor Statistics, Consumer Expenditure Survey, 2000.

FIGURE 7.19 Average Annual Spending on Trash and Wastewater, by Age

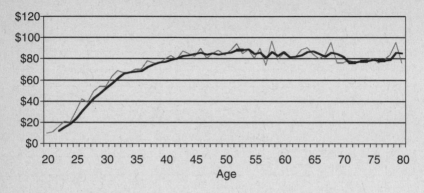

Source: U.S. Bureau of Labor Statistics, Consumer Expenditure Survey, 2000.

trash collection, which is typical of many utility-like industries that peak between the late 40s and mid-50s and plateau into the 60s. We can use these sectors for less risky stock investments once the worst of the crash has hit and our cycles are favorable.

The greatest areas of continued growth will come in Asia. The majority of the world's nonindustrialized populations live in Southeast Asia and India. They will continue to industrialize and see people move from rural to urban areas (especially China) as we mature long term and decline from 2010 to 2022. But the demographic spending trends will continue upward in much of Asia from 2010 to 2020, more specifically in China, South Korea, and Japan. In *The Roaring 2000s Investor,* we looked at the age distributions of the developed countries in Chapter 3 and the developing countries in Chapter 4. You can get a much clearer view of the entire world's demographics by reviewing those chapters.

China's age distribution (Figure 7.20) shows that there will be rising numbers of people moving into their peak spending into around 2020. The country's baby boom lasted about a decade longer than ours in the United States. Note that you have to read these charts backward, starting from the peak spending cohort of 45–49 and counting back to the peak in the population bulge, to see how long spending will grow before it peaks.

South Korea (Figure 7.21) is not only the strongest country for spending growth in the boom, but its spending trends should be up similarly into 2020 before peaking. Japan (Figure 7.22) will finally see another significant spending trend upward with its echo baby boom from around 2005 into

FIGURE 7.20 Age Distribution: China, 2000

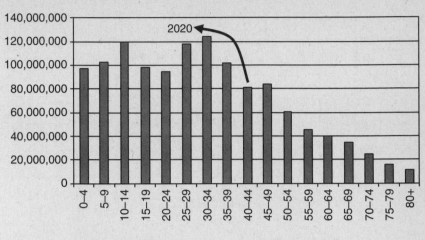

Source: United Nations.

FIGURE 7.21 Age Distribution: South Korea, 2000

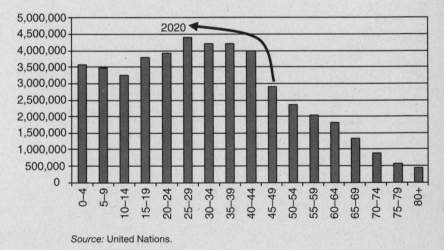

Source: United Nations.

2020. By 2010, the smaller, wealthy countries such as Hong Kong and Singapore will peak similarly to the United States. But the larger, less developed countries will continue to grow in spending power. Figure 7.23 shows Indonesia with growth in spending into 2025–2030. However, we recommend that most investors stay away from developing countries, as the political instability and volatility are too great.

FIGURE 7.22 Age Distribution: Japan, 2000

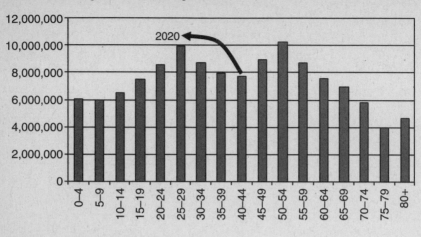

Source: United Nations.

FIGURE 7.23 Age Distribution: Indonesia, 2000

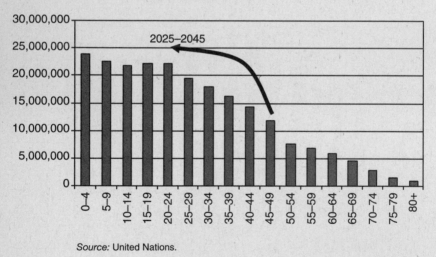

Source: United Nations.

SUMMARY OF INVESTMENT STRATEGIES FOR 2010–2022

We will end this chapter by summarizing the portfolio strategies that we would suggest for the great downturn between around 2010 and 2022. We will be giving much more refined estimates of timing and be adding more refined sector strategies in our newsletter, *The H. S. Dent Forecast,* and in our next book as the time gets much closer and we focus our research more on the downturn. Note that on all of these strategies you could choose to get more defensive (stocks to bonds) in the two four-year cycles from May to October in 2014 and 2018. Also note that when we refer to Asia we see the best potential in China, Taiwan, South Korea, Japan, and possibly India.

AGGRESSIVE STRATEGY: PORTFOLIO ALLOCATIONS, 2010–2022

1. Mid- to late 2012/early 2013: 90% Aaa corporate bonds, 10% T-bills or CDs

2. Late 2012/early 2013 to late 2019: 25% health care, 15% biotech, 35% Asia, 15% newspapers/magazines and/or utilities, 10% Aaa corporate bonds

3. Late 2019 to late 2022: 90% Aaa corporate bonds, 10% T-bills or CDs

GROWTH STRATEGY: PORTFOLIO ALLOCATIONS, 2010–2022

1. Mid- to late 2010 to late 2014: 90% Aaa corporate bonds, 10% T-bills or CDs

2. Late 2014 to late 2019: 30% health care, 10% biotech, 25% Asia, 20% newspapers/magazines and/or utilities, 20% Aaa corporate bonds

3. Late 2019 to late 2022: 90% Aaa corporate bonds, 10% T-Bills or CDs

CONSERVATIVE STRATEGY: PORTFOLIO ALLOCATIONS, 2010–2022

1. Mid- to late 2010 to late 2022: 80% Aaa corporate bonds, 20% T-bills or CDs

Now that you can feel that there is a way to survive and profit during the downturn, in Chapter 8 we focus on how this eighty-year New Economy Cycle will evolve into what we call the "New Millionaire Economy," with wealth and high incomes becoming the norm rather than the exception. It will be our children who most benefit from this new economy, as the baby boomers will be retiring during the great crash and Shakeout Season ahead.

THE NEW MILLIONAIRE ECONOMY

*Creating Wealth by Understanding
the Rise in Mass Affluence*

AFFLUENT HOUSEHOLDS ARE THE NEW ECONOMY

There is more to this new economy than the emergence of new technologies, customization of goods and services, network organizations, and the rising tide of baby-boom spending and productivity. The overriding trend of this emerging new economy, and hence the theme of this new decade and millennium is the rise of mass affluence. Households with greater than $100,000 in income number close to 14 million or 14% as of 2001 and have been growing a little faster than the economy over the last three decades (Figure 8.1). At this rate of growth, we should see 18 to 20 million (or almost 20% of households) in this category by the top of this boom between 2009 and 2010 when we finally see the peak of baby-boom spending. This represents the new upper middle class in the wealthiest country in the world. They will set the trends in lifestyles and business for decades to come. They are no longer "yuppies" (young urban professionals) but have aged into what David Brooks has called "bobos" (bourgeois bohemians). We will discuss the bobo lifestyle trends later in this chapter.

Remember that many of these households have incomes much higher than $100,000. The average income of the top 1% of households today is about $250,000 and the average net worth is $5 million. The average income of the top 10% is $100,000. The top 1% pays 37% of the total taxes, the top 10% pay 67% and the top 25%, 84%. The top 20% of households control over 50% of the income, over 40% of the spending, and over 90% of

FIGURE 8.1 Households with $100,000 or Greater Annual Income, 1967–2001

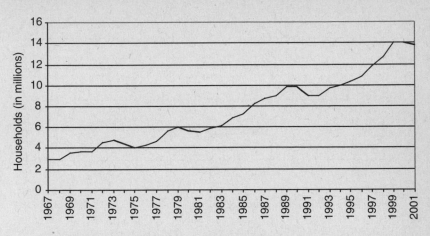

the financial assets outside of home ownership. Their clout will only grow in this and the decades to come as their numbers continue to increase.

The growing standard for the definition of affluence is $100,000 in income and/or $500,000 in net worth (exclusive of personal residence). Figure 8.2 shows the number of households with $500 million or more in net worth exclusive of personal residence. This group similarly reached almost 14 million in 1999 before the stock crash took its toll. Despite the fact that the number of $100,000 income households and $500,000 net worth are nearly the same, they don't always represent the same households. When you combine these two definitions, the numbers here expand to almost 20 million households as of 2001. These numbers would likely reach as high as 30 million by 2009—that is nearly 30% of U.S. households. That 30% will likely control 50% of the spending in our economy by then. This means there is a new affluent class emerging, not wildly wealthy, but well beyond the middle-class standard of living that emerged in the last economic revolution. A new aging affluent class will increasingly be dominating consumer markets and the workplace, reshaping our economy for several decades to come. But they will first determine the business leaders of the new economy in this decade . . . The Roaring 2000s!

Affluence means more than just rising incomes above the most basic living means. Incomes have been rising steadily over the last thousand years and to a greater degree over the last century. There is a critical turning point just above the middle-class standard of living, which today ranges from around $30,000 to $60,000 in income. Somewhere between $75,000 and

FIGURE 8.2   Households with $500,000 or Greater Net Worth, Exclusive of Personal Residence

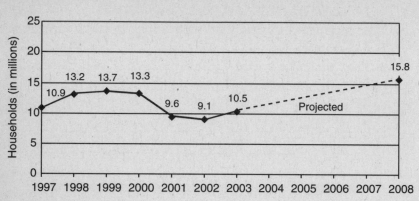

Sources: Spectrem Group Perspective: *The Affluent Investor: Key Attitudes, Behaviors and Demographics: 2003 Overview of Key Trends in the Affluent Market,* Spectrem Group estimates.

$100,000 in earnings there exists enough discretionary income to start saving and investing to a significant degree. Most savings prior to this point go toward down payments on homes or college educations—all investments in the future. But at higher incomes people can actually start planning for the future, creating not only comfortable retirements but also more creative lifestyles and the capacity to fulfill dreams as opposed to simply meeting the necessities of life.

In addition to the escalation in growth of high-income households in this boom, we have seen the rapid emergence of employer-subsidized and government tax-advantaged savings plans, from pension plans to 401(k)s to IRAs to Keoghs to SEPs, which have allowed even more moderate households to save to a higher degree than at any time in history. Why is this so important? The law of compound interest or investment returns means that small amounts of regular savings can accumulate into very large amounts of wealth or net worth, especially in a boom like this, wherein the stock market is growing 30% to 50% faster than in past long-term booms. And of course, the demographic trends from the massive baby-boom generation are driving these unprecedented returns in the stock market and other investment arenas.

As we move to higher definitions of wealth, the growth is higher. The number of high-net-worth or millionaire households has been growing at a stellar 16% a year up until 2000, in line with the long-term growth rates of the stock market (S&P 500 and Dow) in this boom. The Dow has been growing at around 15% from late 1982 throughout this boom as we show in the Dow Channel in Figure 2.15 in Chapter 2. The S&P 500 has grown at very similar rates but will likely grow a bit faster than the Dow as the technology sector continues to grow faster and has a bit higher representation there. We have projected and continue to project that the stock market will continue to grow at that rate into 2009 or perhaps into 2010, in line with the highly predictable demographic trends of baby-boom spending. That would project a Dow as high as 40,000 by late 2009 and an S&P 500 of 5000-plus.

As of 1999, there were more than 7 million millionaire households in the United States (Figure 8.3), or about 7% of households. The stock market crash took its toll here as well, and Spectrem Group is projecting more conservative growth for the rest of this decade with a target of 9.2 million households by 2008, which would suggest well over 10 million by 2010. We think those projections are conservative, given our projections for economic and stock market growth. We think there are likely to be closer to 15 million millionaire households by 2010, or nearly 15% of the households in this country. This is clearly becoming the new definition of the affluent class: a million-dollar net worth and $100,000-plus incomes.

At the extremes in wealth it gets even better. The number of $5 million net worth households (Figure 8.4) reached 590,000 in 1999 and has been growing even faster. Spectrem Group is projecting that this group will grow to 1.16 million by 2008. We think the numbers will be more like 1.5 million to 2 million by 2010. These super-affluent households are more representa-

FIGURE 8.3   Millionaire Households, 1997–2008

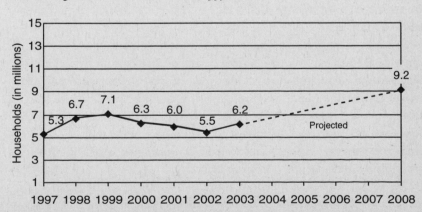

Sources: Spectrem Group Perspective: *The Affluent Investor: Key Attitudes, Behaviors and Demographics: 2003 Overview of Key Trends in the Affluent Market*, Spectrem Group estimates.

FIGURE 8.4　Households with $5 Million or More Net Worth

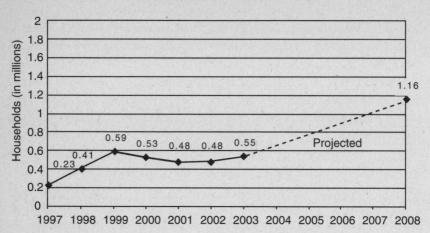

Sources: Spectrem Group Perspective: *The Affluent Investor: Key Attitudes, Behaviors and Demographics: 2003 Overview of Key Trends in the Affluent Market*, Spectrem Group estimates.

tive of the millionaire group that Dr. Thomas Stanley surveyed in *The Millionaire Next Door.* His survey centered on households more in the $5 million to $10 million range of net worth and almost $800,000 in average income.

The critical point of this book is that these new affluent households *are* the new economy, and they aren't typically the frugal "millionaire next door." The real trend in the new economy is that wealth is growing much faster than income. Wealth brings a new dimension of living with greater fundamental financial security that allows the ability not only to invest but to manifest more creative lifestyles as well as entrepreneurial and philanthropic pursuits.

These increasingly affluent households will dominate most of the growth in business over the coming decade of this continuing great boom and set the trends for many decades to come as the new economy fully emerges into the mainstream just as the last economy did from the late 1930s into the 1960s and 1970s. The last economy saw a new middle-class standard of living (10% to 20% of households) emerge from World War I into the Roaring Twenties and that became the norm by the 1960s and 1970s. Even beyond this extraordinary boom, more households will continue to participate in the stock market, business ownership, and profit sharing in the new economy. Professional/knowledge-based jobs as well as entrepreneurial innovation and ownership will continue to accelerate versus factory and clerical jobs.

FIGURE 8.5 Average Household Income: 1950–2060

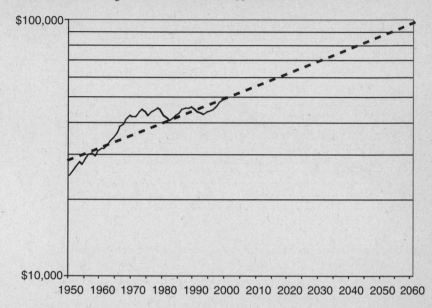

In addition to many more households approaching millionaire status in this boom and for many decades to follow, the average household income should continue to rise at similar rates as it has for many decades (Figure 8.5). The trends in this chart suggest that the average family income will be $100,000 by around 2060. And note that the average family size is declining such that per capita GDP (a much better measure of the real standard of living) is growing even faster, as we show in Figure 8.6.

The greatest gains in productivity and standard of living for most households come for many decades after the tech bubbles that usher in the new infrastructures and ways of living and doing business.

These charts show that such gains did come—and more consistently—after the 1919 and 1929 bubbles and crashes during the last eighty-year New Economy Cycle. That means our children should be very affluent by the time they hit their peak career and wealth cycles—but more so after the downturn from 2010 to 2020! And they should live to 90 to 100 years of age, and some potentially as high as 120 due to the emerging biotech revolution by the middle and later parts of this century! This means a longer productive life cycle in which to learn, earn, spend, and accumulate wealth—and a longer retirement to save for.

FIGURE 8.6   Real Per Capita GDP, 1900–2050

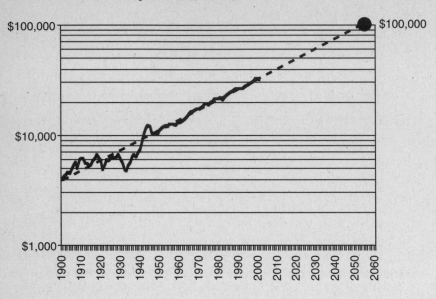

WHAT'S DRIVING THE WEALTH EXPLOSION?

Of course, the greatest overall trend is that incomes are rising to the point that people can have the discretionary income to start to save and invest for the long term, as mentioned earlier. And our average life expectancy has risen from 47 to 78 years in the last century, giving us more time to accumulate wealth. But how we invest is critical. If we gamble it all on Internet stocks at E*Trade, we are not likely to become wealthy. Thomas Stanley's statistics clearly reflected that 97% of the millionaire households he surveyed owned their own home. Home ownership has always been a key to accumulating wealth, but it has been relatively high and expanding more slowly since the 1950s, as shown in Figure 8.7.

Home ownership has risen modestly from 55% to more than 66% since the 1950s after rising more substantially in the first half of the last century. This is an obvious way to build equity and wealth and to get tax advantages, both in deductions and in capital gains. And of course, higher-income households can more readily afford to buy a home and start earlier in their cycle. The new tax laws now allow the first $500,000 in capital gains to be tax-free, increasing the advantages beyond the typical 80% mortgage, which leverages the equity gains five to one. This trend should rise toward 70% by the end of this decade. But it does not completely explain the ex-

FIGURE 8.7 Home Ownership, 1890–2000

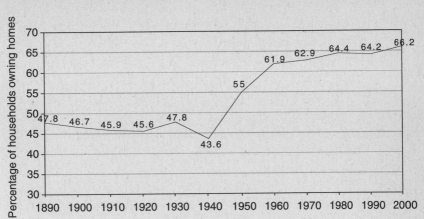

plosion in wealth, especially in the last decade. The second advance kicked in as stock ownership and returns expanded in the 1980s and 1990s.

Hence, a more powerful trend for creating wealth has been the dramatic increase in households that are investing in stocks (Figure 8.8 repeated from Figure 2.19 in Chapter 2). This is clearly a new S-curve trend from the new economy, much like the adoption of PCs, cell phones, the Internet, and broadband—but on a longer time scale. Stock ownership has gone up exponentially compared to home ownership since the late 1970s

FIGURE 8.8 S-Curve of Stock Investing by the Public, 1900–2009

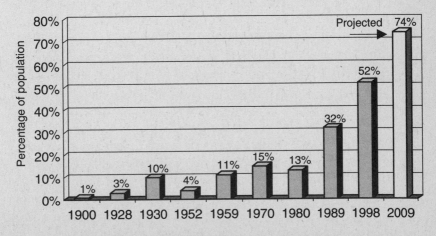

Source: Theodore Caplow, Louis Hicks, and Ben J. Wattenberg, *The First Measured Century*, pp. 252–253.

and early 1980s. At the beginning of the last century, only 1% of households owned stock; in the early 1950s, a mere 7% of households owned stock. At the start of the boom in the early 1980s, only 13% did. But by 1998 the percentage had risen to 52%. We project that the number will rise to 70%–80% (best estimate 74%) by the end of this decade. Of the 65 million Americans who own shares in mutual funds, 70% have household incomes of less than $75,000. So stock ownership isn't just for the rich anymore. The biggest factor behind this trend is again the rise of 401(k) plans (and other tax-advantaged retirement plans such as IRAs and Keoghs), which started with a simple change in the tax codes in 1978—the most important retirement initiative since Social Security.

Most of the households that don't own stock work for small businesses that can't afford the administrative cost and complexity of 401(k) plans. About 50% of employees don't have a 401(k) plan. A staggering 96% of companies with more than 5,000 employees have 401(k) plans. Even 75% of companies with 500 to 1,000 employees have plans. But it drops off rapidly from there. Only 36% of companies with 100 to 500 employees have plans, and a scant 14% of companies with fewer than 100 employees have 401(k) plans. Retirement plans are almost nonexistent in firms with fewer than 20 employees. That is where the most people work! One of the key trends in our economy is the fact that most jobs are continuing to be created in more entrepreneurial small companies—13 million today, as small as one person. The S-curve progression of retirement plans strongly suggests that we will see this small-business market penetrated in the coming decades.

The seeds for this change are already occurring. One of the greatest innovations we have seen in the 401(k) and financial services industry is the advent of low-cost, turnkey, self-administered platforms for 401(k) plans that can be offered by many providers. GoldK (www.goldk.com) was the first company to offer such plans, in the early 2000s. These plans can be set up by a small business at little or no cost in as little as two hours. How can this be? New firms are increasingly automating the bureaucracy of the 401(k) process through software. Employees are generally automatically enrolled and can log on and set up their individual plan in less than an hour.

If your small-business employer hasn't heard of these new low-cost, self-service 401(k) plans, you should let him or her know about them! This is the best tax-advantaged means of building wealth. You are at a distinct disadvantage if you don't have a 401(k) or similar retirement plan. It is not just that your savings accumulate tax-free, but the portion of your salary that goes into the plan is not subject to income tax to begin with.

The investment revolution will ultimately move into everyday households, likely through banks and even large retailers such as Wal-Mart and Costco, which are already starting to offer financial services to their everyday customers. SaveDaily (www.savedaily.com) is a new company that has developed software similar to GoldK's for low-cost investing outside of 401(k) plans. Through this software, banks, credit unions, affinity organizations, and retailers will ultimately be able to offer very low cost, systematic savings plans with very low account fees and no minimum investment. The plans invest people in a mutual fund portfolio commensurate with their risk profile and allow people to have regular deductions made from their bank account or payroll check—$50 or $100 or $200 a month, as David Bach recommends in *The Automatic Millionaire*—or to make random deposits in cash at a retail outlet or at their bank.

David Bach's simple but powerful rules for saving in *The Automatic Millionaire* are: (1) Pay yourself first (make savings just like your rent) and (2) make it automatic (through systematic direct debits to your banking account, paycheck, etc.).

With new platforms such as SaveDaily and GoldK, it is easy to see how millions of new households will be able to do just that and become new equity investors each year for two decades to come, as the S-curve progression in Figure 8.8 suggests. Now everyday households can start to save and invest with amounts as low as $10 a month if that's all they can afford to begin with. They can build more as their discretionary incomes increase over their life cycles.

The first slogan for the new economy would be: Everyone an investor!

THE TREND TOWARD SELF-EMPLOYMENT AND FREE AGENTS

The most important trend that is driving the new wealth paradigm is that more people are starting their own businesses and home-based businesses, creating more participation in income and equity from their own work. *The Millionaire Next Door* and *The Millionaire Mind* by Thomas J. Stanley clearly showed that 80% of millionaires are self-made. Some 32% own their

own businesses and 19% are lawyers or doctors, many of whom own their
own practice or participate more directly in their income stream. Only 16%
were senior corporate executives. The business owners clearly had the highest net worth on average in those surveys.

**The best single way to build wealth is to own your own business,
especially one that can be systematically expanded or sold.**

Daniel Pink, in *Free Agent Nation,* estimates the number of workers
who don't have traditional full-time jobs and breaks them into four categories: microbusinesses, soloists, telecommuters, and temps. But note that
only the soloists and microbusinesses are really self-employed and tend to
have some potential for building equity in their own business.

There are about 13 million microbusinesses. More than half of American companies have less than five employees, and many of these are run out
of the owner's home. A Wells Fargo study found that 69% of all new businesses are located in the owner's place of residence. Many of these are simple businesses revolving around sales, construction, maintenance, cleaning,
data processing, graphic arts, or accounting. We estimate that only a minority of these businesses could be sold to create substantial equity. The
biggest benefit of these home-based businesses is lower costs, less commuting, greater work flexibility—and typically higher income for the owners.

There are approximately 16.5 million soloists. These are one-person
businesses that typically include writers, artists, photographers, plumbers,
management consultants, graphic designers, carpet installers, and computer programmers. There is an obvious overlap with the microbusinesses.
The difference is that microbusinesses have more than one employee and
are more likely to build equity in a business that can be sold. If your business revolves only around you and your talents, how are you going to sell it
when you move or decide to retire? However, even some of these soloists
can sell their clients and name to a new aspiring soloist or business.

The number of people who work for a company but from their homes
is also rising. Pink estimates that there are between 11 million and 14 million, or 12.5 million as the best estimate. These people obviously don't own
their own business, but do get the benefits of more flexible work hours and
less commuting. There is very little opportunity to develop equity here unless you renegotiate with your employer to become an independent con-
tractor and then expand your business to other companies.

And finally, there are about 3.5 million temps. These are people who work for others part-time and have little control over their work and no opportunity to build equity. They often do this not out of choice, but out of the inability to find a stable job. Many others do it for the work flexibility or because they desire only part-time work. In summary, there is a large and growing segment of households that is increasingly self-employed to one degree or another. Only 10% of workers are employed by Fortune 500 companies. This trend toward self-employment and owning your own business will continue to grow in the new economy.

THE FINAL TRUTH: OWNING YOUR OWN BUSINESS IS THE BEST MEANS OF BUILDING WEALTH

The greatest opportunity to build wealth has and will come from starting your own business, more often than not out of your home at first. Every study of millionaire households has shown this to be the most critical factor. In *The Millionaire Mind,* Stanley shows (page 73) that his surveys of the highest-net-worth households indicated that 87% rated "investing in my own business" as either very important (50%) or important (37%). In contrast, only 40% rated investing in stocks very important (12%) or important (28%). But unless you build an organization that can be replicated and/or succeed you, it is hard to recognize substantial equity from owning your own business. Hence, the microbusiness category is the best route for most people. Just as we saw that stock ownership has been rising dramatically since the early 1980s, the wealth trend in the most affluent sectors has grown the most due to the acceleration in self-employment or business ownership as we can see in Figure 8.9.

Among the top 1% income households, the percentage that are self-employed has risen from 37% in 1983 to 70% by 1998. That is another S-curve progression that may be starting to peak for that income category. But for the rest of us, it is the beginning of a major new S-curve trend. For households with $5 million plus in net worth, self-employment rose from 35% in 1983 to 65% in 1998, achieving most of those gains by 1989. The self-employment rates of $1 million plus net worth households went from just under 50% in 1983 to 62% in 1998 and rose more rapidly since 1995. Note that these levels of incomes and net worth are measured in real, inflation-adjusted 1998 dollars. Based on these levels of self-employment among the top households, it would be reasonable to project that over the coming decades about 70% of us will be self-employed.

Since 1983, the percentage of the top 1% of households with the head of

FIGURE 8.9   Self-Employment Among Top-Income and Top-Net-Worth
Households, 1983–1998

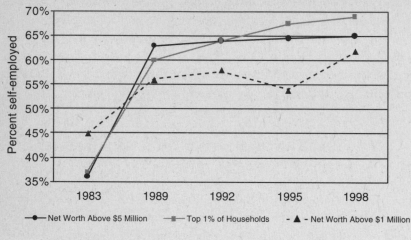

Source: Tim W. Ferguson, "Nouveau Riche," *Forbes*, October 8, 2001, p.78.

FIGURE 8.10   Percentage of Younger High-Income Households, 1993–1998

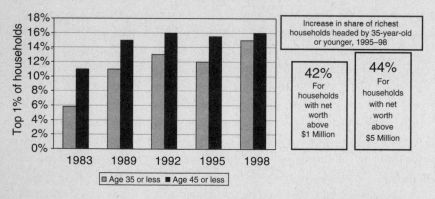

Source: Tim W. Ferguson, "Nouveau Riche," *Forbes*, October 8, 2001, p. 78.

household under age 45 has been rising steadily, although it is still a distinct
minority (Figure 8.10). The under-35 age group has been growing even
faster, showing the entrepreneurial trend in the emerging new economy
and technologies. It is only logical that the percentage of top earners would
be much less at age 45 and below as the incomes of the top 1% of households peak between the ages of 55 to 59, much later than those of the average household, between ages 45 and 49, as we can see in Figure 8.11. The
incomes of the top 5% and 10% of households peak between ages 50 and

FIGURE 8.11 Peak Incomes in the Top 1%, 5%, and 10% of Households by Age, 1999

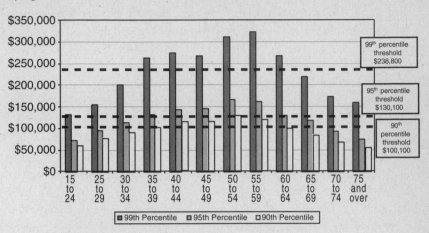

Source: Peter Brimelow, "Keeping Up," *Forbes*, May 1, 2000.
Research: Edwin S. Rubinstein, Hudson Institute.

54. The top 10% of households have peak incomes 2½ times that of the average household and the top 1% approximately 7 times.

> The second slogan for the new economy would be: Everyone a business owner—or a business within their company with profit-sharing.

MOST BUSINESSES ARE MISSING THE OPPORTUNITIES OF THE NEW AFFLUENT MARKET

One of the unique insights from the explosion of wealth is that most businesses are missing this massive and powerful new affluent market. Most businesses continue to cater to the middle-class market with the "lowest-price" strategy where there is high competition and low profit margins. Ask yourself, "Why are people always waiting in line for Mercedes while Mazdas are always on sale?" These new wealthy households increasingly value quality of life over quantity, service over the lowest price, making their own decisions versus being told what to do at work, and making a real difference versus just fulfilling a job description. Their time is valuable, and their sense of self-worth is high. That means new values, new lifestyles, and new work environments. Yet most companies and institutions continue their inherited tradition of treating their customers' time as worth nothing while they optimize their workers' time, yet suppress their strongest motivations and talents. They maximize their shareholders' returns, while service levels to customers continue to plummet.

A new book, *Trading Up*, by Michael J. Silverstein and Neil Fiske, makes the strongest argument for the emergence of the new premium class of products and services that we have been projecting to emerge since our first major book, *The Great Boom Ahead*, in 1992. The top 20% of households have seen greater gains in income and wealth than the average in the past two decades, contributing to the growth of the new premium segments. But Silverstein and Fiske show, as we have, that the discount sector that emerged from the 1970s into the 1990s (Figure 8.12, repeated from *The Roaring 2000s*) has made everyday goods more affordable, freeing up more discretionary income for premium goods even in the everyday household. Most people will now buy premium products in select areas where they have a great interest, such as "Big Bertha" golf clubs from Callaway or Starbucks lattes. And of course, the growing affluent households typically buy such goods across the board, as opposed to selectively. Hence, it is the firms in the middle (or old standard-quality range, such as Sears) that are getting squeezed out. Discount firms have been rising for decades, but premium firms will rise even faster in the decades ahead. It is these firms that will cre-

FIGURE 8.12 Discount, Standard, and Premium Trends, 1970–2010

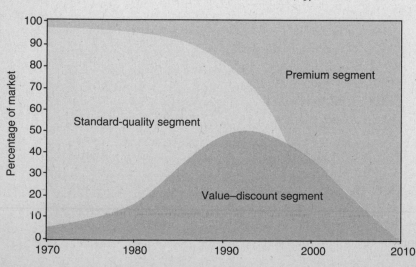

ate the new economy over the next several decades and win the race for leadership by the end of this decade.

Hence, we will see a more radical change toward the more upscale mass-market segments in this decade and beyond than we saw in the 1970s, 1980s, and 1990s. And it's not just the rise in power of this minority new affluent class since the 1990s. In the decades to come most households will achieve this status of affluence, just as with mass middle-class living standards after World War II. Hence, this new affluent class is determining the new trends in commerce, work, and lifestyles not only for the coming decade but also into the middle of this new century and beyond. And of course, these affluent trends will be followed increasingly in emerging countries, Asia, and elsewhere over the coming decades.

That's why it is important for businesses and investors to target this rising affluent class in this "Roaring 2000s" decade. They will determine the race for leadership in the new economy by the top of this boom, as occurred in the Roaring Twenties, when the last revolution first moved mainstream. The lesson from the Roaring Twenties: General Motors won the race for leadership in automobiles by appealing to the rising quality needs of the new affluent generation with trade-up models such as Buick and Cadillac, while Ford kept cranking out low-cost Model Ts.

Many will say that the e-commerce trends of the late 1990s represented just a mania in stock prices and a dream that would not be fulfilled. In *The Roaring 2000s*, we outlined the stages of this technology revolution with the business-to-business (B2B) trend emerging from the mid-1990s into the early 2000s and the consumer revolution emerging from 2002 into 2010. It will be the expansion of broadband Internet connections, the advance of voice activation or speech-recognition technologies (easy access), and the ultimate emergence of video interactivity (real-time, personalized service), that will create the real consumer revolution in the second half of this decade.

The lesson of the Internet bubble and technology crash of 2000 was twofold. First, the consumer revolution that everyone anticipated was still years away. We did not flock onto the Internet for everyday products and services. We are still using it largely as an information and communications tool and have bought only simple commodity products in cyberspace thus far, such as computers, CDs, books, and travel.

But more important, the real revolution was about changing how we organize and do business, as I emphasized in *The Roaring 2000s* (Chapters 5–8). It was about the emergence of radically new business models— bottom-up, not top-down in management; real-time, personalized service, not just lower costs and prices. It was not about creating new brand names overnight with companies run by young people with no business plans or profitability. These were the companies that were bid up to ridiculous prices on the stock market and then crashed, often by 99% or more, by 2002. It is more about leveraging the new brands, technologies, products, and services that emerged in the innovative years of the 1960s and 1970s, in the younger years of the new baby-boom cycle.

The real impact was that most existing leading larger companies were forced to retool for the Internet and to embrace new direct marketing strategies—"bricks and clicks"! These companies will be the ones to win the race for leadership ahead along with a few strong new brand names such as eBay and Amazon. More and more radical new start-ups will see that joint ventures or services to larger or more established companies will be the way to emerge quickly enough to participate in winning this race for leadership.

We also emphasized in *The Roaring 2000s* that every other generation brings the radical innovations that launch a new economy. The generation that follows the new innovations extends and improves the existing technologies, products, services, and industries. The echo baby boom began its Innovation Stage hoping to suddenly change the world and create whole new brand names and companies. The lesson of the 2000–2002 e-commerce crash was that the new trend is about improving and extending the PC and Internet revolution, not creating a whole new set of brands. (Of course, new brands will always emerge over time.) This is what occurred as the Bob Hope generation emerged into its Innovation Stage and ultimately put jet engines onto airplanes and superhighways under cars, and so on. That is the revolution from now on. But it is ultimately more about changing how we work and live to extend these new technologies and products into mainstream affordability and everyday use for increasingly affluent consumers who demand higher quality and service at more affordable prices.

But this revolution will extend beyond consumers. The only way to attract the best workers from this rising class will be by allowing them to run their own businesses within your company or to partner with them as outsource suppliers. Millionaires don't have to work; they will increasingly be attracted to opportunities to run their own businesses and will expect to be able to profit accordingly. And more will want to work from their homes or on a flexible basis, combining home and corporate office and being in the field with customers and vendors as is appropriate.

Mission-based businesses that have meaningful causes beyond financial compensation will rise, as will a rapidly growing and revitalized nonprofit sector fueled by the baby-boom philanthropy wave. This new more entrepreneurial and decentralized profit and nonprofit sector will progressively usurp many of the functions of government beyond the mere privatization trends of the past decades. The new role of national government will simply be to set standards in areas such as education and basic welfare and let the profit and nonprofit economy best achieve those needs at local levels.

The greatest opportunity will come not only by starting your own business or getting a greater equity stake in the business you work for, but by understanding the types of businesses that will win the race for leadership into the top of this unprecedented boom. This is where most of the new millionaires have created and will continue to create their wealth. First, your business must target this new rising affluent class of baby boomers. But even more important, they will lead the radical changes that maturing baby boomers and the Internet will bring to how we design our business organizations, both profit and nonprofit—changes that will allow more workers to gain an equity stake in their businesses.

THE AFFLUENT-CONSUMER REVOLUTION: WHY THE MILLIONAIRE NEXT DOOR IS NOT NEXT DOOR AND DOESN'T REPRESENT THE NEW MILLIONAIRE ECONOMY

Since the bestseller *The Millionaire Next Door* by Thomas Stanley, many of us have gotten the impression that the new affluent class is a bunch of stingy, frugal households that save all of their money and never spend it— "cheap dates," as Dr. Stanley calls them! That is certainly true of a very tiny percentage of our population. But these are not the real trendsetters in our new economy, and they have been greatly overstated by that book. At the time the sequel, *The Millionaire Mind,* came out in early 2000, the book was estimating 4.9% millionaire households versus 3.0% four years earlier. More updated estimates by Spectrem indicate that the number is more like 6% to 7% and growing as much as 16% per year on average, as we showed earlier in this chapter.

The truth clearly is that Stanley's books intensively surveyed only a very small portion of the new millionaire population. Their average net worth was $9.2 million, and their average income was $749,000. This group's affluence is representative of only approximately the top 0.5% or 500,000 of U.S. households. What about the other 6.5 million millionaire households? Stanley professed to having done statistically meaningful research on the millionaire population that my broader research and experience clearly disagree with. Why? He targeted only the very small percentage of traditional upscale neighborhoods that have the highest percentage of millionaires, at 80%. And these people were older, at age 54, on average, more representative of the last generation. They were also more traditional, with average marriages of 28 years and spouses typically not working outside of the household.

We conclude that more of the millionaires to date are not of the lifestyle described in *The Millionaire Next Door* and that the great majority of the rising affluent households that will drive consumer trends in the future are definitely not of that persuasion! That means that the great majority of the projected 25 to 30 million millionaire and affluent households by 2009 will not be the frugal, all-saving, no-spending, low-lifestyle types but more the opposite—bobos.

FROM HIPPIES TO YUPPIES TO BOBOS: THE AFFLUENT BABY-BOOM TREND

Let's start with a very different point of view, confirmed by the broader trends we can witness in this unprecedented boom and in the rising and increasing affluent baby-boomer households that are actually leading this boom. Let's start with a little history summarized from *The Roaring 2000s*. The baby boomers started as hippies in their youthful, idealistic stage of the 1960s and 1970s, transitioned to yuppies as they entered their career cycle in the 1980s and 1990s, and are now maturing into bobos, or bourgeois bohemians, as David Brooks has dubbed them in his book *Bobos in Paradise* (Simon & Schuster, 2000).

They have dramatically changed the economy every step of the way, both because of the size of the generation and their change-oriented versus conformist personality, which comes every other generation. William Strauss and Neil Howe document these generation cycles in great detail in three groundbreaking books: *Generations, The Fourth Turning,* and *Millennials Rising.* These books are all highly recommended reading. But they are for the more serious reader since they are long and very detailed in their accounts of history, despite the simpler overview of demographic trends that ultimately reveal powerful insights.

The baby boomers brought new innovations in lifestyles, products, and technologies from the 1960s and 1970s into new mainstream trends in the boom from the 1980s into the 1990s. They will now bring even more radical and meaningful changes to our economy and society in the 2000s and 2010s, as they mature into their power cycle and have the opportunity to remake society around their more stable new lifestyles. These new "bobos" are very different from the old upper class of the 1950s and 1960s. From the beginning they rose out of a new capital called knowledge, and in the light of it they have questioned every aspect of culture and economics in the search to create a better world that transcends the limitations of the already middle-class, affluent world they grew up in. But it is only since the mid-1990s that they have finally begun to have the collective power to change the world, and they will to a much greater degree in the coming two decades.

After World War II, a college education became the critical ingredient in achieving an upper-middle-class life. The percentage of people with a college degree rose from less than 10% in 1950 to 25% today and that doesn't count the people who attended college or technical schools but didn't graduate. This trend has had the greatest correlation with the explosion of the new affluent class. In fact, with continued increases ahead, the college-educated class tracks my projections of the new affluent class toward 30% by 2009. But what changed in the 1960s and 1970s was the bohemian creative and equality movement. Government and nonprofit education aid programs expanded, and entrance requirements started to revolve more around standardized tests and more objective SAT scores. Hence, a new knowledge class, increasingly rising from the broader middle class, first began their assault on the upper class or "bourgeois" of the past, which revolved more around inherited wealth and class connections.

The old class, as usual, had little interest in changing the system. The new class had every interest in doing so. So they rebelled, largely against the good-old-boy network, but also against ostentatious displays of wealth, conformity, and the very nature of authority and top-down management, increasingly characterized as "the corporation man." New generations have always rebelled against the past establishment as they have entered the workforce. But this generation was much larger and armed with the new secret weapon in the information age: knowledge. Their first revolution was the bohemian cycle: returning to basic values and human pleasures and rebelling against the puritan work ethic and frugality of the past.

But as this new, idealistic generation entered its career cycle and subsequently had families, they became yuppies in the 1980s, spurred by the booming economy that they were driving with their new innovations and spending power. They suddenly weren't so back-to-nature and carefree. The upper-end young boomers were starting new trends in upscale products from new restaurants to espressos to wines to sports cars to trendy downtown condos. They would pay the top price for any product or service of good quality. They were the first gourmet class since the robber barons in the early 1900s, when the Henry Ford generation was in its own "yuppie" phase. They were entering the natural acquisitive stage that comes upon entering the family and career cycle, but they were struggling to reconcile their need to spend with their rebellious ethic against materialism, rationalizing that it paid to buy the best quality. And they in greater numbers for the first time in history had the educated tastes to appreciate such quality.

The showiness of the yuppie trends matured between the late 1980s and 1990s for most, but the appetite for quality and service hasn't. After having been antiestablishment, this new knowledge-based affluent sector of the baby-boom generation has been inevitably maturing into the new establishment. In doing so it has been struggling to create a new lifestyle and consumer ethic that reconciles the two extremes of their experience, the "bohemian," or inner, values of the 1960s and 1970s and the more "bourgeois," or outer success, values of the 1980s and 1990s. Again, this struggle is most astutely captured in *Bobos in Paradise,* by David Brooks. The 1960s radicals advocated dropping out of the rat race and being true to your soul, living simply in smaller, more human communities. In the 1990s, we saw a wave of books on "simplifying your life" that continued that theme. But the rising desire for greater success and more affluent lifestyles for this aging, family-oriented generation has continued to dominate the larger trends.

"Bobos" is Brooks's abbreviation for "bourgeois bohemians." He has documented how this generation went to extremes from the 1960s and 1970s to the 1980s and 1990s, struggling to reconcile them to the point that they have finally and successfully embraced both ideals and integrated both into their lifestyles. This has also been an observation we have had about the baby boomers since the 1970s. They have always striven to question the lifestyle, consumer, and work ethics of the past but then have attempted to create "the best of both worlds" rather than opt for one or the other of the past ideals. This has required a lot of experimentation and soul-searching, which has created and continues to create tension in their lives and in our society. To quote from Brooks:

> But the biggest tension, to put it in the grandest terms, is between worldly success and inner virtue. How do you move ahead in life without letting ambition wither your soul? How do you accumulate the material resources to do the things you want without becoming a slave to those material things? How do you build a comfortable and stable

life for your family without getting bogged down in stultifying routine? How do you live at the top of society without becoming an insufferable snob?

David Brooks, *Bobos in Paradise,* p. 41

TARGETING THE NEW AFFLUENT BOBOS

Out of this four-decade struggle since the 1960s, this generation finds itself in the 2000s with a clearer ethic of "self-actualization" that should endure and mature for the rest of its life cycle and will continue to shape the qualitative side of its needs for consumer service, as well as work environments. Brooks best summarizes the new ethic in consumption as "utilitarian spending." Bobos will spend very lavishly on necessities rather than flaunting obvious luxuries. That means they will spend $200 on a casual "fishing" shirt that is made of very durable and fine fabric—even though they may never actually go fishing. They have incredible gourmet kitchens, even though they may not have much time to cook. They have very well made and appointed SUVs even though they rarely go seriously off road.

As they first learned in their yuppie years, quality does pay, so they also buy less apparently for mere show, except to their peers, who recognize the quality and utilitarianism—and the fine threads in that fishing shirt. So in effect the new ethic is about being wealthy without showing it too much. Less gold plating and shiny marble, more rustic, natural stones and tiles. They also prefer to live in smaller communities even though they are involved in an increasingly global and high-paced economy. They don't like traffic jams or franchises in their small enclaves, and they are increasingly moving into exurban and resort towns to get back to nature and community. But they are still increasingly living the high life by their own new definition, and there seems to be no turning back!

But I certainly don't want to oversimplify here and create an impression that all affluent baby boomers are alike and all fit the bobo lifestyle. They don't. After all, this is the era of customization and choice in lifestyles. That is one of the new bohemian values: that people can be more what they want to be and not have to fit into the very rigid suburban lifestyles, upper and middle class, of the 1950s and 1960s. Here is where another book, *The Clustered World* (2000) by Michael Weiss, is important. This book is a follow-up to his first book, *The Clustering of America* (1988), where he first chronicled the emergence of a new lifestyle science of demographic marketing segmentation pioneered by Jonathan Robbin and Claritas Inc. Note that this was the same geodemographic expert hired by Dr. Stanley to target his millionaire surveys. In 2000, Weiss updated this model and its lifestyle segments, including a look at adaptations of the model around the world.

With this model, which we have been following since the mid-1980s, you can see how diverse the new ethic is—although it has a clear direction. This model now breaks the United States into sixty-two different lifestyle categories, the importance being that households with similar ages and incomes can behave very differently in how they live and what they buy—the difference between who lives in the cities, the suburbs, the exurbs, or old-fashioned rural towns; who buys Mercedes versus Volvos versus Hondas; who drinks light versus domestic versus foreign beer; or who reads *Fortune* versus *BusinessWeek* versus *Money* magazine—and much more, all down to zip codes and neighborhood blocks. This is demographics at its best, and we've been touting it for decades as a marketing tool to businesses, and even as a method for analyzing areas you are thinking of relocating to for lifestyle compatibilities.

FROM SELF-ESTEEM TO SELF-ACTUALIZATION— WHAT A TRIP IT'S BEEN

It's important to understand that there is more going on here than just an expansion of wealth. Rising skills, incomes, and even more so wealth expand people's sense of self-esteem and self-worth. They cause them to look at the world differently and to expect to be treated differently. But at some point of achievement and wealth this self-esteem evolves into a more profound stage of self-actualization. Understanding how people change as they move into self-esteem and toward self-actualization is critical to understanding the qualitative side of this revolution in the consumer markets and in the workplace that is now accelerating.

Human evolution has grown very slowly in history from the four basic stages of psychology, best characterized by Abraham Maslow, from survival to belonging to self-esteem to self-actualization. But that evolution has been accelerating dramatically since the Industrial Revolution. Each stage of growth brings changes in the direction of growth, from self-oriented to collective-oriented. The survival and self-esteem cycles are more self-oriented, building the individual ego first before achieving further advances into greater collective accomplishments. You can't do much for society until you can survive and provide for your basic needs (survival and security stage). But once these basic needs are achieved, people naturally move toward higher needs for socialization or integrating with other people into a family or community or society (the belonging stage). Happiness makes a great leap between these two stages, both because survival is very fear-based and stressful and also because advancing beyond the ego or a self-centered survival mode into a greater level of belonging through marriage, family, tribe, culture, and community is more expansive and more sustainable.

You are not only just your limited self, you are part of something greater that completes you and extends from you. That is the more happy and collective stage of belonging. But just as you have fully achieved this stage of fitting in, the egoistic urge to grow, to be more than just an ordinary member of the clan, resurfaces. "I just got to be me!" This propels you into the difficult self-oriented stage of building self-esteem, which is much like the survival stage, but at a higher level. It's like going through adolescence instead of the early-childhood struggle of the survival stage. As you enter this stage you already know how to provide for yourself and you can integrate into a group of people that have likewise surpassed the survival level and have the need for relationship.

But now you have to begin to leave the safe rules and roles of the clan and rise above, to new levels of achievement—not survival against the odds, but standing out, doing something a bit extraordinary, being your own person. This naturally entails taking some risks and being more self-centered again. But at first you do it more cautiously, still trying to fit into the rules and roles of the clan, like teenagers breaking away from their parents to try to fit into a new peer group with new values. You try to become better at what society dictates is okay. You become better at belonging to the point that you become a manager, a professional, a pillar of the community. You increasingly set and achieve your own goals, live your own life, create your own rules, again like teenagers.

As you mature in this stage, you are increasingly less embarrassed at standing out from the crowd. You don't need all of the rules and roles to fit into. You are more like a young adult in your late 20s or early 30s who is finding your clear career direction in life and understanding your strengths and weaknesses as an individual—what you are suited for and what you are not. There is initially a great freedom here, in that you realize that you don't have to be like everyone else to succeed and be happy. You can be what you actually are and want to be. You start trusting your own instincts and desires but also feel increasingly responsible for your own behaviors and consequences now that you are increasingly determining your own destiny. You are a successful person, you know what you want and how to achieve it. You have learned "how to be me." That is the fullness of the self-esteem stage, a stage that continues to grow and peaks in career and family achievements today for many people in their mid- to late 40s. That is when the midlife crisis, or the beginning of the self-actualization stage, can kick in.

Now that you have achieved success, you realize that you may have done it at the expense of some of your relationships. You start wondering what all of this success and achievement is about since it hasn't brought you the full happiness you thought would be possible if you achieved your goals as an individual. How big a house can you build, how many more "eco" or exclusive vacations can you go on? How many great restaurants can you dine in? You start to realize that you became so focused on "me" that you forgot the happiness and belonging of "we."

You start thinking, now that I feel confidence in my abilities, how can I use them to be a better person, how can I take my success and my understanding of my unique skills and integrate them into a greater role, not just in my family and community, but into society and the world? How can I change my profession or business for the better of society? Or, as David Brooks put it, how can I live at the top of society and not be an insufferable snob? How can I create a family or community within which all members can have their own self-esteem and do what they are best designed to do in life? How can I give others the self-esteem and freedom to be their selves that I have achieved? How can I give back to society and become a part of the greater whole again, as in my belonging days? How can I make a real difference in the world?

Now your point of view of your community is more expanded, because you have more capacities and greater vision than you did as you moved into the belonging stage. I'm okay, you're okay. Win/win is your new philosophy. You can be what you want to be, and I can be what I want to be. A much greater rise in tolerance or relativistic thinking arises. You can see other people's points of view and unique talents. We don't all have to be the same in how we achieve and fit in! If we all maximize our individual talents and cooperate, we are better off than if we all just follow the rules and do what we are told—as if we have no individual talents or initiatives (belonging stage)—or if we compete ruthlessly for self-esteem to merely see who is best (or who survives in the earliest self-oriented survival stage). I don't want to prosper at the expense of others. I want my livelihood to benefit others, not to exploit them (as has occurred through the advancement of wealth for most of history). That is the self-actualization stage, one that flowers into human wisdom and maturity into most people's elder years if they mature fully within their life cycle.

This growth cycle obviously doesn't occur at the same rate for all people. In a prosperous middle-class economy like that of the United States where most people are born into at least the belonging stage, the first stages occur rapidly. Survival just until age 4 or 5, when you become physically functional. Belonging by early or late adolescence. For middle-class people, then, the movement into self-esteem can begin between late adolescence and early adulthood and require the rest of their lives. For the more highly educated and advanced, self-esteem can begin in early adolescence and crest anywhere from the late 30s to the early 50s. Then they tend to move into a whole new stage of human evolution, self-actualization, which will occupy them for the rest of their lives. And there are, of course, some highly motivated people who move out of their less fortunate or middle-class background faster by accelerating their education and/or entrepreneurial development.

We are at an important intersection in history wherein the mass of baby boomers are moving increasingly into their midlife crisis, with a substantial portion of the new affluent class moving for the first time into the self-actualization stage from a longer view of human evolution. Even though most of this new affluent class is still more in the self-esteem stage, the latter stages of this level of growth are clearly starting to lean toward the urge to self-actualization. Why is this so critical? Self-esteem and self-actualization are the human trends driving the new economy, and the present corporate model is not designed to serve these needs of the increasingly affluent consumers and knowledge-based workers.

As the aging baby boomers move firmly into their power cycle in the coming two decades, corporations will be forced to change more radically, beginning with recognizing the imperative of focusing on the exploding affluent markets, the very ones that slowed the most in 2000–2002. As a business or investor, don't make the mistake of thinking this wealth revolution is over because of that temporary crash—or even the greater crash we are forecasting after 2009. This rise in affluence is a long-term trend offering great opportunities for decades ahead. It actually just began in the mid-1990s. The companies that reorganize more radically to meet the needs of this new affluent class will win the race for leadership in the coming decade and tend to continue to dominate for many more decades to come. Would you rather be focusing on Mercedes or Mazdas?

WHY THE OLD MANAGEMENT SYSTEMS WILL FINALLY DIE IN THE COMING DECADES

In Chapter 2 we showed how the radical new infrastructures for the new economy are just emerging into mainstream penetration between 1994 and 2009. In this chapter we have shown how they will continue to emerge much more so into mainstream incomes and wealth in the decades ahead. Hence, we haven't yet seen the real revolution from these new technologies and the eighty-year cycle. As new technologies and economies emerge while old ones are maturing we reach a point of growth and progress where the old system, no matter how much we improve and refine it, simply and utterly fails to work! That only begins to occur when the new technologies emerge to the degree that they can start to offer new ways of working and living—during the 50% to 90% penetration cycle on the S-curve as we are approaching in this decade.

We see this today in our urban congestion. No matter how much we expand our highways and infrastructures, we see greater traffic jams and congestion in our cities, suburbs, and even now in many growing exurban and resort areas. We seem to work harder and longer hours but waste more time dealing with meetings, bureaucracy, management bottlenecks, and corporate reorganization initiatives. We become more affluent and wealthier, yet spend more time waiting on phones and in lines at stores for less and less real human service.

The paradox seems to be that the more that we succeed, the less time we have for our families and communities. As Jimi Hendrix put it: "Is this love—or just confusion?" Is there a way out of this dilemma? Although every new economy and paradigm ultimately presents its own challenges and limits, we clearly see a new paradigm of living and working that is better, higher service, less wasteful and polluting—and, most important, more self-actualized for individual workers. And it is already emerging in the more affluent and innovative segments of society, as we covered earlier in this chapter.

We characterize the present system of society and business as "people waiting in lines," a simple parody of the "batch and queue" or assembly-line production system that emerged in the last economic revolution. That system revolved around creating large productions and inventories of standardized products to take advantages of economies of scale and to minimize costs, and then mass marketing to convince everyone that they needed these products to get rid of them. This is the very system that created the greatest middle-class living standard in all of history, especially in North America. So first you think: How could we fault this system? But then you should think: How could we as people allow ourselves to become the "new inventory" of this system, treated as mass markets of consumers as if we were all alike, standing in lines waiting for mediocre service just as we have the incomes to afford more? Wasn't it the material products and natural resources that were supposed to be organized, waiting in lines and leveraged to our human benefit? It now seems that the oppressors have become the oppressed!

The critical trends that are causing this breakdown in the midst of such progress are the following:

1. Rapidly rising demands for customization and personalization of service among increasingly affluent consumers

2. Rising needs for more entrepreneurial and creative work environments by a fast-growing, more self-actualizing new knowledge class of workers

3. An acceleration of economic growth from the aging of the massive baby-boom generation here and around the world

4. Rising urban congestion from the industrial-age population shift from rural areas to cities and suburbs, now accelerating around the world

5. Rising pollution and environmental degradation from unprecedented population growth, economic development, and the industrial revolution in third-world countries

Our present top-down, managed, commute-to-work, and urban/suburban-based society simply can't manage these rising demands and constraints—and the results in many higher-population third-world cities is looking horrifying many decades ahead of their peak in industrial development! We need a new architecture of society, business, work, and consumption. That is the real importance of the computer, the Internet, and the new information-based technologies: to fundamentally change the way we manage, work, consume, and live. That has been the ultimate impact of every technology and economic revolution in history. But the more profound impact of such changes occurs as the new innovative generations who spawn these technological and social changes in their youth are maturing beyond their peak consumer years into their power years (which peak around age 58 and grow between the ages of 45 to 65), and have the capacity to change the

FIGURE 8.13 The Generation Wave, 1933–2033

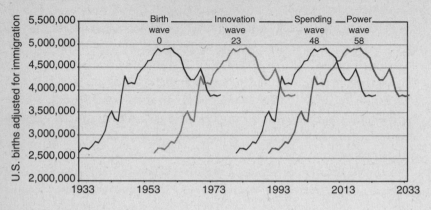

decision-making and organizational processes that govern business and society, as we show in Figure 8.13 updated from *The Roaring 2000s* (and *The
Great Boom Ahead* in the early 1990s).

This paradox of rising wealth and an apparent fall in many areas of our
quality of life is actually a symptom of the success of our economic system
and society, not its failure. But it is more critically a call to radically "reorganize" our fundamental structures to accommodate a higher level of population, wealth, and standard of living—just as living organisms create as
they grow more intelligent and complex in function. Our human systems
and DNA, from brain to skeleton to muscle, are obviously more complex
than amoebas and lizards. This is what occurred in our economic and soci-
etal structures between World War I (the assembly line at Ford) and the
Roaring Twenties, when a whole new model of organization (the General
Motors corporate model) and a new suburban lifestyle began to emerge.
The cities would have broken down under the continuing rise of population and pollution by horse manure and wood burning alone, not to mention congestion.

Such radical revolutions also occurred following all major technological innovations ranging from the printing press to the steam engine to the
railroads and came many decades after most of the new technologies and
brand names first emerged. The real revolution in the emergence of the last
economy occurred only beginning in the Roaring Twenties as the new technologies were moving from 50% to 90% penetration, not in the decades of
great innovation in new technologies that occurred before. And that revolution was about a whole new model for restructuring business and society,
not about a whole slew of new products and brand names emerging over-

night. Again, that's why the dot-com mania was an overreaction to this technology revolution and crashed in 2000–2002. The innovation of radical new products and technologies flowered to the greatest degree in the 1960s and 1970s.

The dot-com crash doesn't mean that the Internet will not accelerate the revolution in business and society. This most critical chapter of the revolution will similarly begin in this decade, which we have termed "The Roaring 2000s" as the new infrastructures have passed the 50% penetration that make them an increasing mainstream phenomenon. Until most workers and consumers get on the new infrastructures, the revolution can't fully begin to manifest in a more radical way. Again, this will happen despite the Nasdaq crash and slowing of the economy that temporarily occurred in 2000–2002. That was a natural part of the cycle of new technologies emerging. We have shown that the same downtrends occurred in the early 1920s as well as at the outset of every decade of this boom, the early 1980s and early 1990s, to a lesser degree. We see the next dramatic surge in stocks and economic growth from 2003 into 2009 or early 2010 and a race for leadership that will determine which businesses dominate in most new growth sectors for decades to come, just as occurred in the Roaring Twenties.

We are about to go deeper into the greatest decade of growth and progress in U.S. and world history as we have been forecasting since the late 1980s based on simple demographic trends around the aging of the massive baby-boom generation into their peak spending and productivity years around 2009–2010. This chapter is about how to position your career and your business to win in the race for leadership that will ensue. Embracing the new, more radical models of organization and service will be much more critical to winning that race than merely innovating new products and extensions. This decade is the most exciting yet in this new economy and revolution. Don't be left behind!

PERSONALIZED, REAL-TIME SERVICE:
SOFTWARE AND HUMAN ADVANCES IN PRODUCTIVITY

We've heard that the key trends driving the new economy are the new-technology paradigms: semiconductor chips are doubling every 18 months, storage technologies every 12 months, and bandwidth every 6 months. We maintain that this new stage of the information or Internet revolution is still the harbinger of a more profound revolution in the progress of our economy and society. It is ultimately about a better way of doing business.

Our approach to forecasting has always focused on the more fundamental human impacts of economic change and growth: how we earn, spend, innovate, work, produce, borrow, invest, and change as we age—and how we benefit over time from new-technology revolutions and the emergence of new companies and brands.

If we look back at the last economic revolution, most of the companies that dominated the Roaring Twenties economy were established as start-ups between the late 1800s and the early 1900s, not in the Roaring Twenties. The great expansion of car companies started between 1904 and 1908 and peaked by 1919, but fewer and fewer survived to dominate into the Roaring Twenties and 1930s (as we showed in Chapter 1). Similarly, most of the PC and software-related companies emerged between the late 1960s and early 1980s, most are gone today, and a strong few dominate most markets. So it shouldn't be a great surprise that out of hundreds of new dot-com companies, only a few survive at this late stage in the Innovation Stage. Now such innovative surges run their course more quickly, as a new breed of large companies is quicker to respond than did the sleepy Fortune 500 of the 1970s. Remember the Netscape threat to Microsoft? It didn't last long! Ultimately what is important about the Internet revolution is that it is about a better way of doing business. It is about leveraging software and human communications to maximize human productivity.

It should be obvious by now that software (or more human applications of technology) and human progress in wealth, incomes, and lifestyles come slower than advances in technologies. Our incomes and wealth have not been doubling every 18 months, like semiconductor chips! However, like technologies, these trends are accelerating faster than at any time in history in this unique time of economic growth and technological progress. Technologies succeed and accelerate so rapidly because they are highly focused in automating more simple human tasks that in turn free us up for higher, more complex human functions and skills. But since we are far more complex than highly focused technologies such as production machinery, home appliances, or computers, we must naturally change, advance, and adapt at a slower pace.

Complexity is our strength, not our disadvantage. Only highly complex and innovative human beings can design such incredibly focused technologies and tools, even though they may exceed our talents at specific tasks. The number of $100,000-earning households is growing faster than the economy. But wealthy households are growing even faster in this boom, more in line with the stock market and rising business ownership. That is a truer indication of real human progress and the advance of our more complex nature that is being leveraged by these high-growth technologies. Why is our progress so much slower? Precisely because we are human and more complex.

Software programs have also obviously advanced much slower than the hardware pace of Moore's Law or the bandwidth equivalent of George Gilder's "Telecosm." As computers become more powerful, software seems to become more bloated and hence absorbs most of the increases of the computing-power advances. This has been the main criticism of Microsoft and the growing complexity of its software, but it represents a human reality. Again, since we are more complex than computers, software evolves, like us, more slowly. But the truth is that the greatest leverage in business and investments has been in software, not hardware, as it meets real human needs and advances real human productivity, income, and wealth. Hence, Microsoft has been a greater winner in business success and has seen much greater growth in earnings and valuation than the PC companies, or even Intel, which has a similar near-monopoly on semiconductor chips.

But the "Wintel," or PC-oriented, model of software is just beginning to give way to a new network-centric model being facilitated by the rapid emergence of the Internet. Software and information can be downloaded when and as needed, onto smaller, more focused, and more often mobile computing/communications devices that simplify the software and hardware at the user or local level. That in turn means that more people can use computers and communications devices for more applications. That means that each computer or end-user application doesn't have to be so complex, housing and coordinating every possible application component. They can focus more on their critical applications and store more of the information needed locally. Otherwise, the growth in Moore's Law would be increasingly overshadowed by the complexity of software programs and human applications.

Yet the whole system will continue to grow in magnitude rapidly and, of course, become more complex. "The network is the computer" is still the new trend. And it will determine the ultimate winners of the race for leadership among technology, telecom, and software companies. But this trend cannot happen without a simplification and decentralization at the end-user and human level. And it cannot occur without a more radical approach to decentralizing decision making in our companies and corporations.

Real-life products and services are where the greatest impacts of new technology are realized and create real benefits in economic growth, productivity, and lifestyles. But this shift in software suggests a radical new logic in business beyond merely tapping this network for better information access and communications. If we can simplify and focus our inherently complex human decision-making processes, especially at the front lines of our complex and still bureaucratic organizations (which persist despite the overhyped reengineering revolution), we can best accelerate the law of human progress. Software and the bottom-up and horizontal communications it fosters will be the key enabler of this more challenging and more profitable trend.

Only this revolution, which ultimately entails making every customer or small segment a market and every individual or team a real business, will have the capacity to create vastly greater numbers of millionaires and affluent households beyond the present level of entrepreneurs who have done so on their own initiative, but at substantial investment and risk! This still will not occur at the rate of our technology accelerators, but it can accelerate to unprecedented levels in line with previous post-technology Innovation Stages like the early 1500s (following the printing press), the early 1800s (following the steam engine), the 1870s (following the railroads, telegraphs, and power plants), and the Roaring Twenties (following electricity, telephones, and automobiles).

How the Last Organizational Revolution Emerged

In the last revolution, Frederick Taylor's time-and-motion studies simplified work and focused it on simple, repeatable tasks, beginning in 1894 with his invention of "Scientific Business Management." His research and work culminated with the publishing of his classic book *The Principles of Scientific Management,* in 1911. Why was this so critical at that time? Back then, most people had only rudimentary education and skills and little capacity to organize themselves and make decisions about their work. Most people were "jacks-of-all-trades," being small farmers, craftsmen, or merchants. There was hence little specialization of labor compared with today's economy. On an approximate eighty-year cycle forward to today's revolution, you could compare Taylor's book of 1911 with *Reengineering the Corporation* by Michael Hammer and James Champy.

But that was just the beginning of the revolution. Henry Ford's moving assembly line emerged in 1914 and followed the standardization of parts and the standardized Model T design in 1907. This radical new production process not only coordinated these simple tasks (from Taylor) into a greater process but also simplified and accelerated that more complex process by moving the work to the worker via powered machinery. That innovation in production design in 1914 would be comparable to the emergence of the Dell model ("real-time production to demand") between 1994 and 1996. The initial emergence of the Internet between 1992 and 1996 was a great enabler of this new model.

But it was Alfred Sloan's innovations in management at the macro scale (starting between 1921–1923) that created the first level of decentralized management that allowed decision making to be simplified by moving it increasingly from the highly centralized level of the railroad era to product divisions and functional levels of support services in a greater assembly-line service scheme—from R&D to production to marketing to sales to service. That time period would correlate with the most critical stage of the management and organizational model we have been touting that should emerge into practical manifestation between 2002 and 2004 in today's New Economy Cycle.

That new corporate model from Alfred Sloan at GM has been expounded and refined by experts and leaders such as Peter Drucker, Taiichi Ohno, W. Edwards Deming, and Jack Welch, and in companies ranging from GE to Toyota to Wal-Mart to Intel. This model of modern management has created unprecedented middle-class living standards in North America, Europe, and Japan that are now expanding around the world. But that highly efficient and refined model are quickly meeting its diminishing-returns stage as we face increasing urban congestion and pollution. Consumer surveys are reporting declining levels of service despite rising corporate profits. More and more knowledge workers are exiting to start their own businesses or to work for higher-growth and more challenging smaller businesses.

This model will not suffice to meet the increasing needs for customization and service required by a new affluent class that is exploding in growth, nor the rising self-esteem and self-actualizing workers this new economy is rapidly creating. Dell was the first major company to launch something more radical—real-time production—in the mid- to late 1990s, almost exactly two generations after Ford's radical assembly line. Not only do most businesses need to master this already proven model and adapt it to their products or industry, but a broader model of organizational design is just emerging that will give an even greater sustainable competitive edge to the businesses, large and small, that understand and implement it in this critical decade in the race for leadership in this new economy.

So let's stop here and review the progress in this new revolution in management and organizational design. Computers have been able to automate many of the left-brain, logical functions of workers, while "reengineering" has simplified aspects of work design, freeing us to make more intuitive human and creative decisions that focus on meeting changing customer needs, much like Frederick Taylor's time-and-motion studies and powered machinery simplified and focused work in the early 1900s. The essence of the reengineering revolution was that it began to organize around processes and end results rather than around functions and specialized tasks (the opposite of Frederick Taylor's revolution in work design). That was the first stage and the focus of business innovation in the early to mid-1990s.

A new model of direct flow, producing only to consumer demand—exemplified by Dell—has emerged, much like the assembly line, for coordinating real-time production through the automation of logistical and scheduling tasks by software. This radical new model allows for the direct ordering and delivery of customized goods at lower cost with smaller inventories and less bureaucracy. And many product companies from groceries to cars are trying to figure out how to adapt this model to their organizations and delivery systems. That was stage two and the focus of business innovation from the latter 1990s into recent years. But the third stage is ahead and will be the most critical to meeting the needs of the new affluent consumer and worker.

THE REVOLT OF THE AFFLUENT:
GREATER CUSTOMIZATION AND SERVICE DEMANDED

Increasingly, what most businesses and consumers need are customized, results-oriented solutions that require the integration of different products, services and expertise—like investments, health care, education, business consulting, and systems design. Hence, the real revolution will emerge, like Sloan's model in the Roaring Twenties, through radically simplifying management by decentralizing decision making to the lowest level, the frontline workers who serve ever-changing consumer needs in an increasingly affluent society that requires real-time, personalized service, not just real-time production.

That is stage three and represents the powerful integration of the previous two stages. This stage should emerge between 2004 and 2005 and will become the most powerful competitive weapon for winning the new markets of affluent consumers of the future. And that stage requires adding frontline, narrowly customer-focused, human "browser" units that can coordinate the many products and services from the backline, produce-to-demand systems, and integrate them into real-time personalized and customized solutions.

For example, you could take Dell's present highly automated backline, produce-to-demand systems and add frontline teams of human integrators that focused on a narrow market of consumers and could design applications to fit customers' needs from those many choices in components, products, and services from the backline providers—and add ongoing services. Hence, instead of just selling a consumer or a business a computer direct at lower prices, a company could deliver an ongoing service starting with a customized solution of hardware and software with ongoing service, maintenance, and consulting.

The real revolution is about real-time, personalized service at lower costs to meet the needs of a rapidly expanding affluent consumer who expects and demands such service, and creating an ongoing service revenue versus a onetime product sale.

But this revolution also meets the needs of the increasingly affluent, knowledge-based worker who is looking for greater challenge and means to emulate the millionaire trends that have resulted from more people owning their own businesses and professional practices and high-level corporate executives who have been given a greater stake in their corporations through stock options and other incentive plans. You can't attract and reward the best talent without giving them an equity-based or ownership interest in their business. You cannot simplify work or create real-time service past a certain point without giving frontline workers the ability to make decisions directly for customers and be accountable for them at the bottom-line profit level, just like a small business owner.

This will occur not at the greater macro level, but more at the micro level of the results each individual or team creates. The dot-com revolution may have failed to create a whole new society of entrepreneurial workers overnight, but the desire is still there in the new increasingly affluent, knowledge-based, self-actualizing workforce. But the most important impact is that this more radical "bottom-up" revolution in our organizations will allow the delivery of a much higher level of personalized and customized service for the rising new affluent class of baby boomers, which is growing much faster than most businesses and investors realize. Again, in human terms, mass affluence is the new economy. And this trend will continue to explode in the coming decades, despite the slowdown of the early 2000s and the greater collapse we forecast in the next decade ahead.

THE SILENT REVOLUTION:
MANAGEMENT IS THE PROBLEM, NOT THE SOLUTION!

As opposed to the highly touted and hyped dot-com revolution, the real revolution is more subtle, less visible in corporate organization charts and reengineering strategies . . . it is a silent revolution. The Internet allows workers and customers at all levels to communicate directly, see information and opportunities, and respond—without the interference of management and marketing propaganda!

Our summary of this revolution has always been "Management is the problem, not the solution."

As the education, skills, and information access of workers have grown dramatically in the past decades, more and more workers don't need managers to plan and coordinate their every action carefully. This not only makes you feel like a child, but it greatly inhibits the ability to respond creatively to real and changing consumer needs in a timely manner.

How will this new revolution really occur? By people like you creating your own business within your corporation, or by creating your own business outside of your company. That in essence is the revolution, and the new technologies merely enable it to occur!

As the ability to access information and to communicate at all levels of an organization increases with Internet-based technologies, you can identify opportunities, access information, communicate with other experts or departments or product/service divisions, and come up with solutions yourself that meet your customers' needs—whether they be internal company divisions that develop solutions for end customers or frontline units that deliver solutions for end customers themselves. In other words, you can become your own business and act in real time without the interference of endless management, approvals, and reengineering edicts and plans. The new economy of real-time personalized service can't work without such spontaneous and accountable decision making by people like you. But it does mean you have to be as accountable as a small-business owner. No longer do you have the luxury of blaming management when things go wrong. That's the price you have to pay for the opportunity to become a millionaire and to have more self-actualizing work.

That is the challenge of today's new economy. There is simply too much management from the top down that is trying to coordinate too many decisions and processes to allow real-time personalized service. You don't stand a chance as an employee of giving such service and customers don't stand a chance of receiving such service! Again, that is why we say that management is the problem, not the solution. Only an organization, large or small, that is designed around the customer and the decision-making needs and accountability of frontline workers can deliver such service. That is what we mean by bottom-up, not top-down, organizations, and that is a radical change—the most radical and productive change for this new economy. It has not happened yet, except in a few companies. But it will be the theme of this decade and many decades to follow!

CUSTOMER-DRIVEN IS THE OPPOSITE OF SHAREHOLDER-DRIVEN

We have seen over two decades of shareholder-driven management philosophies for how to create profits and rising share prices in companies. U.S. companies have led the world in creating this and the recent model of reengineering in management while European, Asian, and other countries have been following. Although this was a natural direction in the maturity of the old economy, we think it is the wrong direction for business management in the new economy! How does it feel for you as a customer to know that the company that serves you values its shareholders first and you by definition last? How does it feel to you as an employee to know that management values shareholders first while insisting that its employees are the company's greatest assets? Who are the shareholders in this economy, anyway? Hordes of mutual fund and institutional investment managers who dominate 80% of the markets—and increasingly, even more fickle individual investors? They will move from company to company in a flash, depending on short-term earnings and progress reports. They are not loyal shareholders.

Why should a public company see its shareholders as its primary constituents? It's not that they are not important. Any business needs access to capital at reasonable prices. But the truth is that the most truly successful businesses, such as Microsoft, have never needed capital past the initial stages of development; their stock price is merely a means to motivate key employees through stock options and to acquire other businesses to grow and expand. In new ventures it is the initial investors who believe in your concept that are critical. After that, it is your customers who decide whether you survive long term and who determine your profit margins—depending on how they benefit from your products, services, and business processes.

We suggest the opposite model of business management: customer-driven, not shareholder-driven.

If you organize around your customers and satisfy their needs on an ongoing basis at affordable prices and costs, you will have high growth and profits—and then investors will find you and bid up your stock! Again, the problem today with corporations is that the people who run them are constantly trying to plan and implement complex strategies from the top down. They try to create a corporate mission that everyone should follow. They try to plan at every level how this mission and strategy will be implemented. They want everyone in the company to march to the same drummer. They say that we all have to be more responsible for satisfying customers and make more creative decisions, yet they already have everything planned for us.

The truth is simply that you can't create real-time, personalized service from the top down.

There are simply too many solutions and options for satisfying customers as they become more individualized, affluent, and demanding in their choices. How could you possibly have real innovation and customer response in such an environment? How can employees working for such a company feel as though they are creating their own destiny or truly satisfying the needs of their customers, internal or external? How could you respond as an employee to the changing needs of customers when you are handcuffed by so many company policies, rules, and reengineering initiatives?

Like the Internet, corporations will become more bottom-up versus top-down in management. That is perhaps the greatest change we will see from this silent revolution, and it will create enormous productivity gains for decades to come and incredible opportunities for workers to create their own business within or outside of the traditional corporation and to create greater incomes and wealth. This is the only way to truly create real-time, personalized service. Large companies are not going to disappear, they will just reorganize more radically into networks of smaller businesses within and subcontractors and vendors without. And many new small companies will emerge, many run from home offices.

In *The Roaring 2000s* in Chapters 5–8, we outlined a new approach to redesigning businesses around the customer, focusing on four new principles for redesigning your company in Chapter 7. We are not going to repeat that approach here, but would refer you back to that book. But we are going to update those four principles in more detail below with twelve key principles for redesigning your business organization to create real-time personalized service at affordable costs, starting with the end in mind: a human network automated by information technologies and organized totally around customers.

12 PRINCIPLES FOR CREATING REAL-TIME, PERSONALIZED SERVICE AND A SUSTAINABLE COMPETITIVE ADVANTAGE

First Paradigm: Organize from Your Customer Back, Not the Top Down

1. Start by designing your business the way your best customers would (around their needs, costs, and priorities—not merely your own—then optimize your costs).

2. Make every customer or significant segment a market and a business (accountable from customer satisfaction down to the profit-and-loss level).

3. Create frontline human browsers or butlers to serve each segment (to coordinate and integrate backline products and services to meet their needs).

4. Make every decision possible on the front lines (automate those backline decisions through software or create real-time response in backline services).

Second Paradigm: Focus on Your Customers' Highest-Value-Added Solutions

5. Only do things that are in the best interests of your end customer (integrity and transparency for building trust and long-term loyalty).

6. Focus only on what you do best and what adds the highest value to your customers (outsourcing everything else to the best and most efficient in their field).

7. Provide total solutions as an ongoing service with recurring fees (don't sell one-time products and then have to resell; make outsourcing to you more feasible and sustainable long-term).

8. Anticipate your customers' needs before they and competitors do (project the next stage in their demographic and S-curve or product life cycles).

Third Paradigm: Create Real-Time Production and Service Systems

9. Design direct-flow, produce-to-demand systems throughout (no waste, no inventories, no time delays, no obsolete products, minimal environmental impacts).

10. Automate all logical, logistical, and bureaucratic decision processes (to focus on high-value-added human service, customization, and quality).

11. Link everyone as necessary in real-time communication systems (to minimize bureaucracy and to facilitate real-time decisions for your customers).

12. Create an internal marketplace within for real-time decision-making (accountable real-time decisions made among frontline and backline units with P&L accountability at all levels).

Again, we recommend that if the subject of corporate reorganization interests you, you go back to Chapters 5–8 in *The Roaring 2000s,* since we don't want to have to repeat them here. But we think that these principles will represent the most important generators of ongoing productivity trends for decades to come and will give the greatest strategic advantage in the race for leadership in this decade that will decide most of the leaders for many decades to come.

The new economy is still emerging, and the most important organizational and long-term productivity innovations are just beginning, like the modern corporate organization innovations of Alfred Sloan at General Motors from the early 1920s on. Making more and more employees of companies into accountable businesses with greater participation in profit sharing will add to the increasing trends in self-employment and new businesses toward the growth of income and wealth in our economy.

Yet for the first time in modern history we are seeing a slowing in birth and demographic growth rates across the world. This suggests new directions ahead for the coming decades and many decades to follow. In the Epilogue we will look at how the ultimate bubble, human population, is projected to peak for the first time in thousands of years due to rapidly falling birth rates around the world. This will cause a massive change in economic growth around the world in the decades and century to come.

We are at an auspicious time in history for both opportunity and risk. The human population bubble that has been building for centuries is getting ready to slow and it will have many consequences for our lives, the economy, and our increasingly global culture. A clash of cultures has begun with 9/11 and it will build over the next two decades. This next consideration should make you even more serious about preparing for the great crash and downturn ahead from 2010 on—and seeing the opportunities it holds, especially in Asia.

THE ULTIMATE BUBBLE

Human Population Is Peaking After Thousands of Years of Exponential Growth

THROUGHOUT THIS BOOK we have been showing that growth is always cyclical and exponential, and hence that bubbles are inevitable—it is always just a matter of degree. The longer we look back at history, the greater the bubbles we will inevitably see. We showed in Chapter 2 (Figure 2.17) how the stock market has been in an increasing bubble boom since the 1780s and the Industrial Revolution and that a 230-year boom may be peaking around 2009/2010 along with the baby boom Spending Wave and the present broadband, wireless, Internet revolution in technologies. In *The Roaring 2000s Investor* in Chapter 6, Charts 6-2 and 6-3, we showed further how we have been in a growing bubble boom since the Crusades around 1,000 years ago as well as a broader Civilization Cycle emerging around the concepts of democracy and science since Greek times 2,500 years ago.

But if we keep looking back in history the most obvious bubble reveals itself: human population has been growing largely exponentially as far back as we can measure it. Figure 9.1 is repeated from Chart 6-1 of *The Roaring 2000s Investor.* This chart shows population growth back 3,000 years to 1,000 B.C. on both a normal linear scale (absolute growth) and on a logarithmic or ratio scale (percentage growth rates). Talk about exponential growth! The linear line on the lower part of the graph shows that population started to accelerate in the mid-1400s (around the time of the printing press, gunpowder, and long-range sailing ships), and has gone ballistic since the Industrial Revolution around 1800. This is clearly a major bubble in the making.

Population is projected to peak close to 9 billion by the end of this cen-

FIGURE E.1 The History of World Population Growth

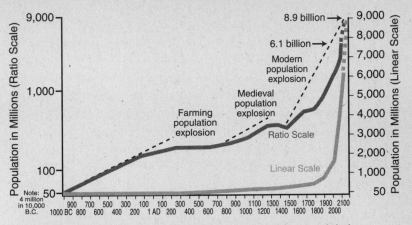

* Ratio scale shows constant percentage growth rate as a straight, upward-sloping
line; linear scale shows equal absolute increase, so steady percentage growth rate to curve up.
Source: Forbes, January 25, 1999, pp. 58–59.
Research: Edwin S. Rubenstein, research director, Hudson Institute, Indianapolis.
Data: Colin McEvedy and Richard Jones, Atlas of World Population History;
U.N. Secretariat, World Population Prospects: The 1998 Revision; Census Bureau.

tury. Note that population trends start to accelerate before major technological innovations, and then such innovations accelerate population
trends until limits to growth set in. Hence, demographic trends are the
driving force in growth and economics, but demographic and technology
cycles are also inevitably intertwined and feed on each other, as we have
showed through our forty-year generation cycles in spending/productivity
and our eighty-year cycles in technologies and new economies throughout
this and past books.

A longer-term view of history and cycles only serves to further confirm
the importance of demographic and technology cycles. On our Web site at
www.hsdent.com (click on "Key Concepts" and then "The Long View"), we
offer an extensive free report you can download on human economic
progress back many thousands of years and more, which shows even more
conclusively how demographic and technology trends have intertwined to
shape human and economic progress in larger and larger cycles over history. Many longer-term cycles point to major peaks around 2010 and later
in this century between 2040 and 2065. So this is perhaps the most important time in history to have a longer view, and information technologies,
including DNA research, have provided us with much clearer information
about the past than ever before.

The ratio or logarithmic line on the upper end of Figure E.1 shows that the percentage growth rates were higher into the early Roman Empire just before the birth of Christ, and then slowed and flattened out just before the fall of the Roman Empire in the mid-400s A.D. As population trends merely flattened, we saw the Dark Ages, the longest bear market or regression period in economic progress (from highly developed urban societies back to largely feudal and rural) in modern history—around five hundred years. Hence, demographic growth is critical to economic growth historically, and the slowing of population growth can have severe consequences. Just before the Crusades, population growth started to pick up again and slowed temporarily after the Great Plague in the mid-1300s. By the mid-1400s growth has become more and more exponential even on a logarithmic scale, which reflects rising percentage growth rates, not just rapid growth in mass.

This means we have seen a clear bubble in population forming since the mid-1400s and more so since the late 1780s, when the stock market started to form its latest long-term bubble boom. When will this greater bubble end? Around 2065 worldwide, and by 2010 in many developed countries today!

Just as we can forecast economic and stock trends on a lag for births decades in advance, birth rates and life expectancy trends can forecast population trends decades in advance. The world's population is forecast to peak around 2065, in this century and our children's lifetimes. But the greater insight is that such population trends have already peaked in Europe and region after region will peak successively with the largest country, China, peaking by 2030 during most of our lifetimes!

History would suggest that declining population trends, first in major regions and then in the world as a whole, will not be a pretty picture economically.

WHY THE SLOWING IN POPULATION TRENDS? PROSPERITY AND URBANIZATION!

Growth occurs exponentially until limits to growth start to set in. The limits to the growth of any population from rabbits to humans will always set in when you hit environmental limits to food supply, pollution, ease of attack by predators, and so on. But humans have no predators as of yet, except within our own species and the wars of the past and even terrorist threats of today. The limits to our growth would certainly include environmental constraints with the rises in pollution and global warming and the decline in land and natural resources that we have seen in past decades and centuries. But there is more to the story given that we have no obvious higher predators or competitors on this planet and that we already have new technologies that can ultimately reduce environmental threats profitably as new technologies have in the past.

The limits to human growth are ultimately psychological, social, and economic. As we grow out of rural/agricultural cultures and urbanize, and as we grow more prosperous with sharply rising costs of raising and educating children, we have fewer children and invest more in educating and preparing them longer. Yet declining birth trends slow the entire demographic cycle from the innovation of the young to the productivity and spending of maturing adults to the saving, investment, and philanthropy of the more elderly.

Modern prosperous civilizations from Rome to Europe to the United States always eventually decline due to increasing urbanization and prosperity, which lead to lower birth rates and lower growth in innovation, productivity, spending, and investment on a lag. Isolated farming cultures have often peaked due to local environmental restraints, which are becoming more a factor worldwide today. But the environment is not the greatest threat, at least not yet. Now the entire world, instead of just one major region, seems to be set in motion to peak and decline by 2065 due to rapidly declining birth trends.

SLOWING BIRTH TRENDS AS THE KEY LEADING INDICATOR

Many people are aware that many European countries and Japan are not reproducing at rates that would sustain their population growth long term. But even so, most people aren't aware how fast major countries from Japan to Italy could decline in population over the next several decades given such trends in birth rates per capita. Europe and Japan are projected to lose 30% or more of their populations in the next fifty-plus years. But the biggest surprise is how fast newly industrialized countries from China to Brazil to India are slowing in birth trends and population growth. Figure E.2 shows how birth rates are slowing dramatically in all major regions around the world, including India and Africa, not just China and Southeast Asia.

Birth rates per capita are the lowest in Europe and Japan, but the U.S. is not far behind. The biggest surprise again is that China's birth rates have

FIGURE E.2 Slowing Birth Trends Across the World

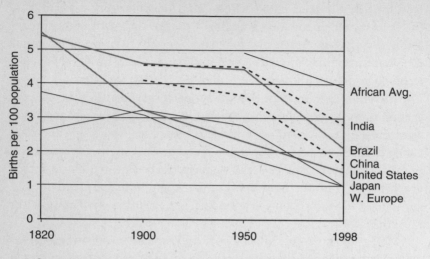

Source: Maddison, Angus. *The World Economy: A Millennial Perspective.*
Development Center Studies, OECD, 2001: Table 1-5A, p. 30.

fallen so far, so quickly. After a huge population surge, China started a one-child-per-family policy back around 1950. But despite not having such declared policies in other developing countries, birth rates are falling every-where, including India and Africa. Why is this occurring? Prosperity and urbanization both increase the costs and time period for raising children and increase social opportunities for the parents.

The advent of TV, and now the Internet, may have been the greatest catalysts for declining birth rates beyond urbanization, industrialization, and prosperity, but are a natural by-product of such trends.

Most people around the world now get a sense through TV news, movies, sitcoms, and the Internet that affluent people have fewer children and greater business, social, and romantic opportunities. Hence, it is our own success that has led to our potential decline—as is typical throughout history. So what are the projections we can make demographically from the declining birth trends around the world? The population of the world is very likely to peak around 2065, unless something dramatically changes in birth or longevity trends. Despite promises from the biotechnology revolu-tion, we have seen no increases in longevity trends beyond the 1.5-year-per-decade increase in average life expectancy in the past four decades and declining birth trends are more than offsetting those advances.

THE PEAKING OF THE POPULATION BUBBLE AHEAD

The greatest reality of this century is that the world's population is forecast to peak around 2065 and then begin declining for the first time in thousands of years of increasingly exponential growth, as Figure E.3 shows. What does that mean beyond cycles of slowing innovation, productivity, spending, and investment growth? It means more, older people depending on fewer workers for retirement and health care benefits around the world. It means deflationary trends at first in the Western world and then decades later in Asia and the developing world (after a new inflationary surge there first).

  Environmentalists will hail the final coming of zero population growth and declining demands on our natural resources and environment, while conversely not understanding how much new innovations from demographic growth have reduced pollution and expanded natural resources in the past. With declining economic environments in developed countries, will the higher numbers of people in larger population areas that are still developing care as much about the environment as more affluent people in the U.S. and Europe do today? Will measures to protect the environment be supported by voters or be cut as they struggle to survive in a new declining environment?

  But the real story of population peaking and demographic slowing comes not from looking at the total population but at the major countries

FIGURE E.3 World Population Forecast, 2000–2100

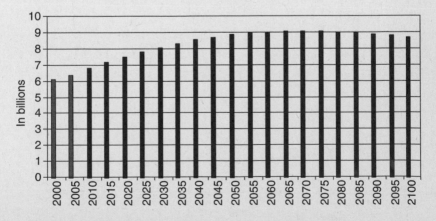

Source: Investor's Business Daily, 4/22/2004, P. A16. *Research:* United Nations.

and regions around the world. Broader Europe, including East Europe and
the former Soviet Union, already peaked in population in 2000, with some
countries from Finland to Romania peaking earlier and others peaking increasingly in the coming decade or two. Japan peaks in 2005 after their
largest Spending Wave peaked in late 1989. Again, many countries in Europe and Japan are likely to see their population decline 30% to 40% in the
next 50 to 100 years. That is dramatic!

China will peak in total population around 2030 and then begin to decline, and their baby-boom Spending Wave will peak around 2020, much
earlier than most people would expect. Then Latin America and India both
peak in population around 2065. But don't expect as dramatic growth from
now to then in these regions, since unlike China and Southeast Asia, they
are already more urbanized and will not get the more dramatic increases
from the movement of populations from rural agricultural areas to urban

FIGURE E.4 GDP Per Capita: Western Europe versus China, 400–1999

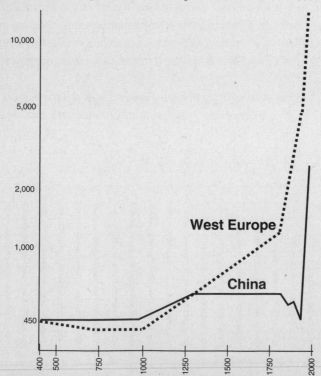

Source: Maddison, Angus. *The World Economy: A Millennial Perspective.*
Development Center Studies, OECD, 2001: Figure 1-4, p. 42.

and industrialized areas that China is experiencing. China is making such a transition in the fastest time frame of any major country or region in history, as Figure E.4 shows.

Western Europe and, increasingly, offshoots of that culture from the United States and Canada to Australia and New Zealand have made dramatic increases in standards of living as measured by GDP per capita in the last thousand years since the Crusades. Most other countries and areas progressed much more slowly. China progressed a bit at first after the Dark Ages, but ultimately regressed in standard of living as it chose isolationism into the mid-1900s. Since 1950, China has been making in just decades the progress that the West has made over many centuries. Southeast Asia, India, and possibly Africa are due to follow, possibly to lesser degrees, in the decades ahead. That spells huge economic growth and an "Asian bubble" after the U.S. bubble in 2009–2010. China is on course to surpass the U.S. in GDP in purchasing-power parity (the value of goods produced versus the price of those goods in their local currencies where they cost less) by 2020 and India should likewise surpass the United States by 2050.

China, Southeast Asia, India, and perhaps Africa are likely to see the fastest catch-up game in prosperity and economic growth in world history in the next two to six decades. But then the world party in economic growth is likely to be over for many centuries with dramatic implications for world economics and the political environment.

Hence, as the Western countries peak in their Spending Waves and population growth mostly around the end of this decade, world growth will shift even more dramatically toward China, Southeast Asia, and India, where the largest populations of consumers live. This will likely cause a final bubble to build between the 2020s and the 2060s that could be followed by slowing population trends and deflationary trends for centuries to follow.

THE GREAT BOOM IN ASIA AFTER THE NEXT GREAT BUBBLE BURSTS

In future books we will look more at the implications of the great bust from 2010 on in the United States and other leading Western nations. But the greatest opportunity after 2010 will come from investing and doing business in the Asian countries from China to Southeast Asia to India (and perhaps Africa if it proves it can join the party) that will be benefiting from this great catch-up trend in industrialization and information technologies and urbanization.

And countries like China, South Korea, Vietnam, and India are exhibiting the highest growth rates today. We are used to investing and doing business in the United States or other more ethnically related developed countries such as Canada or Europe, or Mexico and the Caribbean on our borders. Investments in other countries appear too difficult culturally and politically to most, and are by clear financial measures more risky and volatile.

That will change. Investors and businesses in the United States, Canada, Europe, Australia, New Zealand, and even Hong Kong and Singapore will see maturing economies after 2009 and will be forced to invest in the newly industrializing countries, mostly in Southeast Asia and India. These countries will continue to develop and largely become more stable economically and less volatile over time as the developed countries become more volatile with declining economies and more terrorist threats. Late-stage industries like health care and drugs and pharmaceuticals will also be attractive after the bust in the more developed countries such as the United States and Europe.

After 2010 the investment and business opportunities will shift to China, Southeast Asia, and India.

But again, investors should remain largely liquid and safe in high-quality bonds and fixed-income investments until the first great crash from 2010 into 2012 or late 2014 at the latest. Even the demographically strong Asian and health care sectors will decline when stock markets peak and turn down violently again from 2010 to 2012. Then you can invest in rising demographic trends domestically and around the world at bargain prices. From around 2022 to 2023 on, there will be echo baby booms in the United States, western Canada, and select developed countries around the world, but not in most European countries or Japan, which didn't have echo baby booms. There will be another boom in the United States from around 2023 to around 2040 or so. But it will not rival this boom in economic growth, productivity, or stock market returns. Only companies and stock indices that focus on Asian countries will see another great boom and China is likely to peak after 2020, or by 2030 at the latest, with Southeast Asia and India likely leading after 2020.

THE CLASH OF CULTURES AND
GROWING WAR AND TERRORISM AFTER 2010

The greatest impact of the peaking of many Western countries around 2009–2010 or shortly thereafter will be that the extreme differences that have built up in standards of living and culture around the world will cause greater clashes among cultures and countries than have already occurred in the growing boom in which we have seen the greatest inequality in standards of living perhaps ever across the world. The United States has a hard time getting along with France and Germany, not just Afghanistan, Iraq, Iran, and North Korea as time moves on. The growth of the U.S. and the Western cultures is seen increasingly as a threat to more fundamentalist old-world countries in the Middle East, India/Pakistan, and parts of Southeast Asia. If we see a major collapse in the dominant Western countries as we predict from 2010 on, it will at first heavily impact these developing countries that rely more on us for exports than we typically rely on them. The catchphrase in economics is that when we sneeze, they catch a cold.

The more backward countries whose values and lifestyles our modern and more liberal lifestyles threaten will have more reason to attack our values and institutions when we appear to cause a worldwide bust after 2009–2010. Asian countries like China will continue to grow in economic and military power, while we decline for the first time in many decades. That sets the stage for world instability, changing economic and military power structures, and "a clash of cultures" greater than we have seen in recent times.

We are likely entering a time after a thousand years of expansion since the Dark Ages, when growth will peak in a series of bubbles around the world, much as it did in the late stages of the Roman Empire, and then enter a longer period of change, conflict, and consolidation as we did from the mid-400s to the late 900s. The best strategies will be to take advantage of perhaps the greatest unexpected boom in history from 2005 into late 2009 or early 2010. Then to preserve your wealth by switching into high-quality long-term corporate bonds and fixed-income investments, sell most of your real estate and business holdings that you don't strongly desire to keep long term, and relocate if possible into high-quality exurban/resort areas to survive the great winter ahead. Once the first major crash sets in between 2010 and 2012 or 2014 at the latest, you can start investing in exurban areas and late-stage demographic sectors such as health care and pharmaceuticals, and increasingly in Asian countries from China to India that may grow very dramatically for decades to come.

The one thing that demographic trends forecast is that from around 2010 on, the world and its opportunities and threats will grow and diverge perhaps more than at any other time in our lifetimes. We can't change these trends on a macro scale substantially, since they are already largely cast due to the law of averages and large numbers that makes demographics and other statistical sciences so predictable. But we can adapt as individuals in our personal investment, business, and life decisions and continue to prosper in perhaps the greatest time in human history.

The Return of Globalization

But as we move out of the great shakeout from 2011 to 2022 in the United States and many developed countries, we will see globalization move forward again after retrenching in the global clash of cultures that has been building. After all, globalization is one of the mega trends, along with customization, network communications, and the organizational structures and mass affluence of the emerging eighty-year New Economy Cycle. The Maturity Boom of this cycle and the next stage of globalization will emerge to greater degrees largely because these emerging countries will rapidly catch up to Western standards of living while Western countries will slow in their progress relatively.

We will likely finally see a world where cultures aren't so unequal and different, and we can integrate more into a win/win global economic network. But between now and then expect greater volatility with both a greater boom ahead than anyone expects, and a more difficult downturn and transition to the new global, network-based, affluent economy. And remember that the greatest opportunities come in difficult times for the few people who see them coming. "What doesn't kill you makes you stronger." That is the lesson of natural and human evolution we study in our free special report at "The Long View," under "Key Concepts" on our Web site, www.hsdent.com. Academics, long-term history buffs, and anyone interested in evolutionary trends should make sure to download this more extensive analysis of very long-term cycles in human history that follow the same demographic and technology cycles we cover in this book.

Best of success to you in one of the most opportune and volatile times in human evolution!

Index

baby-boom generation, 2, 15, 48, 94–95, 326
  and forecast for great boom and bust
    ahead, 122
  and investment opportunity of a
    lifetime, 58–60
  life planning and, 178–81, 183–84, 188, 195
  New Millionaire Economy and, 284,
    286–87, 300–304, 309, 311, 313, 319
  and outlook for investment markets,
    207–12, 214, 216–17, 224, 226
  portfolio strategies and, 246–48, 250,
    257–58, 260–61, 278–79
  and projections for last great bull
    market, 98
  real estate and, 19, 30, 134, 136, 138–41, 143,
    145, 152, 156–57, 162–63, 165–68, 171
  and reasons for bubble booms, 104–5
  and recurring cycles to reduce risk in
    volatile markets, 116
  Spending Wave of, 43, 105, 116, 138
  stock market rebounds and, 51–52
baby bust generation, 159, 224
Bach, David, 293
Bakersfield, Calif., 148
bear markets, see downturns
Best Asset-Class Model, 249–50, 252, 256,
  261–64
biotechnology, 37, 102, 132, 204
  population growth and, 330
  portfolio strategies and, 251, 272, 274, 279,
    283
  technology bubbles and, 83
births, birth trends, 129, 165, 312
  key surges and declines in, 179, 181
  life planning and, 179, 181, 187–88
  and outlook for investment markets,
    206–7, 210–11, 214–15, 217, 220
  population growth and, 328–30
  portfolio strategies and, 250, 263
  Spending Wave and, 59
Bob Hope generation, 72
  life planning and, 179
  New Millionaire Economy and, 300
  and outlook for investment markets,
    208–9, 220
  portfolio strategies and, 254, 257

  real estate and, 156
  Spending Wave of, 94, 114
bobos (bourgeois bohemians), 284, 302–6
Bobos in Paradise (Brooks), 302, 304–5
bonds, 4, 11, 13–18, 35, 126–29, 132
  comparisons between stocks and, 222,
    224–25, 240, 254
  and indicators for spotting bubbles
    ahead, 126–28
  life planning and, 177, 189–90, 193–94, 196
  long-term trend of, 14–16
  outlook for, 204, 222–30
  population growth and, 334–35
  portfolio strategies and, 235, 237–38, 240,
    245, 251–60, 262–63, 266–69, 274,
    276–78, 283
  returns of, 222, 224–25, 227, 253–56, 258,
    276–78
  technology bubbles and, 81
  see also Treasury bills; Treasury bonds
booms, boom years, 1–5, 10–11, 14, 20, 28
  forecasting of, 120–22
  interest rates and, 17–18
  oil bubble and, 10
  outlook for investment markets in,
    204–8, 210–12, 216–20, 222
  portfolio strategies for, 238, 240, 242–48,
    253–57, 260, 263–72, 274–75, 280
  real estate and, 29–30
  see also bull market, bull markets
Boston, Mass., 27, 147–48
Bradenton, Fla., 26–27
Brazil, 329–30
Brief History of Time, A (Hawking), 47
broadband, 4, 45, 102, 291, 326
  financing of, 79
  and investment opportunity of a
    lifetime, 75–76
  life planning and, 188, 201–2
  New Millionaire Economy and, 299
  real estate and, 158
  S-curve for, 76
  technology bubbles and, 83
Brooks, David, 284, 302, 304–5, 308
bubble, bubbles:
  asset, 80, 87–88, 91, 94–95

technology, technologies (*cont.*)
 information, *see* information
  technologies, information age
 and investment opportunity of a
  lifetime, 51–58, 60–70, 72–77
 life planning and, 176–78, 189, 198, 201–2
 longer-term advances in, 42–43
 New Millionaire Economy and, 284, 287,
  299–300, 302–3, 310–16, 320
 and outlook for investment markets,
  204, 209, 212, 214, 216, 219–20, 225
 population growth and, 327, 329–30
 portfolio strategies and, 234, 236–37,
  239–40, 244, 246, 249–51, 253, 264–70,
  272–74
 and projections for last great bull
  market, 98, 102
 real estate and, 10–11, 134, 170–71
 and reasons for bubble booms, 104–5
 revolutions in, 3, 43, 52–53, 62, 75–77, 83,
  87–88, 92–95, 117, 120, 170, 202, 234–35,
  237, 239, 253, 299–300, 310–14, 316, 326,
  330
 Roaring Twenties and, 52–53, 134, 138,
  316
telecommuting, 158, 294
telegraphs, 202, 316
telephones, 2, 202, 275, 316
television:
 life planning and, 178, 199
 population growth and, 330
 technology bubbles and, 84
Templeton, Sir John, 51–52, 242
temps, 294–95
ten-year cycles:
 and corrections from 1960 to 2002,
  114
 and indicators for spotting bubbles
  ahead, 125–26
 see also Decade Hangover Cycle;
  Decennial Cycle
terrorism, 41–43
 and forecast for great boom and bust
  ahead, 121
 and indicators for spotting bubbles
  ahead, 126–27

 and investment opportunity of a
  lifetime, 51, 53, 72, 75
 life planning and, 198–201
 oil and, 6–8
 and outlook for investment markets, 205,
  218
 population growth and, 328, 334
 real estate and, 172
 on September 11, 2001, 7, 10, 41, 43, 51,
  198–99, 205
 and strategies for investing in volatile
  times, 128
 technology bubbles and, 81
Tesco, 83
time-shares, 162
Tire and Rubber Index, 67–68
Trading Up (Silverstein and Fiske), 298
trash, spending on, 279–80
travel:
 life planning and, 183, 188–89
 and outlook for investment markets,
  204
 real estate and, 172–73
Treasury bills (T-bills):
 and indicators for spotting bubbles
  ahead, 126
 outlook for, 222, 224, 227–30
 portfolio strategies and, 255, 257, 260–63,
  276, 278, 283
 returns of, 276, 278
 volatility and, 112, 130
Treasury bonds, 13–18
 and forecast for great boom and bust
  ahead, 120
 portfolio strategies and, 276–78
 30-year channel of, 14–16, 18
T. Rowe Price Indicator, 219
trusts, 197, 268–70
twenty-year cycles, 119

unemployment, 53, 72
 and indicators for spotting bubbles
  ahead, 128
 and investment opportunity of a
  lifetime, 67–68
 life planning and, 182, 196, 200

and outlook for investment markets,
209, 212, 227–30
portfolio strategies and, 237
real estate and, 170, 173
see also employment, employees
upper class, *see* affluence, affluent
households; New Millionaire
Economy
urbanization, 328–29, 332–33
utilitarian spending, 305
utilities, 275, 279–80, 283

vacation homes, 2, 4, 37, 134, 137–38, 158,
161–66, 173–74
annual mortgage interest paid on,
163–64
average purchases of, 162–63
housing bubble and, 19–21
life planning and, 184, 188–90, 201–3
prices of, 161, 163–64
total purchases of, 162
value stocks:
comparisons between growth and,
242–52, 257–60
outlook for, 204, 222
portfolio strategies and, 242–53, 256–60,
264
returns of, 242–50, 258–60
valuation of, 246–48
variable annuities, 193–95
variable universal life policies, 193–95
very conservative portfolio, 265, 269–72

Wal-Mart, 83, 188, 210, 214, 293, 317
warfare:
and indicators for spotting bubbles
ahead, 127–28
life planning and, 200–201
population growth and, 328
Washington, D.C.:
median asking price for existing houses
in, 159–60
as terrorist target, 201
waste water, spending on, 279–80
Webvan, 83
Weekly Leading Index, 16
Weiss, Michael, 305–6
Wells Fargo, 294
Wolfram, Stephen, 42, 46–48
workforce, *see* careers; employment,
employees; unemployment
World Trade Center, 1993 bombing of, 198
World War I, 64, 72, 74, 104, 288, 312
World War II, 7, 41, 72, 74, 87, 178, 299
life planning and, 191, 200
New Millionaire Economy and, 303
and outlook for investment markets, 315
portfolio strategies and, 236, 260
and recurring cycles to reduce risk in
volatile markets, 110–11, 113

Yahoo!, 11, 15, 18, 29, 34–35, 83, 85, 123
yuppies (young urban professionals), 180
New Millionaire Economy and, 284, 302–5
and outlook for investment markets, 214

Permissions Acknowledgments

Grateful acknowledgment to the following sources:

Source for Figure F.8 reprinted by permission from Economic Cycle Research Institute (ECRI).

Source for Figure F.10 reprinted with permission from *Irrational Exuberance*, 2nd edition, by Robert J. Shiller, Princeton University Press, 2005.

Information in Figure F.11 © 2005 The Economist Newspaper Ltd. All rights reserved. Reprinted with permission. Further reproduction prohibited. www.economist.com.

Source for Figures F.12, F.13, F.16 and F.20 reprinted from The September 2005 Real Estate with permission of the National Association of Realtors®. Copyright 2005. All rights reserved.

Source for Figure F.17 Copyright USA Today. May 2004. Reprinted with permission.

Source for Figure F.19 reprinted with permission from Barron's, *Hitting the Roof*, March 2005.

Source for Figure F.21 reprinted with permission from Hays Advisory, LLC.

Source for Figures 2.4 and 2.5 reprinted with permission from *Conquer the Crash* by Robert Prechter, p. 80.

Source for Figures 2.6 and 2.17 reprinted with permission from *Conquer the Crash* by Robert Prechter, p. 33.

Figures 2.19 and 8.8 reprinted from Theodore Caplow, Louis Hicks, and Ben J. Wattenberg. 2001. *The First Measured Century,* pp. 252–53. Washington, D.C.: The AEI Press.

Information in Figures 3.2 reprinted with permission from page 186, September 30, 2002 issue of *Fortune;* Chart entitled: "Despite Some Dark Days . . . October Isn't Really So Spooky." Fortune Source: Dow Jones Indexes © 2002 Time Inc. All rights reserved.

Information in Figures 3.3 and 3.7 has been provided with permission from Ned Davis Research, www.ndr.com. The data and analysis contained herein are provided "as is" and without warranty of any kind, either expressed or implied. Ned Davis Research, Inc. (NDR), any NDR affiliates or employees, or any third party data provider shall not have any liability for any loss sustained by anyone who has relied on the information contained in any NDR publication. All opinions expressed herein are subject to change without notice, and diligence before trading. NDR, accounts that NDR or its affiliated companies manage, or their respective shareholders, directors, officers and/or employees, may have long or short positions in the securities discussed herein and may purchase or sell such securities without notice. NDR uses various methods to evaluate investments which may, at times, produce contradictory recommendations with respect to the same securities. When evaluating the results of prior NDR recommendations or NDR performance rankings, one should also consider that NDR may modify the methods it uses to evaluate investment opportunities from time to time. For this and for many other reasons, the performance of NDR's past recommendations is not a guarantee of future results. The securities mentioned in this document may not be eligible for sale in some states or countries, nor be suitable for all types of investors; their value and income they produce may fluctuate and/or be adversely affected by exchange rates, interest rates or other factors. For data vendor disclaimers refer to www.ndr.com/vendorinfo. Further distribution prohibited without prior permission. Copyright 2004 © Ned Davis Research, Inc. All rights reserved.

Information in Figures 4.1 and 4.27 has been provided with permission from Milken Institute, September 2002.

The U.S. Bureau of Labor has provided the information used in Figures 4.2, 4.3, 4.4, 4.5, 4.6, 4.7, 4.9, 4.10, 4.11, 4.12, 4.13, 4.18, 4.19, 4.20, 4.21, 4.22, 4.23, 4.24, 4.25, 4.26, 4.31, 4.32, 4.33, 4.36, 4.40, 4.44, 7.16, 7.17, 7.18, and 7.19. Consumer Expenditure Survey, 1989.

Figures 4.8 and 4.34 reprinted from The 2003 National Association of REALTORS Profile of Home Buyers and Sellers, © 2003 NATIONAL ASSOCIATION OF REALTORS®. Used with permission. Reproduction, reprinting, or retransmission of this excerpt in any form (electronic media included) is prohibited without written permission. For more information, visit www.REALTOR.org/research.

Figures 4.14, 4.15, 4.16, and 4.17 used under license from Fidelity National Information Solutions, Inc. Copyright © 2003 Fidelity National Information Solutions, Inc. All rights reserved.

Source for Figures 4.29 and 4.30 provided by the U.S. Bureau of the Census, 1975. *Historical Statistics of the U.S.; Colonial Times to 1970.*

Source for Figures 4.37, 4.38, 4.39, 4.42, and 4.43 provided by Torto Wheaton Research, an independent research unit of CB Richard Ellis, www.tortowheaton research.com. "Real Estate Cycles and Outlook 2002," January 2002.

Figure 6.10 reprinted with permission from T. Rowe Price Associates using data from Standard & Poor's and Frank Russell Company.

Source for Figure 6.13 reprinted with permission from Robert Prechter, *Conquer the Crash,* 2002, p. 146.

Source for Figure 6.14 reprinted with permission from Robert Prechter, *Conquer the Crash,* 2002, p. 144. Elliot Wave International Global Financial Data and Mark Timing Report.

Source for Figures 8.2, 8.3, and 8.4 provided by Spectrem Group Perspective: *The Affluent Investor: Key Attitudes, Behaviors and Demographics: 2003 Overview of Key Trends in the Affluent Market,* Spectrem Group estimates.

Figure 8.8 source reprinted from Theodore Caplow, Louis Hicks, and Ben J. Wattenberg, 2001. *The First Measured Century,* pp. 252–53. Washington, D.C.: The AEI Press.

Figures 8.9, 8.10, and 8.11 reprinted by permission of Forbes Magazine © 2004 Forbes Inc.

About the Author

HARRY S. DENT, JR., is President of the H. S. Dent Foundation, whose mission is "Helping People Understand Change." In his first book, *The Great Boom Ahead,* published in 1992, he stood virtually alone in forecasting the unanticipated boom of the 1990s. He has since authored two bestselling books, *The Roaring 2000s* and *The Roaring 2000s Investor.* A Harvard MBA, Fortune 100 consultant, new venture founder and investor, and noted speaker, Dent offers a refreshingly positive view of the future with practical applications at all levels.

More Information and Services from Harry S. Dent Jr.

Our Website: www.hsdent.com. Here we feature special reports on demographic trends, real estate and technology cycles; explanations of key concepts; books and audiotapes; speaking services; and free samples of *The H. S. Dent Forecast* monthly newsletter.

***H.S. Dent Forecast* monthly newsletter.** Current market forecasts, buy targets and best sectors for investments, adding short-term technical analysis and cyclical factors to our demographic and technology trends. Expanded quarterly editions include new research updates years ahead of our books. To subscribe to *The H. S. Dent Forecast* visit http://www.hsdent.com/subscribe.html.

Investment Services. Harry S. Dent, Jr., is the chief economist of High Street Financial Inc., located in Tampa, Florida. Mr. Dent and his organization provide investment services including mutual fund and ETF allocations, privately managed accounts and hedge funds to institutions, high net worth individuals, and other investment management firms. Among their partners are Van Kampen, First Trust Advisors, Walt St., AssetMark, Baker 500, and Clark Capital.

H. S. Dent Advisers Network. This group is comprised of a select network of investment professionals throughout the nation who have studied the demographic research of H. S. Dent in order to bring their clients the best information possible. These advisers work with H. S. Dent regularly and attend semiannual educational conferences to keep current. The knowledge they possess and research to which they subscribe allows them to assist clients not only in investment decisions, but also in decisions about many aspects of life and business. To learn more, please visit www.hsdent.com and follow the link to H. S. Dent Network Advisers.

Special Reports at www.amazon.com/shorts. Amazon has a new feature for short stories and reports from top authors in which we are regularly featured. Downloads are only $0.49.

Find out what's on the economic horizon with these other national bestsellers from
HARRY S. DENT, JR.

For almost two decades, Harry S. Dent, Jr., has been among the most prescient and successful economic forecasters.

His comprehensive and uncannily accurate predictions will give you a strategic edge in planning for your financial future.